Praise for "The Legal Analyst"

"Every good lawyer knows that there's a standard set of argumentative moves that are repeatedly made in different legal settings. Farnsworth's book is chock full of the kind of tools that every legal analyst should have in his or her back pocket. This ambitious book is likely to spur a lively debate about what exactly are the essential tools of legal analysis. While some will grouse that their pet tool was excluded, the book points toward a new way of organizing the first-year curriculum. Farnsworth is forging a new pedagogical canon."

IAN AYRES, Townsend Professor, Yale Law School and author of *Super Crunchers*

"This is an outstanding book. It occupies a significant and unique niche in the literature of jurisprudence and legal methodology. The beauty of this book is that it introduces students and practitioners alike to basic methods of analysis of legal rules and outcomes across a broad range of disciplines (economics, psychology, sociology, jurisprudence, and evidence). This should become the ultimate 'toolbox' for those new to, or simply interested in, the profession."

DAVID J. BEDERMAN, Emory University School of Law

"*The Legal Analyst* provides an engaging and enlightening introduction to the most essential concepts of legal reasoning. In exceptionally clear prose, Ward Farnsworth walks the reader through concepts such as the Coase theorem, the prisoner's dilemma, and property rules and liability rules—peeling away the fog of confusion that often envelops them to reveal the deep and startlingly simple insights that they offer. The reader comes away from the book with a toolkit of ideas that can be used to take apart and examine almost any legal issue."

OONA A. HATHAWAY, Yale Law School

THE LEGAL ANALYST

The Legal Analyst

A Toolkit for Thinking about the Law

WARD FARNSWORTH

THE UNIVERSITY OF CHICAGO PRESS *Chicago and London*

WARD FARNSWORTH is professor of law and Nancy Barton Scholar at the Boston University School of Law. He is the coauthor of *Torts: Cases and Questions* (2004, with Mark F. Grady).

The University of Chicago Press, Chicago 60637
The University of Chicago Press, Ltd., London

Printed in the United States of America

16 15 14 13 12 11 10 09 08 07 1 2 3 4 5

ISBN-13: 978-0-226-23834-0 (cloth)
ISBN-13: 978-0-226-23835-7 (paper)
ISBN-10: 0-226-23834-2 (cloth)
ISBN-10: 0-226-23835-0 (paper)

LIBRARY OF CONGRESS CATALOGING-IN-PUBLICATION DATA

Farnsworth, Ward, 1967–
The legal analyst : a toolkit for thinking about the law / Ward Farnsworth.
p. cm.
Includes bibliographical references and index.
ISBN-13: 978-0-226-23834-0 (cloth : alk. paper)
ISBN-10: 0-226-23834-2 (cloth : alk. paper)
ISBN-13: 978-0-226-23835-7 (pbk. : alk. paper)
ISBN-10: 0-226-23835-0 (pbk. : alk. paper)
1. Law—Methodology. 2. Sociological jurisprudence. 3. Law and economics. 4. Law—Psychological aspects. I. Title.
K212.F37 2007
340'.11—dc22

2006039091

⊗ The paper used in this publication meets the minimum requirements of the American National Standard for Information Sciences—Permanence of Paper for Printed Library Materials, ANSI Z39.48-1992.

CONTENTS

PART IV. PSYCHOLOGY

PART V. PROBLEMS OF PROOF

PREFACE

This book is a collection of tools for thinking about legal questions. It attempts to gather the most interesting ideas one learns about in law school—or should learn, or might wish to have learned—and explain them in plain language with lots of examples of how they work. The result is a kind of user's guide meant to be helpful to a wide range of people: law students, lawyers, scholars, and anyone else with an interest in the legal system. An alternative title for the book, *Thinking Like a Law Professor,* might have been more descriptive but was rejected by the focus groups as ambiguous, as it might be construed as a threat rather than a promise.

That is a short account of this book and its purpose. A more detailed one has to begin with the way law usually is taught, which often seems to me to be upside down. There are, in general, two sorts of things one learns at a law school. First, there are lots of legal rules—principles that tell you whether a contract is valid, for example, or when people have to pay for accidents they cause, or what the difference is between murder and manslaughter. Second, there are tools for thinking about legal problems—ideas such as the prisoner's dilemma, or the differences between rules and standards, or the notion of a baseline problem, or the problem of hindsight bias. Some of them are old matters of jurisprudence; a larger share have been imported into the law schools more recently from other disciplines, such as economics or psychology. In either event, these tools for thought are by far the more interesting, useful, and fun part of a legal education. They enable you to see more deeply into all sorts of questions, old and new, and say better, more penetrating things about them.

The problem is that law schools generally don't teach those tools carefully or systematically. One might imagine it otherwise: law school courses could be organized around tools rather than legal subjects, so that in the first year everyone would take a course on the prisoner's dilemma and other ideas from game theory, a little course on rules and standards, a course on cognitive psychology, and so on, and in each of those classes one would learn, along the way, a bit about contract law, a bit about tort law, and a bit about all the other major subjects. But instead law school is carved up the other way around: by legal topics, not by tools. There are courses on contract law, on tort law, and on all the other topics that become familiar; tools for thought are then mentioned here and there while those subjects are studied. Law tends to be taught, in other words, as if legal rules were the most important things one could learn, and as if the tools for thinking about them were valuable but secondary—nice to know if someone happens to explain them, but nothing urgent.

There might well be good reasons for teaching law this way, but a side effect is that most students never really gain the knowledge of the tools that ought to be the largest payoff of the enterprise. It is hard to see why the tools are valuable, much less to master them, unless you see lots of examples of how they make different areas of law easier to understand. But that only happens if the teachers of different subjects coordinate what they say—if the torts teacher explains how the prisoner's dilemma works in that area of law, and the contracts teacher explains it in contracts class, and the teacher of property law explains it there. This generally isn't done. Law teachers don't coordinate their efforts much, and they have different views about what's worth saying in class, so many of the best tools for thought are likely to be mentioned just once or twice during law school—or maybe not at all—and the student ends up never getting the hang of them.

In effect the tools become the property of an inadvertent cognoscenti. Nobody means to keep the ideas behind them secret, but nobody takes the trouble to fill everyone in about them, either. The good stuff is hidden accidentally and randomly—some of it in a course over here, some of it in the library over there, perhaps in an article that not one law student in a thousand (and not one professor in a hundred) reads. And then there is all the work done outside the law schools by economists, political scientists, and cognitive psychologists that has value for people thinking about legal problems. The small share of it that would be of most interest to a student or to a generalist lawyer or law professor—the portion that amounts to a helpful analytical tool, or to an instructive or charming illustration of the use of one—is not always easy to find.

This book is meant as a corrective to the problems just sketched. So far it might sound like an aid for law students, and it is indeed meant to help them; when new recruits ask me what they might read during the summer before law school, I never have been sure what to suggest.[1] But it also is meant for others interested in law, whether professional or amateur. This is the book I would have liked to have read before I went to law school, when I understood almost none of what it explains. But it also is the book I would have liked to have read when I got *out* of law school, at which time I understood about half of it. It even is a book I'd like to have had at various earlier points during my teaching career, as when I wasn't sure about the meaning of a stag hunt or the conjunction paradox.

Now a few disclaimers. First, a book like this can only introduce tools for thought; there is more to say about each of them—usually much more—than can be conveyed in a short chapter. Specialists on the subjects treated here will have no trouble finding imprecisions or omissions. But the goal of the project is merely to say enough about the tools to give you a good sense of their power and to get you started using them on your own. Suggestions for further reading appear at the end of most of the chapters, and those, along with the endnotes (with which they usually overlap), will give you plenty of places to go for more if the chapters have succeeded in stimulating your curiosity.

Second, I said earlier that this book tries to present in one place the most valuable tools for thinking about the law. Now I have to grant that the success of the effort is only partial, for there are plenty of important legal ideas that the book doesn't discuss. It is limited to tools for thought that lend themselves to this format—ideas that can be introduced effectively with a bunch of good examples in a short chapter. Some of the notable omissions include ideas from moral theory, from critical legal studies, and from legal realism (the last one especially hurts, since it is an area where I like to write). I don't discuss theories of constitutional interpretation, either, because they don't have the kind of versatility that the other tools do. They don't illuminate lots of different corners of the law; their value is confined to the area for which they are designed. Not coincidentally, they usually get covered pretty well in law schools, making treatment of them here less worthwhile.

A danger in leaving out these topics is that the book might be viewed as disparaging them by implication. A large share of the ideas offered in this book are economic in their origins. This isn't meant to imply that economic or utilitarian approaches to law are the only valuable ones (a position I have argued against elsewhere at some length).[2] I merely claim that they are very helpful and that they invite an introductory treatment of this sort. Everything will be fine as long as the reader kindly remembers that the book doesn't claim to be a complete collection of the helpful tools for thinking about legal problems. It purports to be a useful start.

Finally, even among ideas that lend themselves to the format of this book, I am conscious of much that I have left out. A chapter on textualism and alternatives to it was left on the cutting-room floor, along with one about social norms. And as I prepare to send the manuscript to the publisher, I already am running across other ideas that I wish I had managed to include. But the book already is longer than it was meant to be, and I console myself with the thought that some of the omissions may become fodder for a later edition if the first one finds an audience.

The book consists of thirty-one chapters grouped into five parts. The first concerns incentives: the effects that legal decisions have on the choices people make afterwards. The second part is about trust, cooperation, and other problems that arise when people work together. The third part takes up subjects from jurisprudence; it introduces some classic tools for thinking about how courts make decisions—rules and standards, slippery slopes, and the like. The fourth part, on cognitive psychology, discusses ways that people may act irrationally (or, as Richard Thaler would say, "quasi rationally") and the implications for law.[3] Last comes a part on ways to look at problems of proof that are common to many different legal subjects. The sorting of the topics into these bins is somewhat arbitrary, and they certainly can be enjoyed out of order. But the later chapters sometimes refer to earlier ones when there are connections to be made, so reading them in the order given will probably be most satisfying.

A final note at my copyeditor's request: I sought to write this book in the clearest possible English. I naturally encountered the problem of choosing a pronoun to refer to someone who could be male or female. I dealt with this by treating the masculine pronoun as referring to anyone of either sex; I find the other, newer ways of handling the problem too self-conscious to bear. I know others have different views, and am sorry for the annoyance that my inclusive use of "he" and "him" may cause them.

ACKNOWLEDGMENTS

The footnote (or, in this book, the endnote) is an overrated institution in legal scholarship, but in this case I really did need to use a lot of them. In this book I weave in my own views without compunction; that was part of the fun of writing it. But my central project is to round up useful ideas developed by specialists and teach them to a more general audience. The authors of those ideas are entitled to credit, which I have tried to give wherever appropriate, and to my thanks, which I offer here—along with apologies for any oversights I have made in attributing the ideas and examples in the book to their most deserving sources.

In three cases the topics I wanted to discuss had already received outstanding treatment somewhat similar in approach to what I sought to achieve here: useful ideas crisply explained, with lots of interesting examples. In those cases I asked the authors of the original works—Eric Posner,[1] Saul Levmore,[2] and Eugene Volokh[3]—if they might join me as coauthors of the chapters covering those subjects. They each were kind enough to agree. The resulting chapters sometimes go a bit beyond the scope of those original articles, but in all three cases the substance of them is attributable mostly, or more than mostly, to my coauthors. I am grateful to them for permitting their work to be adapted here. The book is stronger for it.

Speaking of Saul Levmore, I also owe a large additional debt of thanks to him for providing generous encouragement and suggestions from early in the process of writing this book to the end of it. His work and his conversation overflow with interesting ideas, and the book has been greatly enriched by them at countless points—sometimes in ways reflected in the endnotes, and sometimes not. For reading and commenting on the manuscript or parts of it, I also thank Jack Beermann, Eric Blumenson, Robert Bone, Ronald Cass, Tamar Frankel, Jonathan Koehler, Andrew Kull, Gary Lawson, Gerald Leonard, Steve Marks, Jeff Rachlinski, Ken Simons, and three anonymous referees for the University of Chicago Press; John Tryneski and Leslie Keros, also at the Press, helped the book along in various important ways as well. I received able research assistance on the project from Alon Cohen, Susan Frauenhoffer, Daniel Norland, Sarah

McCabe, Wells Miller, Nick Semanko, Brian Vito, and Graham Foster. For helpful conversations at various points I am grateful to Brian Brooks, Carl Byers, Daniel Cantor, Janet Farnsworth, Ward Farnsworth Sr., Ted Frank, Kelly Klaus, Adam Long, Christopher Roberts, James Sanders, Ted Skillman, and Jack Taylor. The kind and indefatigable library staff at the Boston University School of Law also was a great help, as ever.

PART I *Incentives*

1 ↠ Ex Ante and Ex Post

A thief walks into a bank, puts a gun to the head of one of the customers, and announces that he will shoot unless the teller hands over all the money in the drawer. The teller does nothing. The thief shoots the customer, runs off, and never is seen again. The customer dies of his injuries, and his estate brings a lawsuit against the bank, complaining that the teller should have given the money—it was only $5,000, let us imagine—to the thief. What should the court say?

There are two quite different ways to think about this question. The first looks at the case like this: it is a dispute between the bank and the estate of one of its customers. They've come to court because they haven't been able to resolve their differences informally; the judge serves as an adjuster of last resort, producing an answer the parties agree to accept because it has the force of law. One of them will walk away a winner; the question is *who.* We find the answer by looking back at what happened and asking whether justice requires that the bank pay damages to the plaintiff. Did the bank do anything wrong? If the teller's refusal saved the bank some money, would it be fair for the bank to pay nothing to the party who was injured as a result (or, more precisely, to his estate)? Can the bank bear the economic burden of the customer's death more easily than his kin? We might consult our sense of fairness. And it might be possible to draw analogies to this case from others that seem similar—perhaps cases where a customer slipped on a puddle left behind by the bank's janitor, or where a bank was held liable because one of its tellers tipped off a thief that a customer soon would leave the bank with a great deal of money. We could try to decide this case like others that sort of resemble it.

That much is, again, a first way of looking at the case. But now here is a second one: what happened that day at the bank is unfortunate but of secondary interest at this point; it's *over,* and nothing a court says can change what happened. Money can be moved from one person to another now, or punishments inflicted, but these are just rearrangements, and they are too late to be of any serious consequence. What's appalling about the day at the bank (or any crime or accident) is the *waste* of it:

the lost life, the demolished car, the broken window, or whatever the harm might be. When any of those things happen, the world is made poorer—irrevocably so. This is intuitive and obvious to the family of the person who was killed. They are painfully conscious that nothing the law says can bring him back. But it's also true, if less obvious, after an accident that merely wrecks a car. The car can be repaired, and whoever was to blame can be made to pay for it, and now the car's owner might feel that the law *did* bring back the car: a miracle! It's as if the accident never happened. But it isn't a miracle. It's a waste. No matter how satisfied the owner feels, the world would have been better off without the accident, because it ate up money that would have been better spent on something else—anything else. Just ask the person who ended up paying for it. The point is that the law doesn't *fix* bad things that have happened. It can't: they've happened. All the law can do is redistribute the suffering a bit. That isn't nothing, of course; assigning blame and making the right person pay for it might make the victim feel better, or make the rest of us feel better. But the law's dream—anyone's dream—would be to turn the clock back and stop the bad thing from happening in the first place. That would be much better than quarreling afterwards about who should justly suffer for it. Too bad it's impossible.

Yet in a sense perhaps it *is* possible, for the court may be able to do something almost as good. It might make a rule that would cause horrible events like the bank robbery to be less likely from now on. This wouldn't undo the killing that already happened, but it could stop some killings in the future—and that's equally good, isn't it? Or better than equally good: for we would be stopping lots of bad things, not just undoing one of them. (If they *aren't* prevented, we'll be just as unhappy about those killings after they occur as we are now about the one that already did; we'll wish we could turn the clock back—perhaps to today.) So here we arrive at a different vision of what the law can do about a case. Instead of looking back and deciding who should bear the suffering, it can look ahead and decide what ruling will make the suffering less likely to occur later.

What would this train of thought look like? In the case of the bank, it means asking what incentives people will have after the case is over. Here is an interesting possibility: if the court says that the plaintiff wins, then from now on banks will have an incentive to hand over the money when thieves take hostages (to avoid paying in court again next time). And that, in turn, means that thieves will have an incentive to take hostages. True, thieves might not know the legal rule, but then they might not need to know it. Maybe they would just observe that taking hostages has become wonderfully effective: the teller always hands over the money. The trouble becomes apparent. Letting the customer's estate win might cause *more* hostages to be taken in the future. Perhaps fewer of them would be shot since the thieves would get the money they demand, but it's hard to be sure what will happen once guns have been drawn and hostages taken.

On this view the bank *has* to win the case brought by the customer's estate. It's not a question of what's fair as we look back on the fateful day. It's a question of making the right rule for the future. The bank has to win for the same basic reason that governments won't give in to hijackers of airplanes when they demand money or whatever else. It's tempting to make the payment and save the passengers' lives. You probably would make the payment if you knew it never was going to happen again. But that's the point: not just that it might happen again, but that if you make the payment it becomes more likely that it *will* happen again.

So now we have seen two distinct ways of thinking about a problem. The first can be called the *ex post* perspective. It involves looking back at a disaster or other event after it has occurred and deciding what to do about it or how to clean it up. The second perspective is called the *ex ante* point of view. It involves looking forward and asking what effects the decision about this case will have in the future—on parties who are entering similar situations and haven't yet decided what to do, and whose choices may be influenced by the consequences the law says will follow from them. (The first perspective also might be called *static,* since it accepts the parties' positions as given and fixed; the second perspective is *dynamic,* since it assumes their behavior may change in response to what others do, including judges.) Part of what makes judicial decisions interesting is that courts think in both of these ways when they decide cases, and the two styles of thought can point to different conclusions. Does a court's decision settle the dispute between these parties or does it make a rule for others in the future? It almost always does both.

This chapter (and much of the rest of this book) emphasizes the ex ante perspective because it creates lots of interesting possibilities for thought and argument, and because it usually comes more slowly than thinking ex post. It's only natural to think in an ex post fashion when a lawsuit comes up: here are two parties in a vigorous dispute, perhaps blaming each other for a disaster. Their attention is fixed on the past and what should be done about it. *They* don't care what effect the decision has on others down the line; they just care who wins right now. (That's especially true in a case involving a random accident. The bank in our example may be a little different; it may be worried both about winning the case and about the rule in the long run, because it deals with these situations repeatedly.) But the court has to care about both perspectives, for it will be declaring a winner now *and* making a rule that affects others later.

In fact most courts to consider the problem of the bank teller have found in favor of the bank on the ex ante grounds sketched a moment ago. The Illinois Supreme Court put the point like so: "In this particular case the result may appear to be harsh and unjust, but, for the protection of future business invitees, we cannot afford to extend to the criminal another weapon in his arsenal."[1] In other words, the argument from the ex ante perspective won out over the ex post. The practical challenge is to learn to see that sort of argument every time it's available: to learn to think the ex ante way when a case is full of cues tempting everyone to only look backwards. The simplest way to find the ex ante angle is to picture either side winning the case and then imagine how the parties will think a week later—what either of them might do differently now that they know how the courts will respond. Thus you can imagine the bank learning of the decision and changing its rules to make sure that its tellers hand over the money; and then you can ask how this would, in turn, change anyone else's incentives, starting with the thief. In real life, of course, the parties whose incentives we care about the most probably aren't the ones before the court—*this* bank, *that* thief, and so on. We're worried about banks generally and thieves generally. But sometimes it helps to think concretely about the parties you can see and then try generalizing to the ones you can't.

Another way to come up with ex ante arguments is to imagine how a legislature would think about the problem facing the court. Legislatures make general rules for the future; they don't resolve individual disputes that have already occurred. So if a legislative committee or a government agency were considering a rule about how banks should handle hostage takers, it less likely would be distracted by the equities of any one case. Its role would be to make decisions that have consequences ex ante—going forward. Granted, a court isn't in quite the same role. It is supposed to decide cases according to the authorities on point: statutes, case law, and the like; and in the case of the bank teller, that is where a real court would start its search for an answer. But it often happens that there are no authorities entirely on point. In effect a judicial decision then serves as a little piece of legislation as well as the resolution of a conflict. The balance between these two functions varies among courts, and students of these matters often argue about how the balance should be struck.[2] But judges at most levels of the legal system accept the importance of giving at least some thought to the ex ante effects of their decisions, as do the lawyers who make arguments in their courtrooms. When you hear that a lawyer is making a "policy" argument, that usually means it's an argument from the ex ante perspective—that is, a claim about the effects the decision might have on someone's incentives.

Let's look at some other examples. I build a house. Unfortunately I was mistaken in my measurements, and the structure extends onto your neighboring property by eighteen inches. There is no cheap way to correct the problem; either the house stays where it is or much of it will have to be torn down. What to do? The ex post style of thought accepts the situation as it is and asks how it might best be resolved. Nothing the court says can change the fact that the house encroaches; all we can do now is try to keep the damage caused by the mistake to a minimum. So the natural remedy might be an order that I pay you for the strip of land I built on, perhaps with a little premium since the sale is, in effect, being forced on you. Why waste a perfectly good house by tearing much of it down? But the ex ante perspective is entirely different. On this view it matters little how our particular mess gets resolved. The important question is how the resolution of it will affect our behavior in the future—and the behavior of others like us. From this standpoint an award of damages—a forced sale—might seem a terrible solution. It deals sensibly with the problem we already have, but it doesn't give me or anyone else an incentive to be more careful next time. Indeed, it might create the opposite incentive: if I wanted to build on a bit of your property but were unsure whether you would be willing to sell, my best plan would be to go ahead and build and then let you sue for the value of the land. Even if I have to pay a premium, I still might be better off this way than by negotiating with you.

So the usual rule in encroachment cases is that the plaintiff—the complaining neighbor—gets an injunction entitling him to insist that the house be removed. There is more to say about this case, and we will return to it in other chapters. For now the important point is to see that it's another win for the ex ante perspective. Ex post—after the thing is done—having one neighbor pay the other might seem attractive; ex ante—thinking about the incentives for next time, before anything has happened—payment of money seems decidedly unattractive precisely because it makes the bad thing more likely to happen again.[3] Notice the analogy to making the bank pay damages to the hostage's estate, which might cause the number of hostages to increase.

And notice also that the ex ante point of view is more than just a useful tool for courts to use in deciding cases. It's also important to remember when deciding more broadly how well a rule works. A rule requiring buildings to be torn down when they encroach might look ugly if you just study the cases where the rule actually gets used. All you would see are buildings getting torn down or neighbors demanding extortionate prices from each other to avoid that result. But the consequences of the rule don't appear only in those cases, or even primarily in those cases. The results of the rule also include all the cases where the building never encroaches in the first place because everyone was careful to get a proper survey done—for fear that otherwise the house would have to be torn down later. So new houses that *don't* get torn down are evidence of the rule's operation, too. A rule that looks brutal and wasteful when invoked might actually be working beautifully, if invisibly, by causing the occasions for its use to be rare.

These same trade-offs arise often when courts decide whether to allow evidence into a case. A police officer sees a fellow with a butcher knife chasing someone out the front door of a building. The officer shoots and kills him. Or at least that's what she says happened. The trouble is that no knife was found on the dead man afterwards. The officer has some sessions with a therapist to discuss the incident. Meanwhile she is sued by the estate of the man she killed. The plaintiff demands to see the notes the therapist took during the sessions with the officer. Should this be allowed? Ex post—now that the notes exist and the two sides are arguing about them—the answer might seem clear: of course the plaintiff should be allowed to have them. They might show something important. What if the officer privately admitted that the story about the knife was an invention? What if she admitted that she shot the man because she had a grudge against him? Surely the jury ought to know those things. And if the officer didn't say anything incriminating, what's the harm in finding out? All this might seem a little unfair to the officer if she thought she was speaking in confidence, but that interest pales in comparison to getting at the truth behind the killing, does it not?

To repeat, however, this whole line of reasoning starts by taking for granted that the notes exist. The ex ante perspective doesn't take it for granted. It asks how everyone's incentives will be changed next time if the plaintiff wins this time. Next time the officer won't go to the therapist, or won't be as likely to talk; for a good therapist will start the session with a warning that anything said there can be used in court. Seizing the notes of the therapist, one might say, is an example of a trick that only works once. The trade-off here isn't just between getting all that good information on the one hand and discouraging candid discussions with therapists on the other. That good information will be less likely to *exist* next time if it can be brought into court. This doesn't necessarily mean, of course, that the conversation ought to be kept confidential, or "privileged." That final decision depends on the details—in particular on how important it is for people to talk to therapists and how important confidentiality is in making those conversations happen. In the case of the officer and the butcher knife, the Supreme Court answered both those questions in favor of the officer and said that the notes of therapists are off-limits.[4]

This style of reasoning comes into play often when information of any sort is created.[5] There frequently is tension between the rules that are best for distributing information once it exists (ex post) and for causing it to be created in the first place (ex ante). The information revealed in the therapist's office is one example; information revealed to a lawyer is another: the case for the attorney-client privilege runs along the same lines as the case just discussed. When an attorney knows something important about a case, the court might like to hear about it; but forcing the attorney to talk this time makes it less likely that a client will talk to an attorney next time. The same goes for the rule that you can't bring statements into court that were made during negotiations to settle the case. We'd like very much to have that information (we'd like to have *all* information), but ex ante the effect of allowing this would be to discourage frank settlement negotiations next time, and we want them to occur.

Or leave behind the question of evidence and think of intellectual property. Once I discover a useful drug, it might seem sensible to let you copy it. Your copying the drug doesn't prevent me or anyone else from having it; and why should the first person to combine chemicals in a certain way be able to prevent others from doing the same? Yes, that is the ex post analysis—the analysis that makes sense once the drug exists, two parties are feuding over it, and we take those things as givens. But the ex ante point is that if you can copy the drug freely, other drugs may not come into existence in the first place. People won't have as much incentive to create them. It's a delicate trade-off, and the patent laws are the legal system's current solution to it. They give the inventor of the drug a limited right to the exclusive manufacture and sale of it. The same story could be told about copyrights in books or music. Once books and music exist (ex post), there's a great case for free distribution of them. But then they are less likely to exist at all next time (the ex ante point).

Instead of evidence or a drug or a song, our subject could be a whale. Imagine that we live in the golden age of whaling, and a dispute has come up between a party who harpooned a whale and another who captured the animal later while it still was swimming for its life. Who has the better claim to it? Various ex post arguments come to mind: putting a harpoon in a whale doesn't make you the owner of it; it's still swimming around and might live for years more. We call this an ex post argument because it assumes that everything in the case already has happened: a whale was harpooned, got away, and then was caught by someone else; the question for the court is simply who keeps it. The ex ante angle on the problem is different. It means asking how the decision about *this* whale will affect what other whalers do later—and how the whole industry will fare as a result. The courts that were confronted with these questions in the nineteenth century didn't always answer them the same way, but they always did tend to worry about whether their decisions, however appealing they might have seemed in the case at hand, would create trouble for everyone else down the line. The size of the trouble depended, as usual, on details, such as whether a whaler would be likely to give up the job if he couldn't count on collecting the whales he harpooned.

An extreme example was presented by the finback whale. The usual method of hunting it was to throw a bomb lance, or exploding harpoon, into its back; the whale would disappear, die, and wash up on shore days later. The lance would still be there, and its owner would appear to claim the whale. Then one day a passerby found one of the whales washed up on shore and decided to keep it. The whaler responsible for the kill complained, and the court found his argument unanswerable: if the passerby were allowed to keep the whale, "this branch of industry must necessarily cease, for no person would engage in it if the fruits of his labor could be appropriated by any chance finder."[6] One might find this an appealing consequence of letting the passerby win if one didn't like whaling, but the court unsurprisingly wanted to protect an industry on which many communities in the state depended.

By this point it might seem as though ex ante arguments come up with respect to lots of legal questions. Actually that may be an understatement. About *every* question of law it is possible to ask what the ex ante effects of a decision one way or the other would be. We merely have been looking at examples where that question has great and obvious importance—where there can be no doubt that the court's decision between the parties will affect the incentives of others. The case where the effect on incentives is most in doubt probably is the first one about the bank robber and the hostage; one might wonder whether the court's decision really would have much effect on the behavior of either banks or thieves. As we saw, courts consider the ex ante argument decisive even there; but it's possible that they are wrong, and there are plenty of other cases where the ability of courts to affect anyone's incentives is controversial. Think of a case about a car accident, and an argument that a judgment in favor of the driver on some issue will give bad incentives to other drivers. One can ask how the legal knowledge will be transmitted to those other drivers (might insurance companies have a role to play here?), what other incentives drivers have that might blot out the signals sent by the law, and so forth. Those are good questions, but they can't be asked until one sees the ex ante argument in the first place.

There are those who regard just about every legal question as calling for resolution entirely on ex ante grounds: entirely on the basis, that is, of what decision between the parties will create the best incentives for others in the future.[7] The adherents to this approach write books, hold meetings, and even have their own name: economists. They prefer the ex ante perspective because it is the point of view relevant to the things economists care about. Trying to decide who should win on an ex post basis—that is, just looking back and assigning blame—is basically a distributive exercise. It's a decision about how a stake should be divided, about who should pay whom. Those decisions are of no interest to most economists because their usual goal is to figure out how to increase the amount of value in the world, not how to divide it up once it exists (except insofar as the act of dividing it up affects how much of it gets created in the first place). From that standpoint the ex ante perspective is the only one that matters because it is the court's only chance to do something useful—something that will cause events to work out better next time and thus prevent some waste, instead of just sorting out the blame for a disaster after it's too late.

Meanwhile, of course, the parties to a case naturally care very much about who pays whom, and so does the legal system. That is why ex post arguments are important as well as the ex ante kind, and why the tension between them is interesting. But many of this book's chapters nevertheless amount to lessons in how to think about legal problems the way an economist would. We will be spending time on this because the ex ante style of reasoning is less intuitive to most people than the ex post. It opens the door to fascinating insights about why legal rules look the way they do, and the insights often aren't obvious; they involve subtleties that take some help to see. The next chapters begin to reveal and explain them.

SUGGESTIONS FOR FURTHER READING. The scholarship analyzing legal questions from an ex ante point of view—in other words, by considering the incentives created by various answers to legal questions—is endless, but a classic introduction to this perspective is Frank H. Easterbrook, *The Court and the Economic System,* 98 Harv. L. Rev. 4 (1984). Some sophisticated recent discussions focusing on particular implications of the ex ante perspective are Bruce L. Hay, *Procedural Justice—Ex Ante vs. Ex Post,* 44 UCLA L. Rev. 1803 (1997); Lucian A. Bebchuk, *Property Rights and Liability Rules: The Ex Ante View of the Cathedral,* 100 Mich. L. Rev. 601 (2001); and Mark A. Lemley, *Ex Ante and Ex Post Justifications for Intellectual Property,* 71 U. Chi. L. Rev. 129 (2004). For more skeptical accounts of appeals to incentives in legal argument, see Paul H. Robinson and John M. Darley, *The Role of Deterrence in the Formulation of Criminal Law Rules: At Its Worst When Doing Its Best,* 91 Geo. L.J. 949 (2003); Dan M. Kahan, *The Secret Ambition of Deterrence,* 113 Harv. L. Rev. 413 (1999); and Gary T. Schwartz, *Reality in the Economic Analysis of Tort Law: Does Tort Law Really Deter?* 42 UCLA L. Rev. 377 (1994).

2 ⤞ The Idea of Efficiency

We have seen how the decisions that courts make can affect people's incentives afterwards. Now we need to talk about what sorts of incentives we want people to have. Sometimes it's just obvious: incentives not to take hostages presumably are a good thing, and the judge in the case of the finback whale we just considered was understandably worried about destroying a major industry (though whale lovers may find even this a hard case). But many cases lend themselves to a deeper analysis.

The law uses different rules to deal with attacks by dogs and by lions. A dog's owner pays only if the dog was known to be a biter; if a lion bites someone, the owner pays every time regardless of the excellence of the animal's reputation. (Some states now have stricter rules for dogs, but the rules just sketched were in place in every jurisdiction for a long time and still serve as a good basis for illustration.) Suppose you are sued by your neighbor over a dog bite and the trial judge screws up the instructions to the jurors: they are told that you are obliged to pay, regardless of whether the dog had a bad record, so long as the animal was yours. The jury brings in a verdict requiring you to pay $10,000 to cover the plaintiff's medical expenses. You go to a court of appeals to complain about the mistaken jury instructions. Unfortunately there is a problem: you didn't point out the error at the time it was made; you weren't paying careful attention to it because you thought the legal rule was too obvious for the trial judge to misstate. Since the appellate court is the first place you have raised the issue, your adversary says it's too late. What's the best way to think about this?

You might be able to make a strong argument based on notions of fairness. You have, we may assume, been ordered to pay a bunch of money to the plaintiff that the law says you shouldn't owe; no jury would have made such a decision if it had been instructed correctly. But on the other side there is a powerful argument about incentives—an ex ante point. If you are allowed to complain about the jury instructions now despite not complaining earlier, then in the future there might not be much incentive for others to object early, either. It may seem obvious that everyone is best off objecting promptly, so the incentives created by the courts aren't important; but that might not be so. Some lawyers may have a strategic thought about it: if there is a glitch in the jury instructions, the best plan might be to quietly let it pass. If we win the case, that's great, and if we lose, we'll have a good argument on appeal that the trial should be done over again—an especially encouraging thought if the current trial has been going badly. Complaining early causes the mistake to get fixed and so gives away the lawyer's best hope for a do-over later. Of course *you* weren't thinking that when you let the bad jury instruction go by in our initial illustration. You merely were careless. But then that raises a point about incentives, too. Forbidding you to raise the argument now would be harsh in your case, but it would make other lawyers more careful next time.

In the dog bite case you are almost certain to lose your appeal for all the reasons just given. In federal court there is a rule saying so (you have to complain about jury instructions when they are delivered, or not at all), and state courts have similar rules, whether made by judges or by legislatures.[8] So far this case study sounds much the same as the ones in the first chapter: it's just another example of a decision that seems harsh ex post but has good effects ex ante. But this time we should push a bit harder and reflect on why the ex ante effects are so attractive. What makes it important that objections be raised early—so important that we tolerate brutal results in cases like yours to keep the incentives right for others? The answer has to do with the cost of correcting a mistake. If you notice a flaw in the instructions to a jury and speak up promptly, the problem can be corrected on the spot very easily. If you wait until later, whether deliberately or carelessly, then dealing with the problem becomes much more expensive. The court can't bring back the old jury; a new one has to be picked, and the case retried. It's costly for the parties and the public. Those costs are a waste, by which we mean they are needless, or inefficient. They can be avoided if people point out mistakes when they happen. This is why courts of appeal tend to be very hard on a complaint of any kind that wasn't raised in the trial court, whether it's about jury instructions, a bad closing argument, or a blunder in allowing a piece of evidence into the case.

Here's another matter of procedure that follows a broadly similar analysis. Your adversary—the same neighbor—brings a second lawsuit against you. He's still complaining about the dog bite, but this time he wants compensation for pain and suffering, which he didn't demand in his earlier action (all he sought then was reimbursement of his medical expenses). This time you are the one who can make a powerful objection based on a point about incentives. The plaintiff could have asked for these damages in the first case, and should have. If this second case goes forward now, a new jury will have to learn all about it, just as the first jury did; you will have to pay a lawyer to defend you again, and call a lot of the same witnesses and argue a lot of the same points. It's all a waste. The same claim could have been handled without the duplication of effort if it had been included in the first lawsuit; and though it's too late to do anything about that now, parties planning lawsuits like these in the future would save everyone money and trouble by bringing all their claims at once—claims for their medical expenses *and* for pain and suffering. Again these arguments will win. The neighbor's second case will be dismissed under the doctrine of *res judicata* ("the thing is decided"), which generally forbids one party to sue another twice over the same transaction. "Transaction" is a vague term, but most courts define the word to mean that it would have avoided waste—in other words, that it would have been more efficient—to combine the second case with the first one.

Notice that at bottom the winning arguments are the same in both cases we've discussed here—the one where you try to raise on appeal a problem that you didn't complain about to the trial judge, and the one where your neighbor tries to sue you twice over the same dog bite. The rules violated by these moves are different, but they have a similar rationale. There is a cheaper way to do things and a more expensive way, so the law requires the cheaper way even if it means that some good claims have to be dismissed to keep the incentive strong. Some of the cases mentioned in the first chapter can be looked at in a similar way. Requiring me to tear down a house that encroaches on your land is harsh, just like refusing to hear an appeal that has merit is harsh; but in both cases the harsh answer creates a strong incentive to take precautions next time that will deal with the problem more cheaply: ordering a survey of my land in advance, or complaining about bad jury instructions when they're first drawn up.

The general point is that it's expensive when things go wrong (perhaps this is mostly what it *means* for things to go wrong). One thing the law tries to do—some think it's the main thing the law tries to do—is keep the cost of such situations to a minimum. It does this by penalizing people who make problems more expensive than they have to be, perhaps by holding them liable for the result (as in the encroachment case) or by denying them a recovery they otherwise would have had (as when the appeal from the late complainer is denied, or a second lawsuit about the same facts is not allowed). This is what it means to make efficiency a legal goal. To tie the point to the first chapter: when you are trying to figure out whether a legal decision will create good incentives, try asking whether it will cause the parties, or people like them, to keep all the costs of their situations to a minimum.

Let's talk now about accidents. Every accident is an expensive event. A bunch of costs suddenly come into existence: repair costs, medical costs, lost wages, and so forth. We can count pain and suffering as costs, too; even if they don't directly involve money, they are something that anyone would pay to avoid. So far as the parties are concerned the point of a lawsuit is to decide who will pay for all these things. But so far as the court is concerned the point of the case is larger, because the result in the lawsuit also may influence, ex ante, how large those costs will be for other people in the future. To stick with our theme of disasters involving animals, suppose a cow wanders onto a road and is hit by a car. The car is wrecked and the driver sues the cow's owner to recover his costs. You might think the owner would be blamed automatically for any failure to keep his animals on his property, but it isn't so. The question in the case, at least in most states, will be whether the animal's owner took reasonable care to prevent this sort of accident.[9] Reasonable care doesn't mean perfect care; courts typically say that sometimes a rancher will do everything he ought to do and yet a cow still will escape and cause a collision—and in that case the rancher doesn't pay for it. How can this be? If a cow makes it onto a road, isn't it obvious that its owner *didn't* do everything he should have done?

One answer to these questions goes back to the problem of waste. Suppose the only way to guarantee that no cows *ever* escape is to enclose the ranch within brick walls and post armed guards around the perimeter. This would be, we may safely assume, very effective but dreadfully expensive. It would prevent some accidents, but it would be hard to consider that result an endorsement of the idea; the accidents would have cost less than the measures used to avoid them. The wall and the guards would be viewed as overkill—a waste of money. It would be cheaper to just use barbed wire, which is far less expensive than bricks and still works most of the time, and then let accidents happen once in a while. The crucial step in this line of thought is to consider *all* the costs in the picture: not just the cost of the accident, but also the cost of preventing accidents. If the goal is to keep the entire cost of these ranch-and-road situations to a minimum, the best solution—the most efficient one, we might call it—may be to prevent most of the accidents and then not worry about the small number that still occur and are very expensive to eliminate entirely. We're all sorry about those last few, but trying to get rid of them is more costly than letting them happen. So perhaps the right legal result is victory for the rancher as long as he did everything that was, as the expression goes, cost-justified—e.g., using barbed wire to keep in the cows, even if it didn't work perfectly; in that case the driver bears his own costs. We don't make the rancher pay anything because there is nothing else we wanted the rancher to do.

This way of thinking is jarring to some people because it implies that the legal system is content to see some accidents happen. But on reflection that seems to be our implied philosophy most of the time, does it not? We could reduce speed limits to five miles per hour everywhere; that probably would eliminate most fatalities on the road, of which there are about forty thousand every year in the United States. Evidently we would rather put up with those deaths and drive faster.[10] We would experience the super-slow driving as a waste of time. We can apply the same logic to individual cases; that is what we did in the lawsuit against the rancher. And notice the analogies to the other cases we discussed earlier. The rancher who fails to at least use barbed wire—the cheap solution—is like a lawyer who doesn't object to mistaken jury instructions in the trial court. He failed to do something within his power to keep the cost of the problem low. That's why a rancher who doesn't build a cost-justified fence loses when he gets sued; that's what it means to say that he was negligent. Conversely, if the rancher did use barbed wire and otherwise is found to have done all that was reasonable, he won't be penalized for failing to build a brick wall any more than a trial lawyer will be penalized for failing to repeat an objection twenty times in the trial court. We don't want those things done even if they might help once in a while. On balance they're a waste.

Some observers of tort law think the story just told explains how judges decide accident cases: they ask whether the defendant failed to take any steps that were cost-justified—any steps, in other words, that would have saved money when compared with the costs of the accidents they could have been expected to prevent. If so, the defendant is liable, and otherwise not. The judges might not use those words in their opinions or in their thinking, and they certainly wouldn't be able to put definite numbers on any of the values at stake, especially when a case involves the loss of life or limb. They just apply common sense and rely on intuitions about whether a defendant has done something blameworthy. But (the theory goes) a dread of waste, or, equivalently, a sense of costs and benefits, is precisely what common sense is made of: we feel angry at people when they easily can prevent accidents but don't, not when they pass up a chance at prevention that would have been more trouble than the accident itself.[11] (But then why don't we feel angry when someone spends too *much* on precautions? It's just as wasteful as spending too little, isn't it?) So most decisions in tort cases turn out to be consistent with the idea that judges are worrying about efficiency, even if the worry is unconscious or expressed in different words.

This whole account has its opponents; they deny that the results of tort cases follow such a pattern, or they deny that the pattern is best explained by the value of efficiency. We aren't interested in trying to settle that debate here. Our purpose is just to show what an argument based on efficiency can look like, and why anyone might imagine that judges pursue such a goal in their rulings even when they don't think of their task that way. One value in law, whether or not it's the leading one, is to find the cheapest ways to solve problems, and then to give people incentives to use them.

Our theme in this chapter is waste—what it means, and various ways that the legal system discourages it. Another variety of waste that troubles the law can occur when things that people value go unused, or underused. Let's say I have the mouth of a cave on my property. The rest of the cave extends a long way; some of it is under your land, some more is under the property further up the road, and so on. Who (if anyone) owns the cave, and why do we care? Start with the possibility that *nobody* owns it. Setting aside the problem of how anyone then gets into the cave when the mouth is on my land (maybe there is a public right-of-way), this rule might seem to ensure that the largest number of people will be able to enjoy it: since nobody owns the thing, nobody is excluded from it; the cave is free for everyone to explore. But the results might not be so great after all. A cave may start out having little value; it's dark and full of dangers. Its great potential lies in the possibility that someone will chart its interior, figure out where the safe parts are, and arrange for outsiders—tourists or cave enthusiasts—to come have a look at them. The trouble is that all this exploring and mapping requires a large investment, and nobody will be inclined to spend the time and money required if they can't recoup their costs by charging admission—which can only be done by an owner.

Saying, then, that the cave is owned by no one—that nobody has the right to exclude the rest of the world—tends to ensure that its full value won't be developed, and this amounts to an argument that it's important for the cave to be owned, probably by one person. (Another possibility is to say the government owns it. How do you think these possibilities would compare?) I won't be inclined to do much with it if I know there are a dozen other owners whose permission is required, though the details of this will depend on my ability to negotiate with them. Let's therefore imagine that ownership of the entire cave is mine since I own the land where its mouth lies. We now encounter a second risk, and another reason why the cave's potential might go untapped: I might be all thumbs when it comes to spelunking. In this case there is another solution. I can sell the property to someone who has more aptitude for developing it, and who will value the rights to the cave more than I do because he will have a better chance of turning it into something attractive. And if it later turns out that someone still different can do even better with the cave, then that person can be the *next* buyer.

The cave is a minor example of a major purpose served by the legal institutions of property and contract. Instead of a cave we could have made it a mine, or surface land, or the chemical combinations known as vaccines or other drugs, or anything else in which the law assigns rights of ownership—property rights, that is. A chief reason for letting people own things, not to mention enforcing their rights of ownership by providing courts, police, and the like, is that ownership gives them incentives to get the most out of whatever it is they own and to take care of it. If the cave (or the land, or bandwidth) isn't owned by anyone, it probably won't get developed to the full extent that it could be, and this would be yet another example of waste. No doubt you can imagine situations where it's *better* that a resource not be exploited, and the best treatment of those cases might be different from the best handling of the cave; but there are a lot of cases that do fit the account just given pretty well, including most farms and most residential property. The law gives mixed treatment to more exotic examples—airwaves, intellectual property, and sometimes also caves. The most famous of the cave cases denied ownership of it to the mouth's owner (over a scathing dissent);[12] broadcasting rights get parceled out by the government, sometimes by auction; and intellectual property gets strong protection only for limited periods of time. All these cases can be viewed as involving decisions about what sorts of ownership rights need to exist in a thing to encourage the fullest development of it—and the least waste, or unused potential.

If property rights are useful because they make it worth someone's while to cultivate and take care of land or other resources, then contracts are useful because they make it possible to get the rights into the hands of the someone who can cultivate it best, or anyway at the best profit. Just as an absence of property rights in something can result in waste, so can the inability to make a contract about it. I have something; you value it more than I do; I would like to sell it to you, as we would both consider ourselves better off afterwards. If I can't make that sale, whether for legal or practical reasons, the result can be considered a waste (sometimes also known as a deadweight loss). The measure of the waste is the size of that "better-offness," or welfare, that we had coming from the sale of whatever was at stake, which we probably can measure by the difference in its dollar value to us. Again, there may be cases where it's better not to enforce contracts, and where that is the law's position. But there is a legal presumption in favor of enforcement, and it's easy to understand why. We don't like to see a squandered chance for two people to make themselves better off by their own lights, and to move a resource to a more highly valued use in the process. We want the cave to end up owned by whoever can make the most of it. Contracts are a principal way that a cave or anything else finds such an owner.

That last bit of discussion makes it sound as though the only way two parties *wouldn't* be able to make a contract is if the law wouldn't enforce it. But the more common problems are just practical: sometimes people can't make contracts because there are logistical impediments in the way. We noted in passing that if everyone above the cave owns a piece of it, the owner might like to go to each of them and negotiate terms. But it might not work out. If there are a lot of owners, the negotiations might be time consuming or might be derailed by strategic behavior; maybe each neighbor would resist my offer in the hope that everyone else would agree first, leaving the last one in the delicious position of demanding a big payment not to spoil the whole arrangement. That dynamic, known as a holdout problem, is just one of many difficulties that can ruin a good bargain which would have made all the parties to it better off. (Economists call all such problems transaction costs; we will come back to that term in chapter 8.)

And then there are cases where bargaining is *really* impossible, such as a car accident that neither side sees coming. If the drivers had known they would be at risk of colliding with each other in the afternoon, they would have made a contract in the morning in which they both agreed to drive at a reasonable speed—in which case the party who drove too fast could be thought of as breaking the contract. This example sounds far-fetched, but it helps show the relationship between some of the topics we've been discussing. Nobody advocates for waste; when it does occur, you usually can view it as a departure from what the parties would have agreed on in advance if they could. A lot of legal rules thus make more sense when you imagine the people affected by them all discussing the issue before the arrival of whatever situation they are in. Many times a rule, when seen from that perspective, evidently functions to keep everyone's total costs down before they all know what roles they will end up playing. Again, we will discuss this idea further when we take up the Coase theorem in a later chapter.

To summarize: observe the common thread that runs through all the principal examples in this chapter—the late complaint in the dog bite case, the rancher's possible non-liability for the straying cow, and the rules about ownership of caves or anything else. All of these situations involve risks of waste, whether it's wasted time, misspent money, or resources never developed. The legal rules about these cases can be viewed as ways to stop waste from occurring by giving people incentives to avoid it. The incentives might be legal penalties for failing to use a cheap solution to an expensive problem; they might be freedom from liability once you *have* used the cheap solution; they might be rules of ownership and contract that create rewards for getting the most out of things. We will see more examples of other problems of waste (and solutions to them) in the succeeding chapters, but it will help to see the basic point now. It's very common for legal problems to lend themselves to this kind of inquiry: there are various possible solutions, but some of them will create bad incentives—and thus a risk of wasted time or effort or other resources. The better solution will discourage such squandering.

There are different ways to label these concerns we have been discussing. We have spoken of minimizing waste. We also could have called it maximizing wealth. A trade increases wealth by making the parties to it better off (that's the only reason both sides would agree to it); this is another way to think about a point discussed a moment ago: the value of contracts. People's wealth also is increased by rules that discourage the frittering away of it on duplicative litigation (as in the first examples in this chapter) or on repairs after needless accidents or on overspending to prevent accidents (as in our examples from tort law). We might just as easily refer to these goals as equivalent to the pursuit of *efficiency*. Efficiency can be viewed precisely as the elimination of waste; but there are different ways to think about what counts as waste and thus about what amounts to efficiency. The type of efficiency we will be concerned with in this book is the "Kaldor-Hicks" variety, which holds a decision efficient if it creates more benefits than costs overall. In other words, the people helped by the decision could fully compensate the people hurt by it and still be better off. In practice no such compensation need be paid, so a decision can be efficient in the Kaldor-Hicks sense even if some people are made worse off by it—so long as others are made even better off still. When this book refers to efficiency, that is what it means: comparing the total costs of decisions to their total benefits. (Distinguish this from the weaker notion of *Pareto* efficiency. A state of affairs is Pareto efficient if nobody can be made better off without making someone else worse off.)

We will be treating efficiency as valuable—as something a legal decision can have in its favor, though it need not be the only thing. You should understand, though, that there is controversy about the use of efficiency as a legal goal. To pursue efficiency may be considered a modified sort of utilitarianism, the goal of which is to maximize everyone's wealth rather than utility. But utilitarianism is controversial; and while seeking to maximize wealth may be more appealing in some ways,[13] in other ways it may be less so: increasing the total wealth of a group of people usually will mean increasing their welfare, but not necessarily.[14] And increasing overall wealth is usually considered an unsatisfying ultimate goal for the legal system because that project has to begin from someplace—namely, from the amount of wealth everyone starts with, which can itself be viewed as a product of law. That initial distribution of wealth may be unjust, and in any event it requires some separate defense of its own.[15]

There are other possible objections to using law to try to satisfy people's preferences, which is still another way of thinking about what the quest for efficiency aims to do. The preferences themselves, like everyone's initial distribution of wealth, may partly be products of the legal system (or endogenous to it, as the jargon goes).[16] People may have "adaptive preferences" that reflect the best they think they can get under their circumstances, not what they really want in any sense to which the law ought to defer.[17] Or their immediate preferences may not be in their own interests in the long run, either because they don't understand their interests very well or because they are in the grip of all sorts of cognitive biases and illusions. Or the preferences may include wishes that seem immoral and be entitled to no weight in public debate.[18] In any of these cases some people will conclude that paternalism is called for—or other policies based on a better foundation than just giving people what they think they want.[19]

Some of these considerations will be discussed in other chapters. Others are issues the interested reader can pursue in the references given in the endnotes and in the suggestions for further reading that follow in a moment. For now there are two points to grasp. The first is that the ultimate importance of efficiency as a legal value is open to debate. The second is that you don't need to resolve that debate to use the tools offered in this book for thinking about efficiency. The tools don't presuppose a belief that efficiency is the master goal of the legal system or even that it's always important. A lot of appeals to efficiency are just of a local "if-then" nature that everyone is likely to find agreeable or at least valuable. Pointing out that one decision would create more costs than another, or more costs than benefits, is almost always interesting, and sometimes turns out to be decisive, even if everyone agrees that other things matter, too.

SUGGESTIONS FOR FURTHER READING. Richard A. Posner's book Economic Analysis of Law (6th ed. 2002) argues that most legal rules can be viewed as ways of getting people to avoid waste, or act efficiently. It is probably the most influential book about American law of its times, and it is the first place to go for more examples—endless examples—of the same general sort found in this chapter. As just noted in the chapter text, the pursuit of efficiency raises philosophical issues that some readers might like to explore: questions about precisely *why* maximizing wealth might be considered valuable by the legal system, and whether it is best considered an appropriate moral goal in itself or just a possible means to other ends such as prosperity or liberty. Posner once argued the former view but now has moved to the latter. For the most important entries in this debate, see Richard A. Posner, The Economics of Justice chs. 3–4 (1981); Ronald M. Dworkin, *Is Wealth a Value?* 9 J. Legal Stud. 191 (1980); Anthony T. Kronman, *Wealth Maximization as a Normative Principle,* 9 J. Legal Stud. 227 (1980); Richard A. Posner, *The Value of Wealth: A Comment on Dworkin and Kronman,* 9 J. Legal Stud. 243 (1980); *Symposium on Efficiency as a Legal Concern,* 8 Hofstra L. Rev. 485 (1980); Richard A. Posner, *A Reply to Some Recent Criticisms of the Efficiency Theory of the Common Law,* 9 Hofstra L. Rev. 775 (1981); Richard A. Posner, The Problematics of Moral and Legal Theory 46–47 (1999).

3 ⤞ Thinking at the Margin

Being a smoker sounds simple, but there are many dimensions to it: how many cigarettes a day you smoke, what kind they are, and where you smoke them. Driving to work sounds simple, too, but again it's a bundle of choices, this time involving what kind of car you drive, how often you replace it, what time you go, what route you use, and so forth. Each of these dimensions can be called a *margin;* you might think of each activity—smoking, driving, or whatever—as having a shape, and those choices we've listed are its edges. The first thing to see is that if the law is going to concern itself with incentives in the way we saw in the first two chapters, it might be able to put pressure on some of those margins more easily than others: on where you smoke, but not on how much (as by forbidding smoking in restaurants); or on how much you smoke but not what kind of cigarettes (as by enacting a tax on all cigarette sales). The next thing to see about margins is that sometimes you can make substitutions between them: one can get wider if pressure is put on another. If you can't smoke at work, maybe you decide to smoke more at home or work more at home. If you can't afford as many cigarettes as before, maybe you decide to smoke a stronger kind. A last thing to notice is that each of the general activities so far mentioned—smoking or driving—can itself be regarded as one of the margins of some larger frame of reference. If you can't smoke at all, maybe you chew more gum.

Thinking at the margin, then, means a lot of things. Most importantly it means looking at problems not in a total, all-or-nothing way—smoking versus not-smoking—but in incremental terms: seeing behavior as a bunch of choices about when to do a little less along one dimension and a little more along another. This same style of thought can be applied to populations. You can think about how the average member of a group reacts to legal pressure, or you can focus on the margin: how the most sensitive members react to it. Maybe a tax on cigarettes doesn't cause a slight change in what each person does; but maybe it produces a slight change in what the *group* does by causing a few members of the group—the least resolute, or the least dedicated—to switch from cigarettes to gum. The activities of individual people have margins, in other words, and then groups of people have marginal members. And then this way of thinking can be applied to legal rules themselves, which may be simple affairs ("thou shalt not") or may set incremental penalties or require incremental changes in behavior.

Let's look more closely at why these ideas are useful. If you want to understand the incentives that rules create, it's important to grasp the meaning of margins because margins are where incentives take their bite. Legal rules may not cause entire changes in behavior by anyone, or little changes in behavior by everyone; but they do their work if they cause some shifts at the margins. It's also important to understand margins so that you will know to ask what substitutions a legal incentive might cause. One way to think about incentives is that they are meant to promote good substitutions from one margin to another, but there's always the risk that the actual substitution one gets will be perverse and counterproductive. And finally it's important to understand margins because the best solution to a problem often involves little adjustments—and maybe adjustments of several margins, belonging to different people—rather than just a decision to do something or not do it. We will take up each of these points in turn.

For the sake of illustration, start with one of the incentives discussed in the first chapter. We saw that courts don't hold banks liable for failing to hand over money when thieves take hostages; they worry that liability would cause more hostages to be taken. But is the average thief really likely to change his behavior in response to a shift in policy by banks? And is an average bank really likely to change *its* behavior in reply to a legal ruling like this? The answers may be no and no, but the questions are wrong. The issue isn't what the average bank or thief will do. It's what the *marginal* bank or thief will do—the bank in doubt about what its policy ought to be, perhaps, or the thief who is on the fence about whether to take a hostage. Either way the resulting behavior isn't an all-or-nothing proposition; the legal rule isn't going to cause everyone to take hostages or nobody to take them. The hope, realistic or not, is just that it cuts down on the practice at the margin.

The same reasoning goes for most of the arguments made about incentives created by law. How is it that raising the tax on cars causes fewer of them to be sold? You might imagine that you either need a car or you don't, so the tax isn't going to stop you. But that's thinking in totals, not at the margin; the marginal point is that some people (not all of them—just the ones who aren't entirely committed to buying a car now) will make substitutions. The substitutions will occur between margins of their own. People will still get new cars, but perhaps first some of them will drive their old ones a little longer, preferring to string them out and pay for repairs rather than trade them in at greater expense.[20] The point shades over into law more clearly when we talk about the rules governing tort liability for car accidents. The average person no doubt will drive as carefully under one system of liability—a "no fault" system, let's say—as under any other. But maybe a few people at the margin worry a little less under one rule than another, and maybe the occasionally reduced anxieties result in a few more accidents. Or maybe the no-fault rule creates a slightly more fertile ground for fraud by way of staged accidents and false claims. Again, most drivers will have nothing to do with this. At the margin, a few will. This doesn't mean that no-fault is a bad idea. Nobody is certain about the magnitude of those effects just described. The point is just to see the right questions, which are marginal.

Or more generally you may think that all these arguments about incentives are based on unrealistic visions of how human beings operate. People don't tend to plan their affairs around careful observation of legal rules. They usually don't know enough law for that, and typically they aren't even all that rational; most people are beset by lots of beliefs and preferences that amount to cognitive illusions, as we shall see in part 4 of this book. But again the comeback is the same. We are in search of marginal effects, not average ones. You can question even the marginal effects or their significance; just make sure that is what you are doing. Arguments about what the average person typically does aren't an effective reply to those who are trying to make a dent at the margin.

And the issue isn't just how many people decide to do something; it's how much of it they decide to do. From time to time there is talk of extending capital punishment to rapists or kidnappers. Moral and constitutional considerations to one side, there is an argument against it as a matter of incentives. Once a criminal has committed a rape, he isn't done; there is still a marginal decision about how far to go with the crime. If he faces execution for the crime he already has committed, he pays no additional price for adding a murder to it (and there is a benefit: one fewer witness to worry about). Thus the old saying that in deciding what to steal, one may as well be hanged for a sheep as a lamb.[21] The same reasoning is a source of objection to "three strikes" laws that put a criminal in prison for life after his third felony. He might as well make the third crime something spectacular since he will have "maxed out" on penalties if he gets caught. Many criminals—perhaps most—won't deliberate in this way. But in a large population, whether of criminals or anyone else, there always are some nearer to the center and some nearer to the edge, or margin, of decision. It's this last group that one must worry about.[22]

The worries just described have a name: the designers of criminal penalties have to worry about preserving *marginal deterrence*—scaling penalties so that there is always something more to fear by doing a little worse. We think not just about deterring crime overall but about putting pressure on the margin. How *much* crime, and which crimes? We saw how such reasoning can provide an argument against capital punishment; in other cases it can provide an argument *for* capital punishment, as when a murder is committed by a prison inmate already serving a life sentence. If the inmate already has committed a dozen murders, we still want an incentive at the margin to discourage him from committing a thirteenth. The typical murderous inmate might be indifferent to the penalty, but as usual we aren't concerned with the typical murderous inmate. We're interested in the marginal one who is thinking it over. In one actual case, for example, an inmate at the maximum security prison in Marion, Illinois, had received a life sentence for murder. He murdered a fellow inmate and received another life sentence; then he murdered still another inmate and received a third life sentence. Remarkably enough, he later found a way to commit yet another murder, this time of a prison guard. The court of appeals in his case concluded that "the facts cry out for a federal death penalty for prison murders"[23]—which wasn't available.

We saw at the start of this chapter that one can make substitutions between various margins: more of one thing to make up for less of another. This is a way to think about all those incentives we talked about in the earlier chapter on the ex ante perspective. The purpose of legal incentives isn't just to get people to do things or not do them; it is to get people to make substitutions. We want bank robbers to substitute away from taking hostages—to other tactics, or to a lawful occupation. We don't let people use things said during settlement negotiations as evidence in court; the reason, in the language of this chapter, is that letting people suffer for what they say during those negotiations would make the negotiations more costly, and so cause some parties to substitute away from settlement and toward litigation. We want the substitution to run in the other direction.

Almost any incentive furnished by law can be restated as an effort to get people to make a substitution of some sort, changing the shape of their activity by moving back along one margin and forward on some other instead. A good example involves the choice of tort rules that decide when people have to pay for accidents they cause. The great decision is between holding them liable for negligence—that is, only if it's shown that they weren't as careful as they should have been—or holding them strictly liable, which means that they pay no matter how careful they were. One way to think of the difference involves this question of substitution. If the rule is that people are liable only if they are found to have been negligent, they know they never will have to pay for harm their activities cause so long as they are careful. Strict liability sends a different message. It says that you will be getting the bills for any harm your activity causes, whether you were careful or careless; the implication is that if the bills get too high for your liking despite your best efforts at being careful, you have one recourse: substitute away to some less expensive activity. That is one reason why we have strict liability for activities we aren't sure people should be carrying on at all.

An example will make this clearer. Recall the old common law rule about dog bites mentioned at the start of the previous chapter: the dog's owner doesn't pay unless he already knew the dog was a biter. (The old saw is that "every dog is entitled to one free bite," though no court ever appears to have said such a thing.) But it was different for owners of wild animals—of lions, tigers, and bears. Owners of those beasts were, and usually still are, strictly liable for any damage caused by them, even the first time. Why the difference? We don't want people to stop owning dogs; for dogs—at least the ones thought to be tame—are highly useful animals. They can provide a package of friendship and security that is hard to improve upon. So in effect the first bite a dog gives is subsidized by the victim, who has to bear the cost without getting reimbursement from anyone. But we do want people to think about substituting away from owning lions, since it's difficult to think of important purposes lions serve that can't be achieved in safer ways. We encourage owners of lions to think about that by making them pay for damage the lion does no matter what. If they don't like it, they can trade in their lions—or even just some of them—for dogs or for other assets that will serve whatever purposes the lion did. In some jurisdictions there is an exception to this rule about lions and other wild animals; there is no strict liability if the owner is running a zoo.[24] The reason, at least on the account we're developing here, is that this time we don't want to put pressure on the owner to substitute away from the activity after all—from running a zoo to running a museum or some other amusement involving less liability.

Private owners of lions always are subject to the tough rule, though, because we can't see any harm in the substitutions they are likely to make (from lions to cats, or live lions to stuffed lions, etc.).

This reasoning also can explain why there is strict liability for using dynamite to bring down a building. Sending contractors the bills for any harm they cause with their blasting puts some pressure on that activity, and prompts the blaster to ask whether a substitution might be in order—say, a wrecking ball that will do less damage.[25] In all these cases we don't want to *ban* the activity—blasting or owning lions. That would be a non-marginal approach. Instead we want the full costs of the thing brought home to the people doing it, who are then left to judge for themselves whether to make substitutions. We will continue this train of thought when we discuss least cost avoiders in chapter 5.

There is a danger to think about when you try to force substitutions: you may create unwanted ones. This is a line of criticism of some attempts to protect the liberties of suspects in criminal cases. The famous *Miranda* case held that before interrogating a suspect they have taken into custody, the police have to warn him that he has a right to a lawyer, the right to remain silent, and the rest of the familiar litany.[26] It sounds like a help to suspects, but what are the consequences? One argument against *Miranda* is that it creates bad incentives for substitutions by prosecutors. *Miranda* raised the cost of trying to get convictions against some suspects: the ones who respond to the warnings by turning silent. So prosecutors trying to get all the convictions they can on a limited budget may stay away from the silent types and go after the more talkative ones. Yet the silent types are more likely to be guilty (that's *why* many of them are staying silent).[27] The pressure along one margin causes an expansion of the other—but we don't want an expansion of the other. It's hard to know if this story about substitutions is true. Here, as elsewhere, we don't know as much as we would like about the real consequences of the decisions we're discussing. But unwanted substitutions of this sort are worth considering when you think about the value of a legal rule.

Another possible example of such unintended consequences is the attempt to restrict spending on political campaigns. If you limit what candidates can spend on their own advertisements, you suppress one margin, so candidates and their donors will look to expand along another: now the massive donations are redirected toward political parties or political action committees, which run the advertisements instead—and now there is less accountability because it's not as clear who is responsible for the ads.[28] The government can try to suppress movement at that margin, too, but then it starts gobbling up liberty at an alarming rate. That is a great problem with unwanted substitutions: to stop them you often have to regulate *all* the margins involved to prevent the problem from moving around like a bump in a rug. But regulating all those margins may have great costs, both in conventional expense and in lost freedoms.

The structure of the argument sometimes is similar when people debate the value of employment protections, such as the right not to be fired without cause. Whatever the merits of the idea, it has the effect of suppressing one margin of action by an employer and raising its costs there. It becomes costlier, for example, to hire new people, because it will be harder to ever get rid of them. So we have to ask in familiar fashion about substitutions the proposal might cause, as by inducing the employer to make fewer new hires and instead have the existing employees work longer and harder, or to hire temporary workers or independent contractors who don't get the full protections that employees do. The same substitutions become tempting when employers are required to supply health care or other benefits to their regular employees. Again, our goal isn't to settle any of these arguments; as an empirical matter there is controversy about how the substitutions play out in all these cases. The point is to gain alertness to them.

One view of the danger we are discussing is known as the theory of second best.[29] It's complicated to demonstrate formally, but the thrust of it is this: suppose there is some set of conditions that you would like to create; they are "optimal," or first best. Unfortunately you can't fulfill all the conditions, but perhaps you can fulfill three out of four. Is it clear that you should? Not necessarily; satisfying some of the conditions (but not all) might be worse than doing nothing. To say it in slightly less abstract terms that are relevant to this chapter: ideally—or at least ideally from an economic standpoint—we might like to see the whole world running efficiently. But if we can't get to that result, we should at least make as much of it go efficiently as we can, right? Again, not necessarily. Settling for a "second best" change might actually do more harm than good because it might cause substitutions elsewhere that are inefficient (i.e., that cause waste) and offset whatever good the first change did. That wouldn't be a problem in a first-best world, because in that world there is efficiency at every margin. But in a world where we can only control some margins, changes that improve the ones we can control might make things worse along the others we can't control. And sometimes the bad effects can outweigh the good.

Here is an example of how this line of thinking works, suggested by Thomas Ulen.[30] A man named Tunkl showed up at a public hospital in California. The hospital wouldn't treat him unless he signed a waiver of his right to sue (or his estate's right to sue) if anything went wrong. Tunkl signed the waiver and died in the hospital soon after. His wife sued. The waiver Tunkl signed was held to be unenforceable; the California Supreme Court said, among other things, that the imbalance of bargaining power between the parties was too great to treat the contract as valid. It was a "contract of adhesion," meaning that Tunkl had to take it or leave it; there was no chance to negotiate over the terms, and under the circumstances he might have been likely to sign it no matter what it said.

Was the decision in Tunkl's case efficient? Normally it would seem inefficient to stop two parties from making any sort of contract that suits them, including a waiver of the right of one to sue the other. Presumably they wouldn't sign it unless they both thought it would make them better off, and the loss of that amount by which they would be made better off seems like a waste. To put it concretely, maybe some hospitals won't treat people like Tunkl because they are too afraid of being sued—and that would be a shame if the patients in Tunkl's position would have been willing to waive their right to sue in order to get treated. In that case there would be an outcome—treatment, but with a waiver—that both sides would have liked, yet instead the patient gets no help. But maybe all this is wrong. Perhaps this particular contract might not have been efficient after all because there was no chance to negotiate over it. Maybe if there were time to bargain (imagine that the patient isn't in such a hurry to pick a hospital), no such waiver would ever be signed. In that case it's more efficient *not* to allow these waivers because that is the result the parties would reach for themselves if they were making their decisions in a well-functioning market rather than at the front door of an emergency room.

If this last idea is right, it might seem like a strong argument against enforcing the waiver. And maybe it is. But a possible problem with this analysis is suggested by the theory of the second best. We can control one margin of this situation, but not all the margins. If research hospitals can't get patients to sign waivers that stand up in court, maybe they react to the financial consequences by making other changes: they stop paying their doctors quite as much, and those doctors leave and work at other hospitals with different priorities. Now less research is conducted and fewer discoveries are made. This overall result might be inefficient; the lost value of those discoveries might be greater than the losses you would get if you simply enforced those nasty waivers despite the imbalance of bargaining power. We got rid of a small source of waste but created a bigger one. Maybe to get *real* efficiency the courts should forbid the waivers *and* then the legislature should give larger subsidies to research hospitals. But if it turns out that we can do the former but not the latter, it's not clear that the former is worth doing at all; that is the point of second-best theory. Just forbidding the waiver might appear to be the second-best solution (getting rid of one market failure is better than nothing), but sometimes the second-best solution actually makes things worse because of its side effects (or "external costs"—an idea we will examine further in chapters to come). When you correct one failure of the market, you might just shift more pressure onto some other failure you didn't correct, perhaps because you couldn't.

Here is one more example that we are now in a position to summarize more quickly.[31] Suppose a firm dumps waste into a river. The harm to the river is an external cost to the firm—a case of market failure—since the firm does not feel it and does not take it into account when deciding what to do. A court might correct the problem by holding the firm liable, and this might seem an improvement in efficiency. But maybe it isn't. If the firm still can pollute the *air* with impunity, maybe it does more of that now—and this might do more harm than the pollution of the river ever did. The correction of one market failure put more pressure on another that was worse. Trying to make the situation a little more efficient, but not perfectly so, actually made it *less* efficient.

For reasons that are themselves a matter of debate and conjecture, the side effects of second-best solutions tend not to receive much analysis when people study the efficiency of legal rules.[32] Part of the reason might be the sheer difficulty of it. The application of second-best theory to the hospital case or the case of the polluted river, for example, is just conjecture; the side effects that those sorts of decisions have along other margins can be hard to nail down, especially for a court. It's hard to prove that the bad substitutions will occur, but just as hard to prove that they *won't* occur, and the uncertainty makes it difficult to say whether a legal decision that looks efficient is really helping the cause of efficiency overall. This difficulty highlights the importance of choosing which institutions—courts or legislatures—are in a better position to worry about different kinds of problems. Courts tend to be in a bad position to figure out what the side effects of a second-best solution would be, so it has been suggested that they should confine themselves to worrying about smaller or "local" problems of waste, where the side effects of the solution are likely to be small. Adjustments of margins on a larger scale, with efforts to control all the side effects, are better made by legislatures or agencies. They can gather more information than a judge usually is given by the parties to a lawsuit.[33]

Now let's consider a last aspect of marginal reasoning. When a court or legislature makes a legal rule, there is a general choice to be made between an all-or-nothing approach and a marginal one. Imagine a controversy between an airport and neighbors who complain that it makes too much noise. It may be artificial to restate these things in dollars, but we'll do so to make the discussion work. Suppose the airport creates $10 million in benefits over some period of time, but the neighbors say it creates $15 million in costs (perhaps that is what you would have to pay all the neighbors to make them indifferent to the noise). It might seem natural to conclude that the airport should be shut down; it creates more harm than good. But now look at it from a marginal point of view. Maybe cutting back on 10 percent of its flights—perhaps by stopping the ones at night—would reduce the airport's benefits by $1 million but reduce the harm to the neighbors by $8 million. Then the balance would be different: $9 million in benefits as compared to $7 million in costs. The optimal solution here isn't to shut down the airport; it's to adjust the margins (perhaps with a payment to the neighbors—but that's a separate issue). The same basic story could be told, with the same general lesson, without the dollar figures.

We can retell the account as a lawsuit involving an accident rather than noise. Most law students eventually encounter the famous British case *Bolton v. Stone,* where a ball in a cricket game was hit over the fence and struck one of the field's neighbors on the head. One question in the case is whether the owners of the cricket ground did anything wrong—whether they were negligent in failing to build a higher fence or take other precautions. From this story we can spin out a little example of what a marginal analysis might look like. Suppose the cricket ground was surrounded by a ten-foot fence. The ball sailed just over it before hitting the neighbor; the question is whether the fence should have been, say, fifteen feet high, since then it would have blocked the ball. The neighbor might be able to show that the taller fence would have benefits: the total cost of it would be (let us imagine) $10,000 and it would prevent $15,000 in accidents. It sounds worthwhile. But on a marginal view of the case, again, that isn't the right way to think of it. Maybe most of the benefit of the fifteen-foot fence already is secured by the ten-foot version; only one ball in a million would be stopped by the taller fence but not by the shorter one. Yet meanwhile the shorter one is considerably less expensive to build and maintain. On these facts the answer furnished by marginal analysis might be that the owners of the field got it just right: they did the efficient thing. Yes, a taller fence would have provided more protection, and the total protection it supplied would have been greater than its total cost. But the *marginal* cost of those extra five feet of fence would have been greater than the *marginal* (additional) protection those five feet provided to anyone. It's better that the five feet of fence wasn't built, at least from the standpoint of the costs and benefits involved.

The purpose of that example is just to illustrate what it means to think about marginal costs and benefits rather than in totals. The court in *Bolton v. Stone* didn't talk that way; no court quite does. As was mentioned last chapter, there is debate about whether judges can or do think in explicitly economic terms about accident cases.[34] Regardless of the outcome of that larger debate, though, it's worth considering when and why courts might at least think marginally and when not. One reason to avoid thinking about margins is that one can't do it well. In the examples involving the airport and the cricket field we put made-up numbers on the values involved, but in real life the numbers may be hard or awkward to devise. It's worth emphasizing again that it is possible to think about margins without using numbers. That's what courts usually do when they worry about incentives. But in some cases it may be hard to say anything intelligent about margins if there aren't any numbers to go on. In the case of the cricket ground, the details of the height of the fence, and the resulting benefits from each increment of it, might end up lost in fog; it's all speculation that can't be reduced to anything more reliable except, perhaps, at prohibitive cost. So maybe the court ends up just making a judgment about whether the proposed fence seems cost-justified and leaves it at that, or maybe it abandons concern with costs and benefits entirely in favor of some other type of analysis.

One reason there might be no numbers to go on is that the parties don't really want to supply them. This is another consideration that can cut against marginal thinking in court: the adversarial process may not be very hospitable to it. If there is litigation between the airport and its neighbors, the neighbors likely don't *want* a marginal solution. They probably consider themselves better off with the airport shut down altogether (assuming they don't work there); even if the benefits it generally creates are greater than the harms they suffer, they would rather do without the harms. Likewise, the airport doesn't want to cut back its nighttime flights. A solution by marginal adjustment isn't the first choice of either side, so neither may present the idea to the court or bring forward the information the court would need to see the solution for itself—unless one of the sides comes to believe it is going to be made a loser by an all-or-nothing decision. Then, of course, it may suddenly become open to compromise and negotiation, which is to say adjustment at the margin. Hopefully the lawyer sees this before it's too late. The point is general. If an all-out attack seems likely to fail, what a lawyer must do is find a margin on which to argue: some dimension of the situation where an adjustment seems most in order. It is one of the challenges of a decision maker—whether a judge, legislator, or regulator—to notice the possibility of such marginal solutions when the parties don't see them or won't admit to them.

Sometimes courts *prefer* to think in terms of margins rather than totals even when the sources of law seem to suggest otherwise. The Constitution is full of language that doesn't sound marginal at all. The First Amendment says that Congress shall "make no law . . . abridging the freedom of speech, or of the press. . . ." That's all-or-nothing language, not the language of marginal analysis; yet the courts sometimes turn First Amendment disputes into marginal inquiries. They don't put numbers on the values involved as we did in the examples just considered; they don't approach these cases as problems of comparing costs and benefits, at least not explicitly. But they do look at laws and the cases that challenge them in incremental terms. A law that restricts the "time, place, and manner" of speech without regard to its content is put to a test: it is valid if it serves an important objective, if it's narrowly tailored to meet that end, and if there are ample alternative chances for speech left open.[35] This is the stuff of marginal analysis after all. To restate the legal idea in the terms of this chapter, we ask whether the government could have substituted some other method for the one it chose—whether a different arrangement of margins, friendlier to speech, would have been feasible—and we ask what chances for substitution there are for the speaker. We could give the same account of many other constitutional rules that are phrased in either-or terms but have been turned into tests by the courts—tiers of "scrutiny," as they are called—that serve as occasions for thinking about the margins of everyone concerned. Why do courts so routinely turn absolute language from the Constitution into tests that call for marginal thinking? Perhaps because a constitution has to address such a wide variety of situations over long periods of time. Marginal approaches leave room for easier adjustment in how a constitution is read when changes in the world call for it.

SUGGESTIONS FOR FURTHER READING. Frank H. Easterbrook, *The Court and the Economic System,* 98 Harv. L. Rev. 4 (1984); David Friedman and William Sjostrom, *Hanged for a Sheep—The Economics of Marginal Deterrence,* 22 J. Legal Stud. 345 (1993); Herbert Hovenkamp, *The Marginalist Revolution in Legal Thought,* 46 Vand. L. Rev. 305 (1993). For good discussions of the theory of second best and its application to issues in this chapter, see Thomas S. Ulen, *Courts, Legislatures, and the General Theory of Second Best in Law and Economics,* 73 Chi.-Kent L. Rev. 189 (1998).

4 ↠ The Single Owner

We have seen that a lot of legal rules make sense when viewed as ways to discourage waste. At first this might seem to raise a question about why the rules are needed, for who *wants* waste, and who needs a rule to keep from creating it? The answer is that nobody wants waste—so long as whatever is wasted belongs to them. But people often create waste for others in the course of creating gains for themselves. Suppose that an accident occurs because the defendant skips some precaution: he doesn't put a fence around his ballpark, so balls sometimes break the windows of the neighboring houses. The owner gains by omitting the fence; he saves some money. The neighbors have a different experience of the situation: broken windows. Looking at the situation from the outside in, we can call it a waste if the gains from skipping the fence are smaller than the losses from the smashed windows. We view these things in the aggregate; we decide whether there is waste by comparing the gains to everyone with the losses to everyone. The challenge is to get the ballpark's owner to think that way, too. That is what the law accomplishes if it holds the owner liable for the broken windows. We make the costs experienced by the neighbors costs to *him;* to say it more technically, we force him to internalize the cost of omitting the fence. If he weren't held liable for the broken windows, he wouldn't worry about breaking them, which we then could call an external cost, or externality—a cost of his behavior that isn't brought home to him. Try thinking of that as the point of many legal rules, and of holding people liable for expenses they create: the purpose is to bring home to them the full costs of their choices rather than letting them foist the costs onto other people they don't care about.

There is a nice tool for thinking about this type of situation. It is known generally as the single owner. The word "single" doesn't refer to marital status; it means *sole.* The idea is to picture all the interests at stake in a case having just one owner, and to ask what that single owner of them would do. Think again of the problem involving the ballpark. It arises only because the owner of the ballpark is different and separate from his neighbors, and so doesn't take their losses as seriously as he takes his own gains. We treated it as obvious that he should have installed the fence, but maybe it isn't; maybe the fence would have been very expensive, whereas the broken windows are only an occasional problem. The useful thought experiment is to imagine that the ballpark and the neighboring houses had a single owner. Would *he* have built a fence? Notice how this solves the problem. A single owner of all the properties would take the cost of the broken windows just as seriously as the cost of the fence. He would build the fence if it were cheaper than replacing windows, and otherwise not. Put differently, a single owner of all the interests at stake would be careful to minimize waste, or (the same) to do the efficient thing. On this view the law's goal should be to make a rule that gets the owner of the ballpark to think the way a single owner would when he decides what precautions to take. Making him pay for every window broken by his baseballs (whether or not he builds a fence) might do the trick; that would be known as strict liability. Making him pay only if he fails to think like a single owner—that is, making him pay only if he *doesn't* build the fence, and it's found that the fence would have paid for itself in the broken windows it would have prevented—probably would do it, too. That would be called liability for negligence.

The idea of thinking about what a single owner would do was famously suggested in a nineteenth-century English case, *Bamford v. Turnley*.[36] Some farmers sued a railroad because sparks from its trains had started fires on their land. One of the judges, George Bramwell, said that it "is for the public benefit that trains should run, but not unless they pay their expenses. If one of these expenses is the burning down of a wood of such value that the railway owners would not run the train and burn down the wood if it were their own, neither is it for the public benefit that they should if the wood is not their own. If, though the wood were their own, they still would find it compensated them to run trains at the cost of burning the wood, then they obviously ought to compensate the owner of such wood, not being themselves, if they burn it down in making their gains." It's not clear if Bramwell was making a claim about what would be fair for the railroad to do, or what would be efficient; an attractive feature of the single-owner hypothetical is that it often can be used to capture both concerns.

The idea of the single owner helps clear up what neighbors should do for each other and how railroads should think about the risks they impose on farmers (what would the railroad do if it *owned* the farms?). But it also turns out to have other interesting applications. It can be used to think about cases where one person claims to have been injured by the negligence of another. Law students learn early about the

"Hand formula"—the way of thinking about negligence devised by Judge Learned Hand.[37] If the plaintiff says the defendant should have taken some precaution to prevent an accident, you can compare the cost of the precaution to the cost of the accidents it would have prevented (in other words, to the actual cost of the accidents, but multiplied by the chance that they would happen, since most accidents are low-risk affairs, not sure things). If preventing the accident would have been cheaper than letting it happen (or, rather, taking the *chance* that it would happen), then the defendant is held responsible for it. This is a just a more formal way to express the idea behind the tale of the escaped cow in chapter 2.

A problem with the Hand formula is that judges and juries never have the numbers they need to carry out the calculations involved in a rigorous way. One writer thus has suggested that juries be told to ask not whether the defendant in an accident case was as careful as a reasonable person (which is the usual question asked now), nor whether the defendant violated the Hand formula, but instead to consider "whether a reasonable person with average values in matters of safety and precaution costs—and who values the interests of others on a par with his or her own equivalent interests—would have taken the precaution at issue."[38] Notice that this amounts to asking what a single owner would do, and also to a rough restatement of the Hand formula. A person who owned all the interests at stake in a case—who felt all the costs of any precautions but also all the costs of any accidents—would balance those costs carefully when deciding what to do. That's one pretty good account of what we want people to do all the time, whether the cost of an accident they might cause would fall on themselves or on strangers.

This way of thinking also deals well with a common objection to the Hand formula, which is that it is uncomfortable to compare the dollars involved in taking precautions with the agony that accidents cause human beings. Balancing those things may well be uncomfortable, but people do it all the time—with respect to *themselves,* when they decide how carefully to drive, how much to spend on safety features for their cars and homes, and so forth. The idea is to get them to think the same way, and with the same care, when their decisions put other people at risk. Thought experiments involving the single owner thus provide an attractive link between the golden rule on one hand and economic talk about balancing costs and benefits on the other. They also illustrate the great emphasis the law places on balancing various interests against one another rather than dealing in absolutes. Few people are absolutists in their own lives; everyone tries to strike a sensible balance between safety and economy. The law does not ask for more. It just insists that the balance include the interests of others as well as oneself.

Courts generally don't instruct juries in negligence cases to think in the way we have been describing, but it still may be what judges and juries *do* when they apply common sense (recall the discussion of efficiency as a legal goal in chapter 2). Meanwhile, though, a number of other legal rules are clearer efforts to get people to act as if they were the sole owners of all the things that their decisions affected. Suppose one of your neighbor's oxen comes onto your land and starts to gore one of your goats. The ox is impressive in size and ferocity, and it becomes clear that you will have to choose between shooting it and letting the goat die—so you shoot it. Do you owe your neighbor a new ox? Probably. It turns out to depend on how much the ox was worth and on how much the goat was worth. The neighbor will say that you should be held liable for the tort of conversion, which is the name of the action used to recover when property has been stolen or destroyed (in this case, perhaps, you converted his live ox to a dead one); you will defend by saying that your apparent act of conversion was covered by your privilege to defend your own property: the goat. But in most jurisdictions the question for the jury will boil down to the relative values of the two animals. You will have to pay your neighbor for the ox if it was worth significantly more than the goat; if the goat was worth more than the ox, you needn't pay anything.[39]

Do you see why this amounts to a single-owner rule? The effect of it is to get you to think about the situation in roughly the way you would if you owned *both* animals, the goat and the ox. You would then be forced to choose which one would live, just as you were here. Presumably you would decide to save whichever was worth more, since the death of either animal would be a cost to you. The legal rule arranges its pressures to simulate that same outcome when the animals *don't* both belong to you. If the goat is worth more, you can shoot the ox and won't get in any trouble. If the ox is worth more, you shouldn't shoot it; you should let it finish off the goat and then make your neighbor buy you a new one. In essence the law penalizes you if you kill the more valuable animal: you are committing waste by destroying something more valuable to save something less valuable, and thus you are failing to act as a single owner of both animals would. (We're gliding over the question of how anyone decides what animals are worth. We'll deal with this, too, in a later chapter.)

The rules are a little different, but produce the same basic outcome, if your ship is threatened by a storm and you are trying to decide whether to lash it to my dock without permission. The courts say that since your property is in peril you have a right to save it by seizing my property; this is called the doctrine of necessity. But if the dock is wrecked as a result, what then? This was the situation in the famous case of *Vincent v. Lake Erie Steamship Co.*, where the court held that the ship's owner, despite having an undeniable right to use the dock in a case of extreme peril, had to pay for any damage done to it.[40] The result is to get you, the ship's owner, to think the same way you would if you owned the ship *and* the dock. In that case, as when the ox attacked your goat, you would try to perform a speedy comparison. If the ship was worth more than the dock, you would risk sacrificing the dock to save the ship and would swallow the cost, this being the lesser of two evils. If the dock was worth more (you'll have to imagine that the ship was decrepit), you would let the ship go rather than risk demolishing the dock. The legal rule causes you to internalize the costs of all these decisions—to experience them as if they were all incurred by you—by simply saying that you can choose to borrow the dock but then must pay for any damage to it. This is like strict liability, since you pay for the dock no matter how reasonable your decision to tie your boat to it. When you saved your goat your liability wasn't strict; it depended on whether you made the waste-minimizing decision (or wealth-maximizing decision—it's the same), which was like liability for negligence. Either rule can get you thinking like a single owner would. The difference lies in whether you have to pay anything if you made the right decision. In the case of the dueling animals the answer is no, perhaps because it would rankle to make you pay when you take reasonable measures to defend your animals against intruders who have no right to be on your land in the first place.

Now let's imagine that the boat is in similar trouble but this time is far from any dock. It is out to sea, sinking slowly, and groaning under the weight of its cargo. The natural thought is to start throwing things overboard—but which ones? The cargo probably is owned by lots of different people, and each of them would prefer that you throw someone else's goods over the side rather than theirs. If you pull into port and confess that you jettisoned a piano and several treasure chests to save the ship, the owners of those things are going to be most annoyed if they learn that you didn't push overboard the circus elephant the ship was carrying. They will suppose, perhaps rightly, that you were protecting the animal at the behest of its owner. They may feel obliged to send their own agents along next time to protect their goods against any such future decisions. In the meantime your decisions about what to jettison probably were wasteful, unless it was a remarkably valuable elephant.

This whole mess isn't very appealing, so since ancient times the law of admiralty—the legal name for the law of the sea—has met these cases with a doctrine called the *general average*.[41] It holds that if cargo is thrown overboard to save a ship, the owners of what was saved (including the ship itself) have to chip in to make it up to the person whose goods were sacrificed. Someone who owned a third of all the cargo that was saved (measured by its value) pays for a third of whatever was thrown overboard to save it. (The same goes in the more common modern case where the ship needs repairs to complete its journey, but let's stick to the more interesting problem of what to jettison.) The rule is meant to get you, the captain, to make the same sorts of decisions you would if you owned everything on the ship. Then when you were deciding what to throw overboard you wouldn't be distracted by thoughts of who owns what. You would just think about the weight and value of the things on the ship and try to stop the sinking as efficiently as possible. The rule of general average contribution likewise makes the captain indifferent to who owns what. It doesn't matter: everyone pays for all the losses anyway. The captain again has no reason to worry about anything except finding the most efficient response to the threat that the boat will sink.

Some details of the general average rule reinforce the idea that it tries to get the captain to think as a single owner would. When the court tallies up what was saved by throwing things overboard, it doesn't count cash, expensive jewelry, and the like that people on the ship were carrying on their persons. Why not? Weren't those things saved just as surely as the rest of the cargo? Yes, but we don't *need* to include those things to get the captain's incentives right. He probably won't ever be tempted to seize a passenger's necklace and cast it over the side, since it wouldn't help much; the jewelry is unlikely to have much to do with the threat to the ship.[42] We also don't collect payments from the passengers on the ship whose lives were saved. It might seem obvious that they should owe something to whoever owned the boxes thrown overboard to save them. But again the purpose of the rule evidently isn't to make everyone pay who got a benefit. The purpose is to get the captain to think the right way about what to jettison, and to achieve that we don't need to involve the passengers in the rule; for again there isn't much chance that the captain (single owner or not) will consider throwing *them* off the ship in order to lighten it. Maybe he's all heart; or maybe the benefits of tossing people overboard are very unlikely to be greater than the costs.

⋘--⋙

Next let's consider some complexities and limits of these thought experiments. Suppose the owner of a tall building fails to install a fancy safety cable in its elevator. The elevator plummets and its occupants are squashed at the bottom of the shaft. Their kin sue the owner for negligence, claiming the fancy cable should have been there. On the witness stand the owner gazes earnestly at the jurors and says he rode that elevator when he visited the building on the first Monday of every month; if it was safe enough for him, how can anyone say he was negligent in not buying the cable for the benefit of others? This sounds like a nice appeal to the principle of the single owner: the defendant's own interests were entwined with everyone else's, so he internalized all the costs of his decisions. Or did he? The problem with the owner's argument is that he enjoys *all* the savings from omitting the cable but incurs only part of the resulting risk. There was only a small chance that the elevator would plummet, and—more to the point—the chance was much tinier that he would be in the elevator when that happened because he rode it only once a month. It would be a much better argument if he could say that in addition to being the owner of the building he was the elevator operator and so was riding in it all the time. Or that his wife was the elevator operator; a "single family" hypothetical often works about as well as one based on a single owner, since we usually can assume that most people—and certainly most hypothetical people—value the safety of their family members about as much as their own.

Or think of an officer of a big corporation who is accused of self-dealing in ways that hurt the firm. He protests that he would never do such a thing; he's a major shareholder himself, so the *last* thing he would want to do is hurt the company. Whether the argument is worth anything obviously depends on what he is accused of doing and how many shares he holds. Someone who owns a third of a corporation's shares is still likely to be better off if he can steal some money from it outright. He gets all of what he steals but suffers only a share (perhaps a one-third share) of the consequences. If he were a true single owner—one who owned the entire company himself—then his argument would be strong: for then he would be accused of stealing from himself, which sounds ridiculous.

Asking what a single owner would do is often a good thought experiment for finding an efficient solution to a problem, and sometimes it's even what the law seems to require. But long-run considerations can cut the other way. The prospect of such a solution might make it too tempting for one party to invade the rights of another and thus multiply the occasions on which the solution has to be invoked. Even better than a good solution is not having the problem in the first place.

Recall the rule that if I mistakenly build a house that encroaches on my neighbor's land, he usually can get an injunction ordering me to remove it; the law won't let me wriggle out of the problem by writing him a check. (*He* might decide to let me do that, but we'll come back to that possibility later.) Notice that this rule often will violate the single-owner principle; if a single owner of the two properties built a house on one of them that encroached on the other, he would be most unlikely to deal with the problem by tearing the thing down. The law doesn't use the single-owner principle to guide its solution here because it would create bad incentives. When people choose where to build their houses, we don't want them thinking that if they bungle the decision the law will bail them out by ordering their favored solution—the solution they would have wanted if they owned all the land in question, which they don't. This amounts to saying that tearing down the house is an inefficient solution to a case of encroachment—or, to be more precise, to an *individual* case of it. Tearing down offending houses may well be an efficient solution to the problem of encroachment in general; it may be the rule that keeps the total cost of such fiascos lowest by causing them to occur so rarely. This reasoning might make you wonder whether the single-owner solution—letting the encroacher buy his way out of the problem—should at least be available in cases where it seems clear that there was no such abuse because the extent of the encroachment was tiny and the court is sure that it was an honest mistake. Indeed, most courts do make exceptions for those cases.[43]

Here is another limit on the single-owner principle. Suppose we make a contract in which you agree to supply me with as much rubber as I need at a fixed price for the next five years. A year later the price of rubber unexpectedly skyrockets; the price of most things made out of rubber naturally goes way up, too. But not for me: I can keep getting rubber from you at the same price, so I do; I can't get enough of the stuff. You complain that I'm not behaving the way I would if I were a single owner of all the resources involved—my manufacturing plant *and* your rubber supply concern. If I owned both, I would be conserving rubber because it has become scarce; instead I'm using it like mad. I shrug and say that I made a long-term contract with you so that I wouldn't have to worry about acting like a single owner. The law tends to agree. When we make a contract we are gambling, and sometimes we are gambling against each other. If I started demanding lots more rubber, a court eventually might hold that I'm breaching the contract because the point of it wasn't to let me go wild in this way; but even then the benchmark wouldn't be the behavior of a single owner.

The idea of the single owner does help illuminate some other corners of contract law, though. A good example is the doctrine known as mitigation of damages. If someone breaks a contract with you, you gain the right to send the breacher a bill for the damages; but the law requires that you make reasonable efforts to keep the size of the bill down. Imagine that you simply breach the contract we were just discussing; you announce that no more rubber will be forthcoming. It isn't open to me to sit around doing nothing for want of rubber. I have to make the best of the situation. There are various ways I might do it—by buying the rubber elsewhere, or by making things out of plastic instead. One way to think about the point is that if I were a single owner of your firm and mine, and your firm suddenly went kaput, I obviously wouldn't sit around doing nothing. I would try to keep the resulting losses as low as I could. So that is what the law requires me to do here, too.

Here is a last and strange application. Suppose tax rates go up, so your paycheck gets smaller; as a result you decide that it no longer is quite worthwhile to keep your current job. You switch to something that pays less and gives you more leisure time you can spend doing what you really like best, which is oil painting. The beauty of it is that you're just as happy as before, but you aren't getting taxed as much. Ah, but isn't that *immoral* of you? You aren't acting like a single owner. Hmm—but what could it mean to say that? Well, think of it again as though we were talking about a family. Suppose the father and husband is in the work force, but once he has lots of children he finds that he no longer has as much money to enjoy for himself as he once did. He used to spend a large share of his income on fine wine; now more and more of his money goes to his kids' expenses instead. He concludes that his job isn't rewarding enough to justify the sacrifice, so he switches to something that pays less but allows him to spend more time oil painting. His wife and children are considerably worse off now, but he's having a much better time. Might you not say he is behaving badly? He isn't valuing the interests of the rest of his family the way he values his own. But then isn't that just like you quitting your job and depriving the rest of us of the tax revenues that you could be generating and that we could be spending on all sorts of good things? Perhaps we should raise the taxes we impose on you as an oil painter to make up for it—and to get you to think about the whole of society as though it were your family.[44]

This way of thinking isn't quite how the law approaches the matter—but why? It might be because we can't figure out in any reliable way how much you value oil painting (though as a start we could say that you evidently value it more than the salary of your old job). It might have to do with considerations of liberty: if the tax on an oil painter got to be too high—if the painter's leisure were treated as psychic income, and he thus were required to pay as much in tax as a painter as he paid while at his old job—he might not be able to afford to be an oil painter at all. But a final consideration, partly related to that one, is that we do not always expect people to act the way a single owner would. We don't criticize the owner of plastic pink flamingos for not decorating his lawn the way a single owner of the whole street would (whatever that might mean), nor do we accept criticisms from him toward others on those grounds. For who knows what a single owner would do? It depends on *who* the owner would be. These are matters of taste that we prefer to leave to individuals to make for themselves. The right trade-off between working for money and "leisure"—doing things for the enjoyment of them, like oil painting—may be a similar matter. We don't criticize such behavior, and don't tax it, because we want space to exist where people can act for themselves and not worry about maximizing the good of everyone. The placement of choices inside and outside that space is an interesting problem. When people decide how many children to have, for example, how much should they be thinking about their own interests and how much about the interests of the rest of the world? The law of China answers this question rather differently than American law does. But then how does American law distinguish between choices we're content to see people make for themselves and choices we want them to make while thinking about others?

SUGGESTIONS FOR FURTHER READING. Richard A. Epstein, *Holdouts, Externalities, and the Single Owner: One More Salute to Ronald Coase,* 36 J.L. & Econ. 553 (1993); Stephen G. Gilles, *The Invisible Hand Formula,* 80 Va. L. Rev. 1015 (1994); Harold Demsetz, *When Does the Rule of Liability Matter?* 1 J. Legal Stud. 13, 26–27 (1972); William M. Landes and Richard A. Posner, The Economic Structure of Tort Law 32–35 (1987). For interesting examples of single-owner reasoning applied to some particular problems of procedure, see Bruce L. Hay, *Some Settlement Effects of Preclusion,* 1993 U. Ill. L. Rev. 21.

5 ↠ The Least Cost Avoider

The last chapter suggests that the law should penalize people when they fail to act the way a single owner would—in other words, when they don't act the way they would if they cared the same about all the interests affected by their decisions. But another strategy sometimes gets to the same result more simply: when there's an expense, just send the bill to whoever could have avoided it most cheaply, either by taking precautions or by switching to some activity less likely to create such expenses. The expenses might arise from an accident, or a misunderstanding, or an agreement that fell through. All those events can be costly, and all might be handled the same way: figure out who was in the best position to prevent it—we will call this person the least (or cheapest) cost avoider[45]—and make him pay for the result. Sometimes we might hope he will act differently next time, but not necessarily; the point might be just to force him to compare the cost of paying the bills with the cost of taking more precautions, and do whichever is cheaper. The beauty of this approach is that the law doesn't have to figure out how a single owner would have handled the problem. It tells the least cost avoider to figure it out. Maybe he will decide to let the bad things happen and keep paying the bills, or maybe he will find less expensive ways to prevent them. In either case he will feel the full cost of his decisions and so will make them carefully. This isn't the answer to every problem, as we shall see, but it is an interesting solution to many of them.

The legal name for this approach in accident cases is strict liability. We have seen this before; it means that the doer of some act pays for all the damage the act causes. We don't ask whether he did it reasonably or carefully; we simply send him the bills. It is true that when courts decide whether to impose strict liability on a defendant, they don't ask directly whether he was the least cost avoider of whatever bad thing happened. But when you look at cases where liability is strict, you'll usually find that the defendant is in the best position to reduce the risk of injuries. Everyone's favorite case where liability is strict is blasting with dynamite; if you're using dynamite, you probably are the least cost avoider of any harm the blasting causes to others, since there isn't much for the others to do about the danger except hope you are careful. The same goes if you start building a big reservoir that might burst and flood the neighborhood, as in the old English case *Rylands v. Fletcher.*[46] What are the neighbors supposed to do as they observe you starting your construction? There is little else for them but to wait and hope for the best. All the power to avoid disaster lies on your side—or most of it does. Perhaps the neighbors could move away; but let's assume, plausibly, that this would be more expensive than your being more careful or building the reservoir farther away. If the dam bursts, or if your blasting does some damage, we therefore send you the bill. You can pay it and keep blasting, or you can try to find a safer way to blast or a safer way to knock down buildings; you can pay the bill and keep the reservoir the way it is, or you can make it stronger, or you can move it somewhere else. It is all up to you. The point is that you will think about all the costs that your decisions create—decisions to take precautions or to omit them and pay for any harm done—and so will try to keep them all down. Put differently, you will try to arrange things efficiently, because your own money is at stake.

These examples show one of the great advantages of throwing legal responsibility for harm onto whoever can avoid the harm most cheaply. It's easy. If we had to figure out whether your blasting operation was careful or negligent, it would take time. Testimony would have to be heard; experts would have to be paid. The case becomes a lot simpler—less expensive for all concerned, and easier to settle out of court—if everyone knows that he who blasts must pay for the consequences. Or at least it *can* become simpler. We have spoken as though it were obvious who the least cost avoider is, but it might not be. To make that decision in an accident case, you might need to know what precautions each party could have taken, how much trouble the precautions would have been, and how much they would have reduced the chances of the disaster. Those are a lot of the same things that courts worry about when they *don't* ask who the least cost avoider would have been and instead compare each party's negligence. So if we are going to throw responsibility onto the least cost avoider because doing so is simpler, it will have to be because it's clear who the avoider is or because the courts can reduce that inquiry to general rules of thumb—to presumptions and exceptions to them. The law of strict liability can be seen this way. Liability for blasting is strict, but that doesn't mean it's absolute; the blaster can still get off the hook in certain cases, as when the injured plaintiff assumed the risk of injury. Perhaps he knowingly drew near to the dynamiting operation out of irrepressible curiosity. One way to think of such a case is that the victim then became the least cost avoider after all.[47] He knew what he was getting into and should have stayed away. That is why the law makes an exception here to the usual rule that holds the blaster liable.

This business of the victim's own role in the accident is important. When students first hear about strict liability and the idea of the least cost avoider, they sometimes like the idea so much that they start to wonder why we don't handle all accidents that way: strict liability for everything. But what makes the rule look good in the blasting case is that the blaster so obviously is the one who needs incentives to be careful—the only one. It follows that we might as well throw all the pressure of liability onto the blaster and let him decide what, if anything, is worth doing about it. A lot of accidents aren't like that, though. They are situations where both sides can and should take some precautions against trouble. The best way to stop cars from hitting pedestrians isn't just for drivers to be careful, or just for pedestrians to be careful. It is for both of them to be careful—to exercise "joint care," as it sometimes is called. But to send that message the law can't put all the responsibility onto whichever side could have avoided the accident more easily. In a sense there *is* no single cheapest cost-avoider; the cheapest thing is for both sides to use some care.[48] After an accident the law thus needs to examine the decisions made by both sides. That is what the law of torts does in a negligence case—for example, in cases involving car accidents of almost every kind. The usual rule then is some form of comparative negligence: the jury asks whether each side was as careful as it should have been and splits responsibility accordingly. It doesn't just throw liability on the side that could have avoided the problem more easily, nor does it start with that assignment and then make exceptions where the victim assumed some sort of risk. Instead the damages are divided to give both sides an incentive to do their part. Throwing all the liability onto the least cost avoider of some bad thing tends to make sense when there is just one party whose behavior we want the law to influence, usually because that one party has all the control over whether the bad thing happens.[49]

There also is room for debate about how to define the least cost avoider of something. It could be the person who had the power to avoid the disaster more easily, either by taking precautions or by substituting some other activity altogether. Or it could be the person who would have been able to figure out most easily what the costs of avoiding the trouble would be—maybe the party who deals with the same situation more often.[50] Or those two definitions could be combined or extended in various ways: the least cost avoider is the person who can avoid the disaster most easily, where "easily" is read to include not only the power to take precautions but the power to foresee the need for them, figure out what the options are, figure out who *else* might be in an even better position to take precautions (and then pay them to do so), and so forth.[51]

Those are important details, but details nevertheless. The *general* idea of placing liability on the least cost avoider is powerful and makes a lot of legal problems easier to understand. To stay with tort law for a moment, think of cases where one person is sued for failing to rescue another who was drowning. The usual rule is that the defendant wins; there is no duty to rescue strangers from trouble. Again, one way to think about the rule is that the victim is usually the least cost avoider of the disaster; it's easier for victims to avoid getting themselves into trouble than it is for rescuers to get them out of it. So in effect the victim is held liable for his own fix, which is to say that he can't sue anyone else who might have helped him afterwards but didn't. If this logic sounds right, you still might want to perform a reality check. We have been speaking about incentives, but do incentives matter in rescue cases of this sort? Are you—is anyone—likely to be less careful in Vermont because Vermont *does* have a duty to rescue created by statute? Here we can fall back on the usual appeal to (very) marginal effects; or we could suggest that the lack of a duty to rescue does create good incentives in some situations, and it's too much trouble to sort those from the cases where the incentives don't matter at all; or we might wonder whether the apparent economic argument for the rule could be some sort of argument about fairness in disguise. Maybe here, as also was suggested in the last chapter, economic ideas sometimes seem to line up with the law just because they line up with common sense ideas about right and wrong. Forget about incentives: the usual party most to blame in a rescue situation is the party who needs to be rescued.

In any event, there obviously are plenty of cases where these assumptions don't hold—where the rescuer really could have intervened so easily, and the trouble was so surprising to the victim, that a rescue (rather than trying harder to avoid trouble in the first place) would have been the better solution after all. But it would be cumbersome to test those assumptions in every case, so we don't. We use rules of thumb of the kind mentioned a moment ago. We say generally that when one stranger calls on another for rescue, there is no legal responsibility to respond; but then we also make categorical exceptions for cases where the rescuer and victim have a "special relationship"—innkeeper and guest, sea captain and sailor, or railroad conductor and passenger. In those cases it's easier to generalize that the defendant was in a strong position to help the victim after all, and that "strong position" might just be another way of saying that the defendant was the least cost avoider.[52] Sea captains aren't the same as average rescuers at the beach. They have (or should have, because they easily can get) lifesaving equipment, and anyone who falls off a ship is likely to be more at the mercy of nearby rescuers than is an ordinary swimmer thrashing around in a swimming pool or at a beach. Of course there are many reasons for the rules imposing liability on sea captains and railroad conductors for failing to rescue passengers in distress; it isn't *simply* a matter of picking out a least cost avoider and pinning liability accordingly. But that is part of the story.

This discussion of accidents might make it sound complicated to decide who was the least cost avoider of some mishap or whether to hold him liable. But in many cases only some of the decisions are hard, and in some others they aren't hard at all. There are a lot of easy ones in contract law. Most contracts involve one person paying another to do something. If it doesn't get done, the law treats the contract as breached and makes the performer, or "promisor," pay damages. This result sounds obvious, but notice how different it is from the way the law deals with a typical accident case: by asking whether the defendant acted reasonably. In a contract case nobody cares whether the defendant was reasonable or how hard he tried. He either performed the contract or he didn't. To carry over the language we used earlier, the law imposes strict liability for breaches of contract. It is easy to see why when you consider the logic we have been developing in this chapter. Performing a contract usually isn't a joint activity between the two parties. One pays and the other performs. The performer of a contract thus is akin to the demolition man with his dynamite or the builder of a reservoir. Whether a bad outcome occurs—flying debris in the blasting case, or a broken promise here—is up to him. There is nobody else whose behavior should be compared to his; the victim has no important role to play in avoiding harm. That doesn't mean the law always expects the promisor to fulfill the contract, but it does mean that it makes sense to send him the bill when he doesn't. He can decide for himself whether it makes more sense to perform or pay damages.[53]

What about the less usual case? Sometimes a contract becomes hard or impossible to perform for reasons that the other side (the promisee) might have been in as good a position to deal with after all. In those cases the promisor isn't necessarily the least cost avoider—and the law doesn't necessarily hold him responsible. Suppose you hire one of my horses, and in our contract you promise to return the animal in good condition. While in your custody the horse is found to have spinal meningitis and is destroyed, over your objections, by the local animal warden. Evidently you won't be able to return him in his original shape as you had promised; have you therefore breached the contract? The court handling these facts said no.[54] Usually the promisor—whoever borrows the horse—is the least cost avoider of any harm to it because he is the one using the animal. But with respect to *latent* illnesses you probably aren't the least cost avoider. I am, because it usually is in my custody. We *could* make a contract saying openly that you will be held responsible for the death of the horse for any reason, including disease; but where the contract is silent, the court tries to fill in the gaps with terms it thinks the parties would have wanted. A good guess about what they would have wanted is this: liability for whoever could have prevented the trouble most easily—the least cost avoider.

The doctrines that let you off the hook in the case of the diseased horse are known variously as frustration, impracticability, or impossibility: one way or another, it is no longer feasible for you to perform the contract (e.g., the animal is dead). Sometimes in these situations it is a little misleading to speak of the least cost avoider, because "avoiding" the outcome is impossible—as when performance of a contract has been made illegal by a new act of the legislature. In that case it makes sense to ask not which side more cheaply could have avoided the outcome (since neither of them had that power) but which side more cheaply could have borne the risk of it. Often one party is in a better position to have foreseen an unhappy development and to have taken steps to make it less damaging, perhaps by insuring against it. When we start down this road we find two general issues that might bear on which side is in a better position to insure against a bad outcome: one of the parties might be better able than the other to foresee how likely or severe the outcome would be, and one of the parties might be better able to "insure" against the outcome informally by spreading the risk of the bad development (whatever it was) among all its business dealings rather than going to the bother of buying a policy from an insurance company.[55]

These points about insurance can be made more concrete with an example. The United States made a contract with a firm to ship wheat to Iran. The Egyptian government then found itself at war and unexpectedly closed the Suez Canal, which greatly increased the expense of delivering the wheat by forcing the ships to sail around the horn of Africa. The parties might have allocated this risk between themselves in their contract, but they didn't; so the question arose whether the contract should be set aside—"discharged," as it is called—or enforced. The court enforced the contract. There was no point in asking which side was in a better position to avoid the outcome in a literal sense, since that was beyond the power of either of them. But the court was very interested in which side was in a better position to at least avoid the bad consequences of the canal's closing by insuring against it:

> [The shipping company] was no less able than the United States to purchase insurance to cover the contingency's occurrence. If anything, it is more reasonable to expect owner-operators of vessels to insure against the hazards of war. They are in the best position to calculate the cost of performance by alternative routes (and therefore to estimate the amount of insurance required), and are undoubtedly sensitive to international troubles which uniquely affect the demand for and cost of their services.[56]

As the court noted, the shipping company was in a better position to calculate the consequences if the canal were to close, since shipping was its business; it also has been pointed out that the shipping company was in a good position to spread out the risk of this sort of surprise among all those who hired it to ship anything. The United States government can self-insure in this way, too, since it does a lot of shipping, but perhaps that is a fluke. It may well be that the companies that hire shippers usually would have to buy formal insurance policies if they were assigned the risk of unexpected hazards that caused their shipments to fail. So it might be argued, in any event; and the point of the example is just to show how the idea of the cheapest cost avoider might be turned into an argument about the cheapest bearer of a risk that can't be avoided.

Once you start looking around for least cost avoiders, many puzzling distinctions in the law become clearer. Consider two cases. In the first one an oil painting is stolen, and then sold and resold many times—always for full value, and always to buyers who don't realize that it ever was stolen. Then the original owner discovers the painting in the home of its most recent buyer and demands it back. The original owner wins: the recent buyer never got title to the painting because it was stolen; neither the thief nor any later buyers became its legitimate owners.[57] Now here is another case. An impostor posing as a well-known art dealer persuades the owner of an oil painting to let him borrow it so that he might have it examined and appraised; then he runs off with the painting and sells it to an innocent purchaser. The original owner of the painting finds it and demands its return. This time the law sides with the later buyer, not the original owner.[58] What is the difference between these cases? In the first the painting was stolen; in the second it was acquired by fraud—a misrepresentation. The law treats victims of these crimes differently. The victim of a thief always can recover the stolen property, no matter how many times it has been resold (so long as the statute of limitations hasn't expired). The victim of a fraud is out of luck unless he demands the goods back before they are resold for full value to an innocent buyer—a bona fide purchaser, as he is called.

Why does the law draw the line where it does? In either case there are two parties who *might* have tried to prevent the disaster, and one of them is going to get burned: either the original owner, who could have been more careful to protect his property from criminals; or the last buyer, who might have looked more closely into the painting's provenance. But the ease with which each side can take those steps is different in the two cases we are considering. In the case of the fraud, the original victim of it is in a strong position to prevent the mess by investigating the impostor more carefully. They come face to face. In the case of an outright theft, it isn't as obvious that the original victim could have done better—and perhaps the buyer might have had an easier time determining whether the painting had fishy origins.

Notice that all these generalizations are crude—about the powers that victims of fraud and theft have to stop those crimes from occurring, or about whether and when a buyer should doubt the pedigree of the goods he buys. Of course we could avoid these generalizations and ask, one case at a time, whether *this* particular owner was in a better or worse position than this particular buyer to prevent the bad result. But that would be expensive—a case of high administrative costs (a problem discussed more in the next chapter). The cost of figuring it out from scratch in every case might eat up whatever savings we hoped to get by prodding the parties to be more careful. So we stick with general rules, such as treating victims of fraud less generously than we do victims of theft.

Of course it's also possible that the rules are based on some bad assumptions. Even saying which side *tends* to be in the better position to avoid the bad result in cases like these is hard. Maybe owners of stolen paintings often fail to take good, cheap precautions against the theft; maybe innocent buyers don't really have such great ways to find out where their goods came from—and have no reason to doubt the goods' origins. When identifying the least cost avoider of a problem is hard, it's no surprise that different legal systems handle the problem differently—that in some countries, for example, the victim of a theft can't recover the property once it has been resold to an innocent purchaser.[59]

At this point an objection might come to mind: in these cases don't we really want *both* sides—the owner and the later buyer—to take some precautions? In that sense these cases resemble the negligence problems we considered earlier from the law of torts. But if that's true, why would we throw the entire burden onto the least cost avoider? The answer is that we really don't put the entire burden on him. In the fraud case we say that the original owner loses *if* the later purchaser bought the goods in good faith and (what is pretty much the same thing) for their full market value. Assuming the buyer did his part, the original owner was indeed the least cost avoider. But if the price was suspiciously low, then we blame the buyer after all for being incurious or worse, and the original owner wins back the property. This shows how the idea of the least cost avoider can shed light even on cases where we want more than one party to be careful. It's like letting the blaster off the hook when the victim was injured by the dynamite because he knowingly came too close to it. In all these situations our views of the least cost avoider amount to presumptions, or default rules; they can usually be overcome by a showing that in a particular case someone else was in the better position to avoid the harm after all. The rule that allows such a showing in a strict liability case is, as we saw earlier, called assumption of risk. The rule that allows such a showing in a case of fraud is the requirement that the later buyer be a good-faith purchaser for full value. The names of the doctrines change, but the logic is somewhat similar.

Naturally the thief or con man is in the best position of all to avoid the mess—the "first best" avoider of it—so we put the most pressure on him: the threat of jail. But thieves tend to make bad defendants in suits to recover property or money because they so often are either unavailable or broke, so the rules sorting out the victim's rights against people who bought things from the thief are in practice very important. In these cases it is a question, perhaps, of deciding which is the second-best avoider of the trouble and which the third-best.

SUGGESTIONS FOR FURTHER READING. Guido Calabresi, The Costs of Accidents: A Legal and Economic Analysis (1970); Guido Calabresi and Jon T. Hirschoff, *Toward a Test for Strict Liability in Torts,* 81 Yale L.J. 1055 (1972); Richard A. Posner, *Strict Liability: A Comment,* 2 J. Legal Stud. 205 (1973); Stephen G. Gilles, *Negligence, Strict Liability, and the Cheapest Cost-Avoider,* 78 Va. L. Rev. 1291, 1331–32 (1992); Richard A. Posner and Andrew M. Rosenfield, *Impossibility and Related Doctrines in Contract Law: An Economic Analysis,* 6 J. Legal Stud. 83, 106 (1977); George M. Cohen, *The Negligence-Opportunism Tradeoff in Contract Law,* 20 Hofstra L. Rev. 941 (1992).

6 ➛ Administrative Cost

In chapter 1 we looked at legal rules, including judicial decisions, as ways to give people incentives to hunt whales, but we could have spoken instead of hunting foxes or buffalo. Let's do that now: suppose you spend all afternoon chasing a buffalo; at last you wound it and it becomes sluggish. As you are closing in to finish the job, I appear from the underbrush and administer the killing blow. Who gets the animal? You have a solid argument of the ex ante variety: letting me win this case would discourage anyone from chasing buffalo next time; everyone would then wait around in hopes of being the one who arrives for the kill at the end rather than the sucker who spends all day tiring out the animal for the benefit of someone else. The result would probably be less buffalo hunting. Some people would substitute activities involving less risk, such as fishing—which is too bad, because evidently they like buffalo better. This outcome is intolerable, or so the argument concludes. It might seem strange to say that you owned the animal just because you had wounded it, but it's a classic case where a court *has* to say such a thing to avoid ruining everyone's incentives. It's just a rerun of the finback-whaling dispute we talked about earlier.

Except that courts traditionally haven't said that. They say the buffalo goes to whoever captures it—whoever first reduces it to their possession, which probably will be the hunter who finally killed it, not the one who wounded the animal or tired it out.[60] The question is why. It might seem to be a case where all the worries about incentives give way to philosophical notions of ownership: you can't become the owner of something just by chasing or injuring it. Maybe so, but maybe not; we shouldn't give up so quickly on the analysis developed in earlier chapters. Remember the reason we're reluctant to spoil the incentive to hunt: it would be a waste. Everyone likes eating buffalo, and a single owner of the fields where the buffalo roam obviously wouldn't put up with an outcome like this. He would hunt the animals himself or hire a single team of hunters who wouldn't get in the way of each other. Put differently, a rule that gives the animal to whoever spent the most time chasing it surely is what the parties would all agree to in advance, before they knew what positions they would occupy in the hunt, isn't it? Well, not necessarily, because that rule creates some offsetting problems. For there is another kind of waste we haven't yet considered much: the problem of administrative cost.

The trouble is that in future cases the facts might not be as clear as they evidently are in this one. You will say that you were chasing the buffalo for five hours; I will say that it was more like five minutes. You will say that you had wounded it fatally, and that its death was only a matter of time; I will say that you barely grazed it and probably never would have finished it off. Sometimes my claims will be right, and sometimes yours will be—but how is a court to know which? It will be your word against mine, perhaps along with experts we hire to testify at a judicial hearing about the stamina of buffalo. These hearings will create two kinds of costs. The first is the simple outlay of time and resources involved in arguing about all this when we could have been hunting. The second is that sometimes the court will listen to all the evidence and then make the wrong decision. Every time this happens we might say that an "error cost" pops into existence. The cost is unfortunate in itself, and the threat of it will, again, make hunting less attractive in the first place. You will always have to worry not only about the cost of a lawsuit against someone over the result but also about the chance that you will be in the right but that the court will botch the factfinding and decide against you.

The point is that giving the animal to whoever invests the most in chasing it might not be the rule that best avoids waste. The prospects for such a rule would be better if it could be enforced automatically, but in practice it's much messier than that, and the mess probably is so great that it's better to pick a rule that looks worse but is easier to enforce—such as giving the animal to whoever takes hold of it first. True, even this rule would create some disputes. Maybe we won't be able to agree on who first seized it, or one of us will lie. But the rule still creates fewer margins that are likely to be disputed because it doesn't depend on lots of elements that are sure to be matters of interpretation: how vigorous a chase you gave, how badly the animal was wounded, and so forth. Just asking who possessed the animal first won't get rid of *all* disputes, but it will reduce their number and make the remaining ones easier to resolve.

Against all this you might imagine an objection: it's well and good to keep the court's decision simple, but what difference does it make if in the meantime you have ended the practice of hunting by spoiling the incentive to engage in it? The answer is that nothing the court says is likely to *end* the practice of hunting buffalo. As usual, all the effects are at the margin. If the rule is that the killer keeps the animal, some people won't care, but some others will substitute fishing or other things to avoid getting burned by someone who shadows them and free rides on their labor. If the rule is that the chaser keeps the animal, some people will, again, switch to fishing or other activities that don't involve annoying disputes over how much chasing they did. Either way, some people will keep hunting buffalo and some people won't. If one of those effects was obviously much larger than the other, the case would be simpler—as was true when we spoke of finback whales in chapter 1. The court thought it clear that if the party who lanced the whale didn't get to keep it, the legal rule really would end all finback whaling. That, plus the fact that it was usually easy to tell whether the plaintiff had lanced the whale, made it easy to say the lancer should win. Buffalo present a harder problem: it's not so clear that a different rule would ruin the hunt or that a rule giving the animal to its captor would be so easy to administer.[61]

That is, no doubt, more than enough talk about the rules governing a buffalo hunt. The point to bear in mind is that if we're going to worry about avoiding waste, or about solving problems the way a single owner would, there is another dimension to account for besides how the rule will cause people to act. We have to think about how expensive the rule will be when courts, and the parties to lawsuits, try to apply it. This turns out to be a crucial consideration in a lot of cases. The rule we then get is a compromise between different kinds of waste we want to avoid—wasteful behavior, but also wasteful arguments about it. Let us now, after our usual fashion, tour some other examples.

I carelessly run over your dog with my car. (Sorry.) What do I owe you? Clearly we need a rule that gives me reason to be more careful next time—but how *much* more careful? If we use the single-owner principle, the idea presumably is that I should drive as carefully around your dog as you would (or as carefully as *I* would if the dog were mine), which probably is quite carefully since most people are very fond of their pets. To make me feel the way a single owner would, I should have to pay you whatever your dog was worth to you. Yet I don't. The courts merely will make me pay you the dog's market value, which might be nearly nothing if it was a mutt. It's a brutal result, since you might not have parted with the animal for many thousands of dollars and (really the same point) might have driven much more carefully around it than I did. The rule, in short, rather obviously doesn't put much pressure on me to act like a single owner of the car and the dog. Why not?

The answer again is administrative cost. If we try to figure out what the dog was worth to you—what its *subjective value* to you was—we run into the same general problems we did with the buffalo hunt. First, the court is going to get it wrong a lot of the time. A judge or jury will have to listen to a long speech from you about how much you valued the animal—maybe strategic, maybe sincere, or maybe sincere but exaggerated by hindsight—and then make some guess about what dollar value seems right. That judgment probably will be at least partly wrong every time, and wildly wrong some of the time. Second, all this is going to take a while and cost us both. There may have to be a trial about it, perhaps where I cross-examine you distastefully over your feelings for your departed. The choice of rule also will affect how easy it us for us to settle the case without going to court at all. If you are entitled only to the dog's market value, we can figure that out by consulting some objective measures: classified advertisements for mutts, maybe. There's no need to go to court since a judge is simply going to apply the same methods. We can send our lawyers home early. But if the rule is that you are entitled to compensation for how much you personally valued the dog, it's going to be hard to settle the question without help from a court. Our lawyers can guess at what a jury would decide, and if their guesses overlap we might be able to settle the case. But the guessing would be unguided by any objective measure such as a classified ad; it might just be a matter of comparing the plaintiff's case to whatever cases the lawyers can dig up in search of amounts awarded to other dog owners. There will be a lot of room for conjecture. The result of the conjecture will be disagreement. The result of the disagreement will be more cases that go all the way to trial instead of being settled in advance. This process ends up being more costly to the parties, who have to pay their lawyers—not to mention more costly to the taxpayers who provide the courts, and more costly to other parties waiting in line for *their* chance at a trial.

As harsh as it may seem to award mere market value, then, on reflection maybe that is the rule that people would agree to after all if they were talking about the accident in advance—two dog owners, neither knowing who will be the driver and who the grief-stricken plaintiff. They might decide that awarding subjective value wouldn't cause all that great a shift in anyone's incentives to be careful but would cost them both a lot in fees and trouble that they would just as soon avoid. They might agree to a simple rule that can be applied cheaply and (on its terms) accurately. This train of thought helps explain more generally why the law uses market values as the benchmark for awarding damages in any case involving losses that can be measured that way. We will talk more about this in the last chapter of the book, which discusses problems of value.

The choice between subjective and objective tests is a recurring theme in law. A subjective test generally measures how hard people try to do things or what their intentions are. Objective tests just measure what people *do*—their conduct, not their thoughts—against some external benchmark. Subjective tests often seem preferable until their administrative cost is taken into account. The problem is that it's usually difficult to figure out how hard someone tried to do something or what their intentions were: it takes a long time in court, it's difficult to guess what a judge or jury will say about it in advance (so cases are harder to settle), and when courts do make decisions about these things they will have trouble avoiding mistakes. So there is a general tendency in law toward objective standards. In an accident case the law asks whether the defendant drove the way a reasonable person would, not whether he tried his best to be careful. When deciding whether to penalize a lawyer under Rule 11 of the Federal Rules of Civil Procedure, the law asks whether the papers the lawyer filed had a reasonable basis in law and fact, not—or anyway not primarily—whether the lawyer was acting in good faith. In all these cases, in other words, we avoid asking about anyone's intentions. We ask, one way or another, about reasonableness, which is a classic sort of objective test; it measures behavior of whatever sort against community standards, which are personified by the "reasonable person" to whom the party's behavior is compared. There are various reasons why the law does this, one of which is that trying to measure what someone was thinking or how hard they were trying is time consuming and error-prone, and those problems destroy a lot of the benefits that such tests might be expected to create.

These examples suggest how administrative costs often explain the large structure of rules—why the law so generally uses objective rather than subjective tests. But they also help explain smaller decisions. In accident cases the courts ask whether the defendant used the care expected of a reasonable person. But suppose the defendant is blind or insane. Should his behavior be compared to that of a reasonable person with those impairments or without them? The law's answer depends on which of those problems is involved. If the defendant is blind, his behavior is compared to that of a reasonable blind person. But if the defendant is insane, the courts make no such allowance: his behavior is compared to that of a reasonable person, period. Why this difference between the law's treatment of physical and mental difficulties? Part of the explanation probably involves administrative cost. It's relatively easy to tell whether someone has a physical limitation and to understand its consequences. It tends to be harder—more difficult, and more error-prone—to decide whether someone has mental limitations.[62]

Here is another small example. A few moments ago we mentioned Rule 11, which allows federal judges to penalize lawyers who make arguments that lack a reasonable basis in law. In one well-known dispute involving this provision, a lawyer presented a federal judge with a misleading argument: his brief said that a prior case had established an exception to some rule, when in fact the prior case had merely left open the possibility of such an exception.[63] The question was whether the lawyer's argument violated Rule 11. It certainly was a misstatement, and it might have led the court astray. The court of appeals nevertheless said that the lawyer couldn't be penalized. Why not? The best reason was that reading the rule to call for penalties in a case like this would give rise to too many arguments. Lawyers often stretch the meaning of an earlier case, and even more often can plausibly be *accused* of doing so. If every one of those instances became an occasion to move for penalties under Rule 11, judges would spend a lot of time on those disputes—more time than they want. The point is that the decision about how to read the rule was, indirectly, a decision not only about how the court wanted the parties to act but also about how many future disputes over the question the court wanted to hear. It was a decision about how many resources the court wanted to put into the rule's enforcement; it was a decision, in short, about administrative cost.

These arguments can be very powerful but also easy to overlook. In the Rule 11 case, anyone's first inclination is to ask whether *this* lawyer violated the rule, and to answer the question by consulting the rule's text or case law interpreting it. Those are the right places to start. The formidable arguments we just discussed come next, and they take more imagination: one has to stop worrying about what this lawyer did and realize that the decision about his case will make a rule for others; and then one has to realize the right rule for others may not just be the one that tells them to behave properly. A court may be willing to make some sacrifices for the sake of a reading that will be manageable as a practical matter—both in how easy it is to use and in how often it has to be used. Whether that particular Rule 11 case was decided rightly is, as usual, controversial.[64] The aim of this discussion is only to make the train of thought behind the argument clear.

Now consider an issue that seems unrelated but follows a kindred logic. There are, broadly speaking, two kinds of courts in the United States: state and federal. State courts can hear almost any sort of case; federal courts, though, have limited subject-matter jurisdiction, meaning that they can hear only certain types of cases—the kind Congress has authorized them to hear by passing particular statutes. Probably the best known of those statutes, and one every lawyer learns about early, is 28 U.S.C. § 1331, which gives federal courts the power to hear cases "arising under" the Constitution or a statute passed by Congress. The question is what it *means* for a case to arise under one of those sources of law. A natural possibility is that a case can be heard in federal court if the court will have to interpret the Constitution or a federal statute to decide it. This might seem to make sense; the point of the statute evidently is that Congress trusted federal courts more than the state courts to give effect to federal statutes and to the Constitution. Yet that isn't the rule. The Supreme Court held, in *Louisville & Nashville Railroad v. Mottley*,[65] that a case "arises under" federal law only if federal law creates the plaintiff's right to sue the defendant. Imagine, then, that I sue you for defamation under state law. You admit calling me a scoundrel and a thief but claim that you are protected by the First Amendment—part of the federal Constitution. The entire case will depend, let us suppose, on how the First Amendment is interpreted, which is the very thing federal courts are (by the logic of section 1331) supposed to do. Still, I can't bring the suit in federal court because it didn't "arise under" federal law. Your *defense* comes from federal law, but my initial claim against you doesn't. So the case is consigned to the state courts.

The reading just described might seem a strange way to decide when to open the doors of a federal court, but it has a massive, decisive, and familiar advantage over its competitors: administrative cost. We sketched an alternative test that may have sounded reasonable: let a case into federal court if its resolution will depend on how the Constitution is read. But that isn't always so easy to figure out. Sometimes a defendant will have lots of arguments to make, some of them constitutional and some not. How do you decide which ones are likely to matter? And *when* do you decide this? If you wait until the case is some distance along, and then decide that there aren't any important federal issues in it, the parties have to start over again in state court—a waste. If you try to decide at the beginning whether a case ever *will* have a big federal issue in it, the inquiry will often take a while and the court will get it wrong some considerable amount of the time. The rule of the *Mottley* case has problems of its own; it leaves out of federal court a lot of cases that it might make sense for those courts to hear.[66] But it's easy to use and usually hard to bungle. In most cases a lawyer can tell in about thirty seconds whether the test is satisfied. It just involves asking where the plaintiff got his right to sue. There are a few situations where even this question can be hard to answer, as when a plaintiff sues under a state law that incorporates a federal regulatory standard.[67] But that's like saying that we will still get some arguments if we award the buffalo to whoever finally killed it. There will always be disputes about *any* rule, but the rules we use in these cases produce far fewer disputes than the alternatives.

Notice that this business of administrative cost is especially important when it comes to rules about the jurisdiction of a court, since those rules have to be confronted every time a lawyer files a case there. This is why almost all rules about a court's subject-matter jurisdiction are kept simple, even if the simplicity comes at the expense of their substantive purposes. You tend not to see standards and balancing tests used to decide jurisdictional questions because standards and balancing tests require discretion to apply, and discretion is expensive. It takes some time to ask a judge what the answer is and entails a little risk to guess what the judge would say if asked. Any minor cost of this sort can turn into a big one when it's multiplied by all the cases where lawyers will have to fuss over the question before they can figure out where to file the complaint that starts a case.

Statutes of limitations involve a similar story. They give a plaintiff a fixed period of time and no more—two years, say—to bring a lawsuit about an accident, a breach of contract, or whatever other claims they cover. The usual rationale for these statutes is that cases need to be brought before the evidence in them gets old: after a couple of years memories fade and documents are lost or destroyed. And a time ought to come when potential defendants can relax and stop worrying about being sued—the interest in "repose," as it is called. All this is fine, but none of it necessarily suggests that we must have a severe cutoff at the end of two years. Those purposes might be served more exactly if courts made a direct inquiry into them at the start of a case. Instead of asking whether two years have gone by, they could simply ask whether the evidence in the case has, in fact, decayed or whether it's just as solid now as it ever has been. As for the defendant's peace of mind, the court could ask whether the nature of the claim is one as to which the defendant *ought* to have peace of mind. If it's a serious tort and the evidence still is strong, how can the defendant's wish for peace of mind count for anything against the plaintiff's wish for justice? It's no answer to say that one has to draw the line somewhere and that statutes of limitation serve that purpose. The lines could be drawn by judges one case at a time. In effect that is done already in equity cases under the doctrine known as laches; the judge balances the reasons and costs of the plaintiff's delay to decide whether to let the suit proceed. We could do the same thing in suits that seek ordinary money damages rather than equitable remedies (injunctions and the like).

The difficulty is that here—as in the case of federal jurisdiction—trying to pursue the underlying purposes of the law too directly is an administrative nightmare. The parallel to the discussion of jurisdiction is strong because here again the issue would arise in every case: a court's first question (after it knows that it has jurisdiction) would be whether the case is too late. Sometimes that would be hard to decide because it would involve judgment calls about the quality of the evidence and the kind of wrong the defendant is said to have committed. Different judges would decide these questions differently, which would make the resolution of them uncertain, which would make it harder to settle cases in advance and more expensive to litigate them when they go forward. Instead, then, we use crude deadlines. Perhaps it occurs to you that this trade-off might sometimes be *too* crude: why not make the deadline two years *unless* one of us tries to trick the other into missing the deadline by committing some sort of fraud? The law is ahead of you on this; it has doctrines such as equitable estoppel and equitable tolling that can be used relax the limitations period for good cause. Those doctrines, too, can be expensive to use, but we don't mind so much because they only get invoked once in a while.

One way to think of the patterns in all these cases is that a major purpose of law is to maximize the total wealth of everyone by reducing waste of whatever resources they have. This is done by reducing the *total* of all sorts of costs—not only the cost of accidents but also the cost of taking precautions against accidents *and* the cost of arguing about those things afterwards: the administrative cost.[68]

SUGGESTIONS FOR FURTHER READING. Guido Calabresi, The Costs of Accidents: A Legal and Economic Analysis (1970), is an early and influential treatment of the idea that administrative costs need to be included when analyzing the efficiency of legal rules. Steven Shavell and Louis Kaplow, Fairness versus Welfare (2002), discusses a wide range of legal questions from an economic perspective that includes prominent consideration of administrative costs, as does Richard A. Epstein, Simple Rules for a Complex World 30–36 (1995).

7 ⤞ Rents

Suppose the wreck of a galleon is found on the ocean's floor. Four teams of salvors race to lay hands on a treasure chest the ship is known to have on board; it contains historical artifacts worth ten million dollars. Each team spends about three million dollars trying to get there first. Eventually one of them succeeds, and the others are out of luck. The result is perverse, is it not? A total of twelve million dollars was spent to recover something worth less than that. As a group, the salvors would have been wealthier if the treasure *hadn't* been found in the first place. The result still would have been unfortunate, if a little less perverse, if there had been only two teams instead of four, and six million dollars had been spent to raise twelve. That sounds like a better deal, but it's still a waste. Really, spending *anything* more than the bare cost of raising the treasure is a waste; all the other money just goes into efforts by the teams to beat each other out, and there is nothing to show for it once the treasure is raised.[69] Needless to say, it's not how a single owner would have handled the situation.

This is a simple example of a problem known to economists as rent seeking. The phrase may be unfortunate: "rent" brings to mind images of landlords, and the difficulty we mean to talk about here has only a remote connection to them. Rent seeking means wasteful efforts to gain a prize; it might also be described as competition over the way some good thing ought to be distributed. (There are other, more technical definitions, but these are enough for our purposes.) The trouble with it can be seen by reflecting that there are, in general, two kinds of ways to increase one's pile of wealth. You can do it by producing some good or service that other people find valuable. Or you can do it by fighting over a prize of some sort. The difference between these methods—between, say, competing to run a better restaurant and competing to get to the treasure first—is that the first one creates wealth, or better-offness, on the whole: the customers are made happy, and restaurants gradually improve. Fighting over who gets the treasure isn't like that. The treasure doesn't get any bigger as a result. In a sense it gets *smaller* because so much of the wealth it represents is eaten up in the effort to lay hold of it. Those outlays can be described as sterile, meaning that they don't *produce* anything; their only effect is to move the treasure into the hands of one person rather than another. Think of this on a larger scale and you can see that the more a society spends on rent seeking—on quarrels over who gets what—the poorer it becomes. If that's all that anyone did, everyone would starve in due course.

The waste involved in rent seeking is a worry to the law and helps to explain some legal rules that otherwise seem unrelated. Monopolies are a good example. The temptations of rent seeking are greatest when a prize has a winner-take-all character, as was true of the sunken treasure and as also is true when a firm tries to get a monopoly. The firm knows that if it succeeds it will be able to charge higher prices than it could in a competitive market. Those high prices alone are a reason not to like monopolies, since they are a transfer of wealth from consumers to sellers (free markets work the opposite way: competition between suppliers turns their surplus into consumer surplus as they try to beat each other out to get business). But another objection to a monopoly is that the promise of those high prices will make firms and their competitors willing to spend a lot to gain such a position, and these sums are no better spent than the monies laid out to get to the sunken treasure first. From a social standpoint—a perspective that looks at the total amounts spent, and on what—the monies put into gaining a monopoly are a waste. It is just a case of someone buying a chance to charge more.

When you consider these points, do not limit your imaginings to the conventional monopolies forbidden by antitrust law, as when a firm tries to become the only oil company or software supplier in the market. Suppose a government decides to license one bus line to operate a shuttle between an airport and the city it serves. This arrangement will be a monopoly, though a lawful one. The license will go to the victor in a political process; the government will assign the license to the winning applicant. If the license is worth ten million dollars, then it becomes another case of sunken treasure: it might make sense to spend 90 percent of that amount to win the contract—and perhaps for the losers to spend a lot, too, before finally coming in second or third place. The spending can take all sorts of forms. A firm might try to become more attractive by really improving itself, which is good. But instead it might compare the cost of improving in productive ways with the cost of winning by other means that amount to rent seeking, such as campaign contributions to politicians and fancy dinners for them, and other bribes of a legal or illegal sort. From the standpoint of the rest of the world, these sums are badly spent. The first reason is that they don't create any wealth; they just move wealth around. The second reason is that if the spending does produce anything it is likely to be a corrupt or otherwise bad decision. And now we see a way that the results of rent-seeking become even worse. Once politicians come to understand the dynamics just described, they have incentives to *create* rents: they will want to offer tantalizing prizes that call forth lots of spending to win favor with them.[70]

Nor is the point limited to monopolies. It is a worry about any tantalizing prize available from the government. We saw earlier that one can try to amass wealth by, roughly, producing things or by fighting over them. Another and related great division can be made between efforts to gain wealth through the marketplace and to gain it through the political system, as by lobbying for handouts or favored treatment. The latter path, which again tends not to produce anything, might take many forms: it may involve a tariff imposed on competing goods from overseas, or it might be a statute or regulation, with public and private interest groups pouring resources into persuading politicians or other officials to decide one way or the other. Or the waste can work in reverse: an industry threatened with a burdensome rule may pay in various ways to be *rid* of it. Here the government might be said to extract rents instead of creating them. Either way, all the resources spent may be wasted from a social standpoint. (We hedge with the word *may* for reasons to follow in a moment.)

To pick out one illustration, the Internal Revenue Code is revised on a regular basis. One way to think of the ongoing process of changing tax rates, adding and removing deductions, modifying depreciation schedules, and so forth is that it creates chances for rent seeking. Interest groups hoping to protect "deals" they enjoy in the tax law, and other groups eager to get new and better rules, descend on Washington, contribute to political campaigns, pay lobbyists, and work to make friends in the right places. The cost of the tax system is not only the revenue taken in and perhaps misspent by the government, or the dispiriting or distorting effects that taxes can have on the activities to which they apply. It is also the cost of all this rent seeking the system provokes. And once again, politicians might come to favor frequent changes in the law, or rules that otherwise have little to commend them, because they encourage the attentions of the rent seekers known as interest groups. The rent seeking doesn't create wealth but moves some of it over to the politicians, many of whom naturally welcome it.

These hazards give us a way to understand not only restrictions on lobbying and bribes but more general features of the legal landscape, including aspects of the Constitution. One of Madison's great concerns in the Federalist papers was with factions; this can be restated as a worry about rent seeking by interest groups who claw at one another over distributional advantages and bend the attention of politicians away from the public interest in the process.[71] The results are waste by all sides and, more importantly, bad laws that mostly transfer wealth from losers to winners. So the Constitution throws up structural barriers that make it harder for interest groups to get rent-seeking legislation passed—in other words, redistributive laws (which is not to say that redistributive laws always are bad or always are the result of rent seeking). A simple example is the separation of powers. If a group wants a law that distributes some largesse in its direction, it isn't enough to win the support of enough legislators to squeeze the provision through Congress. The law may be vetoed by the executive, who then also will have to be "bought," to stick with the unfortunate terminology; all it means, though, is that resources of whatever sort will have to be spent to try to bring the president around, too. Then the provision may be passed upon by the courts. One can't lobby judges directly, though lavishing large sums on litigation is a natural possibility.[72]

The efficacy of all these constitutional mechanisms is a matter of lively debate. Obviously they are highly imperfect at best, since statutes that are the result of rent seeking—"pork"—are a common feature of modern legislation. Some argue that the separation of powers really serves to *induce* rent seeking by making it very cumbersome to get those legislative deals reversed once they are in place.[73] It's not surprising that the final results are ambiguous, for the problem itself is ambiguous. Some laws that give rewards to one group at the expense of others are the product of rent seeking that we wish wouldn't occur; some of them are thought to serve real public interests. Some efforts to impress legislators may be sterile and wasted; some may have value in improving the quality of the information behind a decision. It's hard to suppress the bad sides of these games without also raising the cost of the good, so we have a system that produces an unclear amount of each. It isn't always so easy to know rent seeking when we see it.

We have been speaking so far of cases where a private party wants some prize from the government—maybe a license, a regulation, or a statute—and spends wastefully to get it, perhaps in competition with others who are doing the same. Now let's consider how rent seeking might be a concern for courts and the lawyers who appear before them. We can begin by returning to the sunken treasure. The courts prevent waste in that actual case by giving exclusive rights to the treasure to the first salvor who makes a large investment in finding and starting to raise the wreck and can show it will be able to finish the job. The rule is a matter of international maritime law and is enforceable by injunction.[74] It encourages salvors to bother finding wrecks in the first place since it assures them that others won't then be able to rush in and take the goods; but it also prevents a frenzy of rent seeking by forbidding the second, third, and fourth teams from competing with the first and causing expensive jockeying for position. The rule thus causes the amount spent to raise the wreck to resemble the minimum cost of doing it, which in turn keeps the value of the project as large as possible. It probably is a rule that everyone in the salvage business would want if they could be asked in advance of any particular case. Rules that prevent rent seeking often are like that.

Here is a landlocked analogy to the sunken treasure: a firm races with others to create an invention, then gets a patent that gives the firm exclusive rights to the result. The purpose of the patent resembles part of the purpose of the rule giving the wreck to the first salvor. Its point is to give the firm an incentive to create the invention in the first place; research is expensive, and during the term of the patent the inventor can recoup those costs by charging a monopolist's price. But by now we know of some hazards that can come with the promise of a monopoly. It may cause rent seeking, as when different companies compete to be the first to come up with the invention. We're glad to have the invention but sorry about the redundancy and waste occasioned along the way by the firms that were beat out. In a sense that waste actually means the invention is a little less valuable than it looks because it was, in effect, more expensive to create than initially appeared. You have to account for all the resources that were plowed into the project in everyone's quest for the monopoly.

This time there is no rule that gives the party in the lead (by analogy to the first salvor) an exclusive right to finish the job, probably because it is too hard to identify that party when the subject matter is an invention that doesn't yet exist. Or maybe the real trouble is that there would then be a comparably wasteful race to be the first to stake a claim to a promising area of research. But in the details of patent law we do find rules that help keep other sorts of rent seeking under control. The story of a patent is not over once the patent is granted. There are chances then for a rival to announce that it has improved on the patented device—perhaps in a large way, or perhaps in a minor one—and then seek a fresh patent of its own. The firm that owns the first patent doesn't want this to happen (*it* wants to make the improvements), so now we find a new open field for rent seeking: a race to make little improvements to the subject of a patent and call it something new. Here it has been suggested that courts do, in fact, read patents more broadly when inventions lend themselves to lots of slightly modified versions, and that this discourages a duplicative race to create those small modifications. The ironic result is that very elegant inventions may get *less* protection in practice because they don't lend themselves to wasteful diddling with little improvements in the way that inelegant, complicated inventions do.[75] The elegant stuff doesn't invite the same sort of rent seeking, so it doesn't need as much protection for the sake of heading off that particular problem.

Setting individual areas of law to one side, a larger point to grasp about rent seeking is that it tends to be invited when a judge (or anyone) has discretion in making decisions that others care about. The others naturally will want to argue, lobby, or do whatever else they can to get the discretion exercised the way they like. This helps explain why it is so important for legal documents to be written clearly. A will that contains an ambiguity may cause the possible beneficiaries to fight long and hard to persuade a court to read it one way or another, which anyone can see is a bad thing—and which we can now recognize as a species of rent seeking, since the money and labor invested in the feud create nothing and effectively deplete the value of the property disposed of by the will. (A celebrated example is "Jarndyce and Jarndyce," the endless inheritance dispute described by Charles Dickens in *Bleak House;* the legal fees spent on the case end up consuming almost the entire estate that the parties are arguing about.)

The same tale can be told about a badly drawn contract or easement or any other instrument. And then it can be told again about the writing of statutes, or regulations, or the opinions that courts issue. There is a lot to say about the choice between rules and standards, and we'll save most of it for chapter 17, which is devoted to the subject. But here we readily can see one disadvantage of a standard: it will tend to call for a partly discretionary judgment (that's what *makes* it a standard) and thus may provoke expensive efforts by both sides to show that the judgment should be made this way or that. It is one of the reasons we insist on rules, even crude rules, when it comes to certain legal questions, especially those that come up very often—like the rules governing jurisdiction and the statutes of limitations discussed in the preceding chapter. If the tests for these things depended on all-things-considered judgments, both sides would be obliged to pour resources into arguing about them—possibly resulting in a small gain in justice, but at frightful cost and waste in the long run.

We can pursue the point further by leaving the courtroom for a moment and looking at some applications of these ideas within law schools. Exams at the end of courses almost always are graded anonymously. There are a number of reasons for this, but a big one is that if grading weren't blind there would be a strong incentive for students to lobby their professors in various ways during the semester. Not all of those ways would be bad; maybe some students would prepare more thoroughly for class, participate better there, and get to know their teachers in ways that would be good for both sides. (This is the equivalent of a company's efforts to get an exclusive license from the government by creating a better product.) But a lot of the student lobbying would amount to rent seeking. There would be sucking up of a kind that wouldn't edify anyone. Everyone is better off if nobody does it. And it's not just a question of wasting time; it's also that the rent seeking here, as in the legislative arena, might *work* and cause some people to do better than others for reasons having nothing to do with merit. A similar logic explains why spots in crowded courses are usually filled by random lotteries rather than at the instructor's discretion. The latter approach would cause students to try to lobby their way in. The lobbying might produce a small improvement in the number of spots allotted to really deserving students (however they might be defined), but it also would waste a lot of time.[76]

We looked at ways that judicial decisions can cut down on rent seeking. But what about courts as *arenas* for rent seeking? At first they might appear immune to the lobbying and bribes that characterize the political process and so might seem a refuge where lawmaking can occur in a more unspoiled environment. But while judges only rarely are lobbied or bribed, the engines of rent seeking have other outlets, as we noted in passing earlier. Rent seekers can make expensive efforts to get favored judges appointed or elected in the first place. The rent seeking starts again when interest groups invest heavily in litigation—and here interest groups may be defined to include firms and lawyers who have lots of wealth, appear repeatedly in court, and have long-term interests in how the courts decide the matters that affect them. They can make litigation very expensive for the other side; they can overspend on the defense of cases to deter future lawsuits; they can settle cases selectively—all to make sure they squeeze every drop of gain and avoid every chance of loss in the judicial system, just as they do in the political arena. And in one respect winning in the judicial system might be better than winning in the political system: a victory in court creates a precedent, and the doctrine of *stare decisis* may make it harder to overturn such a precedent later than it would be to repeal a similar decision made by a legislature.[77]

The problem can, again, be brought a bit closer to home. When economists talk about the problem of rent seeking, as they often do, their favorite example isn't the hunter for treasure or the firm rushing to get a patent or even the aspiring monopolist trying to get the bus contract at the airport. No, their favorite example of a rent seeker is the *lawyer,* whose job they see as fighting over the distribution of things.[78] A lawsuit is like the race to the sunken treasure, only more acrimonious; both sides spend and spend to claim some ever-shrinking pot of assets. Some view lawyers as encouraging these contests because lawsuits are their livelihood. Lawyers also make the contests more expensive because once one side has a lawyer, the other has little choice but to make the same investment. On this view lawyers *produce* nothing. They only shift money around, frittering away assets in the course of arguing about who is entitled to them. (And then it gets worse, as people shy away from useful activities because they fear they will get sued if anything goes wrong. They fear the onslaught of the rent seekers.)

This is, as I say, the view of some economists (as well as some others!), and it is far too ungenerous. Few lawyers spend most of their time bringing or fighting lawsuits; more of them write the wills and contracts we just discussed, the handling of which is important precisely to prevent rent seeking later on. Or they explain how to avoid lawsuits, or advise people on business matters, or settle disputes, or make deals—all of which create wealth (or—the same thing—reduce waste) for their clients and for others. As for the lawyer who does spend time in litigation, those cases may not produce anything for which there is a market, but they are efforts, sometimes successful, to produce goods people value very much but for which there is no market: justice and rights, for example, as well as incentives for wrongdoers to act more carefully next time—to avoid negligence, to perform their contracts, and so forth. Still, there is no denying that *some* litigation amounts to squabbling that consumes resources without producing anything valuable. Naturally lawyers, like lobbyists and politicians, aren't comfortable with the thought that some of their activities are largely wasteful. They tell themselves stories in which they are serving the public interest (as we did above). The stories are partly right.

All those activities—politics, lobbying, and litigating—are partly wasteful and partly beneficial. It is a question of proportion, and it's well worth worrying about, but we can't settle it here. For now our goal has been more modest. It has been to explain what rent seeking is and when and why it's a problem; for if you understand that much you can make an intelligent start on these questions for yourself.

SUGGESTIONS FOR FURTHER READING. The term "rent seeking" originated in Anne Krueger, *The Political Economy of the Rent-Seeking Society,* 61 Am. Econ. Rev. 302 (1974). For more discussion and interesting applications, see Jonathan R. Macey, *Promoting Public-Regarding Legislation through Statutory Interpretation: An Interest Group Model,* 86 Colum. L. Rev. 223 (1986); Fred S. McChesney, Money for Nothing: Politicians, Rent Extraction, and Political Extortion (1997); Stewart E. Sterk, *Information Production and Rent-Seeking in Law School Administration: Rules and Discretion,* 83 B.U. L. Rev. 1141 (2003).

8 ↠ The Coase Theorem

We have spent several chapters talking about various kinds of waste that are worries to the law. The most basic and most important example is behavior by people that creates some benefits for themselves but more costs for others, like failing to take simple precautions to avoid accidents. The problem is that sometimes the things you do create costs for others that you don't feel, and so may not take into account in deciding how to act. We have seen that sometimes legal rules can be viewed as ways to correct that: they make people act the way they would if they cared equally about all the costs and benefits of what they did. Now let's consider another take on the problem, which is that there might not *be* a problem if the parties can easily make contracts with each other. If you're creating more costs to me than benefits for yourself, I can pay you to stop—and that will be the end of the waste even without help from the law.

The idea sounds simple but is easy to overlook. It was first introduced by Ronald Coase, who later won the Nobel Prize in economics partly on the strength of the point.[79] Coase liked to illustrate his argument with examples from old common law cases, and they are convenient for us as well. Imagine a bakery next door to a doctor's office. The bakery creates lots of noise—banging away with pots and pans and so forth. The doctor finds that this disturbs his medical practice, so he brings a lawsuit claiming the bakery is a nuisance. There are various ways to think about the problem, but one—and the one most congenial to the style of analysis we've been developing—is to ask how we can get the most total value out of the space the doctor and the baker share. If there is great value in doing one of the activities there but not so much value in the other, then on this view the more valuable one should have its way. That is what a single owner would do who ran a doctor's office and an adjacent bakery: leave the more valuable one where it is and move the other. It's like the choice between the ox and the goat that we encountered in the discussion of the single owner in chapter 4.

At this point, though, it might seem that there's a problem: how can a court figure out which of these activities—the doctor's or the baker's—is more valuable? Coase's idea was that the court doesn't have to figure it out for the parties. *They* will figure it out for themselves, no matter who wins the lawsuit. Suppose the location is hugely valuable to the doctor and less valuable to the baker. In that case either the doctor will win the lawsuit and the baker will leave, or the doctor will lose and *pay* the baker to leave: since the location is worth more to the doctor than the baker, it stands to reason that there's a deal to be made between them. To make it concrete, let's suppose the doctor derives $10,000 a month from being there (as opposed to anyplace else), and the baker gains only $2,000—but the baker wins the case.[80] The doctor will say, "See here; don't make me leave. We would both be better off if I simply stayed and paid you, say, $3,000 each month—or a comparable lump sum now—to compensate you for the difference between being here and moving to your next favorite location." By bargaining the parties thus will find their way to the same solution a single owner would have reached. Here is another way to see the point: at first the noise the baker makes looks like an external cost of his operation; it's a cost he doesn't feel (only the doctor feels it). But if the parties can bargain, then the baker *does* feel the cost after all, though in a different sense than we have seen before. He feels it in the form of a $3,000 payment that he will turn down if he stays. Again, this will make him think the way a single owner would.

This vignette illustrates how the Coase theorem works. The theorem is usually said to be that in a world with no transaction costs—a world where parties can bargain and make contracts with no trouble at all—rights naturally flow into the hands of whoever will pay the most for them. The highest bidder will be assigned the rights by the law and will simply keep them, or will buy the rights from whoever else they are assigned to. It's hard to state the theorem more precisely than that, because Coase doesn't offer any theorem in his article; when people speak of the "Coase theorem," they are just trying to sum up the point of what Coase said, and they don't always do it the same way. In any event, the idea just described has lots of implications. Let's think about some of them.

1. If the parties to a case can bargain easily, a court needn't worry about waste resulting from whatever decision it makes; the parties will talk afterwards and make sure there isn't any. In those cases it might fairly be said that the law doesn't matter much. Or rather the law doesn't matter much so far as avoiding waste, or getting to an efficient result, is concerned. The law still does matter very much to the parties and to most of the rest of us, since the legal rule will determine whether either of them has to pay anything to the other. But that is a worry about how wealth is distributed between the parties, and right now we aren't focusing on that.

We're focusing on how to get to a "single owner" solution of a conflict that maximizes the total size of the pie the parties share, however it may be carved up.

This view can also be adapted to a larger scale. For some people the Coase theorem is the source of a general preference for letting markets, or in other words private negotiations, take care of bigger problems than lawsuits. The problems might be matters of pollution or might involve injuries caused to consumers by dangerous products; the "Coasean" instinct in either case is to ask whether there is some way that people can bargain their way to solutions, either by negotiating with the polluter or by demanding safe products as consumers—but in any event without intervention by the government. (All Coase himself insisted on, though, was that the costs of public and private solutions to such problems be understood and compared before preferring one to the other.)

2. The views just sketched start from the assumption that people can easily bargain their way to waste-free results—that transaction costs are low. But in the real world, bargaining isn't always so easy, and sometimes it's impossible. Coase's discussion has been thought to have implications for those situations, too. The court (or the legislature, or whoever is handing out rights) should then try to make a winner out of whichever side values the rights involved more highly—the side that *would* end up with the rights if the two parties could easily negotiate. The idea is that the court should make the contract for the parties that they would make for themselves if they could.

Instead of a baker with a doctor next door, imagine a valuable factory—but a factory that creates pollution. The pollution bothers a thousand of its neighbors, some of whom sue to shut down the factory as a nuisance. The judge concludes that the factory creates a lot more benefits for its owner than costs for the neighbors; the judge is satisfied that if all the neighbors could bargain with the owner, the owner would turn down their most generous offer to pay him to leave or change his operation. A single owner of all the properties thus would leave the factory where it is and wouldn't make any changes. But the judge also doubts that any negotiation of that kind will ever take place if the factory loses the case. It's too hard to get the thousand neighbors together.[81] The important thing then—from the standpoint of avoiding a wasteful result—is to either make the factory a winner or let it pay damages that somehow get distributed to the neighbors. The one thing you wouldn't want is an injunction ordering the factory to shut down. That would be a waste, given the assumption we have been making: the factory would be ready to fully compensate the neighbors in return for the right to stay, but wouldn't be able to do it for practical reasons—difficulties in bargaining, or transaction costs. It would be a shame, on an economic view, to let those impediments prevent a transaction when the court can simulate it by letting the factory pay damages (or simply continue what it has been doing).

This point, like the first one, can be adapted to a larger scale. The problems of waste we have talked about in the past few chapters can be restated as problems of high transaction costs. They would be cleared up immediately if the parties involved could bargain without any cost or friction. Think about the problem in terms of external costs, or "externalities": situations where I create costs for other people that I don't feel myself. There wouldn't *be* any externalities if everyone could make bargains by snapping their fingers. I would then feel all the costs of my behavior after all, because by keeping it up I would be turning away payments offered by all the people I am bothering. (Thus George Stigler's way of stating the Coase theorem: "under perfect competition private and social costs will be equal.")[82] This point can be turned into an idea about a general purpose of law: it's a set of substitutes for the agreements people would reach with each other if making agreements were as easy as thinking about them.

As we saw in the chapter introducing the idea of efficiency, you can think this way about the rules in accident cases. An accident where the defendant is negligent can be reimagined as a breach of a hypothetical contract—the contract the two sides would have made if they had seen the chance for an accident coming. The reason they didn't—to tie the point to this chapter—is that transaction costs were too high. Even the fact that time runs one way can be looked at as a transaction cost: the one-way flow makes it impossible to write contracts about problems that nobody sees coming; the Coase theorem therefore can't operate smoothly, and we resort instead to rules of tort law as substitutes that probably look like what the parties would have thought sensible in advance.[83]

3. Notice that the imaginary high bidder for the rights in a case might not be the party you would expect from common-sense notions of what causes what. If an airport creates lots of noise and so makes its neighbors uncomfortable, it doesn't necessarily follow that the airport should be made to feel their pain by paying some sort of usage fee. That was the type of thinking Coase was protesting against. For it might then be that the airport would move or scale back its operations—but that it *shouldn't,* because the cheapest solution to the problem is for some

of the neighbors to move away. It's tempting to say that *they* are the ones creating the problem, not the airport. But actually it's pointless to talk about who is causing the problem. The problem simply exists; it's a conflict caused by both sides, or by neither side, because they are doing things that don't go well together. Instead of worrying about who is causing the problem, it's better to ask what solution to it is cheapest.

This idea—sometimes known as "reciprocal causation"—sounds counterintuitive to most people. Their intuitive sense is that people have *rights*, and the rights serve as benchmarks for deciding who is causing harm to whom. In this case the home owners have a right to hold their ground in comfort; if the airport makes noise that disturbs them, the airport is the one causing the problem in an obvious sense. There is nothing wrong with that intuition. It is embedded not only in the heads of onlookers but in the legal system, which routinely uses rights as starting points for deciding who causes what. It's just that to Coase and other economists, those rights and intuitions are irrelevant. To them the best solution to the conflict is, as usual, whatever a single owner would do—in this case, a single owner of the airport and the houses nearby. Or it's the solution the airport and the neighbors would reach if bargaining were as easy as thinking about bargaining. If the single owner would move the houses rather than make adjustments at the airport, then that is the solution that creates the greatest *overall* gains; it's the solution the two sides would reach if there were no transaction costs; and (the same thing) it is the efficient answer to the conflict. Maybe the home owners should be compensated, either by the airport or by the government. Again, that's a question of distribution. Various answers to it might be all right, so far as the economist is concerned, but they are beside the point. The really important thing is to not make the airport scale back at great expense in order to save the neighbors *less* expense (with "expense" always defined broadly to include any source of value). That would do more harm than good. Lawyers, of course, worry about distribution as well as about waste, or efficiency. But it helps to understand the difference between the two issues.

4. We have spoken so far as if there are two general kinds of situations—some where bargaining is easy and some where it is hard—and then talked about how the law might respond in each case. But notice that these points aren't really independent. Law can affect *whether* bargaining is easy; and one implication of the Coase theorem is that the legal system should try to make bargaining as easy as possible, and to otherwise help it along. Sometimes this is as simple as creating a clear

property right that people can easily understand and trade. But there are theories suggesting other ways that law might help, as by encouraging people to reveal information to one another.

Suppose we make a contract but leave some parts of it unspecified. Should the law fill in the blanks with default terms that amount to guesses at what we would have wanted? That would be consistent with the Coase theorem: it would save the parties the bother and expense of negotiating over all the terms. But here is another idea: maybe the law sometimes should supply default terms for contracts that probably *aren't* what the parties would want. Why? Because then the parties will be more likely to negotiate over the point (since they don't want what the law will give them if they don't). And perhaps we want them to negotiate because we think that talks between them will lead to better results than any background rule the law might come up with.

Let's go back to our contract. Imagine that I agree to sell you a million widgets but we don't mention the price. The courts will fill in a price that seems "reasonable" at the time of delivery.[84] Now suppose the opposite: we do mention the price but we don't specify the number of widgets involved. This time the court's reply will be different. It won't try to speculate about what a reasonable number would have been; it won't enforce the contract at all.[85] In effect the court fills in the blank with a zero. Obviously this isn't an effort to simulate what the parties would have wanted; zero isn't the quantity that either party to a contract has in mind. But whereas a court can figure out a reasonable price fairly easily (by just finding out what the market price was for widgets), it will be much more trouble to figure out what a reasonable *number* of widgets would have been. The court probably would have to learn all about the situation each party is in. It's cheaper (if not for the parties, then cheaper *overall*) for the parties to take the time to work out the quantity in advance. So the default rule is deliberately made inaccurate—perhaps it's a "penalty" default—to force the parties to do their own negotiating.[86] (There is some controversy about whether the "zero quantity" rule is a default rule or is simply a formal requirement of making an enforceable contract—and indeed about whether there are many, or any, true penalty default rules in contract law.[87] But however that debate ever gets resolved, the example at least illustrates why and how the law might force people to negotiate over a point.)

Or suppose the issue is employment. In the United States the usual rule is employment at will: unless there is a contract saying otherwise, an employer can fire an employee for any reason or no reason. Yet there is evidence that most employees don't realize this.[88] It has therefore been suggested that the default rule be changed so that employees can be fired only for cause—unless (again) they sign a contract saying otherwise. Either way the employer and employee can make any contract they like. But a presumption that an employee can be fired only for cause might have the good property of forcing a negotiation. The employer, who more likely knows the default rule, would be obliged to bring it up if he wanted it changed; and employees would then get clearer information than most of them now seem to have. The default rule might not mimic what the parties want (we may not really *know* what they want—that's the point). Instead it is "information forcing"; it prods the parties to reveal things to each other.[89]

Now let's consider some reservations about the Coase theorem and the implications of it described so far. The discussion a moment ago offered a vision in which people treat the decisions of courts merely as starting points and then are ready to bargain their way to different and perhaps opposite results. That's clearly possible in principle, but it's not at all clear how likely it is in practice. The advocates of this vision of bargaining in the legal process generally do not base it on observations of anything. They base it strictly on the logic of the situation: it just stands to reason that parties would bargain after judgment if the rights were worth more to the loser than to the winner. So it might seem, but sometimes, and maybe often, reality is more complicated.

Begin with the case of the doctor and the baker. An empirical study was conducted of twenty actual nuisance cases that had something like that same structure: they all involved one neighbor suing another to complain about noise, smells, or other disturbances.[90] It turned out that after the courts made their decisions in those cases, there was no further bargaining between the parties in any of them. This might seem to show just that the courts were excellent at assigning the rights to the side that would have paid the most for them (so there was no *need* for any bargaining afterwards); but the lawyers in these cases were confident that there would have been no bargaining if the loser had won, either. The reasons were that the parties detested each other and didn't want to bargain, and that they didn't like thinking about their rights as bargaining chips and didn't view themselves as "in it for the money." Presumably massive enough cash offers would have dislodged the parties from those positions, but no such offers were forthcoming. The parties' enmity and distaste for bargaining weren't endless, but they were bigger than any gains from trade they stood to make by talking. (Another interpretation is that the parties were influenced by what's known as the endowment effect; that idea, and other problems for the Coase theorem created by differences between the prices people pay for things and demand to give them up, are discussed in chapter 22.)

The study just described involved a small sample size, so its results may not be typical, but they nevertheless are suggestive. They show that people's preferences may differ significantly from those of the characters in tales told by economists, and they are a caution against ever assuming that a court's decision won't affect who ends up with the rights in a case. They especially are a caution because of the dearth of evidence on the other side; it's not as if there are lots of well-documented examples of parties bargaining around the decisions that judges make. Whether this is inconsistent with any of Coase's claims, though, is another question. All he said was that a court's decision wouldn't affect the final resting place of the rights *if* there were no transaction costs. The question thus becomes whether enmity between the parties, or their distaste for bargaining, ought to be considered a kind of transaction cost—as a bad thing that the legal system should try to override. Should courts treat hatred between the parties, for example, as a warrant for giving judgment to the party who would buy the rights if it *weren't* for the hatred? It's a hard problem, and the best answer probably depends on details of the circumstances—but those may not be visible to a court.[91]

Then there is a different reply to the failure of parties to bargain after judgment in real nuisance cases: they aren't the parties we should be worrying about. Of course those few who insist on litigating all the way to a final judgment probably do hate each other; litigation isn't known for encouraging tender feelings between the parties. But most people settle their cases earlier, or—much more often—resolve their differences without lawsuits at all. They, too, will encounter legal rules made earlier by the courts, and presumably they will be perfectly willing to treat those rules as the starting point for good-natured bargaining. Yet here again there is evidence that doesn't quite square with the Coasean vision. Consider one of Coase's other examples: ranchers and farmers who are neighbors and have a conflict because the ranchers' cows eat the farmers' crops. The question is what should be done about it. The law has two general choices. It can say that the rancher is obliged to keep the cows contained or else pay for the damage they cause, or it can say that it's up to farmers to protect their crops from wandering cows or else take the consequences. Coase suggested that the law's choice between these approaches wouldn't affect the way the problem ended up being solved. If the cheapest solution was for the rancher to build a fence, then that's what would happen. It would come about in either of two ways. The legal rule might favor the farmer, in which case the rancher would build the fence to keep in his cows and avoid paying damages. Or the rule might favor the rancher, in which case the farmer would pay the rancher to build a fence—a cheaper solution than watching his crops get eaten. (If letting the crops get eaten were cheaper than building a fence, then *that* is the solution the parties would find through bargaining.) The important thing is for the law to assign the rights to whoever would pay the most for them if bargaining were costless.

Again these speculations led to an empirical study, this time of how real farmers and ranchers resolve such conflicts.[92] The result was that they generally didn't *know* the legal rule. They worked out their obligations through informal norms—by which is meant rules enforced socially rather than legally—about what neighbors have a right to expect from each other. The author of the study, Robert Ellickson, suggested that these informal norms were themselves waste minimizing (or wealth maximizing; he uses the ideas interchangeably, as this book does). But the point for our present purposes is that the law wasn't serving the function envisioned for it by some of the economists following Coase. Ellickson treats these results as a warning against the temptations of "legal centralism"—the view that the rules governing people's rights all come from the government.

As before, the cases that were the subject of these empirical studies surely aren't typical of many other situations in the world. Where the stakes are high and parties are sophisticated—perhaps, for example, when they are corporations with expensive lawyers—we might well expect classic Coasean bargaining directly from various legal rules to the identical final results. No doubt there are lots of cases like that, as where the winner of a dispute over a patent ends up selling a license to the loser: the law affects who pays whom, but not what the parties actually end up *doing*. The real lesson of the study of ranchers and farmers, like the lesson of the study of nuisance cases, is humility. The actual likelihood of bargaining, and the role of legal rules in it, depends on the environment in which the parties sit. A lot of the time we don't know much about that and may be in no position to control it.

Where do courts come down on all this? The question is too general to admit of one answer. Efficiency—minimizing waste, or making the size of the pie as big as possible—is a value in law; protecting parties' expectations, notions of fairness, and ideas about distribution are values in law, too. Different judges weigh them differently. It's certainly rare for a court to cite the Coase theorem, and probably not common for a judge even to think about it. Yet it's still a valuable thing for lawyers to understand. It can generate valuable arguments about what resolution of a dispute would be efficient and what would be wasteful. But the more immediate payoff comes simply from understanding that the decisions of courts, and legal rules more generally, need not be treated as settling arrangements in the world once and for all. People can use legal rules and decisions as starting points for bargaining their way to other arrangements that suit them better. Sometimes seeing these possibilities takes imagination and creativity, because it's natural for the law's announcement of a rule to carry a sense of finality.

SUGGESTIONS FOR FURTHER READING. The points in this chapter were most influentially developed in Ronald H. Coase, *The Problem of Social Cost,* 3 J.L. & Econ. 1 (1960). Coase's thesis is famous for getting an initially cold reception from economists at the University of Chicago; the story of that reception, and Coase's triumph over it, is told by George Stigler in *The Fire of Truth: A Remembrance of Law and Economics at Chicago, 1932–1970,* 26 J.L. & Econ. 163, 221 (1983). The literature pursuing the implications of Coase's argument is vast; *The Problem of Social Cost* is the most heavily cited article ever published in a legal periodical. The most interesting of the more recent work is Robert C. Ellickson, Order without Law: How Neighbors Settle Disputes (1991). Other good discussions for the newcomer to try include Stewart Schwab, *Coase Defends Coase: Why Lawyers Listen and Economists Do Not,* 87 Mich. L. Rev. 1171 (1989), and Robert D. Cooter, *The Cost of Coase,* 11 J. Legal Stud. 1 (1982). For a skeptical treatment, see Mark Kelman, *Consumption Theory, Production Theory, and Ideology in the Coase Theorem,* 52 S. Cal. L. Rev. 669 (1979); and for an amusing debate about some features of Coase's article, see A. W. Brian Simpson, *Coase v. Pigou Reexamined,* 25 J. Legal Stud. 53 (1996); Ronald H. Coase, *Law and Economics and A. W. Brian Simpson,* 25 J. Legal Stud. 103 (1996); A. W. Brian Simpson, *Coase v. Pigou Reexamined: An Addendum,* 25 J. Legal Stud. 99 (1996).

PART II

Trust, Cooperation, and Other Problems for Multiple Players

9 ⤞ Agency

With Eric Posner

Think about situations where one person is supposed to work hard for the benefit of another. The obvious examples involve people hired to do things: the lawyer is supposed to work hard for the client; the real estate agent is supposed to work hard for the seller of the house. But sometimes the same problem arises where the relationship is less direct. A company's stockholders want the officers running it to work hard, and voters want the politicians they elect to work hard. The general structure of all these situations nevertheless can be considered similar. First there is a person called a principal—a client, a boss, or a citizen; and then there is an agent—a lawyer, an employee, or a politician—who is supposed to be working to advance the principal's interests. But there is a natural conflict of interest between them. The agent doesn't feel all the benefits he creates by working hard; the benefits of his work go, at least immediately, to the client, to the boss, or whoever else he is serving. So the agent, having no love of hard work for its own sake, would prefer not to work so hard. He would prefer, in a word, to shirk.

The shirking wouldn't be a problem if the principal could just pay the agent according to his efforts, so that the harder the agent works, the more money or other benefits he gets. The trouble comes when the principal can't exactly tell how hard the agent is working. Sometimes all the principal clearly sees are the results of the agent's labors, and they might be hard to interpret; he might not be sure whether a bad outcome is the result of the agent's poor efforts or of something else. The owner of the seafood restaurant wonders if he is losing business because nobody likes his waiters or because nobody likes his fish. Shareholders wonder whether the value of a company's stock has gone down because the CEO is inept or because of competition from overseas. It's hard to know for sure.

Principals need ways to reassure themselves that their agents will work hard when they aren't being watched, whether because watching them is impossible as a practical matter or too expensive to be worth the bother. People who would like to be agents will want those mechanisms to exist, too; for if they have no way to reassure their principals, they will have trouble finding work or getting paid as much as they would like. (Agents also will want some insurance against the chance of bad outcomes that aren't their fault; we will come back to this.) The expense to the principal of watching the agent, and the expense to the agent of trying to reassure the principal, are known to those with a taste for economic jargon as *agency costs.* Also regarded as agency costs are the losses that occur when all those efforts fail: the losses from shirking or corruption because the agent's interests aren't quite aligned with the principal's, and the enterprises that never get off the ground because the needed level of trust between principal and agent can't be established at all. But there are interesting ways in which the problems of principal and agent often do get solved or at least kept under control, usually with the help of legal mechanisms. Those solutions are the subject of this chapter.

We already referred to one way of dealing with agency problems—though probably the least interesting solution, and the one that owes the least to law: monitoring, either by watching the agent or inspecting his results. If the agent's effort can be monitored perfectly, of course, there isn't an agency problem; the principal just pays for what he sees. But when the monitoring can't be perfect, principals sometimes go to lengths to watch what they can. They hire spies to pose as co-workers, or they monitor the number of keystrokes their secretaries make, or they put stickers on the back of their trucks telling other drivers to call and complain if the truck is driven badly. At a higher level they might try to make the agents' meetings and deliberations more visible, or "transparent." They have students write evaluations of their professors and submit them to the dean.

The more interesting solutions to agency problems involve contracts that give the agent an incentive to take the principal's interests seriously. There is a recurring tension in the design of these contracts. The principal wants to tie the agent's pay to the results he produces, thus giving him a big incentive to work hard. The agent would rather be paid regardless of result. True, he might like the idea of making more money if he produces a lot, but a typical agent will be made nervous by a contract in which his pay depends entirely on his results. He will be nervous because he knows that hard work doesn't always produce good outcomes. (If there were a perfect match between them, again the problem would dissolve: he would just be paid accordingly.) He might produce disappointing results because of other people's efforts, or bad luck. He will want insurance against those possibilities—some guaranteed money. The principal will prefer to keep that part of their deal smaller; and the larger it gets, the smaller the bonus the principal will be inclined to pay when good results do occur. Those, in general terms, are the moving parts in a typical contract meant to solve an agency problem. Let's look at some examples of how they get arranged.

Start with the waiters at a restaurant. Assume, plausibly, that the success of a restaurant depends partly on how hard the waiters work and partly on various other things. If the waiters are lazy, the restaurant is doomed; if the waiters work hard, the restaurant may do well if various other things also go right. Consider why some of the obvious contractual solutions here wouldn't work. The owner could pay each waiter a lot if business is good and nothing otherwise. The waiters thus realize that they will make money only if they work hard, so they will work hard (probably—there is a danger that it's a prisoner's dilemma, but we can postpone that idea until the next chapter). Although sometimes they won't get paid, that's better than shirking, in which case business is always bad and they never get paid. But most people won't accept a contract like this because they don't want to risk going home with no money on any particular day, especially when the bad day might not be their fault. Indeed, most people would prefer a flat salary so that they go home with the same amount each day no matter what. But the owner won't do this because the flat salary doesn't give the waiter a strong enough incentive to work hard.

It's a conundrum; but it largely gets solved by that excellent economic innovation known as the *tip*. Think of it not as a favor from the customer to the waiter, or as a way for the owner of the restaurant to push the cost of paying his staff onto his customers (where it always will lie in the end anyway). Think of it as a solution to an agency problem. The owner wants the waiters to work hard but usually can't observe their dealings with their customers, so in effect he lets the customers, who know best, set a large share of the waiter's salary. Of course the waiter doesn't want his salary to depend *entirely* on tips, because the restaurant might have slow nights that aren't his fault. So he gets a small guaranteed salary, too: the insurance side of the arrangement. In effect the waiter's contract gives him a larger payment when business is good and a smaller payment if business is bad. This gives waiters an incentive to work hard but also protects them against bad luck, as when business is bad because of bad weather or a bad chef.

The contract is a compromise between the interests of the owner and the waiter. It manages to align their interests—mostly. But there are a couple of wrinkles to notice. First, as often happens in arrangements to solve agency problems, the incentives created by this device aren't quite perfect. Waiters sometimes can please the customer at the owner's expense, as when they give away free food or drinks and are tipped lavishly for it. Collusion of something like this kind—between the agent and the monitor—is a common nagging problem in agency relationships. A related problem is that agents sometimes can fail to enforce the principal's wishes without creating much visible evidence. A waiter who is rude will probably cause people to complain and leave bad tips. A waiter who simply does nothing when he sees the chef fail to wash his hands will go undetected by customer and employer alike. Passive failures of this kind, such as a failure to enforce a principal's rules, can create agency problems that are especially hard to solve. (Compare police who abuse suspects with lazy police who don't do much of anything.)

The other shortcoming of tips is that waiters, like most agents, have more than one task the principal wants them to do well, and the incentive to work hard at one of them may come at the expense of the others. Tips might make the waiter eager to help the customers at his own tables but not very interested in cooperating with his colleagues; thus the time-honored cry of "not my station" when a waiter is summoned for help by a diner at a table not his own. One way to relieve the problem is to have waiters pool their tips. It gives them reason to be more cooperative with each other and also provides some insurance against the chance that one unlucky waiter will draw all the stingy tippers on a given night. But notice that pooling takes away some of the waiters' incentive to ardently serve the customers at their assigned tables, since now they feel all the costs of working hard but only some of the benefits. This time maybe the owner can relieve the problem by studying credit-card receipts to see how much each waiter was tipped, and then rewarding the good ones in other ways. The details of this story aren't important; the point is just to observe the back-and-forth measures that may be used to compensate for incentives that are helpful in one way but not another.

Here is another example. The officers of a corporation are supposed to serve the interests of the shareholders, but the shareholders generally can't see how carefully the officers do their jobs. The shareholders don't want to give the officers a flat salary because then the officers, like waiters on flat salaries, don't have a strong enough incentive to work hard. So shareholders give the officers bonuses at the end of the year when the value of the stock goes up. And rather than trying to figure out what the bonuses should be each year, the shareholders give the officers stocks or stock options whose value goes up when the value of the firm does. This directly ties the officer's compensation to the firm's performance. At the same time, officers also get a salary to compensate them when the value of the stock goes down for reasons that aren't their fault—for example, a new tax law that eats up the firm's revenues. The law also provides other help besides enforcing the terms of those contracts. It imposes duties of loyalty on the officers, allows "derivative" lawsuits to be brought against them by shareholders on behalf of the corporation, and requires that the corporation publicly disclose lots of information about itself (to make monitoring easier).[1] Problems of agency also can put a good face on takeovers by corporate raiders. A takeover is tried only if the raiders think the current managers and directors are failing to get the fullest possible value out of the corporation. Raiders thus provide a bit more monitoring; whatever their unappealing qualities and the dislocations they cause, they also help solve agency problems.[2]

This account of the incentives in a corporation is only a small taste of a very complex institutional and legal structure. Turn the problem around and imagine that an entrepreneur has an idea and wants to raise money from investors. The investors are afraid that if they give money to the entrepreneur, he will misuse it—perhaps putting some of it into the idea, but giving the rest of it to himself as a fat salary and perks. They respond to these fears in various ways. Some investors will give money to the entrepreneur only if he gives them the right to vote on some management decisions. Those investors are called shareholders. The shareholders might also demand that a board of directors be created; the directors monitor the entrepreneur and may have the right to replace him with someone else if he makes bad decisions. The directors, of course, might shirk as well, so as suggested above they may be given stock options to ensure that they monitor the officers rather than sleep on the job. Meanwhile some other investors will lend money to the entrepreneur without demanding any control but will charge an interest rate that reflects their view of these agency problems. Or perhaps this group of investors will lend money only to buy things that they can recover if they don't get repaid promptly. These lenders, in either event, are called creditors. The law gives the creditors this additional advantage as well: if the company goes under, they get repaid before the shareholders do. Directors, creditors, shareholders, and others also might make the entrepreneur hire an outside auditor to review his finances, with the understanding that the auditor will be independent and have a reputation for making impartial judgments.

Or think of real estate agents. How hard will your agent work to sell your house? More to the point, how will you know? You probably won't;

for if the house doesn't sell for a long time, the agent will be able to offer lots of plausible explanations that have nothing to do with how hard he worked. So the usual solution is to align the seller's interests with the agent's by paying the agent a commission on the sale of the house. The higher the price he obtains for it, the greater his pay. When we look for an insurance component in this particular sort of contract, though, we usually don't find one. The agent sees no guaranteed money if the house doesn't sell at all. Maybe the reason is that most houses do sell eventually, but notice that the agent also has a different kind of insurance: he works for a lot of different principals (i.e., sellers), so even if one house won't sell, he'll get paid when the others do.

Or consider your insurance company and your landlord, if you have one. What do they have in common? You are an agent for both of those parties—somewhat surprisingly, since you are the one paying money to them, which makes you feel like a principal. But recall that an agent is, generally, just a person whose actions benefit (or harm) someone else; and your landlord and insurance company both are affected by how careful you are. The landlord wants you to be careful with the apartment you are renting, and the insurer wants you to be careful with the car or house covered by your policy. But neither can directly see how careful you are. They deal with this through contractual devices that bear a family resemblance to each other: the security deposit demanded by the landlord and the deductible in the insurance policy. In both cases the principal bears most of the responsibility for things that might go wrong (a kind of insurance for the agent—literally in the one case and effectively in the other). But in both of them you, as the agent, have to pay for the first chunk of damage, subject to whatever excuses are written into the contracts. This gives you something to worry about. You aren't just playing with someone else's money.

An agent's temptation to shirk or misbehave, especially in the insurance setting, has its own name: moral hazard. If you have insurance against a bad thing, your incentive to avoid it goes down. Sometimes that's tolerable, as when you have plenty of other incentives to avoid it anyway (life insurance is a good example—so long as you aren't trying to take out a policy on the life of a stranger). But the problem of moral hazard helps explain why you will find it hard to buy insurance to cover any punitive damages that ever may be awarded against you. Punitive damages most typically are given when a defendant has committed an intentional bad act, and we don't want you thinking that you can go around committing intentional bad acts without fear because you have insurance against the results. The temptation to misbehave—the moral hazard, the agency cost—would be too great.

In a moment we will look at some more examples, but first let's reflect on the practical importance these issues can have. As you go through life you are both a principal and an agent all the time. You are an ordinary consumer in the world: in a principal's relationship to restaurants, cab drivers, real estate agents, people you hire to do work at your house, and so forth. You are in an agent's relationship to all sorts of other parties with whom you do business, such as your employer and the landlords and insurance companies we talked about a moment ago—and, again, in other respects you also have a principal's relationship to them. You are a principal because you want them to work hard on your behalf. You are an agent because they want you to be careful on their behalf. So you should think about the contracts you have with all these people—about monitoring, and about trade-offs between incentives and insurance.

If you happen to be a lawyer, all this becomes especially important in two ways. The first is that your clients will themselves be agents and principals many times over. They may not always be conscious of those roles, or perceive their implications, or know the classic strategies for dealing with them. Understanding those things is your job. And then lawyers themselves usually stand in complicated webs of agency relationships. If you are a lawyer you have an agent's relationship to your client, and to your firm, and to the courts in which you practice. They all want you to work hard and carefully but may find it hard to tell whether that is happening, and perhaps hard to reassure themselves about it—especially when the best thing for one of those principals isn't the best thing for the others. Meanwhile you will have a principal's relationship to other parties: to lawyers working with you or under you, to people you hire to help with your cases, or—in a less literal but still real sense—to the judge who presides over your case. It will be important to you that they all work hard and carefully, but this time you may have trouble knowing whether they do or improving the odds of it.

Start with the simple question of how, and how much, a lawyer gets paid when the client wants to bring a lawsuit. First notice the agency problem. The client wants the lawyer to work hard but is in a bad position to tell if that is happening. In this respect the lawyer's position vaguely resembles that of the real estate agent, and one of the solutions here resembles the usual answer there: the lawyer can work, in effect, on a commission—a contingency fee entitling him (after the usual American custom) to one-third or some similar share of whatever the plaintiff recovers. Partly this is a way for plaintiffs without cash to finance their lawsuits; the lawyer takes the case on spec and gets paid only if he wins. But the contingency fee also is an attempt to solve an agency problem by aligning the lawyer's interests with the client's. Here, as in the case of real estate, the insurance side of the arrangement comes not from any one client but from pooling the prospects of all of them. That is how the lawyer explains the large size of his share to the client puzzled by it: the cases he wins pay for the cases he loses. (And of course losing a case outright is a lot more common than being entirely unable to sell a house.)

But the agency problems here are more severe than in the real estate sale. Suppose the defendant in a lawsuit offers to settle the case soon after it is filed. The client might not like the idea of settling; maybe he suspects that putting a year of work into the case would produce a better offer. But the settlement might seem more attractive to the lawyer: he gets a third of it right away, and then is done with this case and able to move on to others. Of course the extra year of work would make the lawyer's share bigger, too, but here his interests aren't fully aligned with his client's after all. Suppose the lawyer thinks that working at the case part-time for another year would produce a settlement or judgment $30,000 larger than whatever the defendant is offering now—but would cost him (the lawyer) $15,000 in time or trouble. He would only get $10,000 for his efforts, so it wouldn't seem worthwhile. Yet the client still would want him to press forward. The law tries to deal with this by saying the final decision about a settlement always belongs to the client, but the lawyer usually has a considerable influence on the client's perception of the offer and his options. The result can be a ticklish situation, which is one reason why contingency fees are banned in many other countries. But paying a lawyer by the hour creates agency problems of its own, as every client quickly realizes when high bills arrive.[3]

Ethical rules like the one just mentioned (giving the client final say) call for some comment of their own. They can be considered a response to the hard agency problem that comes up when a principal hires an agent to do work that involves arcane knowledge, as law and medicine do. A typical client can't easily tell whether a lawyer makes good judgments, just as a typical patient can't easily tell whether a doctor does. The problems are worse here than in the case of the real estate agent or waiter, because here the principal might have a hard time telling good behavior from bad even if it were possible to watch the agents every minute of the day. It is in the interests of both sides of this arrangement to find some way to reassure the principals—the lawyer's clients and the doctor's patients—that their agents are handling their interests carefully. A partial solution in both settings is the creation of professional bodies to make rules and monitor the agents: bar and medical associations. Sometimes courts that award sanctions against lawyers can be viewed as serving this function as well. The judges monitor the lawyers and punish them for acting badly. Clients also have another monitoring device: the lawsuit for malpractice. They hire professionals to scrutinize the work of the professionals who may have blundered. Then there is the problem of monitoring the monitors, and on it goes. All these devices are crude, and can't do much about subtle lawyerly abuses—billing a few too many hours, letting preparation slide a bit, and so forth. Clients often sense the presence of these risks and feel frustrated because they can't find effective ways to avoid them. Some of them respond by getting mad at lawyers generally.

As these examples show, looking at the world through the lens of agency is interesting not only because it reveals such problems everywhere, but because it reveals attempts to solve them everywhere. It has been theorized, for instance, that large law firms help solve the agency problem we have been discussing—the hard time the client has figuring out whether a lawyer is good or making sure that he behaves well.[4] The big firm can accumulate a big reputation that endures over time, and the reputation serves as a kind of assurance of quality that is harder for individual lawyers, or small firms, to match. The claim isn't that the big firm is better or that its good reputation is more deserved. It's that the big firm, by investing in its reputation over a period of decades, has a larger stake to lose if it blunders and besmirches it. The valuable reputation serves as a kind of bond for the firm's performance; the more costly the bond was to create, the more convincing it is as a guarantee. It's like a national restaurant franchise that invests heavily in its reputation. When you are in a strange town you may be attracted to the nearby outlet of the famous franchise rather than to a local restaurant you haven't heard of because you have more confidence in the standards—of quality or of cleanliness—at the place with the famous name. You think the franchise couldn't afford to let a local outlet serve questionable food. Local restaurants and small law firms have advantages of their own, of course, but those are a tale for another time.[5]

Here is another case of a familiar institution that might serve an unexpected role in dealing with agency problems: political parties. The agency problem, on this theory, is that separation of the executive and legislative branches of government can make it hard for voters to know whether to blame the president or Congress when something goes wrong. Strong political parties help solve the problem: voters can hold Republicans or Democrats generally responsible and vote accordingly, without distinguishing between the president and Congress. The parties also help solve agency problems in other ways. They have to maintain good reputations with their constituencies or suffer various consequences. And they make it easier for the president to know whom to negotiate with in Congress when he wants something: the head of the party. You might amuse yourself by drawing analogies between the problems shareholders have supervising the agents running their corporations and the problems citizens have supervising the agents running their government.[6]

The fun can then be extended by asking who are the agents and the principals when judges decide cases, or when government agencies issue rules, or when professors grade exams, and what it looks like when any of these parties shirk, and what might be done to reduce the risk of it. Or reflect on the rules that govern liability for injuries caused by defective products. The law holds the manufacturer strictly liable for them. Notice the principal and agent relationships that might therefore run in both directions. Think about the defenses the manufacturer can raise—assumption of risk or misuse of the product, or claims of comparative negligence into which those defenses may be merged; and then consider whether the legal rules, taken together, might serve as substitutes for a contract meant to give both sides good incentives to think about safety. In short, it isn't hard to find agency problems to think about. It's hard to avoid them.

We just saw one set of interesting puzzles to study once you get the hang of thinking about agency: you can sniff out agency relationships, and devices used to deal with them, in unexpected places. Here is a more advanced line of inquiry: look at the contracts in these cases and ask why we find the particular incentives that we do and not others.[7] For example, why don't real estate agents get progressive commissions, receiving an ever-larger share as the sale price of a house gets higher? We should pause first to notice why commissions of this sort might seem like a good idea; for otherwise you might imagine that so long as the agent gets some commission—say, the usual 6 percent—he always has an incentive to push for the highest sale price he possibly can get. But that isn't necessarily true, for reasons much like the ones we saw when we talked about contingency fees for lawyers. If it would take a lot of work to push the sale price for a house from $200,000 to $220,000, and the agent gets only 6 percent of the extra money, the pushing might not seem worthwhile; maybe it would cost him more than $1,200 in time or in distasteful labor or bargaining. But the extra work might seem worthwhile after all if the agent knew he would get *half* the extra money rather than just 6 percent of it.[8] The owner would still be better off; so why don't owners pay agents larger commissions if they sell their houses for an unexpectedly high price? Why do real estate agents instead get commissions that are fixed regardless of the sale price, and also uniform from one house to the next? Of course one answer is that a fixed, uniform commission is simple. It avoids the need for negotiations at the start of every relationship. But might there be more interesting reasons?

One theory ties the custom to the fact that a real estate agent works for lots of different clients—principals—at the same time. If commissions varied from client to client or depended on the size of the sale, then some clients would have to worry that others are getting more attention because they cut special deals with the agent. So the worried clients might feel obliged to investigate, or compete with other clients, with results that would be a waste; they would amount to a kind of rent seeking.[9] Perhaps it's better just to assure all principals that they are on the same footing. Similar worries of principals also might be held down by the fact that a given real estate agent usually isn't selling houses that are radically different in value. Anyhow, the point here is to see that special problems come up when an agent works for more than one principal, especially when the principals have competing interests, and that those problems sometimes can help explain why we see the particular arrangements that we do.

Another example: The retail seller of a thing usually buys it outright from a wholesaler and then does the best he can to resell it to customers. You might try thinking of this as an extreme form of commission—actually a 100 percent commission. (Or, to turn it around, you can unexpectedly think of commissions as amounting to divided ownership: the lawyer who collects one-third of whatever his client wins really is a partial owner of the client's claim.) But the retail store doesn't repeat the process; it doesn't sell the goods to its salesmen to then resell to the store's customers. Instead it pays the salesmen a commission (or just a flat hourly rate). And yet traveling salesmen sometimes *do* buy their wares outright—the hairbrushes they sell, or the encyclopedia sets, or whatever else—and then resell them door-to-door. Instead of getting a 10 percent commission, they buy and then resell, perhaps at a markup of 10 percent. What explains this variety of arrangements?

An important part of the answer involves a theme we noticed in passing earlier: "bilateral," or two-way, agency relationships—in other words, cases where agents and principals both need each other to contribute to getting a job done (so really both sides are principals and both sides are agents). Retail sales usually are like this: getting things sold takes effort from both the store's owner and the salesmen on the floor. A partial commission, rather than sale-plus-resale, preserves incentives to work hard on both sides. The same idea helps explain why real estate agents don't buy their clients' houses and then resell them for the best prices they can. Part of the explanation is that the agents don't want to take on the risk and the burden of borrowing that the approach would require. But companies that sell used cars set up huge operations in which they do buy thousands of cars from people and then resell them; they don't usually sell your car on consignment. Why do companies that sell used houses act differently from companies that sell used cars? Well, again, notice that selling a house is a case of bilateral, or two-way, agency. The seller needs the agent to work hard and be careful—and the agent needs the *seller* to work hard and be careful in maintaining the house and helping to present it to buyers. A commission keeps good incentives intact for both sides. But once a used car dealer has your car, he doesn't need you anymore. He does need good efforts from his salesmen, so they will probably be on commission.

A door-to-door seller of hairbrushes may be different. At the point of sale there is no bilateral agency; there is no store, so the brush company has no role to play. It might as well sell the brushes to the salesman outright, which then gives him the greatest possible incentive to get them resold. And the same logic explains why retailers buy their goods from wholesalers and then resell them, rather than trying to sell them on consignment. Once the good enters the hands of the retailer, there is nothing further the wholesaler can do to help get them sold. Since the wholesaler's incentives aren't relevant any more, there is no reason to bother with the joint ownership of the goods that would be provided by commission or consignment. As usual, there may be other ways to explain some of these results. For now just take away the idea that when each side of an agency relationship depends partly on the other, you will usually find mixed solutions that don't throw all the incentives for work and care onto either side.

SUGGESTIONS FOR FURTHER READING. Good introductions to the topic of this chapter, more detailed than this one, are Eric A. Posner, *Agency Models in Law and Economics, in* Chicago Lectures in Law and Economics (Eric A. Posner ed., 2000); and Saul Levmore, *Commissions and Conflicts in Agency Arrangements: Lawyers, Real Estate Brokers, Underwriters, and Other Agents' Rewards,* 36 J.L. & Econ. 503 (1993). For interesting application of agency principles to various specific topics, see Geoffrey P. Miller, *Some Agency Problems in Settlement,* 16 J. Legal Stud. 189 (1987); Steven G. Calabresi, *Political Parties as Mediating Institutions,* 61 U. Chi. L. Rev. 1479 (1994); Larry E. Ribstein, *Ethical Rules, Agency Costs, and Law Firm Culture,* 84 Va. L. Rev. 1707 (1998).

10 ↠ The Prisoner's Dilemma

You and a confederate are arrested on suspicion of theft. The prosecutor puts you in separate rooms and gives you the same choices. If both of you confess, he will urge the judge to show lenity and give you each five years in prison. If neither confesses, you both will be charged with lesser offenses that are easier to prove, which you may assume will result in one-year sentences. It's more interesting if your partner talks and you don't: he goes free and you get ten years. The reverse also is true: if you talk and he doesn't, he does ten years and you go free—a tantalizing thought. So you might think like this: if your partner is going to talk, you had better talk (otherwise you get the maximum); and if he doesn't talk, you have even *more* reason to confess: then you walk. No matter what he does, your best course is to confess—which you do. Alas, your partner has the same train of thought and confesses as well. You both end up in prison for five years. It's too bad you weren't able to cooperate; if you had trusted each other, you both could have kept silent and cut your jail time to one year apiece. Here is a matrix summarizing how the situation can play out; in each parenthesis the first figure is the number of years of prison time you serve, and the second figure is the number of years he serves:

	He keeps quiet (Cooperates)	He talks (Defects)
You keep quiet (Cooperate)	(1, 1)	(10, 0)
You talk (Defect)	(0, 10)	(5, 5)

There turn out to be many situations in life that are like this: cases where decisions that are individually rational end up making everyone in a group worse off, including you (the rational actor, let us imagine). If we both cooperate we're better off than if neither of us does, but since we can choose strategies only for ourselves and not for others, the temptation may be enormous for each of us to do the selfish thing—to "defect," as it is called. The result is a kind of waste, or inefficiency: there are gains to be had from cooperating that we don't get to enjoy. This situation is called a prisoner's dilemma. It is the best-known pattern studied in the field known as *game theory*—an amalgam of economics, mathematics, and other sciences, the purpose of which is to shed light on strategic interaction. We will be looking at a few different games in this part of the book.

Sometimes the temptations of the prisoner's dilemma are a problem and sometimes they aren't. The reasons why will lead us to some implications for law. A first reason why the prisoner's dilemma just described ends badly is that it's a problem you face only once. If you expect to be in the same fix every week, you have to worry that if you disappoint your partner he will retaliate next time. This explains a great deal of the cooperation we see in business settings: choosing to "burn" someone by taking payment and then shipping lousy goods is a trick that works once; then the relationship is over. And even if there is no fear of such a result, informal norms may produce the same sorts of cooperation, either by creating a fear of censure by others or because the norms have been internalized into mutual trust enforced by pangs of conscience. Those norms—the sense that cooperating is *good*—are immensely valuable; if they didn't exist, and no one ever cooperated except because they expected to see benefits or feared revenge, life would be far less pleasant. So we train children to believe that taking advantage of other people is a bad thing to do, and we try to pick friends and partners who seem to be trustworthy and to enjoy cooperating.

As this discussion suggests, there is an interesting link between the best formal strategies for solving prisoner's dilemmas and values considered admirable in life at large. Robert Axelrod conducted a famous computer tournament to test the power of various strategies for dealing with repeated prisoner's dilemmas, and found that the winner was *tit-for-tat:* begin by cooperating, then in each round do whatever the other player did in the previous round. The strategy has several properties that Axelrod identified as important for success in prisoner's dilemmas, most of them familiar as virtues in everyday life. It is a "nice" strategy: the player of it is never the first to defect. It is a reciprocal strategy: it doesn't ignore bad behavior by the other player, but its user is prepared to be forgiving as well. It is not too clever for its own good; one's partners can quickly understand it. And it is a non-envious strategy, since it doesn't regard beating out the other player as important.[10] Another way to put the last point is that good players don't treat prisoner's dilemmas as "zero-sum" games where anything good for one side must be bad for the other. It's all very comforting; it's always nice to be reassured that virtuous behavior is useful as well as honorable.

The trouble, however, is that those solutions often aren't available because many prisoner's dilemmas don't involve repeated encounters between the same players.[11] We then have to look more deeply into the dilemma's structure in search of other solutions to it. Another reason the classic dilemma ends badly, besides its one-shot character, is that the two of you aren't able to talk. The dilemma would go away if you could make an enforceable agreement with each other not to confess. And so we arrive at much of the reason for the elaborate machinery known as the law of contract. Think about ordering a product from a seller you don't know and probably will never deal with in the future. You worry about sending him your money. You can't very well threaten never to do business again if he fails to deliver the goods. You aren't going to do business with him again in any event, and he knows it. And you don't know him well enough to tell whether he's the sort who ought to be trusted because of his fine character. These kinds of doubts would paralyze you and many others in commercial life if it weren't for an obvious recourse: a contract in which you each promise to perform and submit to penalties if you don't. Contracts allow people to limit their options if others will limit their own in return; they give everyone a convenient way to beat prisoner's dilemmas and enjoy the gains that come from cooperation. Other contracts provide more sophisticated solutions to more complicated problems that nevertheless have a similar deep structure, as when an escrow agent holds money due from a first party to a second until the second one performs a promise.

Sometimes it isn't possible for the parties to a prisoner's dilemma to make a contract, and the question then is whether the law might impose rules that achieve the same thing. Thus another reason why the prisoner's dilemma turns out poorly: you have no punishment from elsewhere to fear if you double-cross your confederate. We can change that if we want people to cooperate and they can't rely on contracts between them to make it happen; we can adjust the payoffs by making rules that require cooperation on pain of legal penalties. This is a way to understand the law of torts and crimes. Suppose you are deciding whether to pay your taxes and you have nothing to fear from the law. If everyone but you pays faithfully, your contribution won't be missed; and if *nobody* else pays, you certainly don't want to be the one who does. Everyone else reasons the same way. It isn't practical to make contracts with everyone else in which you all agree to do what's best for everyone, so the temptation to avoid paying would be pervasive—if we didn't have rules that punish people as criminals when they "defect" by evading their taxes.

You can tell similar stories about all sorts of crimes and torts: stories in which you start by imagining how much fun it would be to do something bad; you imagine that it wouldn't be the end of the world so long as most other people were behaving. Then you realize everyone else might have that same train of thought about themselves, too. Maybe it will tempt them all to act badly, just as it tempts you. And if they're going to act that way, then you have less reason than ever to control yourself. The more you think about it, the better it sounds to misbehave. But then along come thoughts of criminal and civil liability to quash those fantasies, and not a moment too soon. For although it might be your first choice to be the only bad actor, your second choice is for nobody to be one; and your train of thought was leading you toward a world worse than that—where *everyone* is bad, and rationally so.

We saw in an earlier chapter that many legal rules give us what we might agree to by contract if we could. The new point here is just a clearer reason why we would make those contracts, or rules of tort and criminal law to mimic their results: we want the gains from cooperation, so we need mechanisms that make it rational for each of us to cooperate—to do what everyone should do. We're all better off if nobody steals (or litters, or cheats on their taxes) than if everyone does; but that may not be enough to get each of us not to do those things when we privately decide for ourselves. Conscience is a help then, but perhaps not as convincing as the threat of coercion. Law often amounts to a substitute for trust in situations too complex or dispersed for trust to arise.

This sketch shows how whole categories of law can be viewed as ways to solve prisoner's dilemmas, and indeed an entire theory of the state can be built up from the idea.[12] But the prisoner's dilemma also explains many more particular issues in the law. Let's briefly look at some of them.

1. *Lawyerly abuses.* Lawyers involved in lawsuits soon encounter the process known as *discovery:* the formal exchange of information about a case with the other side. Wouldn't it be great if the lawyers for your adversary told you what you wanted to know while you told them nothing? Unfortunately they have the same hopes, so in high-stakes litigation we often find a shortage of cooperation and civility. It's a prisoner's dilemma, and both sides are defecting. There are other temptations as well. Some requests for information have the side effect of being expensive for the other side to answer; they take research. Sometimes a request may not be worth making for the sake of the useful knowledge it will yield, but

then still be attractive just because of the expense it imposes on the other side and the pressure it puts on them to settle the case. Requests made in the hope of creating these pressures are considered abusive, and there are broadly written rules of civil procedure to forbid and punish them, but the rules are notoriously hard to enforce. I say you stole my secret methods for making widgets, and during the lawsuit I formally request that you produce any documents in your files that ever mention widgets and how they are made. You have three million such documents, and they are distributed here and there among other papers in a warehouse that also contains all your confidential plans for making geegaws. So you will be spending a lot of hours picking out documents for me. Naturally you might complain, but the judge is in a bad position to tell the difference between a fair request for information that happens to be burdensome and requests made mostly *because* they are burdensome. So you retaliate by ordering the depositions of all the major officers in my company, which will keep them busy for several weeks answering questions in front of a stenographer. My complaints are no more effective than yours. We're in a prisoner's dilemma: no matter what you do, I'm better off defecting by making abusive requests, and vice versa—though we both would be better off if we both stopped it.

Some lawsuits last for years; why doesn't the resulting prospect of lots of repeated play, as it were—or in other words the chance for retaliation—cause everyone to behave themselves? One reason is that it's hard to know whether the other side is cooperating—not just for the judge, but for the players themselves. *X* is guarded because she has vague suspicions about *Y*'s intentions. *Y* concludes that *X* evidently has something to hide, and that it is a game at which two may play. *X* considers her suspicions confirmed and becomes more resolute. *Y* decides that *X* needs another lesson, and so it goes. Neither can make credible promises to the other; neither can accurately judge the good faith of the other; any outside rule is expensive to enforce precisely. There is nothing left but for each player to defect and to blame the other. The same pattern may recur on a larger scale as both sides to a lawsuit pour resources into it. Suspicion and a lack of clarity about what counts as cooperation can make a prisoner's dilemma especially hard to solve.

Many lawyers find that it's more enjoyable to practice law in towns and small cities than in big ones. One reason involves prisoner's dilemmas of the sort we have been examining. In a smaller community everyone deals with everyone else more often. As a result the lawyers in town develop trust and have incentives to cooperate; what goes around comes around, at least so long as the parties aren't confused about what their adversaries are doing. In large cities a lawyer may interact with a particular counterpart only rarely, and maybe never again; he thus may have little to fear by way of consequences for any obnoxious acts. Likewise for the firm that boasts of having a national practice. It sounds good and has its advantages, but it also means lots of dealings between lawyers who aren't in the same communities and aren't constrained by thoughts of repeated play. Not that economies of scale always produce worse behavior; it depends on the details. If a big national firm specializes in one sort of case, it may deal repeatedly with other specialists, creating a new community defined not by geography but by interest and so giving rise to reasons for cooperation after all. And big firms with offices in lots of places can cause an adversary to worry that crossing them in one place will result in revenge administered in another place by another lawyer, and this is another way to help solve a prisoner's dilemma. Yet then this story, too, can be undercut if the big firms are full of young lawyers hoping to earn a pile of money and then hurry on to another job. Their horizons may be short and their stake in the firm and community small, so they may again see little reason not to stick it to the other side where they can.[13] We have dilemmas within dilemmas.

Most of this general analysis holds for all sorts of activities, not just the practice of law. As communities get larger and more complex, everyone needs cooperation from strangers more often, and without much expectation that the dealings will be repeated—making it less realistic to rely on informal norms and thoughts of repeated dealings to solve the prisoner's dilemmas that naturally result.[14] For those cases we need contracts and rules; and in situations that don't lend themselves to those solutions, a prisoner's dilemma and the waste it creates may prove unavoidable.

2. *Labor unions and other groups.* People frequently do better by working in groups than by working alone, whether the group is a firm, a university faculty, or a labor union. But the gains can be had only if everyone works at it, which puts each of the members into a natural prisoner's dilemma. Each might think it would be great if he could get the benefits of being in the group without the costs—if he could free ride, as it is called, on the work of the others. This talk of "the work" can be replaced by any of the specific things that have to be done to make groups succeed. In the case of a labor union it might mean paying dues, going on strike when the group so decides, and turning down private offers the employer makes that are good for whoever gets them but not for the group as a whole. Each member may be tempted to defect by avoiding those costs: shirking dues, working during the strike, and quietly making terms

with the employer on the side. Each thinks of how perfect it would be if he could do those things and still have the benefits the union creates. Then it occurs to him that the others may have the same thoughts and may defect as well—and perhaps this confirms his sense that he would be a fool *not* to cheat.[15]

These trains of thought can scuttle a group enterprise before it gets started if measures aren't taken to counter them. So naturally the union keeps a close watch on its members and deals severely and visibly with anyone caught shirking. These steps are its way of solving the prisoner's dilemma. And of course the union has to worry not only about people cheating but about people leaving. Its project is to establish the widest possible gap between the benefits of being a member who plays by the rules and the benefits of cheating or leaving entirely. The smaller the gap gets, the more vulnerable the union becomes to collapse on account of prisoner's dilemmas. The monitoring of members and the punishment of them and all the other efforts unions make may be expensive, but they are considered worth it to get the gains from cooperation—in this case, the deals the union extracts by collective bargaining. The law sometimes helps to keep the gap wide by giving tax breaks and subsidies of other kinds that a group can use to make cooperation more rewarding for its members and to help nail defectors.[16]

Perhaps the employer isn't thrilled with all this. He might like to offer contracts to workers giving them a little extra if they promise not to join the union, and now the dilemma has been refreshed. Each worker might be better off waiving his rights than insisting on them, perhaps hoping that others will still join the union and that he may get some benefits from their efforts. If the others will be defecting, obviously he should, too; and if they don't defect and he does, that's even better. But then all the workers think this, so the union collapses and all of them are worse off. This time the union responds by invoking the law directly, getting legislation passed—the Norris-LaGuardia Act—that forbids such "yellow-dog" contracts in which employees bind themselves not to join unions. One party to the game tries to create and re-create prisoner's dilemmas while the other tries to solve them.

3. *The tragedy of the commons.* Suppose we all make our living by fishing for cod. We know that if each of us catches all the cod we can, soon there won't be any left for anyone. Clearly it would be better for all of us if we each showed some restraint. But if all the others are going to restrain themselves, the best thing for me—just thinking for myself—will be to quickly bring in as much cod as I can. And if the others *aren't* going to restrain

themselves, then I obviously wouldn't want to be the sucker who does. So no matter how anyone else acts, I'm inclined to make my own haul as large as possible—and so is everyone else; after a while all the fish are indeed gone and we are in a bad way. The story can be retold with farmers and their grazing cattle, or hunters or miners or users of other common and finite resources. The problem is that each of them gets all the benefits of overextraction but feels only a smaller share of the costs. This is a particular version of the prisoner's dilemma known as the *tragedy of the commons*;[17] it is an old and standard argument for the virtues of private property, since a private owner feels the benefits *and* costs of overusing his resources and so has incentives to act more prudently.[18] It also is a classic argument for regulation by the government to limit the rate of fishing or hunting or drilling or what not. The regulation works like a contract: by taking away some of our choices it makes us all better off—if it works.

4. *Bankruptcy.* It appears that your restaurant is about to fail. You have five creditors—suppliers to whom you owe money for whatever reason. Each is getting nervous and might sensibly decide to demand payment immediately or sue for it before you go broke. It would be better for everyone if all the creditors refrained from these tactics, since if they held back you might be able to keep your business afloat after all; when everyone insists on payment it ensures that you will go under and perhaps leave many creditors with nothing. But if some of the creditors are going to demand their money, the rest might as well do the same (it would be foolish to be last in line); and if the other creditors *aren't* going make such demands, each will see an irresistible chance to be on the safe side by being the one who grabs what is left while it definitely is still there. So it is in each creditor's individual interest to do what will make them worse off as a group.

The solution to this particular prisoner's dilemma is known as bankruptcy law. When someone goes bankrupt, any payments made to creditors in the ninety days beforehand—the "preference period"—are void and have to be returned to the bankrupt's estate. In this case the creditors are the ones in the prisoner's dilemma. They can't very well make contracts between themselves, so the law makes some attempt to help along the same result by statute. It takes away any benefit the creditors might try to get by defecting and making hasty demands.[19] Or at least that is the legislative solution. It turns out that there are contractual answers as well: creditors can provide for these possibilities in advance, not between themselves but by taking security interests in your assets—in other words, a right to take back your property directly if you run out of money.[20]

5. *Unwanted cooperation.* We have been assuming that cooperation is good. Sometimes it isn't, and of course the prisoner's dilemma can be turned into advice for such cases where you *want* the players to double-cross each other: divide and conquer. It works well when performing interrogations, as the original story of the dilemma shows; we don't want cooperation between criminals, so we sometimes try to structure their incentives to destroy that possibility. Another type of prisoner's dilemma also works to pressure an individual suspect to make a plea bargain—an agreement where he agrees to plead guilty to a crime in exchange for a reduced sentence. Criminal defendants might be better off as a group if they all refused to enter into these deals. Their collective stubbornness would put great pressure on the prosecutor to drop many of their cases because he wouldn't have the resources to press forward with all of them. But since it isn't feasible for suspects to form a union of this kind, they are confronted with payoffs that probably make it rational for many of them to agree to prison sentences in return for confessions, truthful or not. Whether this is a good thing is a matter of fair dispute; if it isn't, perhaps we need legal rules requiring prosecutors to treat suspects as if they did have contracts with each other in this limited respect.[21]

A less controversial example of unwanted cooperation is the sort engaged in by business rivals who get together in smoky hotel rooms and fix the prices of their wares. The purpose of antitrust laws is to instead force them into separate rooms, figuratively speaking, so they will do the individually rational thing, which is to compete vigorously. Forbidding them to make contracts in which they agree to cooperate in setting their prices makes them worse off, but makes a larger group—consumers—better off. We *want* the sellers to be in a prisoner's dilemma. If they do manage to form a cartel, by the way, they end up in a new prisoner's dilemma of their own: each might like to cheat and gain more business while everyone else sticks to the price-fixing agreement. Again this is good; it's a dilemma we welcome, and one that the law won't give them any help in resolving.

SUGGESTIONS FOR FURTHER READING. Robert Axelrod, The Evolution of Cooperation (1984); Douglas G. Baird, Robert H. Gertner, and Randal C. Picker, Game Theory and the Law (1994); Russell Hardin, Collective Action (1982). Lively general treatments of the prisoner's dilemma can be found in William Poundstone, Prisoner's Dilemma (1992), and Douglas R. Hofstadter, Metamagical Themas chs. 30–32 (1985).

11 ↠ Public Goods

One type of prisoner's dilemma is important enough to deserve a chapter of its own. It involves *public goods*. Public goods are things that, once made, are available to everyone; you can't exclude people from enjoying them. The other defining feature of a public good is that one person's enjoyment of the thing doesn't use it up or reduce the pleasure anyone else takes from it. So now you can see what a high quality of air in a country has in common with its army. Once either the air or the army exists, anyone can enjoy their fruits—the pleasures of breathing or of feeling secure against invasion; you can't exclude people who didn't contribute to the cause. And my enjoyment of those pleasures, whether I paid for them or not, doesn't use them up at your expense; my sense of security in knowing the army is out there doesn't leave any less security behind for you. Since we don't have to compete to enjoy these things, they are sometimes called "nonrivalrous" goods.

The structure of these cases means that they both lend themselves to free riding and to a variety of the prisoner's dilemma. You can ask everyone to contribute voluntarily to pay for the cost of an army or an environmental cleanup effort. Some people will do it, but many won't. They will see it as a prisoner's dilemma. If everyone else is going to chip in for an army, there's no reason for me to bother: I'll get all the benefits of it anyway. And if others aren't going to contribute, then there's even less reason for me to bother. We're all better off if we all contribute than if none of us do, but the best (or most economically rational) play for me acting alone is always to figure I will ride for free on the efforts of others. Unfortunately, the others think the same thing, so there *are* no efforts—or anyway not enough. It's more common to think about public goods, though, by turning the problem around and looking at it from a different perspective. Suppose you are thinking about making a public good. Why should you bother? Once it exists, everyone will be able to enjoy it and you won't have any way to charge them (since nobody can be excluded from it); the consumers of it won't pay voluntarily because they will regard it as a prisoner's dilemma. So perhaps you won't provide it at all, and in any event you almost certainly will provide less of it than everyone wants. Instead we will get more public bads than everyone wants—pollution and invasion, for starters.

This account explains why providing for the common defense and protecting the environment are considered classic jobs for a government. We generally can't count on those things to be provided by the operation of a market because the people who would provide them can't capture the gains by charging those who benefit. In earlier chapters we have spoken of the problems that arise when people feel the benefits of their behavior but not the costs, which are imposed on others—external costs, as they are called in economics. The problem for providers of public goods is the opposite: they create external *benefits* for others that they don't feel or enjoy because they can't charge for them, so they don't have as much incentive as they should to produce the goods in the first place.

The legal system tries to solve public goods problems in various ways. One is with taxes, which force everyone to pay for good things that they can't feasibly be charged for individually. Defense, police, the environment, roads, and parks are all examples of public goods that get supplied this way—by giving the right to coerce to a central authority, which then forces everyone to pay for them. Public goods are, indeed, the greatest challenge faced by hardcore libertarians—those inclined to get rid of public government outright or nearly so. They have to come up with other ways to ensure that public goods get provided. Usually the proposals involve making things exclusive that aren't usually regarded that way now: turn all roads into toll roads that nobody can use without paying[22] (likewise with parks and other public spaces), have people provide for their own security by subscribing to private clubs for the purpose that exclude free riders, and so on. Since our focus is on showing how the idea of public goods can be used to shed light on current legal principles, we won't be entering into this debate. But it's worth grasping that the notion of goods from which people can't be excluded isn't to be taken for granted. Some people contest it vigorously.

The interesting project for us now is to look around for other examples of public goods and what role law plays in getting people to create them. Lots of good things that people pay for also have benefits for others who don't pay for them, and these generally can be seen as public goods problems. Perhaps the lobby of your apartment building could use some sprucing up. But the sprucing up will be a public good: once it's done, everyone who lives there will enjoy it whether they helped pay for it or not, and their enjoyment won't take away from anyone else's. So the temptation for others to free ride will be great, and they will decide to let you take care of it. But you will be inclined to let *them* take care of it. Maybe you become exasperated, decide that you've had enough, and just pay for a few improvements yourself. That's nice, but the problem still remains. There is some perfect amount that could be spent on the project; it's whatever amount would keep creating more benefits than costs for everyone who lives in the building. You probably won't spend that much, and the difference will be a waste, a deadweight loss, or an inefficiency—however you care to label it.

There are natural ways to solve this particular kind of problem. They are matters of contract. The landlord, if there is one, can make improvements and then bill all the residents for them, the right to do so having been provided for in their rental contracts; or perhaps the "bill" is included already in the rent. If everyone owns their own apartments, then the solution probably takes a governmental form: majority votes and elections of governing boards and such, the end result being the usual forced payment to get done what all the residents—or perhaps only most of them—want but can't accomplish through isolated decisions.[23]

That takes care of the lobby, but not the outside of the building, which may also be an eyesore. Fixing it up would be another example of a public good: the improved appearance would be enjoyed by a lot of people who don't live there but walk past it every day and can't be billed. Their preferences aren't taken into account. That's one reason why a lot of buildings are uglier than they should be, where "should" means that there are some possible improvements that would create more benefits for everyone in the world than costs for everyone in the world. To the extent that the benefits would be enjoyed by people who can't be made to pay for them, there is a missing incentive for the owners—who bear all the costs—to make the improvements even though the improvements would be efficient. This time it isn't clear what the law can do.

Now consider inventors and the economics that would confront them in a world without intellectual property laws. We have talked elsewhere about the good incentives that those laws create; now the laws can be seen more precisely as solutions to a public goods problem. Once the design of an invention is perfected and is "out there," anyone can make use of it, and without impairing the amount left over for others. An invention, like a new paint job on the apartment building, may create lots of benefits for others that the inventor can't capture, which means the inventor won't have as strong an incentive as he should to make the thing in the first place—where, again, we measure "should" by the total benefits the invention would create for the world. We deal with the problem not through taxation but by creating property rights: a patent that forbids anyone but the inventor to make the invention for an initial period of years. There are real losses to others during those years of exclusivity; think of people who can't afford a brand-name drug and have to wait for the generic version—the version that comes out only after the patent expires on the original. Some costs of that sort are worth incurring to get the drug developed in the first place; that, at least, is the logic of the patent laws. We try to keep the costs of patents down in other ways, as with rules that prevent patents for obvious developments or that allow other inventors to develop new variations on the patented original.[24]

We strike a similar balance with copyright laws that give authors limited rights to control the copying of their work. Notice that a work of art is often a public good: in some cases it's hard to limit the enjoyment of it to just those who pay, and the enjoyment of some isn't rivalrous with the enjoyment of anyone else; so the temptation to enjoy without paying will be great, and the incentive to create the art will be less than it should be. Again the right balance is delicate. A property right in a work of art might help the creator capture some of its benefits, but it also *reduces* the total benefits the art creates; for now some people can't afford to enjoy it. As elsewhere, we deal with this by writing the rules with some subtlety. If we protect the art too much for the sake of getting it created, we especially worry about losing variations, parodies, or other works inspired by the original. So copyright law gives the writer or other artist exclusive right to the *expression* of the idea in the work, but not to the idea itself, which others are free to play with. The line between idea and expression is sometimes difficult to draw, but now at least you can see what purpose the decisions serve when courts struggle over them. The idea is to get public goods created because of all the benefits they create; but the bigger the incentive you create by giving the creator a right to the benefits, the smaller the total benefits for the world once the goods are created. You can create waste—inefficiency—by going overboard in either direction. Notice that the systems of patent and copyright law handle this challenge a bit differently. Copyright protection is easy to get (it attaches automatically to any creative work that meets the requirements set by statute) and lasts for a long time (the life of the author plus seventy years), but it is limited in scope and full of exceptions. In patent law the trade-off is made the other way around: the request for a patent is screened very carefully at the front end, and the protection a patent grants doesn't last as long (twenty years), but the property rights conferred by a patent are more robust than those that copyright provides.[25]

The copyright example shows that expression can be a public good. We can carry the point into constitutional law and its treatment of speech. Speech has value, and the First Amendment is meant to protect it. But not all speech gets the same sort of protection, and one reason may be that some speech amounts to a public good and some doesn't. Saying that some bit of speech is a public good doesn't necessarily mean it's good for the public. It just means that the speech creates benefits that the speaker can't capture because of prisoner's dilemmas among those who will receive the benefits: everyone who benefits could be invited to pay, but most of them wouldn't. The types of speech that most fit this description are the political variety and, again, the artistic. Ideas are public goods. Debate is a public good. There are plenty of examples of ideas and debates we could do without, but agreeing on which those are is difficult and not a job we are inclined to trust to judges or anyone else who works for the government. Instead we make the judgments on a categorical basis: certain types of expression tend to create large social benefits that aren't all (or sometimes *at* all) captured by their makers. So they need to be encouraged, and one way we encourage them is with elaborate rules to prevent the government from imposing costs of any sort on them.[26]

Commercial speech (advertisements) and pornography don't get as much protection, and perhaps part of the reason is that they aren't public goods. Again, that isn't the same as saying they're *bad;* it just means the people who create them usually can capture the benefits by billing their recipients and sometimes by excluding the rest. There's no need for a subsidy or for special efforts to protect them against burdens. Now obviously there are other reasons why we value political speech more than advertisements or pornography, and other reasons why we value speech more generally—reasons involving self-expression and self-government. Commercial speech is just another case of a common type where the idea of public goods doesn't explain everything but illuminates the legal situation a bit, making some features of its structure easier to understand.

Sometimes the idea of public goods helps to explain a public subsidy that otherwise may seem mysterious, such as the immunity the common law gave to charities when they were sued for accidents caused by their employees. Charities produce public goods; the benefits they create by relieving poverty or doing other good works are enjoyed by everyone, or at any rate by lots of people who can't be billed. Some of those people do contribute voluntarily, but others don't because they regard it as a prisoner's dilemma. Making charities immune from tort liability helps compensate for that; it amounts to a subsidy. Charities don't pay for some of the costs they create, which helps make up for the fact that they don't enjoy some of the benefits they create. Those benefits are external—in other words, not felt by the charity—so the charity is allowed to externalize (not feel) some of the costs it creates, too. Most states have abolished immunity for charities, but they are still subsidized in various ways—for example by the tax deductions allowed to people who make contributions to them.[27]

Another example is the subsidy the government gives to people who bring lawsuits. Isn't it odd that courts are provided free of charge to anyone who wants to sue anyone else? The total cost of operating a courtroom, including all personnel and facilities, has been estimated at between $400 and $600 per hour, and that was twenty years ago.[28] When people decide whether to bring lawsuits, they ask themselves whether their prospects of winning a judgment (in other words, the amount they stand to win, discounted by the chance that they will lose) is enough to offset their costs; but they don't figure in those costs to the public of providing the court itself. To the plaintiff those costs are an externality: a cost not felt. The public absorbs it, and thus subsidizes every lawsuit, giving us more litigation than we would have if the players felt *all* the costs and benefits of their decisions. The question is why we would so subsidize lawsuits, which most people regard as an evil.

One reason is that some people with good claims wouldn't be able to bring suits if they had to pay the entire costs of the proceeding. But when you see the public paying for something, it's useful to ask as well whether there are public goods at stake—benefits that wouldn't be provided sufficiently if they were left to people to pay for privately because the benefits would go to everyone, not just to those paying. In the case of litigation there are various kinds of public goods at stake. One consists of the rules of law that courts create when they decide cases. An obvious example is public interest litigation launched to achieve some goal for the sake of the common weal, though the rationale for such cases is complicated by the fact that a lot of suits said to be in the public interest benefit some groups at the expense of others. But the point about public goods goes beyond suits brought directly for the sake of the public. A typical decision by a court is meant to resolve the dispute between the parties, but as we have seen the decision also amounts to a rule for the rest of the world, and this latter function may be by far the more important—yet the parties won't care about it and wouldn't be interested in litigating for the sake of it. The point can be made most easily by reflecting that when private arbitrators are hired to resolve a case, they usually don't produce written opinions. Why not? Because judicial opinions are public goods. Everyone gets the benefit of their guidance, but that benefit isn't at all captured by the parties who hire the arbitrators, so they won't pay the arbitrators to write them. Judges publish written opinions precisely because they aren't working for the parties and so don't care whether the parties think the effort is worthwhile. The opinions can be viewed as a dividend from the public subsidy of the lawsuit.[29]

We have seen a bunch of devices for bringing public goods into existence. Sometimes, especially in small cases, contracts can get the job done (the apartment building). Sometimes the government can supply public goods by taxation (defense, police) or by forcing others to supply them—as by requiring firms to take measures to cut their emissions or by requiring drivers to install catalytic converters on their cars. Sometimes the government can enable the maker of the public good to exclude people from its enjoyment after all (intellectual property laws). Or it can subsidize the production of public goods by letting some of the costs be pushed off onto others (as in the case of charities or the possible case of litigation).

A different strategy, though harder to achieve through law, is to develop norms that cause people to want to create public goods.[30] Sometimes people already do, of course: they contribute to charities, support public radio and television, or make sacrifices during wartime. In these cases the contributors defy prisoner's dilemmas and help create public goods without coercion. Norms that make people feel good about doing those things are another solution to the problem of public goods, but the more interesting point is that the norms *themselves* are public goods.[31] If you help the norms along by praising people who are generous and condemning the litterbug, you contribute to the maintenance of an ethic; the rest of us benefit, and we don't compensate you—and you probably don't get any tangible benefits yourself from delivering the scolding. Why, then, would you do it? Because there's a norm about the norm: you feel good about enforcing it.

Norms, and the norms about the norms, are a powerful and useful way of getting good things accomplished without legal coercion. They tend to be most effectively instilled early. It partly becomes a question of education, which on this view is still another example of a public good.[32] Education creates some benefits that are captured by the educated, but it also creates some benefits for the rest of us, including, among other things, early training in ways of thought that will later increase the supply of public goods. All of which helps explain why the public pays for and requires education for the young.

SUGGESTIONS FOR FURTHER READING. Mancur Olson Jr., The Logic of Collective Action: Public Goods and the Theory of Groups (1965); Jon Elster, The Cement of Society (1989); John O. Ledyard, *Public Goods: A Survey of Experimental Research, in* The Handbook of Experimental Economics (John H. Kagel and Alvin E. Roth eds., 1995); Daphna Lewinsohn-Zamir, *Consumer Preferences, Citizen Preferences, and the Provision of Public Goods,* 108 Yale L.J. 377 (1999).

12 ⤞ The Stag Hunt

The two of us are hunters. We know that if we cooperate we can take down a stag and have it for dinner; if we work separately, we'll only be eating hare. It isn't quite a prisoner's dilemma, for in that game it's best for me if you cooperate while I don't (and your preference is the reverse). Here my favorite result is that we both cooperate and eat stag. But I wouldn't want to hunt stag if you don't; that's my *last* choice. It won't work, and so will be a waste of time and leave me hungry. Of course you don't want to go after stag unless you're sure I will, too. Maybe we can agree to work jointly, but there is risk in it. Unless we have good reason to trust each other, the temptation will be great for either of us to give up on the stag and give chase to any hare that goes by. At least if I do get a hare I no longer have to worry that I'll end up with nothing if *you* decide to go after a hare because you think it's good insurance against the danger that I'll go after a hare because I'm worried that—and so forth.

We owe this parable to Rousseau's *Discourse on the Origin and Foundations of Inequality among Men,* written in 1754: "If a deer was to be taken, every one saw that, in order to succeed, he must abide faithfully by his post: but if a hare happened to come within the reach of any one of them, it is not to be doubted that he pursued it without scruple, and, having seized his prey, cared very little, if by so doing he caused his companions to miss theirs." There are many situations like this where players in a drama do best by all cooperating, but otherwise had better all defect; if they don't all cooperate, in other words, then nobody should—so perhaps nobody does. For the sake of charm and convenience we can refer to every such case, as the theorists of these games do, as a *stag hunt.* Like the prisoner's dilemma it has been made the subject of close mathematical work, but even without the numbers we will see that knowing the pattern lets us find the common structure in many puzzles that look dissimilar.

A mutiny is a fine example. You had best not try it unless you are sure the rest of the crew is with you. The same is true of efforts by passengers on an airplane to overpower an armed hijacker. Something close to full cooperation may be needed for success in either case. These aren't prisoner's dilemmas because it does you no good to defect once the action starts, at least in the usual case. The thought of defecting while everyone else goes forward holds no relish; you want the enterprise to succeed, and are ready to participate *if* everyone else will. An arms race often amounts to another case study. Possibly your country and mine would both be better off not spending our treasure on weapons. But restraint makes sense for me only if I'm sure you will show the same, and vice versa; neither of us is prepared to have fewer weapons than the other. Since I'm unsure I can trust you, I build them; since you're unsure you can trust me (indeed, I've just made it clear that you can't), you build them, too. It might be a prisoner's dilemma if my first choice were to build the weapons while you do nothing. But maybe my first choice, and yours, is for *neither* of us to bother with weapons. I build them only because I worry that you will.

I've stressed the distinction between a stag hunt and a prisoner's dilemma because they are easily confused and have different implications. (Sometimes people see a problem of cooperation and immediately announce that it's a prisoner's dilemma when it isn't.) To repeat: the difference is that in a prisoner's dilemma it's best for you to defect no matter what I do. In a stag hunt that's not true; if I *know* you will cooperate, I'll want to cooperate, too. A prisoner's dilemma tends to be harder to solve because it always is tempting for either side to defect unless constrained by some device of the kind reviewed in the past two chapters—usually some penalty, formal or informal. A stag hunt also involves a risk of defection, but here the defections are entirely defensive. They happen because some players aren't sure what the others will do, not because anyone wants to take advantage of the rest. The problem is just to get everyone cooperating; once they are, and *know* they are, and are sure that it will continue, they won't be tempted to defect. Sometimes a stag hunt is said to be an *assurance game* because that is the true issue. If everyone has good assurances that everyone else will cooperate, they will be glad to do the same. But assurance games do have this in common with prisoner's dilemmas: they, too, often come up because for some reason it's hard for the parties to them to make contracts. Mutineers suspect (correctly) that their contract to mutiny would be unenforceable. Passengers on an airplane do not know to make contracts in advance about their behavior in the event of a hijacking; and anyway that sort of contract probably would be unenforceable, too, since (among many other things) if anyone breaches it, there may be nobody left afterwards to complain.

For distinguishing between the different games we have been discussing, the idea of the Nash equilibrium helps. (It is named for John Nash, well known to many with no interest in game theory as the subject of the movie *A Beautiful Mind*.) The players of any game have arrived at a Nash equilibrium if, *given* what everyone else is doing, none can do better by changing their strategies. In a prisoner's dilemma the players reach an unhappy Nash equilibrium by defecting every time they play: given that I'm defecting, you might as well keep defecting, and vice versa; I can't gain by suddenly starting to cooperate. (If we both cooperate we're better off than if neither of us do, but it isn't an equilibrium—it isn't stable—because either of us still can do better anytime by defecting.) But sometimes there is more than one equilibrium the parties can reach, and a stag hunt is an example of this. Eating hare is an equilibrium. If we take as given that you're eating hare, there's no sense in my getting up to chase stag; if we take as given that I'm eating hare, there is no point in your chasing stag, either. The situation is unappetizing but stable. We *all* could do better by changing, but it wouldn't be rational for either one of us to be the first. So we just keep eating hare. Yet hunting stag also is an equilibrium if we somehow can get there. Once we're doing it—once we're cooperating *confidently*—there's no reason for anyone to go back to having hare.

The challenge in a stag hunt thus is to get from an inferior equilibrium to a better one—from eating hare, which is one equilibrium, to eating stag, which is better; from laboring under the lash of the sea captain, which is one equilibrium, to heaving him overboard, which is a superior one, at least in the minds of the crew. Escaping a bad equilibrium takes some device to convince everyone that everyone else is going to cooperate. Here is where law sometimes comes in, though the solution to any particular stag hunt depends on *why* each player is reluctant to act unless the others do.

Suppose we start to worry that the Bailey Building & Loan may run out of money. There is a run on the bank; everyone demands cash at once. It's a stag hunt. All would be better off—and most of them would be *content*—if everyone were to forbear. But since nobody knows what the rest will do, it seems to make best sense for each to withdraw what he can, even if it doesn't amount to a hundred cents on the dollar—in other words, to eat hare. In this case the reason you don't want to hunt stag is that you might then be left with nothing. So what we need are not penalties but assurances. The law replies with federal deposit insurance, which promises there will be enough left over even if you don't join the stampede. The result is that the stampede doesn't occur; the law takes the risk out of hunting stag. A bankruptcy law of the sort mentioned in the prior chapter might do the trick here, too—and without any promise of funds from the government. If I knew that the money I took out of the bank would need to be repaid to a bankruptcy court if the bank were unable to pay all its creditors, I would have little reason to join a rush to withdraw my assets.

The situation may be similar if a stock market collapses. I don't particularly want to sell my shares, but if everyone else is selling I had better do the same. Again it probably isn't a prisoner's dilemma. My preference is that *nobody* panic. So there may be no need for a penalty to make me cooperate, and indeed penalties might have bad effects since it's hard to separate normal sales from the panicky ones that amount to abandonment of the stag. Instead of penalties, the stock exchanges have rules called circuit breakers that stop all trading if, say, the Dow Jones average falls too far in too short a time. The stop is no guarantee that selling won't resume right afterwards, but it creates a restrained equilibrium and gives the equilibrium a little time to develop strength—a chance, perhaps, for everyone to get used to hunting stag again.

Sometimes one game can turn into another, and different games can occur at the same time. It depends on the incentives of the players, which sometimes aren't all the same. An example of a mixed game has been the process by which federal judges hire clerks—their young assistants who have just graduated from law school and come work in the chambers for a year. The hiring is done while the clerks are still students. For many years the judges would agree that the best time to hire is in the September after the students have completed their first two years of school, as this way the judges have plenty of grades to see before making decisions. But then a few judges would do their hiring early; others would get wind of this, and hurry to hire early, too; and soon the timetable would have collapsed, with most judges done hiring by, say, the previous March. The next year the judges would announce that this time they really planned to restrain themselves. Then a few would hire even earlier and the process would collapse into February. After a few more years most hiring was happening at the beginning of the students' second year of school rather than the third.[33]

What sort of game was this? For most judges it was a stag hunt. Their real preference was for everyone to cooperate; if they knew nobody else would be hiring until the preferred September, they would be happy to do the same and wouldn't be tempted to go earlier. But if that result wasn't in the cards, they didn't want to wait and then be the last to hire. Meanwhile, though, there were a few other judges who really liked hiring first. For them the game was a prisoner's dilemma. Their first choice was for everyone else to wait while they went off and defected. It took only a few judges with preferences of this kind to goad the rest into an equilibrium they didn't want. Finally in 2003 the judges circulated a formal agreement in which almost all of them promised to wait until a student's third year before making a job offer. The vigorous threat of opprobrium for anyone who broke their word has been enough to make it work—at least for the moment.

We also might use our current tool to understand some cases of racial segregation. Suppose that a black family moves into a white neighborhood, and a few years later most whites are gone. Why has this sometimes happened? There are various stories to explain it; one is that it might be a stag hunt. Assume every white family would welcome the idea of an integrated neighborhood. (We'll relax the assumption later.) But each of them worries that *other* white families might not like it. If the others all move out, then maybe everyone's property values will go down, and in that case the important thing is to leave early rather than late. A few do. The others see this and it confirms their fears. They move out as well. It's another stag hunt, or assurance game. If everyone knows that nobody will be rushing away, everyone is happy enough to stay. That's an equilibrium. But if they worry that many are going to flee, then each might conclude it's rational for them to leave, too, and that's another equilibrium: all the members of one race leave. And then in the first place probably not everyone *will* want integration. Some families might not like it at all. For them the game isn't a stag hunt; they just leave no matter what the others do. But those who do view it as a stag hunt might interpret those departures as defections that make them want to follow suit. As we have seen, a working stag hunt can be a fragile thing. If some players don't have the same preferences as the others or see themselves as playing a different game, they can plunge all the rest into a bad equilibrium.

Whether the law can do much about this last pattern isn't clear, but our look at other stag hunts may suggest lines of solution. One possibility, mostly theoretical, is home equity insurance: owners of houses obtain insurance policies to pay them if their properties lose more value than similar houses in places where the racial mix isn't changing.[34] These policies, like the deposit insurance provided to banks, take the risk out of resisting the stampede and so may stop it from occurring. In an even more novel vein it has been suggested that a high tax might be put on sales of houses in neighborhoods found to be in some sort of transition. At first this might seem apt just to end the chances for integration; for if the tax stops anyone from moving out of a neighborhood, nobody new can move in, either. But the proposal is subtler than that; it is to make the first 5 percent of property sales each year tax-free, but then to burden the rest. This allows slow turnover. Most people would want to wait until the next tax-free period to sell their houses, and in the meantime the rule would work a little like the circuit breakers we find in stock markets. It creates a cooling period where an equilibrium that is in everyone's interest might assert itself. Of course there are costs to all these proposals. Insurance is expensive, and the heavy taxes would be hard on anyone who needs to move out for other reasons. The costs of a failed stag hunt have to be compared to the costs of the solutions. Nor is it sure that either idea would have the desired effects (the results of equity insurance, where it has been tried, aren't clear); for remember that all this assumes the problem of segregation is a stag hunt, and maybe it isn't only that or even mostly that. But these proposals still are interesting studies in how such games can be addressed.

A parallel problem may arise if banks decide against loans to develop an area because they suspect other banks won't make loans and that values in the neighborhood therefore are headed down. Maybe they're right: most banks won't be lending—but only because they all are worried that the other banks won't. That's one equilibrium; nobody lends, and then it's irrational for any bank to be the first. It might be different if a bank thought that by being the "first mover" it could win the loyal support of customers who will appreciate its courage for many years to come. But no bank is likely to expect that, and notice why: being a loyal customer, and thus paying more to the bank that went first, is itself not a Nash equilibrium. The customers will be sorely tempted to defect when other banks show up later and offer better rates.

But now observe that another equilibrium can occur where the banks *all* lend, and the lending by each of them makes lending by the others more secure since it all contributes to the neighborhood's wealth. The trick is to get the banks from the bad equilibrium to the good one. This is one way, at least, to think about the problem—and one way to view the point of the federal Community Reinvestment Act.[35] It rates banks according to whether they meet the needs of local communities, and it penalizes the ones that do badly. Whether those ratings and consequences in themselves create a strong incentive to lend is debatable, but on our current view of the matter it might be beside the point. Even a gentle push by the law toward the better equilibrium may be enough to overcome the collective action problem and get everyone to hunt stag.[36] All everyone wants, on this view of the problem (again, of course, there are others), is sound reason to think they won't be left in the lurch. The statute helps give the wanted assurance. It turns the good equilibrium not just into a rule but into a norm around which banks might be able to organize their expectations of one another.

The seasoned student of the stag hunt will find that it recurs constantly. Why are some people so much more willing to support redistributive tax policies than they are to just voluntarily write checks that redistribute their own income to others? Why is it that social and political movements tend to be so hard to get started, but then can display such great momentum once they reach a certain threshold of acceptance and success—including, perhaps, a few legal victories?[37] Why did so many hockey players resist wearing helmets until it was made a rule?[38] To say each case may involve a stag hunt gets us only part way to a grasp of it. One still must ask *why* it's a stag hunt: why many people might not want to participate in the venture until they see enough others doing it. It may be because some ventures are sure to come to nothing unless large numbers participate. Or sometimes the practical effect is the same no matter how few people join but the psychological experience is different. The hockey player worries that he will be regarded as a dork (or some such thing) if he wears a helmet but nobody else does; or perhaps people feel like fools if they donate to some public cause and nobody else does, but feel better about contributing if it's forced by legislation that makes everyone do it. There is a strongly speculative flavor to this sort of theorizing, of course. As a spectator it's often hard to be sure whether you're watching a stag hunt; it may just be a fruitful hypothesis.

To the extent that people have a psychological appetite for reciprocity—for cooperating if others are, but otherwise not—much of the rest of their social behavior may resemble a stag hunt as well. Perhaps they will be less inclined to cheat on their taxes or engage in other corruptions if they think most people don't; there is some evidence to suggest so, which may have implications for law. Measures to convince people that others are behaving themselves (paying taxes, being honest, being generous, and so on) might be a useful adjunct—some might call them an improvement upon—the usual bribes and threats at the lawmaker's disposal.[39] Whatever convinces the players that everyone else is hunting stag will make them all more comfortable doing the same. But again the design of a good solution depends on *why* the players want to participate only if others do.

A last point to see is how the creation of law can itself create a stag hunt. Think of the game played by the courts of the various states when they make decisions about legal responsibility for accidents. Any state that makes its choices after most others do will find itself playing in the late innings of a game, as the West Virginia Supreme Court found in a case about whether car makers were responsible if their vehicles failed to protect people who negligently got into accidents:

> West Virginia is a small rural state with .66 percent of the population of the United States. Although some members of this Court have reservations about the wisdom of many aspects of tort law, as a court we are utterly powerless to make the overall tort system for cases arising in interstate commerce more rational: Nothing that we do will have any impact whatsoever on the set of economic trade offs that occur in the national economy. And, ironically, trying unilaterally to make the American tort system more rational through being uniquely responsible in West Virginia will only punish our residents severely without, in any regard, improving the system for anyone else. . . .
>
> [I]n some world other than the one in which we live, where this Court were called upon to make national policy, we might very well take a meat ax to some current product liability rules. Therefore, we do not claim that our adoption of rules liberal to plaintiffs comports, necessarily, with some Platonic ideal of perfect justice. Rather, for a tiny state incapable of controlling the direction of the national law in terms of appropriate trade offs among employment, research, development, and compensation for the injured users of products, the adoption of rules liberal to plaintiffs is simple self defense.[40]

In other words, there's no sense hunting stag when everyone else is eating hare. It follows that if these rules have gone wrong they are unlikely ever to be fixed by the state courts acting piecemeal. They find themselves stuck in a particular equilibrium for good or ill. If a solution is in order it probably would have to be coercive: an act of Congress to settle the question for every state at once.

How did other courts get themselves into the equilibrium this court joins with such contempt? One answer is that the earlier players just disagreed with the new one. They *like* their rules and think everyone ought to use them. But notice that these choices also have a bit of the prisoner's dilemma about them.[41] Most lawsuits complaining about a defective product are brought by plaintiffs in their home states against firms located elsewhere. By making rules generous to plaintiffs, state courts thus distribute some wealth from out-of-state companies to local residents. If the other states do this, then it might seem silly not to join them, as the court here says—and if the other states *don't* do it, then aggressive tort rules can create a real bonanza for the home state: compensation for its residents but without high prices, since the other states are using more conservative rules that don't drive up the cost of making products—and let us assume that it is unworkable to charge different prices in different states (because consumers can buy things in one state and resell them in another). So we see again how a prisoner's dilemma can overlap with a stag hunt, as different players have different incentives. In the end we often can't be sure why some disagreeable equilibrium takes hold; here, as in the case of segregation or the hiring of law clerks or a hundred other instances, some players may just have different preferences or fears than others. Or they may be playing different games.

SUGGESTIONS FOR FURTHER READING. An influential early discussion of assurance games is Amartya K. Sen, *Isolation, Assurance and the Social Rate of Discount,* 81 Q.J. Econ. 112 (1967). Some applications are also discussed in Jon Elster, Ulysses and the Sirens: Studies in Rationality and Irrationality (1979). (Here is a rule of thumb: if Elster has written about a topic that is of interest to you, read it.) The game also is briefly treated at various points in Douglas G. Baird, Robert H. Gertner, and Randal C. Picker, Game Theory and the Law (1994). Brian Skyrms, The Stag Hunt and the Evolution of Social Structure (2003), is a good general treatment of the subject.

13 ⤞ Chicken

In the past few chapters we have been investigating patterns where everyone gains by cooperating but finds this hard to achieve without some help from the law. Here is another one—another game, as these situations are called. Its name is *chicken,* and it is familiar from, among other places, the old movie *Rebel without a Cause.* In the most time-honored version, two teenagers drive straight toward each other at high speed, with various results then possible. One of them can swerve, neither of them can swerve, or both of them can swerve. If one swerves, he is deemed a chicken and is humiliated; the one who didn't swerve revels in his victory. If neither of them swerves, they both may be killed in a head-on collision. If they both swerve, then nobody dies or gets humiliated (at least compared to the other), but then nobody has the fun of winning, either.

People still are killed every year playing the automotive version of chicken, but those unfortunates aren't our main interest here; once the legal system has declared such contests illegal, which it has, there may not be much more it can do. Our real interest is in finding other situations in life that amount to games of chicken and asking what the law has to do with them. One wants to understand how to do well at games of chicken when they can't be avoided; but one wants to know even more how to solve or avoid them altogether, since their destructive potential is large and obvious. Some legal examples of such solutions are plain enough. The triangular yield sign familiar from the side of the road is a simple example. Without it, every attempt by one car to merge into traffic has the potential to become a game of chicken. If you start driving heedlessly into the lane of traffic you want to join, maybe the person you are cutting off will stop for you. Or maybe he will keep going, figuring that you are sure to back down. Maybe you both will make accommodating gestures to each other and come to an annoying pause; or perhaps you will both charge ahead and be killed. It's hard to say—until there's a yield sign, at which point the problem mostly goes away.

We should look a little more closely at the structure of chicken. This business of yielding to oncoming traffic actually is a little different from the version played by headstrong teenagers, and in some respects it is a better illustration of the usual problem created by such games. In the original version where two cars drive straight at each other, we—the rest of us in the world, watching from the outside—don't really care what happens so long as the cars don't collide. If either driver swerves, that's fine; if they both swerve, that's fine, too. At first it might seem a little worse if they both swerve, since in that case nobody gets the pleasure of winning. But the good feeling one person gets just by beating out another isn't the kind of gain we worry about preserving. For one thing it's just a transfer of good feeling from one person to another: the relish I take in winning the game is offset by the humiliation you feel at losing. But even if I get *more* pleasure from it than you lose, there are strong arguments for taking some human wants more seriously than others—for laundering preferences, as it is sometimes called.[42] We don't worry about the disappointment that thieves feel when better police work makes their lives harder; a thief's successful labors produce nothing that anyone else in the world wants. The world is better off without them than with them. The pleasure one player of chicken gets at the expense of the other is like this, too.

Yielding when two roads merge is different. Obviously we don't want a collision, but we also don't really want both cars to slow down, with each driver then edging forward and making polite hand signals to the other. It's an irritating waste of time. So this time it's decidedly best if both parties don't defer, or "swerve." We want one to drive and the other to wait. A yield sign arranges this. It prevents car crashes when both cars go *and* the waste of time when neither of them goes. It imposes a little cost on the party it disfavors (the merging party), who has to slow down; but there is no unfairness in this, not only because the stakes are low but also because everyone is likely to take turns on the happy and sad ends of these yielding situations often enough. And notice that in addition to stating which party wins the contest, the yield sign also changes the nature of the contest by removing any residual worries about honor and humiliation (and thus avoiding cases of road rage). Yielding becomes a matter of deference to the law, not of deference to the driver of the other car.

At first the game of chicken might look similar to a prisoner's dilemma. Driving straight in a game of chicken is like defecting in a prisoner's dilemma; swerving is like cooperating with your partner, or staying silent. It's bad if both parties "defect"; in a prisoner's dilemma it means they both get more jail time than if they had said nothing, and in chicken it means there is a collision. But the games differ in several respects. It's true that from the standpoint of any given player, the best outcome in both games occurs when he defects and the other cooperates (swerves). And the second-best outcome is when they both cooperate, as by both swerving or both saying nothing to the police. The order of their last choices is different, though. The worst outcome for you in a prisoner's dilemma arises when you keep quiet (cooperate) and your confederate talks (defects). Your worst outcome in chicken occurs when you *both* defect, since then you're liable to be killed.

The more important difference between chicken and the prisoner's dilemma appears when we look at the solutions to the games from the outside—in other words, when we ask what reply to the situation will create the most overall benefits and the least waste. In a prisoner's dilemma or stag hunt, the goal is to get everyone doing the same thing: cooperating. In a game of chicken it's often best if we *don't* do the same thing; it's best—least wasteful all the way around—if there is a winner and a loser, one who yields and one who drives on. The reason is that defecting in a prisoner's dilemma is always bad. It means littering, or breaking a promise, or being negligent (we'll set aside cases where we want two real prisoners to confess). In a game of chicken, "defecting" just means not deferring, and sometimes that's good on the whole: as in the case of merging traffic, we don't *want* everyone to always defer; the overall benefits may be greatest when one defers and the other doesn't, even though neither wants to be in the passive role.

Something else follows from this, too: there may not be a best single solution to a game of chicken. There might be two solutions that both work fine (or even three, in cases like the original game where we're content if everyone swerves). You yield and I go, or I yield and you go. Either is an equilibrium, which means that so long as I keep doing what I'm doing, you can't gain by changing what *you're* doing. If you always yield and I always keep driving, that's an equilibrium—but so is a pattern where I always yield and you always drive on. We just need to pick one, but sometimes that's a problem because I don't know which approach you plan to take. The yield sign solves the problem by assigning roles to both drivers. Another name for this game, and one that might be more descriptive, is *hawks and doves*. One side is going to play the hawk (keep driving), and the other is going to be the dove (wait its turn). Everyone would rather play the hawk, but on the other hand it's important not to play the hawk if the other side does, too, since then we get a collision. Above all, you want to know what the other side is going to do so that you don't do the same.

Various other legal rules can be understood as more subtly resolving problems similar to the ones just described; they amount to figurative yield signs. These include most rules that put people into order for gaining property rights: queues for public housing or doctrines about how property ownership gets established at an earlier stage (such as the general rule that the first person to possess an unowned thing, such as a wild animal, becomes its owner).[43] Those rules serve a lot of functions; they avoid the waste of time and energy that occurs if people have to angle for position or fight over prizes—the concern we raised in the discussion of rent seeking in chapter 7. But the rules also avoid the games of chicken that can easily arise when a contest over some prize—whether it's a thing or a place in line—is left for everyone to work out on their own. People will adopt various strategies in such situations. Some of them will cooperate, but others will try aggressive tactics that create big gains for them if others are bluffed into submitting, and disaster otherwise. Some rounds of play will end one of those ways, and some will end in the other: maybe a grudge, or a brawl, or a lawsuit, or a war. (Games of chicken, with the usual variety of endings, are common in international relations. The reader should have no trouble thinking of examples.) The invisible absence of those outcomes is sometimes a benefit of legal rules that settle rights and questions of priority.

Notice, though, that a legal rule might not end the possibilities of chicken. It also can start a new round, because now each side has a new threat: calling the police, or calling a lawyer. A legal rule, in other words, can create a new bluffing contest of its own about whether the rule will be invoked, and then we can have still more rounds of play. The party who was aggressive in round one, and who dared the person in the other car to stand on his rights and call the police, ends up arrested in round two and is offered a plea bargain. He can yield by pleading guilty and getting a lighter sentence, or he can defiantly announce that he will take his chances at trial and hope that this causes the prosecutor to offer a better deal or drop the case. Maybe it works, or maybe (more probably) it doesn't. In the latter event, perhaps he goes to prison and can play the game yet again when he wants to use the Ping-Pong table at the same time as one of his fellow inmates. Some people need more than one lesson, and one of the functions of the criminal law is to gradually remove from the population people who insist on playing chicken when the rest of us would rather not.

But now let's assume the initial dispute wasn't a criminal matter that summoned the police. It was a civil dispute that precipitated a call to an attorney. Now we enter an area where games of chicken are most commonly played: negotiation, whether over the settlement of a case or the purchase of a car or anything else. To see why bargaining can amount to a game of chicken, review why two people sit down to negotiate about anything. They think there are gains to be had from making a trade: one side has something the other side may want more. Maybe the stake is a house, or maybe it's a promise to drop a lawsuit, or maybe it's an agreement to work rather than go on strike. The distance between how much the two sides value the stake is what we can call the bargaining range. I would be willing to sell you my house (or dismiss my lawsuit) for any payment better than $300,000. You would be willing to pay $400,000 to get that result. So there's a bargaining range of $100,000 (since any agreement between $300,000 and $400,000 will make us both better off), and it seems plain that we will be able to make a deal. But at what price? Obviously I would prefer that you pay $400,000, and you would rather that I accept $300,000. The subject of our negotiations will be precisely this question of how to divide the benefits of the deal.

Perhaps you can see how the game of chicken arises. Suppose I demand that you pay $400,000—the maximum; otherwise I won't agree to any deal at all. This puts you in an interesting position. That isn't the deal you want, of course; but it's better than no deal, which I have presented as your other option. So perhaps you swallow hard and accept my terms. Or maybe not. It depends on how convinced you are that I will carry out my threat. Of course I will be worse off, too, if we don't reach a deal, so maybe I'm bluffing. My job is to convince you that I'm not. This is the most important practical point to understand about how games of chicken, when they must be played, are won and lost: the winner generally will be the one who can commit himself to an aggressive strategy—to playing the "hawk"—most visibly and irrevocably. In the classic example offered by Thomas Schelling (whose discussion is great reading),[44] the best strategy for a driver playing chicken would be to somehow remove his steering wheel and throw it out the window. Once the second driver sees this done, he is forced to accept that there is nothing more the first driver can do; he is committed to going straight. The second driver inevitably will swerve away to avoid being killed, unless his frustration gets the better of his judgment.

The point of the example is that people sometimes gain power by having *fewer* choices and options, surprising as it may sound. If you can convince the other driver that you're crazy and won't swerve, you have great power in an automotive game of chicken. And if you can convince the other party to a negotiation that you won't budge (or *can't* budge), you likewise have put yourself into a strong position. Lawyers often get involved in these tactics when they negotiate on behalf of their clients. There is always the question of how much authority the lawyer has to make a deal. It might seem best to get all the authority you can, but often that isn't true. It may be better in a negotiation to be able to say your hands have been tied by your client: you are *forbidden* to accept less than $400,000. If the claim can be made convincingly (obviously this will depend on the circumstances), it can put the other side into the same position as the second driver in our game of chicken. Once you grasp this principle, you will see illustrations of it in all the little negotiations of everyday life: one side stakes out a position that reflects what he hopes to end up with, and tries to make it sound like he won't or can't bend and that massive destruction will result if the other side takes the same position. The other side then decides whether to go straight or swerve, a decision that will depend largely on how firm he thinks the first player's original position is; and so it goes. Children are great at this. They figure it all out very early, and tend to be ruthless negotiators.

These negotiating games usually are harmless enough because if either side gets carried away, the other can go find someone else to bargain with. There are lots of houses on the market; if one seller douses himself with gasoline and arranges to have a match thrown onto him if he accepts less than $400,000, he has made a credible commitment to his position—but then most buyers will seek out other sellers who are in a more reasonable humor. The greater troubles arise when there isn't a market into which the parties can escape from each other. That is what happens when two sides sit down to discuss the settlement of a lawsuit. There is nobody else to bargain with. The technical term for this situation is a bilateral monopoly, because each side is a monopolist—the only possible seller—with respect to what the other side wants (e.g., getting rid of the lawsuit). If one side commits to a position strategically but has misjudged what the other will be willing to accept—or for that matter if *both* sides try the strategy of utterly committing themselves to extreme positions—the bargaining may collapse despite the existence of some price that would have left both of them better off: the boardroom equivalent of a game of chicken that ends with a collision. This is one reason why professional mediators hired to resolve lawsuits like to put the parties in separate rooms and then take turns visiting them privately. Among other things it avoids the danger that either side (or both) will strategically commit to a position in front of the other that then becomes hard to back down from.

The legal system generally lets people play these games out for themselves despite the risk of collision. The reason probably is that it's too hard to interfere in them without doing violence to other values. The law could make everyone submit their lawsuits to binding arbitration, so as to avoid prolonged cases that result from elaborate bluffs in a game of chicken. But we can't necessarily tell when people are bluffing, and the ones who are sincere—the ones who really do place surprisingly high values on their ability to go to court—have rights we want to respect. So letting them thrash their disputes out for themselves seems the lesser evil. Sometimes, though, the law does take a more active interest, as when the public interest is more dramatically affected by the threat of a game of chicken that turns out badly. In labor negotiations, for example, a game of chicken can develop easily enough: both sides, conscious of all the strategic points we have just discussed, announce their demands loudly and publicly. They do this to make it embarrassing and costly for themselves to back down; like getting rid of the steering wheel, this is supposed to force the other side to capitulate. Alas, the other side already did the same thing, so perhaps the result is a strike, with all of its public and private costs—despite the fact that there was (we may imagine) a deal that both sides would have preferred to a strike if they had been able to find their way to it. The law tries to prevent this by defining such open gestures of irrevocable commitment to a position as bad faith in bargaining. As one court put it, "an employer may not so combine 'take-it-or-leave-it' bargaining methods with a widely publicized stance of unbending firmness that he is himself unable to alter a position once taken."[45]

And eminent domain, or "takings" cases, can be viewed along the same lines. The government wants to build a highway where your house sits. We could instruct the government to simply bargain with you until you agree to sell, which you presumably would do at some price. One of the risks of this approach, though, is that you will play chicken, setting a very high price—higher than you really would need to feel compensated—and figuring that the government will have no choice but to cave in to your demand. But then maybe the government does walk away and decides to route the highway through a less convenient path. The result is a bit of waste: there was a price that would have kept you happy and also would have put the highway where it most belongs, but the deal never got made. The law of eminent domain avoids this possibility, as well as other problems, by allowing the government to force a sale upon you. (The forced sale in turn creates other problems that are discussed in other chapters.)

Games of chicken can arise on a larger scale in the relationships between branches of government. Congress thinks a piece of legislation is allowed under the Constitution; the Supreme Court thinks it isn't. Now what? If both bodies insist on their own interpretations, the result may be a kind of collision—a constitutional crisis in which it is unclear who has the last word. The Supreme Court took a hawkish position on the question in *Cooper v. Aaron,* holding that it has the power and duty to say what the Constitution means and that the other branches must obey even if they disagree.[46] The other branches of government generally have gone along with this, "swerving" by accepting the Court's pronouncements as final. From time to time there are nervous moments, as when Congress tried to reverse one of the Court's decisions about the meaning of the free exercise clause of the First Amendment and the Court reasserted what it had said the first time.[47] Or when the Court ordered President Nixon to give a congressional committee the tapes he made of conversations in the White House.[48] What if he had declined? Nobody was sure what the outcome of that collision would have been, though everyone worried about it; in any event, Nixon swerved and handed over the tapes.

But many people regard the Court as the loser of a game of chicken that it played in the 1930s with President Roosevelt. The Court had struck down a number of the laws Roosevelt pushed through as part of the New Deal. Roosevelt threatened to expand the number of Justices on the Court and fill the new openings with like-minded appointees until the Court saw its way to upholding the statutes he wanted. The Court soon began upholding his programs. The role of Roosevelt's threat in producing that outcome is a matter of debate,[49] but it may have been a game of chicken where one side capitulated once it became worried enough that the other was ready to take a path that would force an even less attractive outcome.

A theme worth repeating here about games of chicken, or hawks and doves, is that there is no single solution to them. They can be solved so long as either side goes straight while the other swerves. There are various ways that parties can get into one pattern or the other. We have seen that legal rules sometimes assign them roles, but in other cases a solution arises by custom. Perhaps one party simply asserted its role first, and then it was in everyone else's interests to go along even if they might have preferred a different set of assignments. That may best explain the American practice of judicial review. There is no rule external to the process (in the Constitution itself, for example) establishing it; and in England, unlike the United States, the legislature plays the role of the hawk: the courts treat its constitutional rulings as conclusive. This is an equilibrium, just as is the American approach. The important thing is for someone to have the last word.

Now you can see why being the first to move can be so important in a game of chicken. Once the parties have found their way to an equilibrium, it becomes very costly for the "doves" to force a change to a different equilibrium where *they* get to win. They can do it only by driving straight, as it were, and hoping the other side will swerve for a change. This possibility sounds scary but sometimes might be worth the risk. When we talk about solutions to games of chicken (such as yield signs), we look for outcomes that minimize the total trouble for the parties—but notice that we don't worry about how the benefits are distributed *between* them. One reason why we might not care—and why yielding drivers don't care, either—is that they take turns in each position. But Congress and the Supreme Court don't take turns, at least not explicitly. The general rule is that the Supreme Court wins. If the game is a repeated one, as it is here, a party who always loses might decide that the cost of a collision would be worth enduring in order to avoid playing the dove anymore and forever—a tempting thought after a long, hard period of submission.

The Supreme Court understands these temptations, and it uses various tools to try to keep them from getting out of hand. The Court uses rules about standing, and the "case and controversy" requirement, to prevent itself from hearing legal challenges at the behest of bystanders. The federal courts won't intervene in a controversy except to resolve a live dispute—a lawsuit to redress an injury brought by someone immediately affected. A common defense of these rules is that they minimize the number of confrontations between the Court and the other branches of government (legislative or executive, federal or state)—confrontations that always carry some risk of a game of chicken which may in turn end badly. And then sometimes the Court will fashion its rulings modestly to reduce the friction they cause with the other branches. In some areas of law the Court is very deferential to Congress, as in the review of laws setting economic policy or in challenges to the scope of Congress's power to legislate under the commerce clause. In this last area we have seen a bit of friction lately, and some onlookers think it is time to revise the terms of the game.[50] The question is worth pondering not only in its own right but also because it is a fine study in the management of the reiterated play of chicken. The task is not just to solve the game; it is to keep it solved by managing each side's schedule of costs with some care. If one always wants to be the hawk, it helps to play the part with some grace.

SUGGESTIONS FOR FURTHER READING. Thomas C. Schelling, The Strategy of Conflict (1960), is the classic treatment of negotiation as a game of chicken. Some interesting recent discussions of the role of law in solving games of chicken include Richard H. McAdams, *A Focal Point Theory of Expressive Law,* 86 Va. L. Rev. 1649 (2000), and Lee Anne Fennell, *Interdependence and Choice in Distributive Justice: The Welfare Conundrum,* 1994 Wis. L. Rev. 235.

14 →→ Cascades

You have job interviews with two employers and are turned down in both of them. At the next one you are asked if you have had any prior interviews. You recount your unhappy recent history, and the employer concludes that the two prior rejections probably meant something. This helps him decide to pass on you. The process continues and accelerates from there; the next interviewer finds you have *three* rejections and has even more cause for concern than the previous one.[51] The process can work in reverse, too: a job candidate gets offers, and the offers create interest on the part of others. Or change the scene of the pattern: everyone wants to go to a particular university because it's hard to get in; from this they infer that it must be excellent—and the inference gets stronger the more times it is drawn, because now admission becomes more difficult still. Crowded restaurants may create the same pattern, and uncrowded restaurants the opposite one; likewise when people conclude that a movie probably is good because so many are going to see it—so they go see it themselves and strengthen the same perception by others. Or a street performer attracts a small gathering. The group gets larger as people with low curiosity thresholds come to see what's going on. Then the crowd really grows as people with normal thresholds see a mass of spectators converging on the sidewalk and can't resist investigating what the fuss is about. The same can happen with decisions about nearly anything. People are unsure whether a diet, a new medicine, a tonsillectomy, or a circumcision create enough health benefits to make them worthwhile; or they aren't sure how many children to have. They rely on what others seem to be thinking, and then others rely on what *they* seemed to think. And so on.

These all are possible examples of *information cascades.* Notice that all the parties to them may be rational. If you feel uncertain about something, it might make sense to defer to others who seem sure; maybe they know more than you do. And if the next player likewise has no firm basis for decision, it might be entirely reasonable for him to see the growing agreement, find it impressive, and go along. But whether reasonable or not, the result is that the belief gains empty momentum: there is growth in its acceptance but not in its likelihood of being true, which hasn't changed and may be small. Since someone usually benefits from a cascade, naturally we find that entrepreneurs sometimes try to start them deliberately. Thus the authors of the business book who bought 50,000 copies in an attempt to get it onto the bestseller lists—where it then stayed.[52] Or the producers who hire audience members to applaud at a performance or go heckle its competitors.[53] And it has been suggested that this is why restaurants with long lines of customers don't deal with the problem by raising their prices a bit. The long lines create a cascade; everyone wants to eat there because everyone else wants to eat there. If the lines suddenly get shorter, that might start another cascade—in the wrong direction.[54]

Your vulnerability to a cascade depends on how much knowledge of your own you have and how ready you are to assume that if others think something is true, it probably is. People vary on these points; some are weak resisters and others are strong. But the point of a cascade—the feature that makes it insidious—is that it takes in the weaker and the stronger alike by enlisting them in order. A strong onlooker who isn't impressed by a consensus of two or three people comes back later to find a consensus of two or three hundred, and this time thinks there must be solid basis for it after all; he starts to doubt his own thinking. But the only development while he was gone was that others, more easily impressed than he was, signed on to the emerging opinion and so made it seem more dominant.

Cascades of this sort shed light on some legal problems. They may help explain bandwagons of illegality. When Napster and other computer programs became available for illegally downloading music, not everyone used them right away. Some were uncertain whether they would get in legal trouble for downloading and weren't sure whether it was ethical. But the greater the number of people who went ahead and did it, the more reassured the others were, until millions of people were emboldened to join by the sense of legal and moral security they drew from their numbers. Other possible examples include the problems of the 1980s with insider trading, the common practice of hiring household help without paying taxes on their wages, problems of looting when civil order breaks down after a natural disaster, and recreational drug use. People draw inferences from what they see others doing, and do the same; now even more people are doing it, and they create a still stronger impression on the rest.

Meanwhile the government and the victims of this sort of behavior have strategies of their own for countering cascades. Recall that ignorance and uncertainty are the best soil for a cascade; people rely on what others think when they have no strong knowledge of their own, and the fragility of the consensus that results makes it easily disrupted by shocks. So the government put outs information about tobacco and other drug use that it hopes will cause people to resist what they hear others say and see them do, and perhaps start a cascade in the other direction. Companies that lose profits from music piracy try to disrupt the cascade by bringing highly visible lawsuits against selected downloaders. And then we have laws such as the Securities Acts of 1933 and 1934, which among other things require a company to disclose various sorts of information before offering stock to the public and to keep reporting periodically afterwards. The requirements help preempt the creation of the cascades known as stock market bubbles, where everyone rushes to buy a stock because everyone else seems so eager to have it. Those statutes were passed soon after the crash of 1929, which illustrated the fragility of a cascade and also its potential to reverse direction. The final point of all these efforts is the same: they are meant to send signals stronger than the ones people get by watching each other.

A different implication for law involves the hazards of sequential decision-making. When witnesses are asked what they saw, they say different things alone than if they first hear how others describe the events.[55] This is why the federal guidelines say that witnesses to crimes should be separated and shouldn't talk to each other.[56] We don't want their testimony to create a cascade. A similar problem arises when jurors vote on a case. Should they vote simultaneously or sequentially? A simultaneous vote has the advantage of avoiding cascades: we don't want the third juror swayed by what the first two did, then the fourth juror swayed by what the first three did, and so on. So the choice of procedure might matter; oddly, though, we leave it up to each jury to decide what to do. The same general question arises again when judges vote. In military courts-martial the officers deciding a case vote in reverse order of rank, so the officer with the highest rank goes last; it has been suggested that this reduces the risk that junior officers will defer to senior ones thought to have more experience or better judgment.[57] Alas, on the United States Supreme Court the Justices vote openly and one at a time, starting with the Chief Justice and then descending to the most junior member, who already knows how all the other Justices voted when his turn arrives.

The risk of cascades repeats on a larger scale in elections. Iowa votes first in presidential primaries; if it surprises everyone by picking John Kerry, onlookers in other states conclude that perhaps Kerry is better than they had thought. This helps him win in New Hampshire a week later, and now even more people are convinced he is the right man. Then there are the public opinion polls that claim just to record public preferences but that are known to have effects on the preferences as well; they can contribute to cascades, as uncertain voters see that a candidate is doing well and conclude that maybe all those people supporting him are on to something.[58] His advantage in the polls increases, and the cycle is on its way. It is why partisan organizations sponsor polls, and why some countries, such as France, Italy, and Israel, ban them in the days or weeks before an election. They want independent judgments, not cascades.

Might a similar cascade arise when courts in different jurisdictions are presented with the same question? The first court to decide writes on a blank slate. The next finds the question difficult and gives a bit of weight to the precedent set by the first. The third court is reluctant to create a division of authority and goes along; the fourth court sees an increasingly monolithic body of case law and defers to it; etc. So the notion of cascades might be consistent with what courts do—but this doesn't necessarily mean a cascade is actually occurring. There is no way to prove that such agreement by courts reflects a cascade rather than independent agreement among them; courts say they value consistency with one another but say as well that they have a duty to render independent judgments. So whether "precedential" cascades occur is an interesting but unsettled question.[59] The same point holds for most of the examples we have considered. Cascades are a plausible and intriguing account of much human behavior, but their existence is hard to prove conclusively outside the laboratory.

There are other types of cascades besides the informational variety; let's consider two more briefly. An *availability cascade* is a variation on the theme just considered. It starts with the fact that when people try to decide how likely something is to be true, they often ask themselves how readily examples of it come to mind—how easily it is "available" in the mind's eye. (Psychologists call this the availability heuristic.) A problem with this way of assessing risks, apart from its inaccuracy, is that the sense of availability may cascade. The more that people talk about an example of some problem, the more everyone has it in mind and repeats it, and the more important the problem may come to seem, though its actual importance hasn't increased at all. It's another case of empty momentum. Political campaigns can be viewed as great contests by each side to try to make its virtues, and the flaws of its rivals, as available as possible by putting them before voters in a form—television commercials—that is vivid and calculated to provoke impressions that will cascade.

A troubling result for law, it has been argued, is that availability cascades may cause people to clamor for regulation of hazards that they have heard a lot about and can imagine vividly, such as leaking toxic waste sites or Lyme Disease or plane crashes, but to be unmoved by other hazards that may be more serious but that don't come to mind as much—like cars running into moose.[60] The public sense of which risks are worth worrying about gets determined either arbitrarily or by entrepreneurs who make hazards "available" by marketing memorable examples of them. Those who want tort reform pick a case—the case where a woman won a huge judgment after spilling a cup of coffee on herself, perhaps—and talk about it all they can. Some of those within earshot bring it up at the office water cooler; eventually it ends up in the newspapers; and now the case comes to represent a problem that seems common and urgent. Again, the more people talk about it, the more people talk about it. Those who don't want tort reform counter with horrible cases of unredressed wrongdoing by doctors or corporations that they hope may likewise cascade in the public imagination.

The same account could be given of debates over abortion, affirmative action, economic analysis of law, the problem of "activist" judges, or any number of others. If one side succeeds in getting its favored vignette into circulation and causing its familiarity to cascade, it also will be more likely to persuade people of the importance of the problem or model the story represents. This also helps explain why it's politically so hard to take strong measures against disasters before they have happened at least once. Until they occur they aren't available enough to the public imagination to seem important; after they occur their availability cascades and there is an exaggerated rush to prevent the identical thing from happening again. Thus after the terrorist attacks on the World Trade Center, cutlery was banned from airplanes and invasive security measures were imposed at airports. There wasn't the political will to take drastic measures against the possibility of nuclear or other terrorist attacks of a type that hadn't yet happened and so weren't very available.[61]

In a *reputational cascade* the problem is different. It isn't that I'm trying to form an accurate belief and am tempted to rely on others; it's that I'm trying to get the others to like me. I do this by saying things I think they will find agreeable. Then you arrive on the scene, and you, too, want to be liked. Now that I've joined the others you have even more reason than I did to conform; and once you join there will be still another person saying and not saying the same things, which raises the apparent cost to anyone who might be tempted to do otherwise. Soon it's remarkable how much general agreement there is and how rare and timid other opinions have become.

There can be little doubt that reputational cascades occur. They are a nearly complete account of most fads and especially of fashion in clothing. Not everyone cares about fashion, but those who care the most conform to it first, then bring in those who care a little less; together they bring in others, and the effect is the familiar herding pattern set in motion by the skilled and wealthy cascade makers known as designers. The question for us is how well the model accounts for the spread of ideas. It's clear enough that ideas often succeed for reasons separate from their truth, and that this sometimes happens because people modify what they say to protect their reputations. But the reputational cascade is a slightly more distinctive theory than this: the first group adopts ideas for whatever reason—self-interest or their perceived truth; the second adopts the ideas to preserve their reputation with the first; members of the third group, who perhaps weren't much concerned about their reputations at first, now see a larger consensus to worry about and a more serious danger of social penalties, so they, too, knuckle under. And now the pressure has become that much greater on group number four.

Again this vision isn't provably right. It may explain a little or a lot; possibly it is the key to understanding what a lot of people think about most things most of the time. It at least seems a compelling explanation of many cases where beliefs appear to be held in place by pressures of conformity that are resented by many of those laboring beneath them. The rise of political correctness from a small movement to a pervasive one in many universities is an apparent case of reputational cascades. Expressing certain views comes to be seen as hazardous to one's reputation. As a result they are said less and less. As a further result anyone who does say them stands out even more and incurs greater social penalties than before. The same dynamic can occur in academic departments or in any other communities. And sometimes the pattern can interact with information cascades, as when one group adopts a view for reputational reasons and then others go along because they assume the earlier group knows something they don't; or as when people come to believe that views they started to hold for the sake of conformity really are true.

Cascades aren't always bad. Sometimes an informational cascade is correct; this is one way to understand the widespread confidence that the earth is a sphere despite most people having little direct evidence on the point.[62] And reputational cascades have their upside, too: they help explain manners, many of which serve useful purposes. But the reputational cascade has an especially nasty potential because it so easily can come at the expense of truth. It creates incentives for people to deliberately suppress what they believe or know; Timur Kuran refers to this as "preference falsification" and suggests that it is the stuff totalitarian societies are made of and on which they depend.[63] This is the most important point to grasp about reputational cascades: their power to distort discourse and enforce a fake consensus.

Some of the more specific implications of reputational cascades overlap with points already seen; they, too, have implications for voting of various kinds. We saw, for example, that informational cascades are a reason to make votes simultaneous rather than sequential. The threat of reputational cascades cuts in favor of also making votes *secret.* Of course secrecy can destroy accountability, and that risk has to be traded off against the danger of reputational cascades. The balance between these worries explains why votes in general elections are secret, votes in a legislature aren't, and the secrecy of votes in intermediate settings—faculty meetings, say—may be a matter for negotiation.[64]

But the most interesting application of law to reputational cascades involves efforts to impose a stigma on bad behavior or remove it from good. Lawrence Lessig has argued that this is a subtle but frequent purpose of lawmaking and that it is one way to understand the passage of the Civil Rights Act of 1964, which forbade racial discrimination in various settings. Some Southern white businessmen wanted the law because it helped rid them of the stigma associated with serving or hiring blacks.[65] The stigma might be restated as a reputational cascade. Those who wanted segregation scared some others into complying with their preferences; that first wave of compliance reinforced the pressure and toppled some other resisters, until finally few whites wanted to stand out by integrating. The civil rights statute interrupted the cascade with a legal command. It also changed the way the reputational signals operated by allowing whites who wanted to integrate to say they were obeying the law, not their preferences.

Another case cited by Lessig involves dueling with pistols, which for a long time in the South, as well as elsewhere, was a customary way of revenging insults. All we can do is speculate, but the custom might have been bound up in reputational cascades: even people who weren't sure dueling was a sensible way to resolve problems wouldn't want to say so because they would risk being called cowards, and their silence would then contribute to an apparent consensus that made it still harder for anyone else to resist. Against these pressures, laws to ban dueling often weren't successful. A little more effective, though, were laws that disqualified duelers from public office, because these provisions got to the heart of the matter, which was honor. They disrupted the cascade by allowing someone to avoid a duel on new grounds that were reputable: he wouldn't want to disqualify himself for public service for which he might be needed.

There are lots of other examples where a law addresses the power of reputational pressure in social life. Laws forbidding street gangs to loiter have been defended on the ground that loitering lets gangs openly flaunt their dominance and helps them impose reputational costs on those who won't join.[66] It might be a cascade; it might be a case where everyone in the neighborhood pays respect to the gang even though they privately hate them. Initially the gang cows one subset; the next is more easily subdued because the first is in the fold; finally it becomes too risky for anyone to dissent. In this case as in most others, the reputational point is only part of the law's story, and even then one can worry about reputational pressure without worrying about the particular problem of cascades. But where reputation is a worry, cascades probably should be as well; for cascades often are a means by which threats against reputation get turned into large and powerful mechanisms of social control.

SUGGESTIONS FOR FURTHER READING. Timur Kuran and Cass R. Sunstein, *Availability Cascades and Risk Regulation,* 51 Stan. L. Rev. 683 (1999); Abhijit V. Banerjee, *A Simple Model of Herd Behavior,* 107 Q.J. Econ. 797 (1992); Sushil Bikhchandani, David Hirshleifer, and Ivo Welch, *A Theory of Fads, Fashion, Custom, and Cultural Change as Informational Cascades,* 100 J. Pol. Econ. 992, 992–94 (1992); Lisa R. Anderson and Charles A. Holt, *Information Cascades in the Laboratory,* 87 Am. Econ. Rev. 847 (1997); David Hirshleifer, *The Blind Leading the Blind: Social Influence, Fads, and Information Cascades, in* The New Economics of Human Behavior (Mariano Tommasi and Kathryn Ierulli eds., 1995).

15 ↠ Voting Paradoxes

We now turn to a different sort of problem involving coordination between people. It often happens in law that we want to take the views of more than one person—maybe the views of a lot of people—and amass them into a general preference or judgment. The views could be those of everyone in the country, or all the members of the Senate or some other legislature, or all the Justices of the Supreme Court. So the members of those groups vote, and we say that the result reflects what the largest number of them want. But there are problems below the surface of these procedures that make them trickier than they seem.

The first basic difficulty is known as the *Condorcet voting paradox,* for the Marquis de Condorcet (con-dor-SAY gets the pronunciation close enough; we look briefly at another of his ideas, the jury theorem, in the discussion of reasonable doubt in chapter 28). It arises when people are picking among more than two choices. To illustrate the basic idea, consider a presidential election like the one held in 1992. There were three main choices: George Bush (the first one), Bill Clinton, and Ross Perot, a popular independent candidate. Think of the election being decided by three people, or three groups of people, who have the following preferences:

	First choice	Second choice	Third choice
Voter(s) 1	Clinton	Perot	Bush
Voter(s) 2	Perot	Bush	Clinton
Voter(s) 3	Bush	Clinton	Perot

Which candidate should win? Clearly not Clinton, for although he is the first choice of the first voter, the other two both would prefer Bush over him. But it wouldn't make sense for Bush to win, either, because the first and second voters both would prefer Perot to him. So evidently Perot should win—except that voters one and three both would rather have Clinton. Now you see the trouble: the preferences of a group don't work the same way as the preferences of a single person. When you deal with one person, you generally can assume that his preferences are transitive—that if he prefers *A* to *B* and *B* to *C*, he also prefers *A* to *C*. When you deal with a group, there is no such guarantee. In the case of the presidential election, *A* is better than *B*, *B* is better than *C*—and yet *C* can be shown to be better than *A*. The result is that no matter who wins, two-thirds of the voters will be unhappy and might clamor for a recall: a problem known as cycling.[67]

The implication of the paradox is that after an election like the one just described, it is impossible to make a coherent statement about what the will of the people was. There was just a procedure and an outcome, which was arbitrary. This isn't to say that the outcome in 1992 was arbitrary, though it may have been; it depends on the actual substance of everyone's preferences, which we don't know. Clinton won, but maybe a majority would have preferred Bush (but some members of that majority voted for Perot); maybe a majority also would have preferred Perot to Bush (but some of them voted for Clinton); maybe a majority also would have preferred Clinton to Perot. Each of these statements could be true, though it's also possible that they all are false. The important principle is just the *ABC* point: when you're dealing with a group in an election like this, you can't assume the group's preferences work logically (or are transitive); you also can't assume, just from the victory of one option in an election, that it actually expresses some sort of true preference of the group.

Kenneth Arrow made these points more formal. He showed that as much as one might like to arrange things so that a group produces the same well-behaved, transitive sets of decisions that a single person would, it can't be done. Or at least it can't be done if you also make some other assumptions about the process that everyone probably will be happy to grant: for example, that no one person gets his way (in other words, there is no "dictator"), and that if one voter's preferences change in one direction, the preferences of the group—the social preference—will not move in the other direction as a result. There are a couple of other conditions, but for now we can dispense with them and with Arrow's proof of his resulting "impossibility theorem"; they are easily found elsewhere.[68] The point is that if you create a system of voting that is rational in other respects, it is bound to also have the potential to generate perverse outcomes—a potential which prevents us from saying anything confident about the meaning of the group's decisions when it picks from more than two choices.

Various methods have been devised to try to soften or avoid these paradoxical results. You can try letting people cast first-place, second-place, and third-place votes, and then weight the votes accordingly, though this can create a wide field for strategic behavior by the voters. Or you can have people cast votes between a series of pairs, and then consider who does best—who gets the most votes in all those pair-wise contests (an idea associated with Jean-Charles de Borda), or who has the least bad negative showing in any of them (the preference of the Marquis de Condorcet; a candidate who can beat each of the others in head-to-head competition is sometimes known as the Condorcet winner). But any of these methods can be shown to still have a potential for cycling.[69] Or everyone can vote on a bunch of options and then have a runoff election between the last two candidates standing, whether the candidates are people or proposals. But runoffs can naturally create their own perverse results, since the third option—the one eliminated before the runoff—might have been preferred by a majority to one of the survivors. In any event, all of these proposals are novelties not found very often in American voting processes, which usually stick with simple majority rule regardless of the number of choices.

Everyone accepts the logic of the voting paradox in principle, but there is dispute about the size of the problem it creates in practice. Some analysts think the paradox makes democracy an illusion; in real life there almost always are more than two choices—often many more—and in those cases it's just wrong to think that the outcomes of simple votes really express what people want (the votes may routinely give a majority of them what they really *don't* want).[70] Others suggest that even if those problems exist, democracy still beats the alternatives, and anyway that if the problems were serious we would see more cycling of the kind suggested by the model: every outcome would immediately be condemned, and perhaps overthrown, by a majority of those who participated in it; that majority's choice would then be attacked by a different majority; and so forth. We generally don't see that happen in legislatures,[71] which structure their voting in various ways that make cycling unlikely as a practical matter.[72] It has been argued, though, that cycling is common in many other environments—as when family members try to make decisions (think about ordering at a Chinese restaurant), or students in a classroom are polled on their preferences regarding the format of an exam, or perhaps in political primaries. In those cases the voters usually have more options than are presented to a typical member of Congress when voting on a piece of legislation.[73] Cycling may also be kept under control because deliberation in legislatures and other groups makes their preferences more coherent before the voting occurs (though long conversations can also generate *more* alternatives than everyone thought they had at first, and thus make cycling an even bigger problem). Or it may be that people are bluffed into accepting group decisions without realizing the limits of their meaning—or that people understand that such decisions may not be as meaningful as they appear, but accept the results anyway, even if arbitrary, just for the sake of finality.

One widely accepted payoff of the paradox, however, is the importance of controlling a group's agenda—in other words, the order in which it considers its options. Imagine running a committee that will choose one of three options. It could be a choice of flavors of ice cream, regulatory ideas, or military options; but for convenience let's consider it again a matter of choosing between Clinton, Bush, or Perot. You reasonably suggest that we begin by straightening out everyone's preferences between Clinton and Bush; we can get to Perot in a moment. The result is that, according to the chart we made earlier, Bush wins. Now we turn to the remaining matter of Bush versus Perot—and Perot wins. It all might seem fair enough, but in fact the result is arbitrary. If you had *started* by comparing Bush to Perot, and then comparing the winner to Clinton, the result would have been a victory for Clinton. Indeed, any candidate can be made a winner through careful handling of the agenda.

So the first lesson is to think hard about agendas and who controls them when you are involved in a group's decision. But the second lesson is larger: when you are presented with the decision of a group—perhaps a large and important one to which you weren't a party—you should wonder what role the setting of the agenda played, or whether you are in a position to tell. The implications of these lessons for law can be great. In disputes over the meaning of a statute, it is common for each side to make appeals to the intent of Congress. But there may be no such intent in any useful sense. Perhaps it is obvious that a group can't have an intent in the same way that a person does;[74] but the less obvious point is that it might not even have an intent in the more limited sense one naturally would imagine from a record of its votes. The legislation such a group produces may not accurately reflect even the wishes of a majority. It could just be the result that happened to pop out of the machine because of the order in which the choices were presented at the front end. A further possibility is that the more a political outcome depends on these sorts of procedural points—on how the agenda is set, how issues are bundled, and the like rather than on the expression of clear, stable preferences that groups hold—the more enticing the situation is for interest groups who engage in rent seeking. Rent seekers will see ways to get big returns by manipulating the order and packaging of everyone's choices, which might be quietly done without offending constituencies that are focused on substance rather than process.[75]

And now what about courts? Groups of judges, too, don't behave the same way individual judges do. Whether the exact paradoxes discussed by Condorcet and Arrow are problems for judges has been the subject of some debate,[76] but there is a slightly different paradox that clearly can arise in courts with several members. It comes up when a case contains more than one issue. Imagine a typical appellate court with three judges. They are presented with an accident case where the defendant has lost at trial and now makes two arguments on appeal. His first argument is that the plaintiff's claim was brought too late: the statute of limitations had expired. His second argument is that it's a case of mistaken identity; the plaintiff sued the wrong person. The judges consider his case and arrive at the following positions, where a "Y" means the judge agreed with the defendant's argument named at the top of each column:

	The plaintiff sued too late	The plaintiff sued the wrong person
Judge 1	Y	N
Judge 2	N	Y
Judge 3	N	N

Should the defendant win the appeal? Apparently not: each of his arguments is rejected by a vote of two to one. On the other hand, two of the three judges—namely, judges 1 and 2—think the defendant should *not* be held liable, though they reach this view for different reasons: judge 1 likes the defendant's argument that the lawsuit was filed too late, and judge 2 likes the defendant's argument that he was the wrong person to sue. So the outcome of the case depends on how the votes are counted: should the judges be polled issue-by-issue (in which case the defendant loses) or simply asked what final outcome they prefer (in which case he wins)?

Surprisingly enough there isn't an entirely settled answer to this question, but the usual practice in American courts is to tally up the judges' preferred outcomes. A good example is the *Tidewater* case, decided by the Supreme Court in 1949.[77] First a bit of background: As noted earlier in this book, federal courts can't hear just any case. Congress writes statutes that allow particular cases to be heard by them; Congress gets the power to write those statutes from the Constitution, Article III of which lists all the different kinds of cases Congress can assign to the federal courts if it wants to. One of the most important types of federal jurisdiction—and the one relevant to the case here—is known as *diversity of citizenship*. It means that a lawsuit can be brought in federal court if the parties are citizens of different states and the amount at stake ("in controversy") is more than $75,000.[78] The Constitution allows Congress to create jurisdiction of this kind, and Congress has done it. But what about people who live in the District of Columbia? Do *they* get to bring lawsuits under the diversity jurisdiction, too? Congress tried to say yes, but then along came the argument that this violated the Constitution. Article III lets Congress put cases in the federal courts involving citizens of different *states*. The District of Columbia isn't a state; it is simply—a district. What to do?

The Justices' reactions to that question produced a voting paradox of the kind just described. Three Justices thought that although the District of Columbia isn't a state, Congress had the power to put cases involving its citizens into federal court anyway because a different part of the Constitution—Article I—gives Congress the power to regulate the District's affairs. Two other Justices disliked that argument but said that jurisdiction was all right because D.C. actually *should* be considered a state for jurisdictional purposes. The remaining four Justices didn't like either of these arguments; they thought that extending diversity jurisdiction to people in D.C. was unconstitutional. In the end there were five votes to allow jurisdiction—three based on one theory and two based on another. To put it differently: name any argument in favor of jurisdiction over citizens of D.C., and you can be sure that at least six of the nine Justices (and maybe seven of them) thought the argument was bad. The final result? Jurisdiction nevertheless was upheld, 5–4.[79]

The practice of voting on outcomes has been condemned as producing arbitrary results. Reconsider the tort suit described a few moments ago, and this time suppose that the appeal on the first question—whether the defendant brought the suit too late—was taken up earlier in the case than the second question. Perhaps the defendant succeeded in getting the plaintiff's complaint dismissed by invoking that ground when the case was only a month old, and the plaintiff promptly appealed. The appellate judges, holding the views shown in the table a moment ago, voted against the defendant and sent the case back to the trial court for more proceedings; for two out of three of the judges thought the timing of the suit was fine. Okay; now suppose that a year later the case finally goes to trial and the defendant is held liable. He appeals, this time raises his second argument (that he should have had judgment as a matter of law because the plaintiff clearly sued the wrong person), and again loses: two judges reject his theory. Yet if he had been able to bring both arguments to the court of appeals at the same time, he probably would have won, since two out of the three judges would have said the case against him should be dismissed (though for different reasons). So the result depends on whether the defendant can bring his arguments all at once or has to bring them separately, and this seems arbitrary.

But there are problems with voting issue-by-issue, too. The principal one is that it isn't necessarily obvious what the different issues are. We saw two different arguments in our tort case: whether the suit was late and whether the plaintiff sued the right defendant. But both of those issues could be broken down into others. The first argument, for example, might really involve two questions: whether the clock started ticking on the plaintiff's right to sue at the moment he was injured or when he discovered the injury, which might have been later; and then whether the time limit should be extended because the defendant (let us imagine) took steps to derail the plaintiff's investigation. Should the judges be polled on each of those theories, or just on the general question of whether the suit was too late? Who decides how many distinct arguments there are and which way the voting should work? The outcome might depend on those decisions, which would seem arbitrary in its own right: yet another case where substantive decisions get made by whoever creates the agenda for discussing them.[80]

These issues aren't just a problem in civil cases, of course. We could have imagined a criminal case where the defendant was convicted of murder. On appeal he makes two claims: that the police violated his rights when they searched his house without a warrant (a violation of the Fourth Amendment) and that his confession was coerced (a violation of the Fifth Amendment). The resulting chart might look the same as the one given earlier: both arguments get rejected, yet a majority of the judges think the defendant's rights were violated and that he shouldn't have been convicted. The usual but not universal practice, again, is to reverse the conviction, even though each of the arguments for reversal (considered individually) was rejected. Is the case for voting issue-by-issue stronger in the criminal setting than in accident cases or other civil matters? Perhaps we should be most ready to take votes on outcomes when a defendant's liberty is at stake, for the same reason we have a higher standard of proof in those cases[81]—but now we edge toward matters best postponed until we take up reasonable doubt in chapter 28.

SUGGESTIONS FOR FURTHER READING. Kenneth Arrow, Social Choice and Individual Values (1951); Daniel A. Farber and Philip P. Frickey, Law and Public Choice: A Critical Introduction (1991); Frank H. Easterbrook, *Ways of Criticizing the Court,* 95 Harv. L. Rev. 802 (1982); Lewis A. Kornhauser and Lawrence G. Sager, *Unpacking the Court,* 96 Yale L.J. 82 (1986); Saul Levmore, *Public Choice Defended,* 72 U. Chi. L. Rev. 777 (2005). The literature in this area is massive; these sources, as well as the others referenced in the endnotes to this chapter, will provide many helpful references to it.

16 ⇝ Suppressed Markets

With Saul Levmore

This chapter differs a bit from most of the others in the book. It does not describe a tool primarily useful for understanding cases or legal doctrines (though it has occasional applications there). It explains ideas useful for understanding *institutions,* some of them legal. The discussion belongs here because it involves general questions about how legal and other rules affect life in groups, which is one way to think about the subject of this part of the book. It also belongs here because we have just spent many chapters looking at tools for thinking about law that mostly are economic in their origins. It is fitting to end this part by thinking about when and why we pointedly try to limit competition and suppress the ruthlessness of markets—and with what consequences.

Why is it so hard to get into a good university, but then also so hard to get thrown out? Why is the same true of countries? It sometimes seems that we rely everywhere on markets to sort the better from the worse and squeeze value out of resources. But then we also form communities in which we aren't so sure we want the bargaining, competition, and threats of expulsion that markets bring with them. Instead we say that we want to live and work as equals committed to one another without condition. These ideas intersect in interesting ways. The same communities that want to treat everyone as equals may also want the good effects that competition can produce, and they may have to worry as well about competition from other places. The wish to balance these things creates patterns that recur in communities the size of a nation or the size of a workplace. The members put limits on the competition allowed within their walls because they want everyone inside to be on the same footing, but on inspection this ends up pushing the competition elsewhere—into less visible forms, with interesting side effects. Those are the themes of this chapter; let's make them concrete by making the customary tour of some examples.

Think first about the community known as the United States. The terms of admission are set by immigration law. Some people think we should admit more newcomers than we do, whether out of sympathy for the bad conditions in their home countries or because they hope for more of the economic and cultural gains immigration has produced in the past. Others say we let in enough immigrants already, or too many; they think about the costs to the workers already here if millions more come from other countries. So here is a possible compromise: allow more immigration on the condition that the extra newcomers pay their way in. Those who would like to see more immigration would get it; those who want less would see the country compensated in payments that might be redistributed to those displaced by the influx. People could be admitted in return for cash or for promises to pay after they have made good; they could be subjected to higher tax rates; they could participate in tournaments where temporary rights to visit turn permanent for those most successful during a trial period, thus creating chances for those not already rich. The losers would be sent back. It might seem to make perfect sense. We have what others want desperately. In that circumstance the normal thing is to sell it, and if quantities are limited it is best sold to the high bidder or to those who have proven themselves in fair competition.

Proposals of the kind just outlined don't attract much support. The question is why. It is natural to suppose the reason is that it would just be wrong—appalling, really, for the privilege of citizenship to be distributed according to wealth or to success in anything so cold as a tournament. Yet on reflection that sometimes *is* how we distribute the privilege. In granting visas to aliens the law gives preferences to those who have impressive credentials or can commit a million dollars in investment capital to a commercial enterprise that will employ at least ten Americans.[82] So in a sense we do sell some immigration slots, and we even depend on tournaments to decide who will get them. We just don't manage or see the tournaments; we prefer that they be conducted in the home countries of the players, who compete there for wealth and credentials. The winners present themselves to us for consideration on a take it or leave it basis. In other cases, an alien is given a visa and some years later the government decides whether to renew it or make a citizen out of its holder. People who are given visas because they are engaged to marry Americans or have arrived with investment capital may not be allowed to stay if they lose their assets or their plans change; they go through a proving period of the kind we are unwilling to offer more broadly.[83] The dynamic repeats more clearly when we take illegal aliens into account. Some fraction are able to prove themselves economically, politically, or socially; and then by various means they may be allowed to stay, as by successfully applying to be considered permanent residents after being in the country for a long enough period, even illegally.[84] They are players in a hidden tournament.

The point is that we do use competition and bargaining in immigration law, just not too openly. It's a case of a suppressed market. The choice to hide those things reflects interesting cultural preferences. Bargaining is crass; open competition is brutal; shipping people back is mean—or so we feel. We prefer to think of those seeking entry in ways kinder and less judgmental. We like to live by egalitarian norms, which hold that everyone who lives here ought to be regarded equally, and communitarian norms, which hold that everyone here is part of a group. There are permanence norms, too, holding that those who are here should think of themselves—and be thought of—as loyal and committed to the enterprise. Of course these norms are far from absolute; they are compromised in various ways all the time. But they have force, and one result of them is that we don't want a class of citizens in our midst who pay higher taxes because of their national origins or who live in fear of expulsion if they fail to impress. So we push the competition between them outside our gates, or we let it inside but describe it in other terms. We say that we have illegals within our borders, not second-class citizens desperately competing to stay.

As clear as it is that those norms have value, the price paid for them ought to be considered squarely. If we ran our own internal tournaments, they might well be fairer to the players and also produce better results for us—more immigrants of the sort we would like to have—than the informal competitions that now sort winners from losers in their home countries. To the losers living in dreadful places, our refusal to offer a straightforward chance to compete may even seem cruel. One way to think of these points is that they are a price required to build the sorts of communities we like. We want to clear a space inside our walls where our relationships can be unconditional and founded on a sense of equality. But then we also want to be choosy about who gets in. A direct solution would be to give immigrants a try and then expel them if they don't work out, but this would spoil the ambiance we mean to create. So we have little choice but to push all the competition to the front end, in effect telling outsiders to compete ruthlessly at remote tournament sites and then try for admission here, with the winners let in for good. It's very imperfect, but there is no other way to be selective while preserving the atmosphere we want inside.

All this is plausible, but then we also should consider another and more skeptical account of why we suppress competition inside the gates. Maybe we just prefer to impose costs on those we can't see rather than on those we can. It would be uncomfortable to see people compete in plain view and then force out the ones who don't make the grade. The opposite pain, that of limiting immigration or avoiding forms of it such as tournament play, is dispersed and, to most of us, invisible. It is absorbed by people we do not know and who cannot organize. (This is a common theme in the literature on "public choice," a school of thought that applies economic theory to the political process: interest groups tend to get their way at the expense of opponents who may be more numerous but aren't as well organized and visible.) Our communitarian sensibilities thus may turn out to be selfish in their consequences, whereas open markets, which seem to reward selfish behavior, actually may function less selfishly. They work to the benefit of people far away in literal or political space. Whether or not this account and its implications have much appeal, there is a general point to take away from it: the decision to push competition out of view creates winners and losers of its own. It's always worth asking whether the identity of those winners and losers, and an underlying wish to help the one group at the expense of the other, is a *cause* of the decision to push the competition out of view, and not just a consequence of it.

Now let's compare the arrangements found in the much smaller communities we call universities. There is a trend toward graduating almost everyone who attends them; many colleges and law schools advertise the high percentage of their students who end up with degrees. They are exclusive only at the front end. Here, as with immigration, there would be advantages in sorting people more aggressively after they arrive. Law schools used to do this; they would flunk out lots of students after the first year. Now they have pushed the entire question of membership out beyond the front gate. They choose who gets in by looking at their undergraduate grades and scores on tests (again, think of these as results from remote tournament sites); once admitted on that basis, the school never again questions the fitness of most students for membership in the community. It is a cruder way to decide who will get the degree, and probably a less efficient way to find the best students than by having them audition during the first year, but it also is less brutal and more consistent with the norms of community and permanence that have become the schools' priority. It has come to seem faintly barbaric to threaten students with the equivalent of deportation if they get low grades, and evidently we value those feelings. Evidence of academic wrongdoing follows a similar pattern. It is ruinous to one's chances for admission to a university in the first place, but then many schools are remarkably protective of students who act dishonestly once they are inside. It's hard to get in; once in, it's hard to get thrown out.

So the admissions policies of elite schools resemble those of wealthy countries. In both cases a perfectly functional approach to gatekeeping might call for testing periods followed by sorting and rejection, but in each case the community's norms cause it to push some of the testing to less efficient earlier periods outside its borders. At the front gate there is screening based on the evidence of promise, however questionable, that a candidate has assembled through hard competition elsewhere; then within the gates distinctions are frowned upon and exclusion is almost out of the question. And in both cases these decisions have a price that is partly hidden from view. Applicants rejected because the school wasn't sure about their abilities might have preferred the chance to prove themselves inside, even at the risk of failure and expulsion; and the community would have been better off learning more about them before turning them away—and also better off not feeling obliged to graduate nearly every student who clears the initial hurdle of admission. But we are about as eager to flunk out half our students as we are to deport millions of aliens: not very.

We see similar trade-offs—markets suppressed, and costs of this pushed elsewhere, for the sake of other norms—in many of the smaller arrangements found inside universities. They allocate dorm rooms and seats in popular courses by lottery rather than auction. Students who major in physics or classics typically pay the same tuition as those who study history or sociology, even though the cost of educating the students is higher when their work requires laboratories or the classes are smaller. But then when cutbacks come they may hit some departments more than others, at which point it might seem that ongoing user fees would have been kinder after all than a more egalitarian approach followed by amputation. And notice that the competition absent within the university is present not only on the other side of the gate of entry but just beyond the exit door. Some graduates end up unemployed, and this is more likely among students in some disciplines than others. The ones left in the cold may regret choosing to study in unpromising fields that their universities encouraged in a spirit of even-handedness. But the schools strive for equality only within their jurisdiction; they do not promise it once you leave.

The balance between competition and community is struck differently in different places, and differently in the same places over time. We said earlier that universities used to screen people more carefully after they were inside; why is the trend now the other way? Some of the likely reasons have an economic structure of their own. The evolution may reflect the rising cost of education. As the price of tuition goes up, it becomes harder for even the best schools to convince people to invest their time and money in an enterprise with a large risk of failure, especially when upstart schools may tempt them with more security. This helps explain why the dropout rate is substantial in doctoral programs in the arts and sciences. Tuition is lower there and often gets defrayed by fellowships, and the master's degree provides a nice way to soften the process of sorting and early exit: the student and the university have a chance to try each other out, and if it does not go well the student leaves with a little something by way of credential. The point of these speculations is that anti-economic norms may evolve not just of their own force but as a result of economic pressures. It might be a happy story, or it might not. When serious competition exists among communities, as it does among universities in certain respects but perhaps not so often among countries, there is the potential for a kind of race to the bottom—or at any rate for a race toward norms and practices that create benefits everyone can see with costs that are less perceptible.

Now consider still another environment: the workplace. Most firms compete fiercely with one another but want a sense of community within their own walls. This creates tension. They may want to avoid ruthless competition and exclusion among their own, but trying to suppress it isn't always in the clear interest of their employees or clients; so again we find suppressed markets, with the expected—and interesting—compromises, costs, and evasions. Compare the elite, egalitarian law schools we have discussed to the big firms where their graduates often work. The firms, like most commercial workplaces, amount to tournament sites.[85] Young associates are hired with the knowledge that they probably won't be promoted to partner and then will have to find work elsewhere. There is an audition within the walls of the firm followed by a tough sorting process where most of the lawyers lose and then leave—exactly the sort of arrangement not found in the law schools. Why the difference?

The explanation no doubt is that firms exist in a far more savage competitive environment than the schools do. Perhaps they can't afford the same communitarian norms. The best lawyers would go elsewhere if the superb and the mediocre all were kept and all were paid the same. So would their clients. It might be different if firms could use no lawyer for more than three years; then they probably would come to more closely resemble law schools and judicial clerkships, with competition before and after but not during one's time inside. But so long as a lawyer may stay in the same place for decades, the firms have to confront the costs of a relaxed approach to pay and retention. They respond by making their associates compete and then showing most of them the door. It is another example of how economic forces can shape the space allowed to anti-economic norms; perhaps the norms themselves may be said to compete. Meanwhile it is no accident that in the more egalitarian workplaces where lawyers are found—law school faculties, civil service settings, and courthouses—there are fewer competitive pressures. Those employers have monopolies or don't operate for profit, so they aren't punished in the market for indulging communitarian ideals. The ideals are given effect through customs and legal rules that regulate pay and make it hard to fire anyone. The result is that people who work for those sorts of enterprises do not worry as much, enjoy their work more, but are paid less—the good and the bad of working where the market and its norms are at bay.

Another difference between firms and the other communities we have considered involves captivity. The less captive the members of a community, the more likely competitive pressures will make tastes for communitarianism expensive to satisfy. Paying everyone in a firm the same salary might create a good atmosphere, but it won't last long if the best lawyers leave for better pay elsewhere. Making it hard to fire anyone likewise will make everyone feel better—until the firm loses its clients to rivals who perform better because they aren't afraid to sack bad employees. A different way to see why captivity matters is to look at situations where it is entirely absent. Think of restaurants and people who eat at them as an informal community. Anyone can enter and try to sell meals, but the diners will favor only a few and disqualify the rest; most restaurants fail. It's a tough business, but any other way of ordering the community would mean bad restaurants. If we wanted to protect those bad restaurants, perhaps out of concern for the feelings and good intentions of their owners, we would need to control the people who eat at them (otherwise they will just dine where they like), but that doesn't sound like much fun. Notice that it's harder for the people inside countries and universities to come and go freely, so their hosts can give effect to communitarian sensibilities without as much fear of collapse or extinction whenever an outsider offers incentives to defect.

The importance of captivity can also be seen by looking at when and why some closed communities do tolerate the openly unequal treatment of insiders. Labor unions sometimes bargain for one set of protections and wages for existing members and less generous terms for new hires; it agrees to sort its members into different classes. But a normal union does not consent to such things when its position is strong. It consents to unequal treatment of its members only when it has to fend off threats from nonunion competitors and threats that its members will lose their jobs. It forfeits an egalitarian norm just when—and because—competition threatens to penetrate its captive market: the employer's firm. The union tries to hold its position, and keep its market partly captive, precisely by letting the employer do a bit more of what it could if the market operated freely and ruthlessly: sorting people out and treating them differently.

But even the most competitive firms put limits on the use of market mechanisms within their walls, and they accept some costs of doing so. Thus it is rare for a law firm or any other employer to offer one of its workers a choice of leaving or being demoted. Some firms have started to offer a new rank to lawyers disappointed because they weren't made partners; they can become permanent associates. But the firm still won't try to talk an associate in his fifth year into accepting the sorts of terms given to those in their second year. At first the loss of morale the offer would cause seems distinct from the questions of equality and community that may deter bargaining in other places, but in fact they may be related—for notice that a bargained demotion is much more common when directed at a large group of employees. A labor union may agree to a collective giveback, and officers in the military during a period when the military shrinks all may consent to a demotion. The results can be hard to take, but since the whole group is treated the same way there at least is no threat against its sense of community or any one member's status in it.

By this point it is predictable that where we find competition and bargaining suppressed for the sake of communitarian norms, we find side effects as well. To the extent their hires and promotions are made irreversible, employers naturally are more inclined to hire temporary workers or, in the case of the law firm, to create permanent associates rather than new partners. They assign work to outside contractors even when it might have meant bigger rewards for employees already there; by hiring a contractor the firm can make hard demands and economic decisions that wouldn't be so easy among its own members. Earlier we saw that university faculties enjoy the benefits of suppressed market pressures, but here too displacements can occur—as when the communitarian atmosphere of a faculty is valued so much that it becomes excruciating to deny tenure to a young hire. It is well known that it is easier to get tenure at most schools than it is to be hired later from the outside, and the norms we have been discussing help explain why. One resulting risk is that the school may end up giving tenure to weak professors, and in the long run this can make the better ones restless to leave. So a contrary trend also is possible: the school stops hiring young faculty, realizing that its attempts to sort them out after they arrive have been made untrustworthy by the warm atmosphere of the place. Instead it tries to let other schools do the sorting and hopes to then hire their faculty away in the middle of their careers—perhaps on the basis of visits by the professors where they aren't yet considered members of the community to whom all those friendly norms are extended. Some schools may be able to get away with those strategies because they have high status, which serves as a kind of capital they can spend for the sake of their norms. Other schools get away with it because schools are so weakly disciplined by the market. They can get worse and barely feel the costs because the reduction in quality may make little immediate difference to anyone inside and takes a long time to be noticed by anyone outside. Law firms do not have those luxuries.

We could continue this look at various communities and the ways they use or suppress market mechanisms. Marriages, clubs, apartment buildings, and most of the other circles people draw to organize their common life involve competition at some stages and not others, and these preferences find expression in a mix of law and custom. But by now the tools for analysis this chapter is meant to offer have become familiar enough. Much of our private law is about bargains, and how to facilitate them or imitate them. Much of our public law is about the suppression of bargaining and other market mechanisms that aren't wanted for various reasons. In corners of life where markets have thus been subdued, we have a set of questions to ask that may help us see deeper into the reasons and results: whether the suppression may be for the sake of norms that help build a sense of community among the players; whether there may then be costs and evasions of the sort that often follow when we tame aggressive private ordering and push economic forces out of view; and who the gainers and losers turn out to be.

PART III *Jurisprudence*

17 ➳ Rules and Standards

The police arrest someone on suspicion of murder. They take him to the station house and have a vigorous discussion with him, and eventually he confesses. Can the confession be used against him in court? The Fifth Amendment says that no person "shall be compelled in any criminal case to be a witness against himself." But that language is a bit general; judges trying to enforce it need a set of practical instructions to follow. One possibility is to have a judge hold a hearing to consider what happened at the police station and decide whether the confession was voluntary or "compelled." All the circumstances might be considered: what the police said to the suspect, what he said in return, whether he understood his rights, whether he was hungry, whether he was hanging from the ceiling by his ankles. For a long time that was the way American courts did enforce the Fifth Amendment. They simply asked whether the defendant's confession was coerced, and they answered the question by looking at all the facts.

Then there is a different way to handle the problem: the way that American courts handle it now. They ask whether the defendant was read his rights. If he wasn't, then his confession generally can't be used as evidence. As we saw in chapter 3, this is the rule of *Miranda v. Arizona,*[1] in which the Supreme Court devised the famous warnings that go by the name of that case: the suspect has to be told he has the right to remain silent and the right to a lawyer, with the refinements familiar to everyone from movies and television shows. We say the confession "generally" can't be used without a warning because there are possible exceptions, as when public safety requires that the questioning occur right away because a bomb is about to go off or a weapon may be nearby and needs to be found.[2]

The choice between telling police to issue *Miranda* warnings and telling police not to coerce the defendant into talking is an example of choosing between rules and standards. Asking whether there was coercion at the police station amounts to the use of a standard: it requires someone—in this case, a judge—to apply the law to all the facts and make a judgment about whether the standard was satisfied. *Miranda* warnings are different because they amount to a rule. Either they were given or they weren't, and once that factual question is settled there usually isn't any judgment to exercise (unless the defendant claims he was pressured too much *after* the warnings were given, in which case we may be back to using a version of the coercion standard to decide the claim). That is the general difference between a rule and a standard: the consequences of a rule are triggered once we settle the facts; a standard requires a judgment about the facts before it kicks in.

The distinction between rules and standards can be fuzzy at the edges. In the case of the confession there might be disputes about whether the warnings were given clearly enough; in this way the elements of a rule can themselves become little standards. The exceptions can amount to standards, too: if we ask whether public safety really was at stake and justified dispensing with *Miranda* warnings, we are applying a standard (in order to decide whether to apply the rule). Yet the inquiry into public safety can itself be turned into a rule, for we might say the exception applies only if there was a weapon within the suspect's grabbing range—but then we may need to say a bit more about what counts as a "weapon," and again must pick between a rule and a standard for the purpose. So we can have standards within rules; and we also can have rules within standards. In the days before the *Miranda* warnings were devised—the days when courts always applied a standard (was the defendant coerced?)—there were situations that would cause the judge to automatically decide in favor of the defendant, as where the police beat him until he talked. In those cases the reasoning of the courts amounted to the use of a rule after all. So the distinction between a rule and a standard sometimes is a matter of degree, and mixtures are common: presumptions, guidelines, tests based on factors, and lists of exceptions. A legal directive that starts out in one form may be transformed into the other. One school of thought holds that this has pretty well happened to *Miranda* itself—that it started out as a rule but has now been festooned with so many exceptions, and its protections made so easy to waive, that today it amounts to a standard.[3]

The choice between rules and standards comes up all the time in law. Most laws—whether made by legislatures, courts, agencies, or anyone else—can be understood as if-then statements. Usually they are commands enforced by penalties if they aren't obeyed. Whoever drafts the directives has to decide whether to put them in the form of rules or standards or some combination, whether it's a speed limit, a judicial decision about free speech, or a determination that the defendant in a case involving a car accident was negligent and should pay damages. The problem of coerced confessions is merely a useful place to start thinking about the question because it involves a lot of the classic trade-offs encountered in these debates. Let's consider a few of them.

1. *Potential for abuse.* First, rules can provide stronger protection than standards—or weaker. If we're worried that defendants often don't know their rights and so get manipulated by crafty police officers, the *Miranda* rule helps reduce the gamesmanship by making it clear to everyone what has to be said. Rules usually are better than standards for controlling subordinates or other parties who aren't perfectly trusted; standards create discretion, and discretion creates chances for rent seeking and agency problems (ideas explained in chapters 7 and 9). Yet a rule also may provide less protection by introducing a different *kind* of gamesmanship: the efforts to see what one can get away with by tiptoeing right up the edge of what the rule allows.[4] Those efforts have furnished grist for television shows like *NYPD Blue,* where every week the police would read suspects their rights and then use every device imaginable to discourage the exercise of them. So one thing to consider in choosing between rules and standards is which danger is greater—the abuse of a standard's vagueness or of a rule's precision.

2. *Precision and notice.* A related trade-off involves what gets caught by a rule and a standard. Rules tend to be clear in advance but crude in application. At their edges they often cover some cases one wishes they would miss, and miss some cases one wishes they would cover. In the classic shorthand, rules are overinclusive and underinclusive. Think of a criminal suspect who already knows his rights but decides to confess anyway to a long string of serial killings. The confession is freely given; there is no coercion at all. But then he comes to regret what he said, and perhaps finds that he has a way out: the police forgot to give him his *Miranda* warnings. The case falls outside the purpose of the rule but within its terms, so perhaps he goes free, and perhaps this is costly.[5] The rule was overinclusive; if a standard had been used, a judge could have looked at the facts and decided there was no reason to suppress the confession. Or on the other side—the side of underinclusion—the *Miranda* rule can allow a confession into evidence so long as the magic words were spoken, even if the defendant didn't understand them well. Again, a standard reduces these risks because it calls for a more personalized administration of justice. Sometimes that is important; sometimes the important thing is to try to get every case right. But use of a standard makes the result less clear in advance, and the uncertainty can create costs of its own. Giving everyone clear notice makes it easier to comply with the law and easier to resolve disputes without help from a judge.

3. *Blame and accountability.* Rules gain ground in another respect when it comes time for their enforcement by a court. A judge confronted with an odious defendant might be inclined, consciously or not, to bend the application of a standard—"voluntariness" or "coercion," perhaps—to make sure the scoundrel stays in prison. Or the judge might worry about the public outcry that will ensue if the standard is applied generously and the defendant goes free.[6] A rule helps avoid these risks. It leaves less room for discretion and its abuses not only by those it governs but by the judge called on to enforce it, and it gives the judge a way to enforce the law without worrying about blame: he isn't doing much; he merely is applying the rule, and the rule, or perhaps its authors (anyone but the judge), should bear any blame from the public.[7] By the same token the existence of a rule makes accountability easier. When a standard is applied, a judge can blame its author for blundering in the writing of it, and the author can blame the judge for blundering in its application. Rules tend to make it harder to point fingers back and forth in this way.

And yet it also is possible for rules to have the perverse effect of pushing discretion out of view and thus making its exercise *less* accountable. A standard often requires the users of it to explain their thinking; a rule doesn't.[8] And if a rule seems a bad fit to a case, the enforcer may be tempted to bend its interpretation, or bend the facts, or bend the exercise of discretion, to avoid applying it. A possible example is the Clean Air Act, in which Congress imposed large, rule-based penalties on anyone who used pollutants listed by the Environmental Protection Agency. This sounds severe, but it arguably backfired by leading the EPA to stop listing pollutants at all.[9] Draconian criminal sentences may lead judges to fudge the finding of facts in a case to avoid the force of the categorical rule, or lead the jury to "nullify" the law by finding a guilty defendant innocent. This last point was one of the reasons why the Supreme Court held it unconstitutional for states to impose the death penalty automatically once a defendant has committed a certain crime: studies suggested that juries sometimes avoided finding defendants guilty of first-degree murder if they knew the result would be execution. The Court thought it unacceptable that a state's rule might, in effect, make the penalty depend "on the particular jury's willingness to act lawlessly."[10] So here as elsewhere, the trade-offs between rules and standards can be subtler than first appears.

4. *Uncertainty and conflict.* Sometimes it makes sense to proceed case-by-case because we aren't ready to settle on a rule. Maybe we can't yet figure out what the right rule would be and would rather try to close in on it one situation at a time; good judgments require the sort of information about

the facts that a trial judge will have but that is beyond the reach of rule makers further away from the action. Or maybe we *disagree* about what the right rule would be but can agree on what outcome is best in particular cases; we would rather go case-by-case and make do with "incompletely theorized agreements"—in other words, agreements on results that might not extend to agreements about first principles.[11] Taking one case at a time, rather than insisting on a clear rule, can be a helpful way of getting through the business of life, and of government, despite deep political conflict.

5. *Costs of creation and application.* The choice between rules and standards also has a more explicitly economic side. For example, it often involves trade-offs between accuracy and finality, or—roughly the same thing—how seriously one worries about administrative costs. Standards are more precise than rules, but they also are more expensive to use. We find famous examples in the area known as choice of laws. It sometimes comes as a surprise to legal novices that if one brings a lawsuit in Maine complaining about an accident, the court will not necessarily apply Maine law. If the accident occurred in Texas, the Maine court might instruct the Maine jurors to apply Texas law, as strange as that may sound. It depends on Maine's rules for deciding what law to use when a lawsuit involves acts in other states. In accident cases the rule in most places used to be (and sometimes still is) *lex loci delicti:* the case is governed by the law of the place where the wrong was committed, subject to various exceptions. But by the middle of the twentieth century many courts came to dislike the rule; they thought it led to arbitrary results or that its exceptions allowed courts to manipulate it so much that few rule-like virtues were left over. So they substituted a standard: the law governing a case would come from the state that has the most significant contacts with it. The judge thus would consider where the parties are from, where the wrong occurred, the nature of each state's interest in the case, and various other factors—a standard rather than a rule.

Was the "most significant contacts" standard an improvement on the old rule? It depends what weight one puts on the different things the two approaches do well. The rule was simpler, easier to understand, clearer in advance to everyone, and cheaper to apply. The standard may be more likely to produce results that seem fair on all the facts, which is a point in its favor—maybe a decisive one. But then someone—chiefly the parties, but also the public—has to pay for all the extra efforts to be fair. The standard also makes cases less predictable and harder to settle. Here and elsewhere, standards thus are more expensive than rules; that is why an increase in the use of standards is sometimes associated with an increase in the wealth of a society.[12] When resources are in short supply, there is less interest in spending them on arguments about choice of law or any other feature of litigation. It is easier to live with rules that sometimes produce wrong answers than with standards that cause some of the pie to be destroyed by the efforts to carve it up too precisely.

It is important to think about not only how expensive a standard will be to use but how *often* it will need to be used.[13] That is why, as we saw in the discussion of administrative costs in chapter 6, statutes of limitations are framed as rules rather than standards: it would be very expensive to ask in every case whether the plaintiff waited an unreasonably long time to bring suit. And it helps explain why even in areas where rules seem important, they often have exceptions that amount to standards like "public safety." Since the standards don't apply in the usual case—only in the exceptional ones—the costs of fussing over them are only incurred from time to time.

There can be hidden costs to rules, too. They have to be made in the first place—a process that takes time and investigation, especially if the rules are going to apply to lots of situations with different details. If one proceeds with rules rather than standards, there often have to be many *more* rules, and they will be less intuitive; compare the standard of "reasonable care" in tort law—a single idea used to judge just about every mistake a driver can make—to all the formal rules of the road, the violation of which will result in criminal penalties.[14] Rules also have to be rewritten more often than standards to keep up with changes in the world.[15] A standard delegates that task of adjustment to judges or whoever else applies them on the front lines, which might be the cheapest way to go if the adjustments have to be made often, or if the rule is hard to work out in advance, or if the rule makers face a large risk of botching it when they try to get too precise.[16] And then sometimes rules reduce costs for a court but shift them elsewhere. Think back to *Miranda:* its rule reduces the need for hearings after a confession is made, which sounds like a great savings; but it also forces police to issue lots of warnings, even when the defendant doesn't need them because he already knows his rights—a small cost that gets multiplied many times.

Many of the points just considered suggest a general and useful way to think about rules. They involve three parties: one who makes the rule, another who applies it, and another to whom it is applied. So a constitutional convention might make a rule; the rule might apply to the president; and it might be enforced by courts. Or the rule might be made by a legislature, applied to citizens, and enforced by an agency. Sometimes the maker and enforcer of the rule can be the same, as when a court makes a rule one day and then applies it the next; but even then the rule usually gets carried out by at least some actors besides the ones who wrote it—other judges, perhaps. As a result of these divided functions, sometimes the costs of using or avoiding a rule aren't fully felt by the party who makes it.[17] Using standards rather than rules might sometimes sound good to a court, which then leaves itself wiggle room in future cases; but the standards might create costs for others—for example, litigants trying to settle their cases—that the court doesn't feel or (to say it in economics) internalize. It often is hard to get rule makers to act like "single owners" of all the interests affected by the process.

Another consequence of the divided manner in which rules are made and applied is that that the wishes of the maker may not get expressed accurately once the rule falls into the hands of the enforcer. A Constitution can offer things that sound like rules: Congress shall make no law abridging the freedom of speech; no state shall make any law that denies the privileges or immunities of American citizens. Indeed, the United States Constitution says both of those things, but then it fell to the courts to apply them, and they were turned into standards of various sorts. The First Amendment has become a series of standards and presumptions (it is discussed a bit more in chapters 3 and 27), and the Court has read the rule-like privileges or immunities clause of the Fourteenth Amendment to mean almost nothing, preferring to enforce the original purposes of that clause through a different one—the clause requiring "equal protection of the laws"—which more plainly is a standard. These decisions raise questions about whether and why courts might tend generally to turn constitutional commands into standards: whether this maximizes the power of judges in ways that they like; or helps them avoid the constraints that the rule was meant to place on them; or enables them to do justice, or give effect to the Constitution's purpose, in ways too attractive to turn down. In any event, the point here is that one may not know whether one quite *has* a rule or standard until it has actually been put to use by the enforcer.[18]

Now let's consider what we might learn from one last example: accidents. As we noted a moment ago, people generally have to pay for damage they cause by their failure to drive with reasonable care. But the idea of "reasonable care," like the notion of a coerced confession, can be reduced to either rules or standards. The "standard" version amounts to asking from scratch in every case whether the defendant was reasonable—which is what American courts traditionally do. In the nineteenth century Oliver Wendell Holmes predicted that this approach wouldn't last; after seeing the same sorts of accidents happen over and over again, courts wouldn't need to make fresh inquiries into who was to blame for each of them.[19] They would finally settle on rules—perhaps saying, for example, that if one driver hits another from behind, the one in the rear is always to blame. But the trend Holmes expected hasn't appeared. When he was on the Supreme Court he advanced his view in an opinion saying that if a car is hit by a train, the car's driver is always to blame if he didn't stop, look, and listen, and (if necessary) get out of his car for a better look, before crossing the tracks.[20] But it was Holmes's approach that didn't survive. A few years later the Supreme Court reversed the decision, concluding that there were too many cases where it fit badly.[21] A driver might get out of his car to look for a train, but the train might appear while he was on his way back to the car. So the rule was thought to be too overinclusive and was discarded. Most efforts by judges to make rules of that kind in accident cases have met the same fate. (You might play with this question: should a driver who falls asleep at the wheel always and automatically be held liable for any damage that results?)[22]

Why do judge-made rules seem unattractive to courts in accident cases but more appealing in cases involving criminal procedure? The latter point isn't just illustrated by *Miranda*. The Fourth Amendment forbids "unreasonable searches and seizures," and the Supreme Court has sometimes turned this standard-like language, too, into rules, such as the one forbidding police to search a home without a warrant unless there are exigent circumstances (in other words, some important goal that would be defeated by waiting for the warrant). Granted, the "exigent circumstances" exception amounts to a standard, just like the exception to the *Miranda* rule when public safety is at stake. And there are plenty of other of standards elsewhere in criminal procedure. Judges are told to consider the "totality of the circumstances" to decide whether probable cause for a search exists, for example, and they decide whether a search occurs by consulting the defendant's reasonable expectation of privacy—yet another standard (though again in many situations the content of those expectations has been settled in rule-like fashion; the Supreme Court has held that nobody has a reasonable expectation of privacy in trash they leave out on the curb). But it's still true that courts are more interested in making rules about criminal procedure than about accidents, and there are good reasons why. Think back to the arguments for the *Miranda* rule; notice that they aren't all equally present in tort cases. In criminal cases, but not so much in tort cases, we worry that judges might succumb to their own biases or the fear of public outcry; the judges work for the same government, and may feel answerable to the same public, as the prosecutor. In accident cases the judge—and also the jury that makes the decisions about whether either side was negligent—is less likely to be in such a position because the court has no natural alliance with either of the parties.

Another reason why courts sometimes prefer rules to standards has to do with notice. Rules tell people in advance what consequences will follow from their acts, and clarity of this kind is more important in some areas than others. It is very important when the law imposes criminal penalties, which is why they generally take the form of rules: you get in trouble—and a prescribed amount of trouble—for driving more than fifty-five miles per hour, or for selling a certain amount of cocaine, or for taking things that don't belong to you. The law prefers rules in these situations because the costs of criminal prosecution and conviction are so immense for the defendant. They shouldn't be incurred by surprise, or at the discretion of a representative of the government; people should be able to plan their affairs without the worry that they will unexpectedly end up in jail. To turn the point around, this reasoning may help to explain one of the many reasons why we generally don't put people in jail for negligence. We have trouble defining it crisply in advance, so we have grave reservations about taking away anyone's liberty for committing it.

SUGGESTIONS FOR FURTHER READING. Antonin Scalia, *The Rule of Law as a Law of Rules,* 56 U. Chi. L. Rev. 1175 (1989); Frederick Schauer, Playing by the Rules: A Philosophical Examination of Rule-Based Decision-making in Law and Life (1991); Louis Kaplow, *Rules versus Standards: An Economic Analysis,* 42 Duke L.J. 557 (1992); Kathleen Sullivan, *The Justice of Rules and of Standards,* 106 Harv. L. Rev. 22 (1992); Cass R. Sunstein, *Problems with Rules,* 83 Cal. L. Rev. 953 (1995); Richard A. Posner, Economic Analysis of Law 555–60 (6th ed. 2002); Duncan Kennedy, *Form and Substance in Private Law Adjudication,* 89 Harv. L. Rev. 1685 (1976).

18 ⤞ Slippery Slopes

With Eugene Volokh

Slippery slopes are familiar to anyone who has spent more than ten minutes arguing about anything. You suggest that people should have to register their handguns; I reply that it's a slippery slope: next thing you know, everyone's handguns will be confiscated. Someone says they favor gay marriage, and back comes the argument that it will put us on a slippery slope toward legalized polygamy. Or perhaps you favor assisted suicide, or a ban on hateful speech, and in either case your antagonist describes a "parade of horribles" that could follow—mercy killings, or a ban on other kinds of speech. You are warned that after the first decision the camel's nose will be under the tent, or that the decision will serve as an entering wedge for a worse one, but the slippery slope will do fine as a placeholder for all those metaphors. The general structure of it is always the same. The decision at hand—"decision one," let us say—is acceptable (or so we may assume), but it might lead to a second decision later that sounds scarier: confiscating everyone's guns, making polygamy legal, and so forth. But of course the people who want decision one say that it by no means must lead to decision two, and they dismiss the concern about slippery slopes as a cliché. So how do you know when worries about them are just a distraction from the issue at hand? In this chapter we'll think about some answers to these questions—some reasons why a first decision can make a second one more likely later.

1. *The first decision lowers the cost of the second one.* The first reason is quite practical: sometimes decision one makes decision two less expensive. If everyone registers their handguns, then confiscating them later will be easier. We will know where the guns are; we will be able to find them right away. It still might not happen, of course; the fact that confiscation is easier need not change anyone's view of other parts of the question—the moral side, the constitutional side, and so on. But the costs and benefits of a decision are always an important feature of it. And remember that decisions get made at the margin. In this case that means the question won't be the *total* cost of confiscating guns; it will be the additional, incremental cost. In other words, decisions about confiscation will begin, "well, as long as we've *already* got them all registered . . ."

And then remember too that these decisions usually aren't made by one person. They are made by the voting public, or a legislature, or a set of bureaucrats, or some other group with lots of people in it. If *some* of those people—not necessarily now, but later on—consider the question of cost decisive, they might end up supporting confiscation and causing the balance of votes to tip that way, even if most people on both sides of the issue consider the cost a secondary point, and even if those swing voters worried about cost would have opposed confiscation earlier because (before all the guns were registered) it seemed too costly in various ways.

Of course none of this is meant to show that registering handguns necessarily is a bad thing. Maybe you *like* the idea of banning and confiscating handguns, in which case this discussion might make registration of them sound better than ever. (A complete or near ban on handguns has indeed followed registration in some places, such as England, Australia, and New York City.) But instead of guns we could have talked about letting the government put video cameras in public places (but only if the films are erased promptly unless a crime is reported), or letting it keep track of personal information that it intercepts on the Internet (but only to hunt down terrorists). The point is just to see one way that allowing any of these things can lead to further steps—keeping the films made by the video cameras for a long time and using them to monitor people more widely, or using the information found on the Internet for investigations that have nothing to do with terrorism. Once the first steps are taken, the costs of the second ones are lowered, so the second ones will seem more appealing. Thus the slippery slope.

Notice that the first decision can lower the cost of the second one in other senses besides conventional trouble and expense. Confiscating everyone's guns might be impossible as a legal matter if the police don't know where the guns are to be found; for then they would have to search everyone's house, and the Fourth Amendment wouldn't allow it. But once guns are registered, such a wide search for them might not be needed. The police could just look at the registration lists, check to see who on the list hasn't turned in their guns, and apply for a warrant to search the houses of those people. Whether a warrant could be obtained on those facts is an open question, but it would be a lot more likely in that case than if the police wanted to search every house in town. You can think of the legal obstacles to a search as one cost of trying to carry it out—maybe a prohibitive one. In that sense the removal of legal obstacles makes searches easier, or less costly—another, less obvious way in which decision one (registration) can reduce the expense of decision two and so make it more likely.

Slippery slopes of this general variety—in which the first decision changes the costs and benefits of a later one—bear a relationship to the phenomenon known as *path dependence.* Sometimes an initial decision affects later ones by sending everyone down a path that becomes expensive to leave. Some theorists have suggested that this happens easily in common law systems: early courts make decisions, and notions of *stare decisis* and the value of consistency cause those early decisions to have a disproportionate effect on the decisions by courts that reach the same issue, or variations on it, later.[23] There is a resemblance between this vision of slippery slopes and the cascades discussed in chapter 14.

2. *The first decision affects the attitudes brought to the second one.* Here is another mechanism that can create a slippery slope: the first decision might change the way people think or feel later about the second one. The reason is that the law can influence people's beliefs and attitudes.[24] Some people get their ideas about what is good and bad partly from what the law says about what is legal and illegal, and those ideas can cause one legal decision to have spillover effects on other decisions later. First, smoking is banned in restaurants; once everyone gets used to that, smoking seems a more disreputable activity and the idea of banning smoking in all public places (or—who knows?—banning it entirely) later comes to seem more sensible.[25] This also was Charles Krauthammer's reason for supporting registration of guns: "Its only real justification is not to reduce crime but to desensitize the public to the regulation of weapons in preparation for their ultimate confiscation. . . . De-escalation begins with a change in mentality."[26] (He *wants* the slippery slope.)

These kinds of slippery slopes are notably hard to predict—and may be hard to recognize after they have happened. The influence of law on private beliefs about right and wrong is incomplete and hard to specify. The law leaves room for choices about morality outside its rules; we have to distinguish, as David Friedman points out, between our society and the anthill in T. H. White's *The Once and Future King,* where everything is either forbidden or compulsory.[27] In countries where prostitution is legal, not everyone considers it a good thing. Has it nevertheless had some side effects on how people in such places think about sex or about women? Perhaps. How many, and of what sort? It is hard to say. (Nor has the *illegality* of prostitution concluded the question of its morality elsewhere.)

In any event, here is another way that a legal decision can affect attitudes that then bear on other decisions later: once a legal decision is in place, many people may be inclined to treat it as a "given"—as a starting point for further discussion, and not itself open to question. After the terrorist attacks of September 11, 2001, there was much public discussion of various proposals to allow the government to keep track of people's activity on the Internet: Web sites visited, e-mail addresses used, and so forth. Many of those discussions used, as a starting point, a 1979 decision by the Supreme Court saying that police could keep track of what phone numbers a person had dialed (using a device called a pen register) without violating the Fourth Amendment.[28] The question about monitoring people's Internet usage easily became a debate about whether it was any worse than keeping track of the phone numbers people called.[29] One argument you didn't hear much was that the decision about pen registers was itself wrong and shouldn't be extended. Of course that is a possibility, but once a decision is "on the books" it may easily be regarded as presumptively correct and as setting a new baseline for deciding what is both lawful and desirable.

Fear about these sorts of slopes is the source of various claims about gay marriage, such as the argument that it would lead to expanded protections for gay rights generally. The idea is that the law's attitude toward gay marriage may affect people's attitudes toward gays generally. Over time it may encourage people to think there is nothing wrong with homosexuality; having reached that conclusion under the law's influence, they may end up supporting laws that go further in the same direction. Some consider that possibility one of the best things about gay marriage, others one of the worst. This model of the slippery slope also helps explain the claim that recognizing gay marriage now may lead to legalized polygamy later. The concern—or one version of it—is that gay marriage will come to be treated as the baseline against which judgments about polygamy have to be made. Perhaps the question here (as with the case of the pen register) will become whether the two situations can be distinguished, not so much whether polygamy is a good or bad thing on its own. Or the thought process can play out in a different way: some people may view the law's recognition of gay marriage as support for the idea that it's none of their business who someone else marries; since that is the law's position (or so it may seem), it sinks in widely; and then the idea of making polygamy legal doesn't sound as crazy as it once did. Whether these changes in attitude are likely to occur is a question of sociology or psychology that we need not pursue. The important thing here is to understand the structure of the argument. The law does affect attitudes, and those attitudes then affect the law. The result of this dynamic *can* be a slippery slope, though the operation of the dynamic is hard to predict with much confidence.

A final example involves the use, against people suspected of terrorism, of coercive forms of interrogation—physical and mental pressure that falls short of "torture," though obviously there is a lot of room for debate about where that line gets drawn. One argument against using any such pressures at all is an appeal to the slippery slope: if we get used to putting physical pressure on people, we will become numb to its horrors and dangers and will be inclined then to move on to more aggressive methods that would more obviously amount to torture; or we will start using torture elsewhere—against people suspected of other things, or against people *convicted* of crimes whom we want to punish regardless of whether they have any useful information. (The "we" here might refer to the police who do the pressuring or to the public at large.) All these things could happen, but it is hard to prove that they *will* happen. The advocates of coercive interrogation reply by pointing to other steps already taken that might have been expected to have similar brutalizing effects but haven't seemed to produce them in practice. Capital punishment has been widely adopted in the United States without leading to a slippery slope in which people call for it to be applied to crimes besides murder (though that may be because the Supreme Court has forbidden such extensions). The police are allowed to shoot people in some circumstances; this hasn't led to a slippery slope in which they do it too much to be worth the benefits (or has it?).[30] A challenge of thinking about slippery slopes again becomes apparent. Not only is it hard to predict when the law will cause changes in attitudes that will lead to bad things; it can be hard to look back and be sure whether it has happened already.

3. *Ideas about equal treatment require the second decision to be made like the first one.* Sometimes the problem is this: between the first decision and the scary second one lie a series of distinctions that courts (or others, but it's usually courts) find hard to draw as a practical matter. The point isn't—or shouldn't quite be—that scary decision B necessarily follows from decision A as a matter of principle. If that were true, the problem with decision A really wouldn't involve slippery slopes; it would be that decision A commits us to decision B on the spot once the principle at stake is understood. The slippery slope we mean to describe here occurs when there are distinctions between the two decisions in theory that do not hold up in practice, so the possibly legitimate reasons for separating the two cases in the beginning turn out to fail in the end. The reason might be that courts lack the appetite or ability to draw the distinctions effectively; or it

might be that the distinctions are rickety and can be easily overridden by other preferences of later judges or other decision makers.

This sort of slippery slope lies behind some of the arguments about the end of life. First comes a decision to allow people to refuse medical treatment if they are terminally ill and in great pain. Next comes a proposal to allow assisted suicide by others who also are terminally ill and in great pain but who can't refuse treatment because there is no treatment for them to refuse. Why should a person's power to choose his time of death depend on whether he is hooked up to a machine that he wants to disconnect? If this much is granted, along comes someone who is not terminally ill but is in similar chronic, irremediable pain; he wants to know why he, too, shouldn't have the right to end his life, and why his choices should be more limited than someone who is more certain to die soon. Then comes someone whose agony is mental rather than physical.

A path of this kind, with the right to die expanded in each case, was followed by courts in the Netherlands.[31] The first decision by itself might not have seemed to imply the last one, but each step between them turned out to be slippery. This might have been so because norms of equality—of treating like cases alike—made it hard to draw lines between any two of them; in that case we might question whether it was a true slippery slope or just a case where the implications of the first decision weren't fully appreciated until later. But it's also possible that distinctions between these cases are available and plausible yet hard to draw in practice: each case presents heart-rending facts, and judges may not have the stomach or, perhaps, the moral confidence to say that any two of these situations are different enough to deny relief. If so, the result could amount to a true slippery slope: a case where decision two really was not thought to follow from decision one when decision one was made, but did follow from it after all.

We probably find similar examples in a line of religion cases from the Supreme Court. The Court started by protecting the rights of people in mainstream religions to practice their faiths even if the practices ran afoul of general laws.[32] At first the protections were given to beliefs that were consistent and central to the religions at issue; then over time the Court extended the protections to cover practices and beliefs that may have had more dubious claims to consistency or centrality.[33] There were distinctions available in principle here, but in practice the Court didn't feel comfortable second-guessing people's claims about their religious beliefs. When the first decisions were made, the fringe cases might have seemed distinguishable ("not to worry—we'll be able to decide those cases differently because the beliefs involved probably won't be central or consistent"); but such distinctions ended up being too distasteful or otherwise difficult to make on the front lines. The result is a kind of slippery slope.

A different sort of slope, but related enough to consider here, occurs when distinctions between the first case and the later, scarier one *could* be drawn, both in principle and in practice, but they are too weak to withstand the press of the policy preferences held by whoever is making the later decisions. This is how some people think about *Griswold v. Connecticut,*[34] the 1965 decision in which the Supreme Court struck down a law banning the use of contraceptives by married couples; the law was said to violate constitutional rights to privacy. On its face the case didn't appear to create broad rights of sexual autonomy, and a majority of the Justices who voted to strike down the law indicated, there or elsewhere, that they didn't think they were creating such rights. But then eight years later in *Roe v. Wade,*[35] the Justices—or rather a majority of them, several of whom had not been on the Court for *Griswold*—used *Griswold* as a basis for striking down laws against abortion. How best to think about these developments is a controversial question, but it seems clear enough that the decision in *Griswold* did not require the decision in *Roe.* There were distinctions between them that might have been drawn, and that seemed persuasive to some of those who decided *Griswold* (and so caused them to think they weren't starting down a slippery slope). But the distinctions weren't robust enough to stop the decision from being extended by other Justices who considered abortion rights fundamental. The point is simple. The fact that a distinction *can* be drawn, or even that it would be drawn by an advocate of the first decision, is no assurance that it *will* be drawn by others later when they are making the second one.[36] The others—for example, the later judges—might find that the first decision enables them to do something that seems attractive and that the distinctions between the earlier case and the present one, while possible, are merely matters of discretion that have no constraining power.

4. *The first decision affects the power of those interested in the second one.* Sometimes a first decision creates an interest group, or gives power to a group that already exists, which in turn affects other decisions later and thus creates a variety of slippery slope. "If we legalize marijuana, next thing you know there will be advertisements trying to get people to smoke more of it." In principle, of course, it doesn't at all follow that legalizing marijuana would mean lots of advertisements for it. We could legalize the drug but forbid the ads. A possible problem, though, is that if marijuana

is legal, an industry will emerge to supply it. That industry will have a massive economic interest in finding ways to advertise. Its members will lobby in Congress; they will make campaign contributions; they will try to convince the public that some advertising in appropriate places wouldn't be a bad thing. Whether these efforts would succeed is anyone's guess, and as usual this illustration isn't our way of hinting that marijuana ought to be kept illegal. It's just an example of how decision one might affect decision two by changing the world in which decision two gets made. A similar story might be told about decisions to spend lots of money on certain sorts of military contracts or on construction projects or even on school vouchers. In every case one consequence may be to create a new constituency that will then work hard to cause more money to be sent in its direction. And then there are more obvious cases where extending voting and other political rights to a group naturally can result in the group voting itself still more of them, or other goodies.

The student of slippery slopes should be familiar with two other points about them: some prominent false alarms, and a possible antidote. (Both amount to studies in when and why slippery slopes *don't* occur.) A striking example of a false alarm was *State v. Bell*,[37] an 1872 case in which the Tennessee Supreme Court refused to recognize an interracial marriage solemnized in another state:

> Extend[ ] the rule to the width asked for by the defendant, and we might have in Tennessee the father living with his daughter, the son with the mother, the brother with the sister, in lawful wedlock, because they had formed such relations in a State or country where they were not prohibited. The Turk or Mohammedan, with his numerous wives, may establish his harem at the doors of the capitol, and we are without remedy. Yet none of these are more revolting, more to be avoided, or more unnatural than the case before us.

Yet as time went on, the courts did manage to distinguish between interracial marriages and harems. The court here might have been concerned less with a slippery slope than with the immediate reach of the principle it was considering, but it also is possible to interpret the court's statements along some of the lines sketched in this chapter—that the distinctions would be impossible to draw in practice, or that recognizing the interracial marriage would cause changes in public attitudes that would lead to later recognition of harems. It might, in short, give people ideas; perhaps sons will start marrying their mothers. The fact that the problems didn't occur shows that the operation of slippery slopes usually depends, as we have noted, on details about human behavior and reaction that are hard to predict, or easy to predict badly. When someone is hostile to a decision for other reasons, it is easily for the hostility to get expressed in exaggerated or overconfident claims about where the decision might lead.

Here is another example. Traditionally, American juries in both criminal and civil cases had twelve members. But during the twentieth century many states began to experiment with juries having six members, and the experiments were challenged in the Supreme Court. A possible slippery slope appeared: if six members was enough for a jury, why not five? If five was enough, why not four? It is a modern version of a classic puzzle devised in Ancient Greece by Eubulides—the paradox of the *sorites* (heap): if you remove a grain of sand from a pile, you still have a pile; and again when you remove another grain, and so forth—until there is only one grain of sand left, yet still a pile, because you never were able to identify a grain of sand that made the difference between having a pile and not having one.[38] (Of course you can turn it around, too: one grain doesn't create a pile; adding one more surely doesn't make the difference; so you never have a pile no matter how many you add.) This in turn can be viewed as a restatement of one of the legal patterns we explored earlier: cases where there definitely is a distinction between having a pile and not having one, but it is hard to draw the distinction in practice when a court is presented with one case after another. But when it came to juries the Court fended off the paradox by simply announcing that no number smaller than six would do. The choice between five and six may have been arbitrary, but sometimes an arbitrary solution to a slippery slope is a solution nevertheless—especially where, as here, there is no ongoing constituency clamoring for anything different.[39]

And now a final word about a nonarbitrary antidote to slippery slopes. Sometimes they can be avoided by constitutional or other foundational rules that more or less guarantee the slope will not be slippery. Suppose someone suggests a minor restriction on abortion. Some of those who strongly favor abortion rights might think the restriction reasonable but object to it anyway because they think it might result in a slippery slope. Perhaps once people get comfortable with the small restriction, they will then be ready to accept more restrictions until abortion rights are eroded entirely. So the proposal fails—and this might be regarded as a shame, since both sides thought the proposal in itself was all right. We can consider this a kind of inefficiency, or waste: an arrangement that would have made both sides better off (or at least would have been preferred by one side and acceptable to the other) fell through because a certain kind of trust was impossible. But if the advocates of abortion rights were confident that the rights they cared about most *couldn't* be badly eroded because they were the subject of reliable constitutional protection, then perhaps they would be more willing to compromise after all. A dependable constitutional rule in the background, in other words, creates a safe environment in which two sides can compromise without fear of a slippery slope. The same logic can be applied in various other areas—to a reliable, though not absolute, constitutional right to certain kinds of speech, or to bear arms, or to other sorts of liberties. The more reliable the right, the more confidently those who enjoy it may be prepared to tolerate small losses at its outskirts. The constitutional guarantee is, among other things, insurance against slippery slopes, and the insurance allows bargains and efficient results that otherwise might be impossible.

SUGGESTIONS FOR FURTHER READING. Eugene Volokh's sequel to *The Mechanisms of the Slippery Slope,* 116 Harv. L. Rev. 1026 (2003), is *Same-Sex Marriage and Slippery Slopes,* 33 Hofstra L. Rev. 1155 (2005). Other interesting general discussions are Frederick Schauer, *Slippery Slopes,* 99 Harv. L. Rev. 361 (1985); Mario J. Rizzo and Douglas G. Whitman, *The Camel's Nose Is in the Tent: Rules, Theories, and Slippery Slopes,* 51 UCLA L. Rev. 539 (2003).

19 ↠ Acoustic Separation

The many chapters of this book that talk about incentives are built on a simple idea: people know how the courts will react to various things they might do, and they take this into account when they decide how to act. If the courts hold restaurants strictly responsible for bugs and other unwelcome critters that turn up in the food they serve, for example, restaurants will understand this and worry about it when they prepare meals. If courts won't allow the attorney-client privilege to protect conversations lawyers have with clients in crowded elevators, lawyers will know this and will do their talking elsewhere. But sometimes the situation may be more complicated. Jeremy Bentham suggested that laws might be split into two types of commands—the ones that tell people how to act, called *conduct rules,* and the ones that tell judges how to decide cases, called *decision rules.*[40] On the surface these two sorts of rules usually look the same. If we say that restaurants will always be held liable for things in their food that don't belong, we are giving a command to restaurants about how to behave *and* a command to a judge about what to do when someone comes to grief by eating a bug. The decision rule *is* the conduct rule; to the restaurant there is no difference, because it decides what to do—at least so far as law enters into it—by asking its lawyers what will happen if someone eats a bug and then brings a lawsuit. We could try making the messages different: telling restaurants they always will lose, so they have a great incentive to be careful, but then quietly letting them win if they come to court and we think they tried their best to keep the food bug-free. But that probably wouldn't work for long, because restaurants would hear about the quiet decisions (there's no such thing, is there?) and would realize the strict rule is a sham.

The interesting question is whether there sometimes *can* be differences between the rules told to people in the world and the rules that courts actually enforce—and whether any such differences are a good thing. Meir Dan-Cohen proposed a thought experiment to illustrate the idea: imagine that the law gave completely different instructions to the public and the courts, and that neither could hear what was said to the other; imagine, in his phrase, acoustic separation between those audiences.[41]

Might this not be useful—and sometimes possible? His leading example is the necessity defense in criminal law. Sometimes committing a crime is the lesser of two evils, and in that case letting the defendant off seems attractive; by hypothesis he did the right thing. But it's worrisome to announce this rule in advance, because then people might be too eager to take advantage of it when deciding whether to commit a tempting crime. They will exaggerate the other evil—the one the crime was meant to avoid—in their own minds, and then in court when they are prosecuted. The really good claims of necessity are the ones where someone chooses to commit a crime despite thinking that there *wouldn't* be any defense available. That proves that they really did consider the crime the lesser evil; they thought they would get punished but did it anyway. So let's not punish them. Well, but if we don't punish them, then the next person in the same fix will know there was no punishment last time, so their decision to commit the crime won't be as impressive a piece of evidence that the crime really needed to be committed.

You see the problem, and presumably you see that it would go away if there were acoustic separation—in other words, if we were able to tell people that we never admit the "lesser of two evils" defense but then secretly allow it after all. Dan-Cohen's suggestion is that in fact we do (and should) allow defenses of this kind precisely in those situations where there is some acoustic separation—where the law can permit the defense without worrying much that it will be known and relied upon in the future by people planning their affairs. Suppose you set up a shotgun so that its trigger is tied to a doorknob in your house, and then you leave; you are hoping the contraption will shoot any thieves who try to break in. You succeed; it does. You will be held criminally liable. The courts will be firm in rejecting your "lesser evil" defense. But then suppose you *personally* kill a thief attempting to burgle your house. Most courts will allow your defense this time.[42] What is the difference between this case and the one with the shotgun tied to the doorknob? Actually there are several differences; one, for example, is that courts don't like unattended traps because they could kill children, fire fighters, and so forth. But another distinction may be drawn along the lines suggested by Dan-Cohen: allowing the defense in the second case is less likely to set a bad example because the people who find themselves in a position to shoot burglars are less likely to know the legal rule or have time to look into it. With respect to *them* there is acoustic separation: when they are deciding what to do, they won't know what the courts have said or are likely to say. People who set up traps are different. They have time to talk it over with their lawyers. We can't allow some of them to win without sending a bad message that others will hear. The distinction is imperfect, of course, because some people who kill burglars do plan ahead; they buy guns for such occasions. So whether there is acoustic separation may depend on the details of the situation.

Another example is the maxim that ignorance of the law is no excuse.[43] Everyone has heard this, and it is good for them to hear it because it gives them an incentive to learn the legal rules before they do things that might violate them. But in fact, whether ignorance is an excuse can be a complicated question; sometimes it might be, as when one relies on an official pronouncement that turns out to be misleading, or in some situations involving interpretation of the tax code.[44] But if we advertise that ignorance sometimes is an excuse, we dilute the incentives to avoid it. Notice that acoustic separation can have different sources. In the illustration a minute ago we had partial acoustic separation because people who shoot invading felons don't have *time* to learn the law. That isn't as likely to be true in cases involving claimed ignorance of the law; but this time the separation is created by the repeated utterance of a maxim that most members of the laity can well understand, followed by a tangle of distinctions in practice that hardly any of them can understand. The maxim is publicized but not the exceptions, which creates a kind of acoustic separation.

The idea of acoustic separation has been applied outside the criminal law as well. In contract law, for example, it has been argued that the legal system has conflicting goals. From the standpoint of efficiency we want to enforce rather strictly the terms of the agreements people make, so they will think hard about their contracts before entering into them. But in some cases there may be an interest as well in giving relief from agreements that have a whiff of unfairness about them. It is hard to have it both ways, but a degree of acoustic separation might relieve the tension between those wishes. The general message sent by the law is that contracts almost always get enforced without reference to the sense of fairness in the particular case; there are standard defenses you might raise, but you won't get very far by claiming that you didn't understand the contract before signing it or that enforcement will be hard on you. At the same time, though, those last considerations may be treated as relevant to a court's choice of *remedy*—whether to limit the winner to an award of money, or to make an order of specific performance requiring that the defendant actually carry out the contract. The second option is known as an *equitable* remedy. As a historical matter, specific performance was available only from a court of equity; now that there are no separate equity courts in most places, the greatest significance of the "equity" label is that courts can take into account a wide range of considerations in deciding whether to order the remedy. The practical point is that contracts very commonly aren't strictly enforced, at least not in the sense that one *must* perform them. The disappointed party usually just wins money, and often will find in this something less than the full benefit of the contract. But these details of remedy are beyond the understanding of many parties operating outside sophisticated commercial settings, and perhaps that bit of acoustic separation is for the best. Let people enter into contracts with the thought that enforcement is strict, and let any lenity come as a surprise.[45] Hide the role of fairness in a maze of obscure doctrines of equity that most parties won't learn about in advance. The conduct rule is clear: honor your contracts. The decision rule is mumbled.

Other examples of differences between conduct rules and decision rules are found in corporate law. Directors of corporations have various legal obligations: to act in good faith, to put the interests of the corporation ahead of their own, to use due care in making decisions that affect the corporation's interests. Those are rules of conduct. But when directors get sued, the courts often use rules of decision more lenient than the rules of conduct would suggest—the business judgment rule, for example, under which courts essentially presume that decisions by directors are in the corporation's interests unless clearly proven otherwise. In effect, many courts treat the law as imposing liability only for gross negligence, though the meaning of that term is itself unclear.[46] The question is whether there are sources of acoustic separation that prevent these differences between the conduct rules and decision rules from collapsing into the latter, and being regarded by directors as amounting to this: avoid gross negligence and you have nothing to fear. The answers are not certain, but it may be that because the conduct rules are simpler to understand than, say, the business judgment rule, they do influence directors in many situations where they are making decisions without seeking much formal legal advice.[47] Or it may be that sometimes the stiffer conduct rules have moral force of their own, even if the rules of decision are more relaxed—though this may not be quite the same as a case of acoustic separation. And then there are others who deny there is any acoustic separation here to speak of, and indeed blame the relaxed decision rule for many important cases of misconduct by corporate directors.[48]

Acoustic separation, even in the limited forms we have considered, is open to various ethical objections, such as the claim that people have the right to know what the law is in advance so that they can plan their affairs. It seems illiberal to have secret laws, or to convince the public that the law is one thing when it really is another.[49] But those concerns tend to be at their weakest in the cases we have been discussing because those cases generally have involved giving people the benefit of more lenient rules than they might have expected, not surprising them with unexpected punishments. Someone still might be upset about feeling tricked; "I thought ignorance of the law was no excuse, and so spent a lot of time learning it; imagine my annoyance upon learning that it *might* have been an excuse." Our sympathy with this sort of disappointment evidently is limited, maybe because the person making the claim seems to reveal an uncomfortably keen interest in coming as close to violating the law as possible without going over the line.[50]

A different sort of objection arises from another species of acoustic separation. We have been speaking of three usual parties to these situations: the author of the rule, the enforcer of it, and the party to whom it applies. But there may be a fourth party consisting of the body politic; members of the public may take an interest in the law not because they are concerned about how it applies to them personally but because they are wondering if the law ought to be reformed. Acoustic separation between the courts and the public in its political capacity is therefore a possibility, and it can have troubling consequences. One commentator in the criminal area believes this is the story of American criminal procedure in recent years.[51] In the 1960s the Supreme Court made various famous decisions expanding the rights of criminal defendants. The Court turned more conservative in the decades afterwards, but it didn't overrule those famous cases—*Miranda v. Arizona,* for example. Instead it chipped away at their significance by making decisions that took back some of what the big cases had been thought to accomplish. In various cases the Court held that evidence excluded because it was obtained without a warrant, or without a full reading of warnings to the defendant, or outside the presence of the defendant's lawyer, might be admissible after all if other conditions were satisfied (good faith on the part of the police, for example). The acoustic separation arises because the police understand all this but the public does not; the public thinks those old decisions still stand with all their old force, because the chipping away the Court has done has been too subtle and technical for most people to grasp. On this account the important point isn't that defendants are under the wrong impression about the strength of the protections they enjoy. It is that the rest of the public is under the wrong impression about it, and so clamors for longer prison terms, less discretion for judges in sentencing, and other measures meant to counterbalance those pro-defendant decisions that they think are as strong as ever. This is just one story about the Court's criminal procedure cases, and it may be flawed. But it shows another risk that can arise if one accepts the loss of transparency that acoustic separation implies.

SUGGESTIONS FOR FURTHER READING. Meir Dan-Cohen, *Decision Rules and Conduct Rules: On Acoustic Separation in Criminal Law,* 97 Harv. L. Rev. 625 (1984); Carol S. Steiker, *Counter-revolution in Constitutional Criminal Procedure? Two Audiences, Two Answers,* 94 Mich. L. Rev. 2466 (1996); Cass R. Sunstein, *Problems with Rules,* 83 Cal. L. Rev. 953 (1995); Melvin A. Eisenberg, *The Divergence of Standards of Conduct and Standards of Review in Corporate Law,* 62 Fordham L. Rev. 437 (1993).

20 ↠ Property Rules and Liability Rules

A primitive way to think about law is that for the most part it simply creates *rights*. You have the right not to be mugged, the right not to be run over by a driver who isn't paying attention to the road, the right not to be disappointed by someone with whom you make a contract, and so forth. A first step toward sophistication is realizing that rights are only as good as their protections, and that rights like those just listed can be protected in different ways; the penalties for people who violate them vary not only in degree but in kind. A mugger is put in prison, but an inattentive driver just pays for the damage he causes. Someone who breaks a contract probably just pays damages, too, but occasionally a court might order him to perform his promise or else be held in contempt of court, with heavy monetary penalties or even jail time then a possibility. We will talk about these examples and some others in a moment, but the important initial idea is just the perspective: you can understand law better by looking not so much at the rights it creates per se as at the remedies it gives when rights are invaded. Experiment with the idea that remedies *define* rights.

Perhaps the most famous law review article ever written is *Property Rules, Liability Rules, and Inalienability: One View of the Cathedral* by Guido Calabresi and Douglas Melamed.[52] The article suggested that we might think about remedies in ways that go beyond the usual boundaries between legal subjects; instead of thinking about remedies in property cases versus tort cases, for example, we might carve up the remedies used in both of those areas, and others, into two major categories: property rules and liability rules. A right is protected by a property rule if it can't be invaded without its owner's consent. A right is protected by a liability rule if someone can get away with destroying it so long as he pays the cost. The rules don't apply to things; they apply to situations. Thus your car is protected against outright taking by a property rule: a miscreant who steals it will be arrested. The same car is protected against accidental damage by a liability rule: a careless driver who demolishes it will have to pay damages. In effect the careless driver can force a transaction on you that you might have declined. He damages your car and writes you a check—and the legal system is satisfied. But the system isn't satisfied if the thief gets caught and writes you a check. He goes to prison.

So property rules and liability rules differ in the extent to which they require permission from their owners before they are invaded. But we also just saw another way of looking at the difference: the consequences one suffers for infringing them. If a right is protected by a property rule, invasions of it are punished, whether with jail, fines, or punitive damages. A liability rule requires only that the violator of a right pay for whatever damage he has caused. Nobody likes to do that, but it isn't considered *punishment.* Punishments try to force people to behave in a certain way, whereas holding people liable doesn't necessarily do that; it just puts them to a choice: respect the right or pay for the costs created by invading it. Of course one *could* look at punishments the same way. Someone might choose to break a law and accept jail time as the price of the disobedience. But punishments generally aren't designed to encourage that sort of thought. We don't set the punishment for theft at, say, ten years in prison because we want people to steal from others if they think the benefits of the theft will offset the penalty. Rather, we don't want people to steal at all, and the punishment is set to make it unattractive (the fact that it is only ten years, and not more, is the result of other considerations: the cost of imprisoning people, the need to have marginal deterrence,[53] perhaps a sense of mercy, and so on). Now compare the law's instruction not to break a contract, which is enforced just by a liability rule. Some would say this means there really *isn't* an instruction from the law not to break contracts. There merely is a choice: perform your promise or pay for the damage caused when you don't.[54] On an economic view, the rule invites you to compare the cost of keeping a promise with the cost of breaking it, and to do whichever is cheaper. (Breaking a contract because that's cheaper than performing it is what economists sometimes call *efficient breach.*)

This description has made it sound as though there are only two possibilities: property rules and liability rules. But we also can arrange them on a spectrum. In between are mixed possibilities, including some we have not yet hinted at. If you invade someone's rights you might be forced to pay compensatory damages (which sound like the stuff liability rules are made of) but then also punitive damages (which usually are thought to enforce property rules). Or you might be required not to go to jail but to pay a fine; and it may be debatable whether the fine invites you to violate the rule if the benefits to you are greater than the costs of paying. Think about parking in an illegal spot because you're in a great hurry, and simply accepting that you probably will be ticketed; have you done anything wrong? Why is that different from cheating on your taxes, and accepting the fine that might result if you are caught, because you really need the money? Or, to take another hybrid, you might be made to pay damages and then also be subject to some sort of stigma, or to side consequences, whether public or private—a bad reputation, or higher insurance premiums mandated by law, or suspension of privileges in professional associations that may savor of both public and private interest.[55]

How should the legal system decide which way to protect a right? How should a *judge* decide in cases where there is a choice? Why do we put people in jail for petty thefts but not for causing terrible accidents? Or why don't we allow a payment of damages in both cases? There are lots of possible answers to these questions, and some of them can be connected to ideas we talked about earlier in the book. First is the idea of efficiency: the notion that it's a good thing for rights to be in the hands of whoever values them the most (see chapter 2). Of course the people in charge of the legal system often may not know who values rights the most, and that leads to a second idea familiar from earlier in the book: the Coase theorem, which holds that rights will automatically end up in the hands of whoever values them most if people can bargain over them easily. The high bidder will win the rights in court or buy them from whoever does (see chapter 8).

What do those ideas have to do with the choice between property rules and liability rules? Well, if goods can change hands easily through bargaining, there is a natural argument for protecting them with property rules. That means they can be taken from their owner only with consent; so they will pass from me to you only if you offer to pay me enough. The great thing about this, at least so far as efficiency is concerned, is that when we consent to a trade of this kind we *know* the goods are moving from someone who values them less to someone who values them more. Otherwise we wouldn't have agreed to whatever exchange we made. The world could be run differently; we could say that if you want my things, you can just take them, and then I sue you for the value: they all are protected just by liability rules. One problem with this idea is that if you drive off with my car, we don't know that you valued it more than I did. We only know that you valued it more than the price the law will make you pay for it—its market value.[56] There are some other problems as well. I might decide to take the car back, and things go downhill from there: we take turns stealing the car from each other and demanding damages; we then resort to expensive defensive measures and countermeasures; and so on. It's all a waste of time and money.[57] Using property rules breaks the cycle. Someone who tries this sort of thing is coerced to stop.

This line of thought also suggests reasons why we don't *always* use property rules—why we sometimes do let people take or destroy the entitlements of others and just pay damages afterwards. It's because they *can't* bargain; it's not feasible for them.[58] If for some reason I really want to smash the front of your car with a sledgehammer, I ought to ask first. If I don't ask and do it anyway, I go to jail. If I'm going to *mistakenly* demolish the front of your car by backing into it with mine, again it would be nice if I asked first, but this time it isn't realistic. We're talking about an accident; if I had the foresight to ask about it in advance, I would have had the foresight to avoid it altogether. That's an obvious example, but there are subtler situations where the law recognizes that bargaining isn't realistic and so allows one person to "take and pay" from another without consent. If I feel like mooring my boat at your dock but won't meet your terms, I'll go to jail if I insist on doing it anyway: your rights are protected by a property rule. But if it's an emergency—a case where there's a vicious storm and I *need* to borrow your dock to save life or property—the courts say that you *must* let me do it.[59] I have to pay my way, but that is all; in this case your rights are protected only by a liability rule.

You might think the last case is explained best by pointing out that the stakes are high: your interest in the dock naturally has to yield to my higher interest in saving my life or my much more valuable property. But that isn't quite so. Such an argument once was tried by homeless people in London, who tried to take over vacant public housing for themselves as "squatters." They pointed out that the stakes were high: they and their families desperately needed shelter. The court nevertheless held them to be trespassers.[60] What's the difference between this case and the boat threatened by the storm? The case of the boat involved a sudden, acute emergency, neither very easy to foresee nor very likely to recur in the life of the boat's pilot. These facts are important because they mean that it wasn't realistic to expect the owner of the boat to bargain in advance with the owner of the dock. In the case of the homeless people their distress was easy for them to foresee and it was chronic. It was a simple matter for them to approach the government and ask for public housing, or to negotiate with the owners of private apartments. A simple matter to *ask,* of course, but not a simple matter to succeed. That is what makes the case troubling. The squatters didn't have enough money to make the negotiations work. But if not having enough money to satisfy the market were treated as a sufficient excuse to seize property without consent, there wouldn't be much left to private property. That was the court's view, in any event. Taken together these two cases show that courts relax property rules in favor of liability rules not just when the need is great but when there are practical impediments (as opposed to financial ones) to working out a voluntary exchange.

Here is another famous situation where courts sometimes have to choose between property rules and liability rules. Suppose my factory is spewing pollution onto your nearby house. You sue me, and the court agrees that I'm creating a nuisance; I'm interfering unreasonably with your enjoyment of your property. The interesting question is what the court will do about it. The usual remedy is an injunction: an order that I stop. This is a form of property rule. If I defy it, I can be held in contempt and fined or sent to jail. Of course, as with any property rule, I can approach you and try to buy you out. Your right to stop me from polluting becomes like your right to your car or your house or anything else. It's a kind of a property that you can sell, and we can hope that it will find its way into the hands of whoever values it more. If that's me (the owner of the factory), I will buy the rights from you; if it's you, you will keep them and I will scale back my factory's operations or move it elsewhere. The court doesn't need to figure out who values the rights more. *We* will figure it out. As you no doubt perceive, this is, again, a simple use of the Coase theorem.

So far, so good—but if bargaining is difficult, should the injunction still issue? Here again we need to think broadly about what "difficult" might mean. In our prior examples (the car accident and the boat in the storm), bargaining wasn't practical because there wasn't time. In the case of the nuisance created by my factory, there is, we may assume, plenty of time, but bargaining still might be hard if there are a lot of plaintiffs. Perhaps you aren't the only one my pollution affects; perhaps it annoys everyone else in your neighborhood just as much. In that case I might be able to avoid the injunction only by buying all of you out. The problem with that idea isn't the expense of it. If I can't afford to pay everyone enough to make the injunction go away, then the lesson is clear: I shouldn't be polluting so much; the clean air is worth more to the neighborhood than the right to pollute the air is worth to me. No, the problem is that even if I can *afford* to pay everyone enough to keep them happy, getting the deal done might be difficult as a practical matter. There might be holdout problems of the kind we talked about in chapter 2; in brief, a lot of people might wait to agree to terms because each of them wants to be the last, and thus in a position to make large demands. So maybe the deal never does get made, or gets made after long, expensive delays.[61]

Economists consider holdout problems a type of transaction cost—an obstacle to getting a deal done that would make everyone better off. Some people argue that courts should award damages, not injunctions, in cases like this where there are large numbers of parties involved. The damages are meant to approximate the price at which everyone would agree to sell their rights if there were a good market for them—for notice that the holdout problem arises because there isn't really a well-operating market for the rights. The owner of the factory has to make terms with all these neighbors or with nobody; he can't threaten to "take his business elsewhere" in reply to whatever strategic threats any of them may make. So maybe a liability rule—in other words, a payment of damages rather than an injunction—should be used anytime strategic behavior is a serious danger. This can include cases where there is only one party on either side, as where it is just you suing me. In that case we have what is called a *bilateral monopoly*, familiar from the chapter on games of chicken: we can bargain only with each other, so again each of us might bluff and hold out for a big share of the gains from bargaining.[62] Perhaps you say that you will only sell your rights for a dollar less than the cost to me of moving my factory; I reply that I will buy your rights only for a dollar more than their value to you. But each of us is just guessing, both about the value the other puts on the rights and the likelihood that the other will cave in. Maybe a deal finally gets made and maybe it doesn't—even if there really is some price at which a bargain would have made us both better off. And even assuming it eventually does get made, it may be after a lot of wasted time. We can avoid all these problems by protecting the rights involved with liability rules, so that the court simply makes one side pay the other an amount set by the judge. But then we have a new problem. The judge might set the wrong amount—an amount that doesn't resemble the actual value of the rights to their holder.

Within the legal academy there is a cottage industry devoted to analyzing these kinds of problems and arguing about when damages or injunctions are best—about which promotes bargaining better (for notice that parties can bargain their way around a bad award of damages as well as an injunction),[63] about why parties in these cases might not bargain (the reasons might be strategic, but they might also be matters of enmity or other sorts of distaste toward bargaining),[64] about whether the reasons they don't bargain should be of concern to courts, and so forth. We won't go any further into those complications, it being enough for our current purposes to alert you to the questions involved. In truth the active debate on these issues within law schools tends not to be matched by comparable interest in the courts, or for that matter opportunity in the courts. Problems of pollution involving large communities tend now to be resolved by regulations rather than by nuisance claims, so judges don't get very frequent chances to experiment with all these wonderful theoretical ideas—or at least not in that particular area of law. But courts and (more often) legislatures and agencies still have to make rules and decide what happens to people who break them; and when they think about those questions, the framework we've been discussing suggests something useful to consider: whether people might be able to bargain their way to something better than the law says, and how the law might be written to make that process easier.

There is a similar payoff to another innovation Calabresi and Melamed offer: the infamous "Rule 4." When we think of how a dispute over rights of any sort might end, we usually think of three possibilities: the plaintiff wins, and his rights are protected by a property rule (an injunction, say, or prison for the invader); the plaintiff wins by operation of a liability rule—in other words, the plaintiff wins money; or the defendant wins, and nothing happens to him: he doesn't owe the plaintiff anything and isn't subject to an injunction or prison or anything else. The last case—"defendant wins"—amounts to saying that the defendant gets the benefit of a property rule. If the plaintiff loses the nuisance case brought against the factory, in other words, the factory in effect ends up with a right to pollute as it has been doing, and nobody can stop the factory without its consent. (If the plaintiff tried to climb onto one of the smokestacks and cover it up, he would be carried away as a trespasser.) But this way of thinking leaves out another possibility that is available, at least in principle—Rule 4. The defendant could win the case but have *its* rights protected merely by a liability rule. Thus the plaintiff could be permitted to stop the defendant from polluting (or whatever else the defendant is doing) but be required to compensate the defendant for the costs of this; he can make the factory move but has to pay its way.[65]

Most people find Rule 4 counterintuitive because one does not generally think of a plaintiff being required to pay a defendant. Usually we imagine that either the defendant pays the plaintiff or nothing happens at all. So perhaps it is no surprise that Rule 4 rarely has been used in litigation; there is only one nuisance case on record where a court has employed it,[66] and this on facts where the justice of the approach might seem unusually attractive: the plaintiff had built houses close to a cattle feedlot, then complained about the odors. The court concluded that the plaintiff had a right to be free of the nuisance but that under the circumstances the defendant was entitled to payment of its costs of moving. (The case was decided at about the same time as Calabresi and Melamed's article; neither the judge who made the decision nor the authors of the article were aware of each other.)[67] The scarcity of Rule 4 in practice has caused it to be dismissed by one commentator as "a novelty item from some academic rubber goods catalog,"[68] but it also has been defended as a common approach to many problems of public law—as a tool used in relationships between the government (especially government agencies) and the businesses they regulate. Thus sometimes the government makes corporations do things without their consent—and pays them. Melamed offers as an example a statute that required local phone companies to make their facilities available to rivals but then allowed the local companies to compete for business in the long-distance market; in other words, the statute made the companies do something, but it compensated them. Perhaps this can be roughly analogized to saying that the victim of a polluter can insist that the polluter leave but then has to pay the polluter compensation, too.[69]

Rule 4 has inspired other ideas, some of which seem even stranger but are interesting to think about. Maybe a polluter who is sued should be able to voluntarily stop polluting but then insist on collecting, as a kind of damages, money that reflects the benefits the neighbors will enjoy once the pollution has been stopped.[70] Sounds bizarre, does it not? Here is the reasoning, broken down into steps:

- Remember that the economic goal, as usual, is to see the pollution continue only if it (or rather the activity creating it) does more good than harm. We might like the polluter to be the one to make that comparison because he knows best what the benefits are.

- The simple and familiar way to make the polluter draw on his knowledge is to order him to pay damages to his neighbors. Notice how this will force him to think: if the polluting creates more benefits than costs, he will pay the damages and keep doing it. If it creates more costs than benefits, he will close up shop; it isn't worth staying and paying the neighbors.
- But that might seem hard on the polluter, and unjust, if the residents moved next door to *him*. We want him to make the right choice about whether to keep polluting, but why must we force him to suffer (by paying damages) as a way of getting him to make the choice? A way to avoid this problem, and still have the polluter make the decision (because he knows best what benefits his factory creates), would be to give him a different choice—one he will like better: he can keep polluting and collect nothing, or he can stop polluting and collect from the neighbors.
- If he stops, the amount he will collect from the neighbors is just the amount he normally would be required to *pay* them in the scenario drawn a minute ago—in other words, their damages. Again, notice how this will force him to think. He will compare his choices and pick whichever makes him better off.
- He will stay and pollute if the pollution creates more benefits than costs; for in that case he would rather have the income from the pollution than whatever he would collect from the neighbors if he stopped. But if the pollution creates more costs for his neighbors than benefits for him, he will stop—because then the neighbors have to write him a check in the amount of those costs they were suffering (but now get to avoid).
- The difference between this approach and the earlier one is that here the polluter will get paid if he stops, instead of the neighbors getting paid if he continues. It's a weird idea, but it does seem to pressure the polluter to make the efficient choice (pollution only if it's worthwhile) while not penalizing him at all—and finding a way to do that was the point of this little gymnastic exercise.

Mind you, no court ever actually does this. It is mentioned here just to give you a sense of the speculations that can be triggered once you start pondering various uses of property rules and liability rules. If you have an appetite for more such delicious complications, you can pursue them in the references in the endnotes and at the end of the chapter.

To return to more practical matters, you now are in a better position to understand the powers of eminent domain enjoyed by the state and federal governments: their ability to take your house, write you a check for its market value, and build a highway where the house used to stand. To state the implication in the language of this chapter, your house is protected by a property rule against being taken by your neighbor, but only by a liability rule against the government. Some say the government needs these powers to overcome holdout problems of the kind described a moment ago; this is discussed more in chapter 13. But maybe some of the people in the path of the highway would have held out for big payments not for strategic reasons but because they were just very attached to their houses; they valued them much more than the market price would suggest. That extra value gets snuffed out by the eminent domain power.

This last problem is the classic difficulty created by any liability rule. The party who takes and pays (in this case the government) might not really value the rights taken more than their owner did. Why do we sometimes let people take and pay anyway? Because we have to balance the risk just mentioned against other considerations: the risk of holdouts or the spectacle of one homeowner with idiosyncratic values frustrating a project that the public wants very badly. Whether the courts have allowed the eminent domain power—the government's "liability rule" power, so to speak—to be extended too far is yet another subject of vigorous debate, the frontiers of which are far from exhausted. One commentator, for example, has suggested that the logic of eminent domain be extended to violations of constitutional rights: this would allow the government to respond to risks of terrorism by making mass detentions so long as it pays the detainees for their trouble, a case of protecting liberty with a liability rule.[71] It is always nice to end a chapter on a provocative note.

SUGGESTIONS FOR FURTHER READING. Guido Calabresi and A. Douglas Melamed, *Property Rules, Liability Rules, and Inalienability: One View of the Cathedral,* 85 Harv. L. Rev. 1089 (1972); James E. Krier and Stewart J. Schwab, *Property Rules and Liability Rules: The Cathedral in Another Light,* 70 N.Y.U. L. Rev. 440 (1995); Saul Levmore, *Unifying Remedies: Property Rules, Liability Rules, and Startling Rules,* 106 Yale L.J. 2149 (1997).

21 ⤚ Baselines

The law school where I teach has wireless Internet access in the classrooms. This has turned out to create a hazard: distractible students sometimes will use their laptop computers to check their e-mail during class, read the news, and so forth. Soon enough, I went to a faculty meeting where someone suggested turning off the wireless signal during class hours. A colleague then rose to his feet with a lively riposte: turning off the signal would be paternalism, and he opposed it; students should be left alone. Those were interesting claims, and odd ones when you stop to think about them. Why not install television sets in the classrooms, too, and have them display movies during class? Is it paternalistic *not* to do that? How do we know? And then what does it mean to leave the students alone? Wouldn't it be better to leave them even *more* alone by turning off the wireless signal rather than bombarding them with temptation?

This story is an example of two related difficulties that come up often in law, both involving baselines. To say whether *A* is paternalizing *B* you need to ask, what is the starting point? We need to know what the natural or normal state of affairs for students is supposed to be before we can say what kinds of interference with it amount to paternalism. We can call this a simple baseline problem. It isn't insoluble by any means. It just requires a conversation, rather than a slogan, to solve. But then something else was said, too: that students should be left alone. This, too, raises a baseline problem—not the simple kind, however, but more likely of the hopeless variety. Leaving students alone means leaving them on some baseline. The trouble is that the baseline position of the students, whatever it is, is created by the same law school that is trying to decide whether to send in the wireless signals. Leaving the students alone thus isn't really an option, unless it means sending no professors to teach the classes, or perhaps getting rid of the classrooms altogether. More to the point, letting students log on to the Internet during class isn't a case of leaving them alone. We might summarize the problem by saying the students are surrounded by the university, so to talk of leaving them alone is vacuous. This doesn't mean that wireless signals should or shouldn't be sent into the classrooms. It just means that the idea of leaving people alone is no help. The issue will have to be decided on other grounds—perhaps how the benefits of wireless access in the classroom compare to the costs, or some such train of thought.

Baseline problems arise often in legal settings; let's look at some examples from constitutional law. The Constitution generally puts limits on what the government can do when it acts, not when it doesn't act. It says, for example, that the government can't abridge the freedom of speech, or take property without due process of law; those are problems that can arise when the government passes statutes, sends around the police, or does other affirmative things. But if the government simply does nothing, then apparently we can't have any of those constitutional problems—or can we? "Doing nothing" is one of those expressions like "leaving people alone" that requires a baseline: we need to know what counts as action and inaction. Many people imagine that the government is doing nothing—is leaving them alone—when they go about their ordinary business: buying and selling things, watching television, and so forth. In a sense they are being left alone, but in a sense they aren't: all their conduct is played out against a background of laws and regulations. The regulations aren't visible most of the time because they create fairly simple boundaries within which those activities take place. But you probably would notice right away if the boundaries weren't there. Someone would steal your television or break a contract with you—or not enter into the contract in the first place because they have no reason to think you will go through with it. The rules of property, contract, and criminal law are a deep part of the state of things that we take for granted, and they are responsible for everyone's ability to walk around feeling unmolested most of the time. They also are a necessary condition for some people amassing large amounts of wealth while others don't end up with as much; for large amounts of wealth usually involve lots of contracts to create, and require protections of the criminal law to be kept secure. Of course we might find similar inequalities—or greater—if those rules didn't exist; but the winners and losers probably would be different. Anyway, the point is that the government is engaged in a certain sort of acting all the time, even if you don't notice.

If all this is true, how do we know when the government is "acting" in ways that trigger those constitutional limits mentioned a moment ago? To make the problem concrete, suppose Archie Bunker offers to pay his neighbor *not* to sell his house to a black family. The neighbor agrees, and now the property is subject to a thing called a covenant. But then the neighbor sells the house to a black family anyway, so Bunker sues him to enforce their agreement. Is there a constitutional problem if the court enforces it? The state isn't doing anything; Bunker and his neighbor are the ones doing something. Well, but the state *would* be doing something: it would be enforcing the covenant. The Supreme Court famously held in *Shelley v. Kraemer*[72] that this was indeed a case of state action, and that for a court to enforce a racially restrictive covenant violates the Constitution.

But the famous case gave rise to a famous objection: where does the principle stop? Suppose Bunker calls the police to remove someone from his house because he dislikes the guest's race or religion, and the police oblige; is that a case of state action that violates the Constitution, too?[73] Few people seem to think so. But now you can see the difficulty of the baseline problem. The government is constrained when it acts—but when it "acts" is a hard question. An action is a departure from some state of inaction, but it's hard to find any situation where the government is entirely inactive. Yet if the government is always acting, then does that mean it's violating the Constitution when a radio station fires one of its hosts for making politically offensive statements on the air? True, the government didn't fire him; but the government gives the radio station its license, enforces its contracts, and all the rest. At present, anyway, nobody quite thinks this is a good constitutional case, either. But how *do* we figure out whether the government is "acting" if it isn't as simple as asking whether it is visibly in motion?

We observed earlier that the government regulates behavior all the time by its rules of contract law, property law, criminal law, and the like. One reason some baseline problems are hard is that those rules barely seem noticeable when they do most of their work. They aren't rules that require people to fill out forms, report to bureaucrats, or otherwise come into direct contact with the government. But another reason those rules don't feel like regulation is that so many of them weren't made by legislatures passing statutes. They were made by courts in England and in the United States, one case at a time over hundreds of years. Those decisions taken together we call the common law. Its basic principles are so familiar that it's tempting to think of the common law as though it were the state of nature—as though its enforcement amounts to leaving people alone, not to action by the government. It is so tempting, in fact, that many people think the Supreme Court took that position early in the twentieth century when it struck down various state laws that set a minimum wage or a maximum number of hours for workers of various sorts; the latter case, *Lochner v. New York,* is the best known of them.[74] On this view the Court regarded the parties as being free from interference by the state when left to their rights at common law; those were baseline rights protected by the Constitution and subject to invasion only by use of the state's "police power," which was said not to justify the state laws that the Court struck down. These decisions became a great obstacle to legislation that tried to relieve the Great Depression of the 1930s, and they were attacked vigorously by scholars called legal realists. They said that since workers and employers owed their bargaining positions to law—to the whole set of rules entitling the employer to amass wealth and keep it, for example—the states ought to have wide latitude in changing their laws to modify those positions.[75] In the late 1930s the Supreme Court overturned the earlier decisions and began upholding statutes that interfered with common law rights of contract, though the role of the realists' arguments in producing that outcome is a matter of dispute.[76] The practical result now, in any event, is that the courts have largely abandoned efforts to declare constitutional baselines in economic matters such as when and how the states can restrict employment relationships. Those questions are left to legislatures to decide.

Here is a somewhat similar baseline problem. The Fifth Amendment to the Constitution requires the government to pay compensation when it takes someone's property for public use. But we can't know whether the government has performed a "taking" of my house until we know what the baseline looks like: what rights are mine in the first place. Don't think of ownership as an obvious, monolithic state of affairs where, since something is *yours*, nobody else can interfere with it in any way. It is conventional in law to instead think of ownership as involving a bundle of rights (actually a bundle of sticks is the stock metaphor) that includes some powers but not others. Ownership of land, for example, includes the right to keep trespassers off of it—most of the time, but not always, as we saw in the case of the dock in the preceding chapter. It usually doesn't include the right to keep sound waves out of your airspace, unless they are unreasonably loud. So to know whether the government owes you any compensation, we need to know whether it took away a stick that was ever in your bundle in the first place. It's considered an easy case if the state tears down your house to build an airport. You get paid. But suppose the state instead passes a law forbidding anyone to build houses on the beach—and you own a piece of beachfront property, the value of which has just collapsed because of the new rule. Does the government owe you compensation? It depends on whether the baseline against which we measure "takings" includes the possibility that the state will regulate away the value of your land.

Again, an easy place to look for an answer is the common law. We could ask—and the Supreme Court *does* ask—whether the uses newly forbidden by the state's rule could have been forbidden by the state courts under its common law of public or private nuisance.[77] If so, then you bought the land subject to that risk and you can't demand payment now that the state has achieved something similar by passing a statute. But if the rule forbidding you to build a house is new and unexpected, then whether it is a taking is, unfortunately, hard to say. It's clear that you win the case if the regulation has reduced the value of your land to zero, but the intermediate cases have to get litigated on their facts and without clear rules of decision to guide them. Almost nobody is quite ready to say that the government should have to compensate home owners every time a law is passed that reduces the value of their property in some way unknown to the common law. But nobody is ready to say, either, that since regulation by the government is pervasive, there is no such thing as really "taking" someone's property. After all, the Fifth Amendment speaks explicitly of private property, so there must be such a thing for constitutional purposes. The problem is that all private property has a bit of the public about it, because everyone knows the public makes a lot of rules about its use. So figuring out the baseline—that is, deciding when the government is taking something from you and when it's just fiddling in ways that have to be expected—is hard.

The realists' argument that law is everywhere, so there is no clear and principled distinction between public and private property or between state action and inaction, is a little like the notion in our earlier example that students are surrounded by the university. To say the law can't establish a minimum wage because it should leave the parties to their liberty of contract is like saying the law school can't turn off the wireless signal because it should leave the students to their own devices, so to speak. The law school turned *on* the signal, and created the rest of the classroom arrangements; the students aren't left to their "own devices" in any event—and workers and employers aren't left to their own devices without minimum wage laws, either, because they owe their circumstances to a legal architecture that invisibly surrounds them. The realist claim thus is that the idea of state action (and inaction) presents a baseline problem of the hopeless variety. There is no way to talk sensibly about when the state is acting and when it isn't. It *always* is. We should just talk directly about what the state ought to be doing or not doing; we should make no reference to fictitious notions that people have a right to be left alone.

Perhaps you sense a troubling potential in these arguments. It might be made more specific (and, depending on your tastes, more clearly troubling) by looking at what the arguments can achieve when the topic is the law of search and seizure. Normally the police need a warrant to search a place of business, but the Supreme Court said in *New York v. Burger*[78] that the requirement didn't apply when the police did an "administrative" search of a junkyard without a warrant and arrested its owner because they found contraband. But why not? Isn't a junkyard a piece of property owned by someone? Yes and no. The Court said that junkyards are so heavily regulated that anybody who gets a license to operate one has to understand that it may be subject to search without a warrant. At first the rules in this area seem to present a simple baseline problem. The police need a warrant if they invade someone's reasonable expectation of privacy, because that counts as a "search." But to make sense out of the rule, we have to puzzle over where to set the baseline: what expectations of privacy are reasonable. Not an impossible question, but a difficult one. Yet the baseline problem might go from simple to hopeless when the Court says the police can always search a junkyard because it's so heavily regulated and the defendant owes his right to operate it to a license from the government. Lots of things are regulated and licensed, not just junkyards, and some of them might well be hiding places for contraband, too. Why not extend the reasoning to searches of cars? While we're at it, why not extend the reasoning to houses?[79] They, too, are heavily regulated—by the common law, and to some extent by statute and ordinance. In the end we may owe all of our privacy to the protections of the law; but if the government in effect *gives* us our privacy, can it take some away as it sees fit? Does the legal system—whether through the common law, or statutes, or the Constitution—give us our privacy, or do those instruments merely protect a right to privacy that somehow existed already? But if the latter, then where did it come from and who gets to decide how broad it is?

The problem we encounter here is recurring. The trouble is that for a lot of purposes everyone still likes old-fashioned distinctions between public and private, and between the superficial notions of action and inaction supplied by common sense. Even if they are illusory or don't hold up under close analysis, they have been useful in separating where the government can go from where it can't. But the arguments of the realists have weakened those distinctions, making it harder for anyone to rely on them in an argument—at least in their simple form. It's still possible to say that the old-fashioned distinctions are the best source of baselines, not because they mark off areas of privacy and inaction that are "real" in some natural sense but for other reasons. Maybe the best reading of some parts of the Constitution is that it *does* mean to treat the common law as a source of baselines.[80] Or maybe treating the common law as a baseline is convenient: it gives us the kind of liberty we want, or confines the courts to the kinds of decisions we want them to make, and so forth. But once baselines are viewed as a matter of convenience rather than reflective of a deeper reality, it's easier to chip away at them—to argue that it would be even *more* convenient to set some of the baselines just a bit differently than the common law might have done. Yet once we start hashing out these issues case-by-case, and not by reference to clear and general lines, the consequences can be unpredictable, confusing, and hard to contain.

These points have implications not only for the resolution of cases but, as suggested above, for *who* resolves them. Policing a line between state action and inaction based on the common law, however incoherent it may have been, was something that courts felt able to do. Answering the harder, more substantive question of how much economic liberty people ought to have is something courts generally don't feel able to do; so most of those matters are left to the political process, where they can be compromised openly on the basis of considerations—expediency, changing needs, or the squeaky-wheel principle—that courts are poorly positioned to take into account. Meanwhile the baseline problems that courts do keep to themselves are subject to heated debate and, sometimes, unsatisfactory resolution. This is one of the reasons why constitutional law is difficult. There are many areas where nobody is too sure anymore where the baselines are.

Now let's consider a kindred baseline problem from outside the constitutional area. A lot of law, and a lot of the economic analysis of it, proceeds from the idea that legal machinery ought to be arranged to give effect to people's preferences. The preferences are considered private—as existing before or outside of law; then along comes law to help them get expressed, whether by enforcing the contracts people make or by passing regulations that give them more of what they want. But should the law accept everyone's preferences as a given when they are invoked to justify a rule? What if other things the government has done are responsible for the preferences in the first place? Letting the preferences justify the rule might be circular. Classic examples are civil rights laws that prevent people from expressing their preferences for discrimination. The laws can be justified on various grounds, of course; maybe we just don't like those preferences. But it also has been suggested that the discriminatory preferences are suspect, and entitled to less than the usual weight, because they often seem likely to have roots in other things the government has done. It's hard to disentangle people's views of blacks and women from the centuries of unequal treatment they received from the law.[81] The point can be made more general. If people's preferences depend on law in a way vaguely analogous to the way their wealth depends on it, then we might wonder why the preferences should be considered a solid justification for legal rules. But then there is the matter of finding a suitable alternative: for if preferences don't deserve deference from law because law helps make them, then what other justification—what other baseline—is any better? Deferring to the preferences that individuals hold has the great practical advantage of not putting too much authority into the hands of anyone in particular. Skeptics about the weight to be given to people's preferences usually have grand plans of their own about how the world *really* ought to be ordered, and it is reasonable—urgent, even—to show skepticism toward grand planners. So perhaps this is another case where a baseline (private preferences this time, rather than the common law) may have a weak theoretical pedigree but serve some important practical purposes very well. Ah, but once the baseline is admitted to be a matter of convenience, it again becomes vulnerable to piecemeal attacks—and so it goes.

Baseline problems come up in lots of places (if that weren't so, we wouldn't be spending time on them), but this chapter is long enough. We will resume this train of thought in the next chapter when we discuss the endowment effect.

SUGGESTIONS FOR FURTHER READING. The most influential modern discussion of the issues raised in this chapter is Cass R. Sunstein, *Lochner's Legacy,* 87 Colum. L. Rev. 873 (1987); see also Cass R. Sunstein, The Partial Constitution (1993). Earlier development of the "baseline" language can be found in Duncan Kennedy, *Cost-Benefit Analysis of Entitlement Programs: A Critique,* 33 Stan. L. Rev. 387 (1981), and Jeremy Paul, Searching for the Status Quo (book review), 7 Cardozo L. Rev. 743 (1986). Classic critiques of the distinction between public and private include Robert Hale, *Coercion and Distribution in a Supposedly Non-coercive State,* 38 Pol. Sci. Q. 470 (1923); Felix Cohen, *Transcendental Nonsense and the Functional Approach,* 35 Colum. L. Rev. 809 (1935); and Morris Cohen, *The Basis of Contract,* 46 Harv. L. Rev. 553 (1933). For discussion and references to these and other sources, see Joseph W.

Singer, *Legal Realism Now,* 76 Cal. L. Rev. 465 (1988). For some interesting modern applications, see Jack Beermann and Joseph W. Singer, *Baseline Questions in Legal Reasoning: The Example of Property in Jobs,* 23 Ga. L. Rev. 911 (1989), and Louis Michael Seidman, *The Problems with Privacy's Problem,* 93 Mich. L. Rev. 1079 (1995).

PART IV *Psychology*

22 ↠ Willingness to Pay and Willingness to Accept: The Endowment Effect and Kindred Ideas

People often seem to value things they have more than things they don't have—even when the things are the same. The most famous example, though probably not the most interesting, involves an experiment performed on students in two classrooms. In the first, the students were offered the chance to buy coffee mugs and asked to say how much they would pay for them; in the second, the students were given the mugs for free and then asked how much they would demand to part with them. One might have expected the average prices in the two classrooms to have been about the same, but in fact there were discrepancies: the students given the mugs valued them considerably more than the students asked what they would be willing to pay for them.[1] Another study found subjects willing to spend just over a dollar to purchase a small amount of extra safety in pesticides they were buying; but when asked how much they would demand to *sell* the same amount of safety—in other words, how much they would need to be paid to accept an increase of the same amount in the pesticide's risk—the average demand was nearly three dollars, and many people refused to name a price altogether.[2]

These discrepancies are most commonly referred to as a difference between what people are willing to pay for something and what they are willing to accept for it—"WTP" vs. "WTA," as some writers say, but I won't be using those abbreviations here because I prefer words. (The difference also is sometimes known as the "offer/asking problem.") The difference has implications for the legal system. As we saw in chapter 2, when economists think about law, one of their goals is to get rights into the hands of whoever values them the most. But when we try to measure how much people value things, we have a baseline problem: what starting point should we use? Do you ask how much people would *bid* for whatever is at stake? Or do you ask how much they would *demand* to give up the rights if they already had them? The choice wouldn't matter if the answers to those questions were the same, but in many cases they aren't.

Let's begin with an example from environmental law. Imagine a proposal to auction off rights to pollute to the highest bidders. (There are real proposals, some of which have been enacted, to assign rights to pollute to companies and then allow the rights to be sold or traded;[3] this is a hypothetical variation on those rules.) The high bidders in the auction might be companies that want to do a lot of polluting, or they might be people who want to buy the rights and then not use them because they like having clean air. (Set aside the difficulty those people might have getting themselves organized.) This sounds efficient. The rights should end up going to whoever values them the most; if the polluting firm outbids everyone else, evidently the benefits it gets from polluting are larger than the costs to the people who don't like it, so the polluting is worthwhile.

But not so fast. There are studies suggesting that clean air provokes the sort of differences just discussed: people may not want to pay much for it out of pocket, but once they have it they are stingy about giving it up; their willingness-to-accept prices, in other words, are much higher than what they say they would be willing to pay.[4] What if that's not true for firms—for corporations that, let us suppose, don't experience much difference between what they are willing to pay for something and what they will accept for it? (There is evidence that such discrepancies do get smaller as a party's sophistication and experience in the market become greater, as probably would be true of most big firms seeking permission to pollute.)[5] In that case, auctioning off the right to pollute may be a questionable strategy after all from the standpoint of efficiency. Firms that bid the most for the rights at auction (because they are willing to pay a fair bit to pollute) might still value the rights less than the victims of the pollution would value them *if* they were given the rights from the beginning.

The question, of course, is which measure—willingness to pay, or willingness to accept—ought to serve as the baseline for measuring value. Some have suggested that the solution is clear: figure out how much people value things by using whichever measure is higher—their willingness to pay or willingness to accept.[6] Cutting the other way, at least in many cases, is an administrative point. What someone would be willing to accept to give up rights is notoriously hard to measure, except by simply giving them the rights and waiting to see what they do—but that's circular if we're trying to figure out who should get the rights in the first place. An auction, however, provides a good, clean way to see what anyone is ready to pay for them. This concern might overwhelm all others in the choice between the two measures; possibly a second-best measurement that we can make easily is better than a more meaningful one that we really can't make accurately at all. (In some situations, though, an auction isn't feasible; claims of how much an ordinary person is willing to pay *or* accept when it comes to clean air may be equally hypothetical.)

Another problem with asking people what they would demand to part with environmental quality is that some of them are liable to name enormous or infinite figures, since in setting this price they aren't limited by the amount of money they happen to have. From an economic standpoint the fact that someone puts a huge value on something—even idiosyncratically huge—is no argument against giving them the rights; if they really do value them much more than the market does, so be it. The problem is that uttering a huge number is one thing, and proving that it really would be one's reservation price is another.[7] Maybe the people who say these things are exaggerating, or maybe they are sincere but wrong: their fantasies of what they would charge wouldn't hold up if real money were involved.

Here is a simpler application of how differences between willingness to pay and accept can bear on the choice of a legal rule. As we saw in chapter 8, an American employer generally can fire an employee for any reason or no reason at all, unless the two sides make a contract saying otherwise. This is called employment at will. Is it efficient? Put differently, is it the rule that the two sides would agree upon if they could negotiate? Well, that's a silly question; they *can* negotiate, and usually they nevertheless leave that background presumption in place. So evidently it is indeed what they want. But maybe not; perhaps one reason employment at will tends not to be modified is that employers start out with the entitlement. Employees don't want to buy it away from them because their willingness to pay for job security isn't all that high (and employers would demand a lot to give up their right to fire). But if employees *started* with a presumption of job security supplied by law, it might then be hard for employers to buy it away from them—because now the employers would be the ones with a small willingness to pay, and the employees would be the ones demanding a lot to relinquish their rights.[8] (It might occur to you that if things really do work this way, they seem a strange fit with the Coase theorem. That's right, and we'll talk about this point later in the chapter.)

The right way to handle problems like the ones just discussed might depend on where the discrepancy between willingness to pay and willingness to accept comes from; the possible reasons might have different legal implications. The trouble is that the source of the difference often isn't clear. Sometimes the reason might involve *wealth effects.* Once someone has an entitlement—once ownership of something has been assigned to them—they may in effect be wealthier as a result and unwilling to part with it for *x* dollars even if *x* dollars is more than they could have afforded to bid for it before it was theirs. Health care is probably like this for many people, and this is a common argument against leaving the provision of it to the market.[9] Its price is more than some people can afford; but if a right to health care were given to them, they wouldn't sell it for that same price. Environmental protection might be similar. If you ask someone how much they would pay for it, they worry about how much cash they could afford to spare for the purpose. If you ask them to assume they *have* the protection and to decide how much they would demand to give it up, they aren't constrained in the same way.

Another well-known explanation for the difference between willingness to pay and accept, and one that has wider application than wealth effects, is called the *endowment effect.* The idea is that things come to seem more valuable to people once they own them—once the things (for example, the coffee mugs) become part of their "endowment." But then where does the endowment effect come from? Sometimes it might involve fear of regret: once you own something, you might worry that after you give it up you will kick yourself. Of course you might suppose the opposite would be equally true; you might just as well kick yourself for failing to sell it when you had the chance, or for not buying the thing in the first place. But psychologists have studied regret in some detail, and it seems not to work so symmetrically. People feel worse about acts that turn out badly than they do about *failures* to act that turn out badly, even if the act and the failure to act seem logically indistinguishable—for example, deciding to sell a stock or deciding not to sell it.[10] Perhaps this is some small part of the reason why the common law generally does not hold people liable for failing to do simple things that would help others, such as throwing a rope to someone who is drowning. Rationally or not, omissions just don't seem as culpable as acts. (The cognitive effect is reversed in interesting ways in the long run; people looking back on their lives seem to regret things not done more than things done.)[11] And the anticipation of regret tends to be a bigger influence on decisions than the anticipation of a similar chance for delight.[12] Even putting regret to one side, people fear losses more than they relish gains, and so tend to cling to the status quo (a phenomenon known as *loss aversion*).[13]

Some of these points about regret are useful for lawyers to understand when they counsel clients; in that role it helps to understand both what economic rationality looks like and how the attitudes of real people sometimes differ from it. The points just explained have been used to suggest, for example, that the terms initially offered in a contract—the default language—end up being harder to change than one might have expected. The parties are prone to worry that a change in the terms might lead to a bad outcome, and this seems scarier than the thought that a failure to change them would lead to a bad outcome—and it isn't offset by the thought that changing the terms might lead to a *better* outcome.[14]

Let's return to our earlier question about which is the right baseline for measuring value. If regret theory and loss aversion account for the differences between what people are ready to pay for rights and what they would be willing to sell them for—if, in other words, people demand higher prices for things they own because they worry they will be mad at themselves later if they sell them—then maybe it is best after all to give rights to whoever will bid the most for them. That way the fear of regret never comes into existence, because the person who would feel that way never gets the rights in the first place. They don't feel regret, fear of regret, or anything else, so there is no value lost.[15]

But fear of regret is just one way to account for the discrepancies we are considering, and for the endowment effect in particular. Sometimes the endowment effect may arise from the option value people put on things once they own them—on the knowledge that they can decide later whether to sell, after they have more and better information.[16] Or maybe the endowment effect has some deep genetic root; maybe people who were more reluctant to give up things once they were in hand did better in the evolutionary derby than those who were not so reluctant.[17] Or perhaps it has to do with shame: social norms leave people feeling guilty if they say they would sell environmental quality for some modest price, but not if they decline to pay the same price to preserve it; selling things makes people feel more responsible for the results than merely declining to buy them.[18] If social norms are the problem, then we should talk about what standing those norms ought to have in the legal system. What the outcome of that conversation would be is hard to predict, but the point for us is, again, just that the best response to the endowment effect might depend on the reasons for it—and there are several candidates, some of which have clearer implications than others.

Discrepancies between the amounts one is willing to pay and accept for something also can create problems for the Coase theorem. As explained in chapter 8, the general idea of the theorem is that no matter where the law assigns a right, it will end up in the same hands—the hands of whoever is ready to pay the most for it—so long as transaction costs (impediments to bargaining) don't get in the way. But endowment and wealth effects suggest otherwise (unless *they* are considered transaction costs, but usually they aren't). Sometimes rights may stay wherever the law first puts them, simply because their owner will value them more than others do—though the others would have valued the rights more if they had been made a present of them. In chapter 8 we saw an example of a result that is hard to square with the Coase theorem: parties to nuisance cases didn't bargain after judgment to see whether the loser might have liked to buy the rights away from the winner. There are various ways to think about that result, but one is that the endowment effect applies to *judgments:* once you have won something in court, you are likely to demand more for it than you would have been prepared to bid if you had lost.[19]

If you start looking for examples of these apparently counter-Coasean results you will find them often, though sometimes their workings are hard to understand precisely. I live in Boston, where tickets to Red Sox baseball games are popular and scarce; the whole season's supply gets bought up a few days after the tickets go on sale. The Coase theorem might suggest that Fenway Park will be filled every day with the fans willing to pay the most for tickets: they will buy the tickets at the sale window, or they will buy the tickets away from whoever beat them there. But that isn't quite how it works. Many people are happy to go to a game if they are able to buy tickets the day they go on sale, but they are uninterested in buying tickets from scalpers; they say, for example, that good tickets might be worth $100 (their face value), but certainly not the $500 one might have to pay on the open market.

Notice what a strange state of affairs this might seem to be from an economic standpoint. If you *really* value your ticket at $100, and it would change hands on the open market for $500, then why would you go to the game? Why not instead sell your ticket? Equivalently, if you think a ticket "isn't worth" spending $500 to buy, how can it be worth using the ticket when someone would be willing to pay you $500 for it? (Well, in effect you're turning down only $400, because you had to spend $100 to get the ticket in the first place, but set that point aside.) One point of Coase's famous article is that these situations are economically identical: if you go to a Red Sox game, then in effect you *are* paying roughly the same high price for your ticket that the scalpers charge (because you forgo that payment in order to attend), even if you don't think about it that way because you bought your ticket at the box office. This also means that if you don't manage to get tickets at the box office, you should be about as ready to buy them at a scalper's price. In effect that's what you were going to do anyway.

Now of course some people do operate in the way just described—buying tickets and then reselling them, or buying them from scalpers—but many don't. The interesting question is why not. The reasons might involve the endowment effect. Or they might involve the ethical distaste some people have for dealing with scalpers, which is reinforced by legal warnings or warnings from some sellers of tickets, including the Red Sox, not to resell the tickets for more than their face value. No doubt some people are affected by these concerns, but, again, others aren't. Some people wouldn't want to spend $500 on a ticket from a scalper (it sounds too expensive), but wouldn't mind selling a ticket for that price themselves if they ended up unable to attend the game.

A different and important explanation for this pattern involves the distinction between out-of-pocket costs and opportunity costs. The out-of-pocket cost of a decision is the amount it actually causes you to spend. The opportunity cost is the value of the best alternative you passed up by making the decision you did. Every decision to use resources has costs of both kinds, and it is important to perceive them—especially for lawyers, since sometimes opportunity costs are overlooked by their clients. Thus law school is even more expensive than it sounds; for in addition to the out-of-pocket costs (tuition, books, and so forth) you also have to remember the opportunity cost: the money you could have made, but didn't, if you had been working full-time instead of attending school.

To economists these two kinds of costs count the same, but ordinary people do not seem to experience them that way.[20] In the example of the baseball ticket, the out-of-pocket cost of the ticket is obvious: it's the price paid for it at the box office. But the opportunity cost of attending the game includes the price that a scalper would have been willing to pay you for the ticket; that is why, on an economic view, everyone who attends the game *did* pay a scalper's price to be there. They paid it in opportunity cost. But they don't feel like they paid it. It's easy to think of other examples. Richard Thaler suggests these two plausible scenarios:

> Mr. R bought a case of good wine in the late 50s for about $5 a bottle. A few years later his wine merchant offered to buy the wine back for $100 a bottle. He refused, although he has never paid more than $35 for a bottle of wine.

> Mr. H mows his own law. His neighbor's son would mow it for $8. He wouldn't mow his neighbor's same-sized lawn for $20.[21]

In both of these cases, as in the case of the baseball ticket, you can think of various reasons why the people involved treat opportunity costs differently than out-of-pocket costs. It might involve the endowment effect. It might involve social norms about scalping tickets or mowing lawns,[22] and in the case of scalping the social norms might also have legal backing. Maybe these sorts of discrepancies can be expected to go away if the stakes are higher or if the parties involved are corporations. Maybe they can't. These sorts of questions are worth patient study. Lawyers spend a lot of time helping their clients think about gains and losses, so good lawyers also are keen students of the psychology of value.

To circle back now to law and the Coase theorem, notice that whatever the reason why people treat opportunity costs and out-of-pocket costs differently, the discrepancy will tend to confound some of Coase's suggestions. If I spew pollution onto someone else's land, it looks as though I'm just foisting costs onto them without feeling the harm myself. But one of Coase's points was that if transaction costs are low, then I *will* feel the cost of the pollution because I'll be passing up payments that my neighbors would offer me to stop. This is just like paying out of pocket to pollute, isn't it? Well, probably not. It's different partly because of norms or attitudes or practical difficulties that make people reluctant to pay each other to do things or not to do them. But it's also different because people don't feel the same way about opportunity costs and out-of-pocket costs. You can argue about whether these feelings ought to be considered kinds of transaction costs, or market failures; if that's how you regard them, then maybe Coase was right after all (for remember that his predictions all involve what would happen if transaction costs were zero). But whatever the answer to that question, the practical point is to be cautious about imagining that voluntary payments will produce the same results no matter what the law says—even when bargaining looks easy as a practical matter. Sometimes entitlements are sticky.

SUGGESTIONS FOR FURTHER READING. Russell Korobkin, *The Endowment Effect and Legal Analysis,* 97 Nw. U. L. Rev. 1227 (2003); Elizabeth Hoffman and Matthew Spitzer, *Willingness to Pay vs. Willingness to Accept: Legal and Economic Implications,* 71 Wash. U. L.Q. 59 (1993); Herbert Hovenkamp, *Legal Policy and the Endowment Effect,* 20 J. Legal Stud. 225 (1991); Duncan Kennedy, *Cost-Benefit Analysis of Entitlement Programs:*

A Critique, 33 Stan. L. Rev. 387 (1981); Mark Kelman, *Consumption Theory, Production Theory, and Ideology in the Coase Theorem,* 52 S. Cal. L. Rev. 669 (1979); Daniel Kahneman, Jack L. Knetsch, and Richard H. Thaler, *The Endowment Effect, Loss Aversion, and Status Quo Bias,* 5 J. Econ. Persp. 193 (1991); Richard H. Thaler, Quasi Rational Economics (1991).

23 ➛ Hindsight Bias

Once something happens, people tend to think it was more likely to occur, and easier to foresee, than it really was. This is known as *hindsight bias.* A famous demonstration of it was provided by a study in which researchers told their subjects about a nineteenth-century battle between the British and the Gurkhas of Nepal.[23] The circumstances of the battle were described, and the subjects then were asked to estimate the probabilities of various outcomes—victory for the British, victory for the Gurkhas, or some sort of stalemate. Then other groups were given the same information, but they were also told which one of those outcomes *did* occur. They again were asked to estimate the likelihood in advance of each possible result. The subjects who were told the result of the battle tended to rate the actual result as much more likely than those who weren't told anything about it; thus people who were told that the British won the battle tended to say that the British were likely to win all along. The probability that something would happen should be the same regardless of whether it happened in fact, but humans have trouble keeping the issues separate. The problem isn't confined to judgments about obscure historical events. The bias has been documented extensively in decisions of all sorts. The precise reasons are a matter of dispute, but may involve "creeping determinism": once the outcome is known, the mind begins to focus on all the reasons that contributed to it and to deemphasize the factors that would have seemed salient if the result had been otherwise; the mind searches for a satisfying story to account for the ending. Once it is found, it makes the ending seem inevitable.[24]

Hindsight bias has many applications to decisions in the real world. Here is an example from medical practice: researchers gave doctors information about some patients along with five ways the patients might be diagnosed. The doctors all were told to rank the five possible diagnoses in order of their likely accuracy; but half of the doctors also were told which diagnosis had turned out to be correct. They still were instructed to say what the right rankings would have been ex ante—in other words, before knowing which diagnosis turned out to be correct. Their judgments were strongly infected by hindsight bias. Half of the doctors who were told which diagnosis was correct also said that it would have been the most likely diagnosis beforehand; but only 30 percent of the doctors ranked it as most likely when they didn't know which would turn out to be right.[25]

Hindsight bias is important in law because the legal system spends a lot of time scrutinizing decisions and the foresight that people show in making them. Many accident cases are like this. Usually the plaintiff says that the defendant failed to take some precaution that a reasonable person would have used. But whether a reasonable person would have taken the precaution often will depend on how likely the accident was to occur—or more precisely how likely it would have appeared in advance to that same reasonable person. The problem is that the jury is asked to make judgments about that question after already knowing that the accident *did* occur. Hindsight bias will make it harder than it ought to be for the jurors to conclude that the accident was too unlikely to warrant precautions against it.

The problem is especially acute if you take an economic view of tort law—a view along the lines explained in the early chapters of this book. The idea there was that some accidents are worth preventing but others aren't, because the expense of stopping them is greater than the expense of letting them happen. The Hand formula, discussed in chapter 4, can be used to put that idea into practice: you compare "B" (the burden, or expense, of the precaution the defendant didn't take) with the expected cost of the accident: its probability multiplied by its cost. Everyone understands that you can't put precise numbers on these things, but Hand's way of thinking still has many adherents as a general picture of how courts should think about accident cases. The implication of hindsight bias, though, is that courts systematically will exaggerate "P"—the likelihood that an accident will occur—because they always will be asking the question while knowing that the accident did happen in the case at hand. So defendants will lose too often, and sometimes they may even be held to a kind of strict liability for damage they cause despite the legal system's claim that it holds them liable only if they were negligent.[26] The extent of this pattern is not settled, but there is some experimental evidence suggesting that jurors and judges do indeed display significant hindsight bias when they lay blame for accidents.[27]

Here is another legal example; it bears a bit of resemblance to the medical study described a moment ago, and shows how it might carry over to the courtroom. The *Tarasoff* decision, which all first-year law students encounter in their course on tort law, holds that if a psychiatrist has reasonable grounds to think a patient threatens violence to someone, the psychiatrist has to give the victim a warning. If no such warning is made, the psychiatrist can be held liable if the victim gets attacked.[28] Lawsuits under *Tarasoff* call on juries to decide whether an attack should have seemed likely to a defendant therapist, but the jury decides this after knowing that the attack occurred. A controlled study of such a pattern was conducted with mock jurors. They all read case studies involving psychiatric patients who were potentially violent. Some were told nothing more; others were told which patients actually became violent. The result was analogous to the one found in the medical study: the subjects in the second group were more likely to say that the violent outcome was foreseeable before it happened.[29] The point is clear and by now familiar. Once you know about an outcome, it's hard to accurately imagine how likely or foreseeable it was before it happened.

These tendencies are exacerbated by the related but separate problem of *outcome bias:* people tend to condemn decisions that turn out badly. A companion study to the one just mentioned asked subjects to evaluate whether a therapist had done enough to stop a violent patient by calling the police or taking other measures, or whether she should have done more. The subjects were more likely to condemn the therapist's decision after being told that the patient had, in fact, gone on to commit a violent act. And it appears that the more severe the injury involved, the more tempting it is to find fault in decisions that failed to prevent it—even if the decisions seemed correct to people before knowing what outcome they would produce.[30]

You might imagine various reasons not to worry much about hindsight and outcome biases, but most of the natural candidates for consolation end up being of questionable help. You might suppose, for example, that judges could police the problem if juries seemed too affected by it, but the evidence on whether judges can avoid the problem is mixed and controversial.[31] Nor is it clear whether warning people about these biases helps. Most studies suggest not,[32] but some research with mock jurors has suggested that they do respond to exhortations not to play the role of "Monday-morning quarterback."[33] Other research has found helpful effects when subjects who know about the bad results of a decision are asked explicitly to also think about better outcomes the decision might have produced and estimate the likelihoods that they might have occurred. The estimates might be wrong, as we have seen, but the exercise of producing them nevertheless caused the subjects to then rate the initial decision more favorably.[34] This is something to think about when you are presented with the rhetorical challenge of defending a decision that turned out badly. Taking the time to imagine and estimate the chance of better outcomes the decision might have had seems to put people in a more generous frame of mind.

Another natural response to these biases is to look for objective ways to find out whether a decision seemed sound at the time it was made, rather than asking courts to figure that out from scratch. Sometimes evidence of custom can serve that purpose: if the defendant did what most other people were doing in the same situation, perhaps that was reasonably thought to be enough at the time, however bad it may look in hindsight. But courts usually don't treat compliance with custom as a good defense. They worry that the customary precautions, instead of being solid evidence of how likely the accident seemed in advance, might just be an instance of a whole industry shirking its duties, with each member then benefiting from the negligence of the others.[35] This might not be a problem if all the defendants were businesses and all their victims were customers with whom they had contracts; for then we might expect the customers to pay the firms to take the extra precautions, and the precautions used in the end to reflect what everyone really did think was appropriate at the time.[36] But a lot of accident cases aren't like that.

One area where courts do defer to custom, however, is medical malpractice. In that sort of case it is a complete defense for the defendant to say he did all that was customary in the profession. (The same usually goes for legal malpractice.) The reason given most often for the rule is that medical decisions are too complicated for jurors to evaluate for themselves; they need some benchmark to rely on, such as medical custom, that doesn't call on them to make freestanding judgments about what a good doctor would have done. But notice that using custom to set the standard of care also does a bit to help curb hindsight bias. If the doctor did what was customary, he wins; the jurors aren't asked how likely the accident was to occur, so the bias isn't given as much room to operate.[37] But it still can come out in other parts of a medical case—in decisions about causation or anyplace else where the law takes an interest in the problem of foreseeability.

There have been various other suggestions about how the law might cope with hindsight bias. Some have suggested that trials in tort cases be bifurcated more routinely (it already is done sometimes), with the question of liability tried separately from the question of the plaintiff's damages; for hearing about the damages might make jurors more likely to think the accident was foreseeable and the result of negligence.[38] A more exotic proposal is that jurors be asked to assess the choices the defendant might have made before knowing what choice the defendant *did* make.[39] Still others have suggested that the role of the courts, and the ex post perspective they naturally take, be decreased outright in favor of legal bodies that take an ex ante view: regulatory agencies that say in advance what decisions about safety are best—and then preempt any litigation afterwards.[40] And some more modest features of the law in this area can be viewed as efforts to keep self-serving bias at bay, such as the rule of evidence saying that if a product causes an accident and the defendant later improves it, the improvement can't be offered as evidence that there must have been something wrong with the product in the first place.[41]

The problems of hindsight bias, though probably most serious in tort law, pop up elsewhere, too. One can't get a patent for inventing something obvious; but once an invention is made, hindsight bias might create the impression that anyone could have done it. The problem is especially bad because of the time lag involved between the invention of something and a court's decision about whether it was obvious to a "person having ordinary skill in the art"—the PHOSITA, as he is called; the court might make its decision twenty years after the invention was made, and by then there will have been so many advances in the field that in retrospect the invention looks as though it must not have been very hard to create.[42] So courts don't make judgments of obviousness on the fly. They discipline the process by asking subsidiary questions—accounting for "secondary considerations," as they are called—such as whether the invention, however obvious it might seem in retrospect, had commercial success or met a need "long felt but unsolved"; and they impose stiff requirements on the challenger of the patent who tries to put forward evidence of "prior art" that anticipated the new invention.[43]

A final good example comes up in the field of civil procedure, when one party seeks sanctions against another under Federal Rule 11 or similar state provisions. As we saw in chapter 6, these rules penalize lawyers who file papers with the court that lack solid factual or legal support. The hindsight hazard arises when a lawyer files a motion of some sort that gets denied. Once the court has turned the motion down, hindsight bias can cause the outcome to seem more likely in advance than it was; and if it comes to seem *too* likely, the lawyer ends up paying a penalty for wasting everyone's time with a motion that was "doomed" to fail. But the revisions to Rule 11 made in 1993 largely solved this problem. The rule now says that after Rule 11 sanctions are sought, the filer of the paper that is the subject of the complaint has twenty-one days to withdraw or modify it—a safe harbor, as it is called. As a practical matter this means that a Rule 11 complaint generally has to be filed *before* a judge makes a decision on the merits of the motion at which the complaint is directed; so the decision about whether the motion had plausible support doesn't get infected by a decision already made about whether the motion turned out to be a loser.[44] This wasn't the primary reason for adding the safe harbor period, but it's a pleasant side effect.

SUGGESTIONS FOR FURTHER READING. Baruch Fischhoff, *Hindsight [not=] Foresight: The Effect of Outcome Knowledge on Judgment under Uncertainty,* 1 J. Experimental Psychol. 288 (1975); Jeffrey J. Rachlinski, *A Positive Psychological Theory of Judging in Hindsight,* 65 U. Chi. L. Rev. 571 (1998); Kim A. Kamin and Jeffrey J. Rachlinski, *Ex Post [not=] Ex Ante: Determining Liability in Hindsight,* 19 Law & Hum. Behav. 89 (1995); Chris Guthrie, Jeffrey J. Rachlinski, and Andrew J. Wistrich, *Inside the Judicial Mind,* 86 Cornell L. Rev. 777, 799–805 (2001); Reid Hastie and W. Kip Viscusi, *What Juries Can't Do Well: The Jury's Performance as a Risk Manager,* 40 Ariz. L. Rev. 901 (1998); Richard Lempert, *Juries, Hindsight, and Punitive Damage Awards: Failures of a Social Science Case for Change,* 48 DePaul L. Rev. 867 (1999); Philip G. Peters Jr., *Hindsight Bias and Tort Liability: Avoiding Premature Conclusions,* 31 Ariz. St. L.J. 1277 (1999).

24 ➛ Framing Effects

Sometimes decisions are affected by the way they are framed: how the alternatives are described, or in what order they are arranged. The simplest example is sometimes known as the *compromise effect*—the attraction people feel to a middle option, even if its "middleness" is the result of arbitrarily surrounding it with other choices. In the classic experiment the subjects were instructed to choose cameras from a catalogue. If they were given two choices—a midlevel model and a low-end one—they divided about evenly between them. But the subjects who were given a third choice—a high-end model—showed quite different tendencies. Of course some preferred the fancy camera, but the interesting result was that they tended to abandon the low-end version: of those picking between the middle and low model, 72 percent picked the middle choice. The addition of the new option at the top dragged people from the bottom to the middle.[45] *Contrast effects* are similar. An option is less appealing alone than when set against another option that is clearly inferior. This time the best-known experiment involved offering subjects a choice between a fancy pen and a payment of six dollars. Most of them took the money. But when a third choice was added—a *lousy* pen—significantly more subjects chose the fancy pen rather than the cash. It evidently looked more impressive sitting next to a lesser specimen of the same kind.[46]

The value of understanding these points for advertising executives and consumers is obvious. Their significance for lawyers also is large, and is illuminated in a fine set of studies showing how the same questions of context can affect the negotiations to settle a lawsuit. The subjects in one of the experiments were given a mock case to try to settle; they were told to assume they were representing a plaintiff with a nuisance complaint against a noisy nightclub next to his house. The subjects were to pick between settlement offers from the nightclub, two of which were initially put on the table: (a) an offer to reduce the nightclub's noise and (b) an offer to compensate the plaintiff with cash and a stay in a nice hotel on weekends. The subjects divided about evenly between these. Then to another group a third proposal was offered: less cash, but some vouchers that could be used at other nightclubs. This offer was designed to seem plainly inferior to the cash-plus-hotel offered in (b), which it somewhat resembled, but not plainly inferior to the offer to reduce the noise caused by the nightclub. The result was what you might now expect: the number of people choosing (b) went from 47 percent to 74 percent. The cash-plus-hotel, like the fancy pen discussed earlier, looked more impressive when put alongside an inferior option of the same kind.[47]

These points can also arise in court, as when a judge in a criminal case gives the jury various options to consider. This time the construction of the best study was a little different. The subjects were told to serve as mock jurors and to pick a prison sentence for a man who shot a security guard to death in a dispute at a shopping mall. All of the jurors were given three options to choose from, but the details differed. The first group chose between involuntary manslaughter, voluntary manslaughter, and murder, with each sentence more severe than the last. The second group's choices were voluntary manslaughter, murder, and "special circumstances" murder, again in order of severity; this was a stiffer set of punishments than the first batch. The jurors in the second group were considerably more likely than those in the first to convict the defendant of murder. For the second group of jurors, murder was the "middle" option, and it drew votes away from the voluntary manslaughter choice; in the first group, voluntary manslaughter was the middle option, and it was more likely to draw support.[48]

In a sense these results just confirm what lawyers in criminal cases generally understand already: juries sometimes are attracted to compromise verdicts. But as the authors of these studies point out, they also suggest the possibility of unexpected or perverse consequences when more choices are added to the menu of punishments. If a legislature decides to allow capital punishment for certain crimes, for example, it may also increase the likelihood of convictions for noncapital murder, which will appear to be a compromise position in some cases where it previously had been the most extreme option.[49] This possibility also is a lesson to those who style themselves "moderates" in decisions of all kinds. The look of moderation in a choice often is comforting, but it tends to be an artifact of the other options that are set around it—which in turn may be arbitrary and easily manipulated.

Now let's think about some subtler framing effects. Preferences for risk and certainty tend to change depending on whether the outcome involved is good or bad. The first thing to understand is that, as noted a couple of chapters ago, most people are loss averse: their displeasure at losing a sum of money is a lot greater than their pleasure at gaining a comparable amount.[50] (So they are likely to feel that concessions they make in bargaining are more impressive than similar concessions the other side makes.)[51] The next important point is that when considering various good outcomes, people are more likely to grab a sure thing than take risks in hopes of doing even better; but when thinking about bad outcomes, they usually are more inclined to gamble and risk a worse outcome than to take the sure thing. Thus in the simplest experiments, people were offered a choice between $240 and a 25 percent chance of winning $1,000; 84 percent of them took the sure thing. But when given a choice between a loss of $750 and a 75 percent chance of losing $1,000 (with a 25 percent of losing nothing), 87 percent of them preferred to gamble.[52] In either situation the two choices are the same from an economic standpoint (in the first one the gamble actually is a little better), but people evidently are much more "risk averse" when it comes to gains than they are when it comes to losses. Interestingly enough, however, these preferences change when the odds of the outcomes are remote. Most people would rather pay $5 than take a gamble on a 5 percent chance of paying a $1,000 fine; but they would give up a promise of $5 in favor of a 5 percent chance of a $1,000 prize.[53]

All these results are from the corner of psychological research known as *prospect theory*, which studies how people react differently to gains and losses. What does it have to do with law? Think again of settlement negotiations. We saw that a party's judgments may be affected by the way the choices are arranged, but they also may be affected by whether the party experiences the outcome as a gain or a loss. Prospect theory suggests that settling a case out of court will tend to seem more attractive to a plaintiff than to a defendant. For a plaintiff, a settlement means a sure gain rather than a gamble on a lawsuit that may or may not produce an even better result. But for a defendant a settlement is the opposite: the acceptance of a certain loss rather than a gamble.[54] Studies of behavior in settlement talks are consistent with these speculations. In one of them the subjects were assigned roles of plaintiff and defendant in a copyright dispute. Each was given a choice between a settlement and going to trial, and the numbers were arranged to make the two options economically the same: the settlement would involve a payment of $200,000; going to trial would mean a 50 percent chance of the plaintiff winning $400,000, and a 50 percent chance of winning nothing. Most of the mock plaintiffs found the settlement offer more attractive than the trial. Most of the mock defendants found the trial more attractive than the settlement.[55] In other words, the defendants were more interested in taking chances with their losses than the plaintiffs were in taking chances with their gains. These results show why cases sometimes take a lot of trouble to settle, or don't settle at all.

Jeffrey Rachlinski, the leading legal scholar in this area, argues that the results just considered should make Americans reluctant to adopt the English rule on attorney's fees—the rule that the loser pays the fees of the winner's attorney, rather than each side bearing its own costs; the latter is the usual approach in the United States. Prospect theory suggests that the English rule would make cases harder to settle because it would raise the stakes of losing and make it riskier to go to court. That would make going to court more attractive to defendants; the greater the loss they face (not only paying a judgment to the other side but paying its fees as well), the more inclined they will be to gamble rather than accept a sure (bad) thing. But it will make going to court less appealing to plaintiffs: the settlement is a sure thing, which comes to seem more attractive as the risk of going to court gets larger. Since they have different reactions to the increased risk, the parties will be less likely to settle outside of court and more likely to litigate, which is expensive for everyone. This claim may not be right (the data are inconclusive),[56] and even if it is right there are other considerations that might still make a "loser pays" rule attractive. But it's an interesting argument.

We have been speaking as if it were obvious who gains and who loses from a settlement. Notice, though, that sometimes a result can be viewed as a gain *or* as a loss; it depends what point of reference one chooses for comparison. The choice is important, for sometimes just describing a result one way or the other can have a great effect on how appealing it seems. This is a place where a lawyer can make a significant difference: in helping a defendant to view a settlement offer in ways that get away from the "loss frame" and thus make it seem more attractive; for if the defendant views settling as losing, prospect theory suggests that he will feel some cognitive inclination to take his chances instead.[57] But paying to settle a case might seem like a gain after all when it is compared to the defendant's worst-case scenario rather than to his best hopes, or when all the costs of going to court are taken into account. This isn't to suggest that settlement is always a good thing that necessarily should be encouraged. The point is simply to recognize the role a lawyer can play in encouraging a client to look at a settlement (or anything else) in ways that don't come naturally—for example, in ways that make gains seem more like losses or vice versa, and that therefore trigger different attitudes toward the risks involved. How best to do that—how to do it in a way that best serves the client's own real interests—is a deep question that is hard to answer in a general way. It depends on a broad view of what those interests are, and they won't be the same for everyone. Sometimes part of a good lawyer's job is simply to help clients realize what role frames are playing in their thinking and to offer alternatives.

It may be possible for a trial judge to likewise lend a hand in getting the parties to look at their positions differently, but then again maybe not. In a similar study where trial judges were invited to make recommendations to the parties in a mock case, they showed the same tendencies just described: they were more inclined to recommend that a plaintiff accept a settlement offer than to recommend that the defendant put forward the same one.[58] The moral of the story is that these reactions to gains and losses run deep. They even can affect the judgments of third-party observers who don't themselves have anything at stake. Sometimes lots of experience with such impulses may make them less powerful, as often is true of the effects we are considering in this chapter. But they aren't just the mental habits of the weak or untutored.

This business of framing an event as a gain or loss has applications beyond settlement negotiations, of course. And sometimes the framing is simply a matter of words—the "cash discount" that is more attractive to customers than a penalty for using a credit card, though they are the same thing; or, to take a legal example, the difference between a tax exemption for doing something or some sort of or penalty for not doing it: again these may be the same, yet they can provoke quite different reactions among taxpayers.[59] Or consider two ways of describing the risks and benefits of surgery for lung cancer: out of 100 patients who undergo the procedure, (a) "90 live through the postoperative period and 34 are alive at the end of five years," or (b) "10 die during the postoperative period and 66 die by the end of five years." They are the same in substance, but patients are far more likely to go forward with a procedure when it is described in the first way.[60]

This medical example has legal implications when a doctor is sued for failing to disclose all the risks of an operation to a patient. In those cases a big question is whether the patient would have gone ahead with the operation even if he had been fully informed; if so, he has no case, since the failure to inform him didn't make a difference. But the answer to the counterfactual might depend critically on how the risks would have been presented, or framed: as we just saw, patients often react differently to risks stated in terms of loss than they do to risks stated as gains. Alas, after the operation is over there is no telling how the doctor would have described the risks. This has caused some commentators to argue—as yet unsuccessfully—that the law should abandon the question of what the patient would have done if properly informed, since it can't be answered without knowing more than we can find out about how the information would have been framed. Instead patients in such cases should be awarded damages regardless of whether anyone thinks that more disclosure would have affected their decisions; they should get damages simply because their right to give informed consent was violated.[61]

SUGGESTIONS FOR FURTHER READING. Daniel Kahneman and Amos Tversky, *Choices, Values and Frames,* 39 Am. Psychol. 341 (1984); Mark Kelman, Yuval Rottenstreich, and Amos Tversky, *Context-Dependence in Legal Decision-Making,* 25 J. Legal Stud. 287 (1996); Jeffrey J. Rachlinski, *Gains, Losses and the Psychology of Litigation,* 70 S. Cal. L. Rev. 113 (1996); Chris Guthrie, *Framing Frivolous Litigation: A Psychological Theory,* 67 U. Chi. L. Rev. 163 (2000); Chris Guthrie, *Prospect Theory, Risk Preference, and the Law,* 97 Nw. U. L. Rev. 1115 (2003).

25 ⤐ Anchoring

People prefer not to make judgments from scratch; they find it more comfortable to take some point of reference—a suggestion about the answer from elsewhere—and then adjust it until it sounds right. This isn't so much a deliberate strategy as a psychological temptation, and it is hard to overcome. The practical result is that an initial suggestion about how a judgment might be made can have a large influence on how it *is* made, even if the suggestion is arbitrary or poor. These are the implications, at any rate, of the research into what is called *anchoring*: the ways that initial points of reference serve as anchors for thoughts that follow them. Half the subjects in an experiment were told that 50,000 people die in auto accidents each year; the other half were told that 1,000 people per year are killed by electrocution. All were then asked to estimate the annual deaths from various other causes. The subjects who started out thinking about the auto accidents tended to give higher estimates than the ones who started out thinking about electrocutions; they evidently used the 50,000 deaths per year in cars as some sort of benchmark to help them with their other guesses.[62]

We find the same effect even if the subjects aren't told anything but are merely invited to answer questions that make them think along certain lines. Thus two groups of subjects were asked to estimate the chance of a nuclear war between the United States and the Soviet Union. The ones in the first group were asked to say whether the chance was more or less than 1 percent; the ones in the second group were asked whether the chance was more or less than 90 percent. Then all the subjects were asked to give their own actual estimates. The average from the first subjects was about 25 percent; from the second subjects, about 10 percent.[63] And the effect can hold even if the original suggestion is obviously arbitrary. In another study the subjects were told to estimate the percentage of African countries participating in the United Nations. But first the subjects were told whether the correct answer was higher or lower than the number produced by a wheel spun randomly. If subjects were told the answer was greater than 10 percent, they tended to give answers of their own that averaged around 25 percent; if they initially were told the answer was less than 65 percent, their own answers averaged around 45 percent. Subjects in yet another test estimated the average price of textbooks in a student bookstore; their guesses were higher when they were first asked just to say whether the average price was "greater or less than $7,137.30." The number was so high as to be obviously preposterous, but it nevertheless increased the size of the ballpark in which the later guesses were made.

Anchors no doubt are less important when you have a firm sense of your own about a question, but law is full of situations where no such firm sense is available and where the effects of anchoring therefore can be dramatic. The most straightforward examples involve awards of damages for pain and suffering or loss of society—noneconomic headings, as they are called. As we shall see in more detail in chapter 31, it is hard to calculate these sorts of damages because there is no market where one can look for numbers to put on them. So jurors have to pick whatever numbers feel right, and an exercise so unguided naturally lends itself to reliance on anchors. Lawyers are happy to oblige by supplying suggestions. The simple truth evidently is that asking a jury for a lot of money tends to yield a lot of money—not as much as one asked for, but more than if one had suggested less.[64] The most vivid study was one in which mock jurors were shown a reenactment of a trial where the defendant was sued for causing the deaths of two children in an auto accident. Some jurors saw the plaintiff's lawyer request $2 million in damages; the other group saw the lawyer request $20 million. The jurors in the first group made average awards of just over $1 million, while the average award from the second set of jurors was just over $9 million.[65]

Eventually a point comes where increasing the size of a demand may hurt rather than help because the lawyer loses credibility; but even extreme demands seem to produce higher results than leaving jurors to their own devices, and the demands sometimes have strong effects despite the bad impressions they create of their makers.[66] Thus the study where two sets of mock jurors were told that the plaintiff got cancer from her birth-control pills. When the jurors were told that the plaintiff requested $1 billion in damages, they liked her less, but they still awarded her significantly more than other jurors who were told that the plaintiff demanded $5 million.[67] Of course it is a game at which two can play. A defendant's lawyer can propose a counteranchor in the form of a low suggestion of damages. When such a counteranchor is supported by testimony from an expert, it tends to drive jurors toward an award midway between the suggestions of both sides.[68] There is some evidence indicating that a plaintiff's demand tends to serve as a more powerful anchor than what the defendant suggests, but it still seems clear that defense lawyers make a mistake if they decline to suggest a specific alternative figure to the jury.[69]

The same potential for anchoring exists in settlement negotiations when each side throws out a figure that may serve an anchoring function even if it is sure to be rejected. And notice that here anchoring can run in both directions, signaling not only the high value one puts on one's own case but the low value one puts on the case of an adversary. Thus an early settlement offer can create an anchor that affects the reception of a later one; a $2,000 opening offer has been found to make a later offer of $12,000 seem more attractive than it does when the first offer is $10,000.[70] The low offer created an anchor—a low ballpark—that made the higher offer seem more generous. This is known in psychology as the "door in the face" technique. The initial suggestion is dismissed as ridiculous—its maker gets the door slammed in his face, as it were—but it turns out to make the slammer more receptive to a less extreme suggestion made soon thereafter.[71]

You might suppose that the subjects of these experiments are merely exposing a want of savvy, but similar effects have turned up when judges are tested. In one study judges were asked to say how much they would award a plaintiff in a personal injury case. But some of the judges were first asked to rule on a hypothetical motion to dismiss the case on the ground that less than $75,001 was in controversy, thus making the case ineligible to appear in federal court under the diversity jurisdiction. The motion to dismiss seemed frivolous, since the plaintiff in the case had lost the use of his legs; so it was no surprise that 98 percent of the judges rejected it. But the judges who saw the motion went on to (hypothetically) award the plaintiff 30 percent less, on average, than judges never confronted with the motion to dismiss—a jarring result.[72] The authors of the study hasten to say that they don't think it implies lawyers should file frivolous motions, since they may be subject to sanctions if they do and since in real cases any decision on damages will come long after the motion to dismiss is decided; the time lag probably would reduce the anchoring effect. We can hope so.

The effects of anchoring seem to go beyond the use of suggestions to drive damage awards up or down. Anchors in one sort of calculation can affect the making of others. Consider again the problem of awarding damages for loss of society or consortium—the lost pleasures of having the victim around, as in a case where the plaintiff's spouse was killed by the defendant's act of negligence. Let us compare two cases. In one, the jury awarded a surviving wife $5 million for the loss of her husband's society; in the other, the jury awarded the surviving wife less than $400,000. What could account for such a massive discrepancy? Had the companionship of the one husband been ten times better than the other? Probably not; it was probably an instance of anchoring. The first case involved the death of an oil executive in an airline disaster;[73] the second involved the death of a carpenter as a result of medical malpractice.[74] The oil executive's wife won $9 million in damages to compensate for her husband's immense lost wages. The carpenter was unemployed much of the time, so his wife's award for his lost earnings was less than $400,000. In principle those awards for lost earnings should have nothing to do with the size of the awards that juries make for loss of society, which are formally separate and ought to be conceptually separate as well. If anything, one might suppose that the more time the spouse spent making money, the less he was contributing to the household in the other, nonpecuniary ways that an award for loss of society is supposed to reflect.

It seems obvious in these cases that the jurors were at sea with the task of putting a dollar value on lost companionship, so they groped around for a frame of reference—an anchor—and fastened onto the salaries of the husbands. The numbers used in one part of the case influenced the thinking in other parts. There is impressive evidence that jurors do the same thing when they calculate punitive damages. In principle, the compensatory damages and any punitive damages sought by a plaintiff are supposed to be separate items. Compensatory damages are meant only to restore the plaintiff to the position he had before the tort was committed; the badness of the defendant's conduct is irrelevant to the calculation of them. Punitive damages are the opposite: they're meant only to punish the defendant; the size of the plaintiff's compensatory damages is generally not relevant to them. But the research suggests that jurors do let the size of the *compensatory* award they make influence their judgments about the correct amount to award as a *punitive* matter.[75] There have even been some experiments suggesting that a large request for damages can influence the jury's inclination to find the defendant liable at all: yet another disquieting possibility.[76]

We have seen that anchoring can occur even when the anchor is known to be arbitrary. We can go farther: like most of the behaviors discussed in this part of the book, anchoring is hard to avoid even if one tries. Here the best study again involved judges.[77] They were told to make damage awards to the plaintiff in a mock civil suit. But beforehand they also were told about settlement demands the plaintiff had made during a conference in the judge's chambers. As can be expected by now, the judges were divided into two groups. Some were told the plaintiff had made a low settlement demand ($175,000); some were told the demand was high ($10 million). The judges in the second group went on to award the plaintiff, on average, about twice as much as the judges who heard about the lower settlement demand. So far this won't seem surprising; it might not even seem objectionable, since the size of the settlement demands might have sent useful signals about how serious the plaintiff considered his own injury to be (not all anchoring is irrational). But the kicker of the study was that the judges were explicitly told not to let the settlement offers influence their decision about how much money to award; they were told that taking settlement offers into account was forbidden by a federal rule of evidence (as, in fact, it is).[78] The result is something unpleasant to consider next time you hear a jury told to ignore a piece of testimony it has heard.

All these findings about anchoring have naturally provoked ideas about how the legal system might constructively respond. Some have suggested that the role of juries in awarding damages, and especially their role in awarding punitive damages, be reduced or eliminated; for while judges are vulnerable to the same biases, perhaps their resistance is at least somewhat stronger.[79] Others have proposed giving juries guidelines for making damage awards—a schedule of the allowed range, or information about what plaintiffs in similar suits have received, perhaps in hopes of displacing anchors supplied by lawyers with information that has a less arbitrary or strategic origin. But the work on anchoring also has less expected implications. It suggests that reforming damage awards by capping them at some maximum can have perverse consequences, since the cap itself may serve as an anchor that drives up awards; experimental work suggests that jurors unsure about how much to award sometimes fasten onto a cap as a natural answer—though the exact effects may depend on the size of the cap.[80] Likewise, the plaintiff may use the cap as an anchor in deciding how high an award to expect from a jury, and thus become less likely to settle.[81] The same reasoning has led another commentator to suggest that the liability limits in insurance policies may have the inadvertent effect of driving up the size of the settlements that insurance adjusters make when trying to compromise lawsuits against their clients. It is easy to grasp for the anchor and suggest a settlement for whatever the policy limits may be.[82]

So far we have spoken only of the effect of anchoring on judgments about numbers, but anchoring can occur in other ways, too. It has been suggested, for example, that anchoring occurs when parties write contracts.[83] If contract terms become "standard," the parties can, of course, nevertheless change them to almost anything else. But the standard term may well serve as an anchor that colors either side's sense of what is reasonable, and so cause any negotiations over the contract to produce a quite different result than would be expected if the term hadn't existed at all. The point applies to all sorts of drafting. Control over the first draft of any document—an agenda, a brief, an article, a judicial opinion—usually means great influence over the final version, because subsequent contributors will treat the initial draft as a point of reference; they will spend their time adjusting it, rather than thinking and writing from scratch, and even if the adjustments are massive, the influence of the anchor is still likely to leave a signature.

Finally, consider two different ways law gets made in the United States. Sometimes it is made by courts; they decide one case at a time, working out rules to govern each situation as it arises. The result is called common law. But of course law also is made by legislatures when they pass statutes. The statutes amount to rules that say in advance how a class of problems will be handled when they arise. Into this second category we can also put decisions by agencies or other bodies that amount to general proclamations in advance rather than case-specific decisions made after a conflict arises. Which way of making law is better? Naturally it depends on the problem involved; each has its advantages. But the question relevant to this chapter, and to this part of the book, is which method of making law is more vulnerable to anchoring, framing effects, and other cognitive habits that can distort judgments.

Fred Schauer has critiqued lawmaking by courts on precisely these grounds.[84] A famous strain of thought in American law celebrates the common law because it calls for each decision to be made by a court in a rich factual context; the judge sees the situation in detail before pronouncing on it and so gains a kind of intimate familiarity with the problem it involves that a legislature can't obtain when it debates a question in more abstract terms. Thus Holmes's claim: "It is the merit of the common law that it decides the case first and determines the principle afterward."[85] But such close encounters with the facts of a particular case might also make judges prey to cognitive distortions. The problem is that when a court decides the case at hand, it makes a rule that will also affect other cases—cases that involve the same general question but have different facts. Therein lies the danger. The facts of the case at hand might not be typical, but seeing them up close might cause a judge to treat them as a kind of anchor; estimates about the probabilities involved in the general problem may be influenced too heavily by striking features of the facts in the immediate case, which might serve as a point of departure for larger judgments. Other cognitive quirks, such as framing effects (discussed in the previous chapter) and the availability heuristic (mentioned in the next chapter), might influence judicial lawmaking in similar ways. A judge may be tempted, for example, to overestimate how well the facts of the case at hand represent the facts of a whole class of situations.

Against most of these claims there are plausible counterarguments. Legislation can be subject to cognitive distortions, too, as when a prominent disaster causes a rush to pass laws in response. And decisions by courts are smaller in scale than decisions by legislatures; cognitive glitches by one judge can be corrected by other judges later as they collectively work their way toward general rules, whereas a piece of legislation tends to be written once with fewer chances for adjustment later to correct for overestimations and the like.[86] These trade-offs are too complex to be resolved here. The point for now is just to see them—to notice the cognitive side of the choice between lawmaking by courts and by legislatures. For detailed discussion of the issue, and examples of judicial decisions where some of the tendencies discussed here may have been at work, have a look at Professor Schauer's article and the replies to it, references to which appear below.

SUGGESTIONS FOR FURTHER READING. Amos Tversky and Daniel Kahneman, *Judgment under Uncertainty: Heuristics and Biases,* 185 Sci. 1124 (1974); Cass R. Sunstein et al., Punitive Damages: How Jurors Decide (2002); Neil Vidmar, *Experimental Simulations and Tort Reform: Avoidance, Error, and Overreaching in Sunstein et al.'s* Punitive Damages, 53 Emory L.J. 1359 (2004); Andrew J. Wistrich, Chris Guthrie, and Jeffrey J. Rachlinski, *Can Judges Ignore Inadmissible Information? The Difficulty of Deliberately Disregarding,* 153 U. Pa. L. Rev. 1251 (2005); Mollie W. Marti and Roselle L. Wissler, *Be Careful What You Ask For: The Effect of Anchors on Personal Injury Damages Awards,* 6 J. Experimental Psychol. 91 (2000); Frederick Schauer, *Do Cases Make Bad Law?* 73 U. Chi. L. Rev. 883 (2006); Emily Sherwin, *Judges as Rulemakers,* 73 U. Chi. L. Rev. 919 (2006); Jeffrey J. Rachlinski, *Bottom-Up versus Top-Down Lawmaking,* 73 U. Chi. L. Rev. 933 (2006).

26 ➛ Self-Serving Bias, with a Note on Attribution Error

When you are better off if something is true, you are more likely to believe it. That is a capsule description of self-serving bias. It is common in everyday life. People habitually credit themselves for their successes and blame others for their failures. Most drivers consider themselves above average in their level of skill behind the wheel, while almost nobody thinks they are below average in their ability to get along with others.[87] We see it in the frequent belief that what is fair or right is whatever serves one's own interests. The phrase itself—self-serving bias—is perhaps unfortunate; people tend not be served well by the bias at all (though we will consider some possible exceptions later in the chapter). They would be better off if their beliefs were true, but they aren't better off *believing* they are true when they aren't. Perhaps a better term for it, where it applies, is *optimism bias,* though not every case of one is a case of the other.

These sorts of biases are especially important for lawyers to understand because lawyers are supposed to help clients avoid them. People tend to be overly optimistic about a very long list of things: their likelihood of being sued, for example, or their likelihood of being caught when they break the law, or their likelihood of being in accidents, which in turn affects how much insurance they buy and how many precautions they take.[88] This last point may be a cause for helpful lawyerly advice, but it also is a standard rationale for regulating risks to safety rather than letting the market take care of them; for the people making decisions in the market will be unlikely to perceive risks accurately if they are in the grip of undue optimism.[89] The inaccuracies can run both ways; sometimes people make the opposite mistake of exaggerating remote risks because they are salient, or "available" in the mind's eye, such as the chance of being attacked by a shark. While that type of error mostly is a story for another time,[90] it does suggest a possible antidote to the problem we are considering here—the problem of too much optimism. The bias is quite stubborn; simply warning people about it or giving them better information about odds doesn't seem to help.[91] But it has been suggested that optimism bias might be countered by telling people about possible bad outcomes in ways that are easy to visualize, for people tend to consider things more likely when they can picture them readily.[92] In this way the source of bias known as the *availability heuristic* (closely related to the availability cascades discussed in chapter 14) might be used strategically to help offset a bias toward optimism. There is a certain charm in using one cognitive glitch to help beat another.

Lawyers, meanwhile, have self-serving biases of their own to worry about. The risks can be made concrete by considering a study in which the subjects—law and business students—arbitrarily were assigned roles as plaintiffs and defendants and told to try to settle a hypothetical lawsuit.[93] They showed immediate signs of bias: the plaintiffs valued their claims more than did the ones who had been assigned roles of defendants only moments earlier. This is a very common phenomenon; it's hard to resist seeing your own case as stronger than the rest of the world does. Overcoming this tendency is one of the most important jobs of a negotiator. As part of that same study, some of the subjects were given "debiasing" instructions warning them of the temptation to exaggerate the merit of their claims. Those subjects then displayed less bias than the others. The authors thus suggest that lawyers be forced to write out statements of the defects in their own cases as a corrective to their natural biases. There are reasons to pause before turning that suggestion into a legal requirement, starting with practical objections to asking a lawyer to offer to the court a statement of the flaws in his case. But it's certainly fine advice to follow privately.

Another family of responses to self-serving bias within the legal system involves penalties for indulging it. A prominent example is Rule 68 in the federal system.[94] Suppose you are a plaintiff in a lawsuit. The defendant offers to settle the case for some amount of money. You turn down the offer—but then at trial you win less than the settlement would have given you. Of course you might feel foolish for turning it down, but that isn't enough. Rule 68 then requires you—even if you won the case—to pay the defendant's costs incurred after the offer was made. The rule punishes plaintiffs whose estimates of their prospects are skewed high by self-serving bias (or for that matter by simple bad judgment).

You can imagine intriguing variations on these rules. Each side could certify a prediction of the outcome of a case that is headed to trial; whoever's estimate is farther from the actual result pays the attorney's fees for the other side.[95] Or there could be larger penalties for being wrong, not just payment of the defendant's costs. Why doesn't the law resort to such aggressive measures? First, piling on more sanctions against parties who succumb to bias might not cause comparable reductions in the amount of it. Self-serving bias is insidious in that it denies its own existence,[96] and it's hard to deter people from being influenced by a bias to which they doubt they are subject in the first place. Second, we don't have perfect confidence in the system about which the parties and their lawyers are making their predictions. If every legal result were sure to be correct, perhaps a party's failure to accurately forecast it could be considered an unambiguous error. But there is some variation in the outcome of legal cases, so a prediction that turns out to be wrong may still have been a good guess at the most likely outcome. And finally it sometimes is hard to tell the difference between self-serving bias and other reasons why parties might turn down settlement offers that turn out to be better than what they win by litigating. If a plaintiff declines a settlement offer of x and goes on to recover slightly less than x, he may consider his decision a success if he values a victory in court at some amount greater than his cash recovery. In effect, Rule 68 penalizes litigants who pursue litigation to vindicate nonpecuniary values.[97]

Rule 68 can be viewed as part of a general set of tools for "fee shifting"—making one side in a case pay the costs or attorney's fees of the other. We talked in chapter 24 about the English rule, which requires the loser to reimburse the attorney's fees of the winner, and about the American rule, which leaves each side to pay its own way. How might your view of these rules and their effects change if you assume people are hindered by self-serving bias? The English rule would (again) probably make cases harder to settle. Each side will overestimate its likelihood of winning; since the English rule makes the prize for winning more exciting, the difference between the way each side looks at the case may be increased still more, making it harder for them to agree on a compromise.

The most common strategy for fighting biases in the legal system isn't to penalize decisions that appear to be infected by them. It is to avoid the circumstances that bring the biases about—to forbid conflicts of interest, rather than to urge those who labor under them not to succumb to temptation. Hence the aversion in the legal system to letting parties serve as judges in their own causes: one branch of government checks the other; judges recuse themselves when they have any sort of stake in a case; prosecutors, not victims of crime, decide whether and how to bring criminal charges against one person who is said to have wronged another. If formal separation of this kind isn't possible, we try to distance people from their decisions in other ways, as by pressuring them to hire lawyers—even if the clients themselves are lawyers who know how to try cases. (As the old saw goes, the lawyer who represents himself has a fool for a client.)

Another example: insurance companies usually require that an insured hand over control of litigation to collect for an injury that is covered by one of its policies;[98] one reason is that the insurer is less likely than the insured to be afflicted by self-serving biases, since any judgments about the insured's conduct in the case don't reflect on the insurer. Yet another possible tool for stripping out bias is assignment, meaning the sale of the claim to a disinterested party. The surprising thing is how infrequently such assignment is allowed. It generally can be done in contract but not tort cases; in Texas, a rare jurisdiction that permits the sale of tort claims, it is still not done often.[99] A practical reason is that the plaintiff's cooperation as a witness normally will be needed to successfully press a lawsuit; a plaintiff who sells a claim has little remaining incentive to cooperate in the prosecution of it (a problem of agency; see chapter 9). Besides, many people *want* to litigate their own disputes. They aren't just seeking compensation; they want to participate in the ritual of vindication, and no assignee is going to pay them for that.

A variation on the theme, and a possible reason to doubt that assignment of tort claims is needed, is the contingency fee.[100] As we also saw in chapter 9, a plaintiff's lawyer typically takes a case in return for some percentage of the final recovery—perhaps one-third. The contingency fee is an ambiguous deal from the standpoint of self-serving bias. It might seem a poor idea because it gives the lawyer an untoward interest in winning the case. Now predictions of a big victory serve his self-interest in a way that they wouldn't if he were working for an hourly fee. But if we assume lawyers are good at resisting self-serving bias, the contingency fee might be a helpful antidote to such bias in the client, for it makes a professional with more detached judgment a part owner of the claim and a fuller partner in the perception of its prospects.

Here is another legal angle to consider: what sorts of claims are likely to create the greatest risks of self-serving bias? Suppose you set out to design legal rules *most* likely to provoke self-serving bias in people's estimates of their claims. How best to proceed? The most important elements would be a legal standard that calls for subjective judgment,[101] rather than for a determination of facts that can be readily verified, and then criteria that call for value judgments about either side's behavior. Employment discrimination claims are examples. In a typical employment case the defendant is accused of basing a decision on grounds condemned by norm as well as by statute; especially in a case of alleged racial discrimination, the stigma attaching to a guilty party is considerable. Meanwhile employees who get fired may *want* to believe they have good claims, since that provides a reason for their misfortunes unconnected with the quality of their work. The decision in the case usually will depend on the employer's motives, and there often is no way to settle this objectively—no "smoking gun" document where the motives are spelled out. It is a question of whose protests to believe, how to interpret evaluations of the plaintiff's work, and what inferences to draw from remarks the defendant may have made. The strength of these signals is liable to be too weak to withstand the press of wishful thinking by either party. Of course it finally will fall not to the parties but to the trier of fact to say what the defendant's motives must have been; but at the stage where the parties bargain over such a claim, they may have trouble distinguishing their predictions about what a court will think from their own opinions.

Are there ways to advance the goals of such laws without the high risks of bias? Here we find an example of a classic strategy mentioned a moment ago: inserting a measure of independent judgment between the plaintiff and the courts. An American plaintiff wanting to sue an employer for discrimination must first file the claim with a federal agency, the Equal Employment Opportunity Commission. The EEOC can't stop the plaintiff from eventually suing, but it can delay the process several months while administrators make attempts at "conciliation"—i.e., convincing either or both parties that their position is not as strong as they may think, and that they should compromise or give in. The approach is tougher still in another area of employment litigation: claims under the Fair Labor Standards Act, alleging for example that an employee was fired because of union activity. Here the employee's only right is to complain to the NLRB; he has no right of his own to sue. The reasons for this policy again are many, but one function it serves is to take away from the employee the power to decide whether his own self-serving perception that he was fired for bad reasons should be turned into legal costs for the employer.

Let's take a moment to connect self-serving bias to a larger problem: what psychologists call *fundamental attribution error.* When a person has a role in making something happen—an accident, an achievement, a decision, anything—there are two places where you might assign blame or credit: to the person's inner qualities (for example to their virtue or ability, or lack thereof) or to their circumstances. Attribution error means exaggerating the importance of the personal qualities and underrating the importance of the circumstances.[102] This kind of mistake is very common. A famous study asked subjects to rate the attitudes toward Fidel Castro held by two speakers. One of the speakers praised Castro while the other denounced him, but it was explained to the subjects that the speakers' roles had been assigned by a coin flip. The subjects still tended to conclude that the one who spoke in favor of Castro liked him better.[103] They couldn't overcome the impression that the things he was saying must have reflected on him and not just on his circumstances.

Attribution error has been thought the source of various problems for the legal system. When an accident occurs, many people find it hard to accept that no one might be at fault in a legal sense. *Somebody* must be blameworthy; the bad result couldn't have just been the result of circumstances. This is bad news for defendants in accident cases.[104] Attribution error also is bad news for defendants in criminal cases who claim they were entrapped by police in an aggressive sting operation. Jurors are likely to overrate the role of the defendant's moral failings and underrate the importance of whatever temptations the government offered.[105] It also has been suggested that attribution error makes jurors more likely than they should be to blame the victims of rape or other crimes for their misfortunes.[106] Indeed, you can use this model to think about the whole penalty phase of a case in which the government wants a defendant to be executed for committing a murder. The prosecutor tries to convince the jury that the defendant committed the crime because of the type of person he is. The defendant's lawyer tries to convince the jury that it was more a result of his circumstances—his upbringing, or the provocation he received from the victim, or whatever other facts the lawyer can rally. The risk of attribution error becomes an advantage for the prosecutor.[107] These risks may also have some bearing on the choice, discussed in the previous chapter, between lawmaking by courts and by legislatures. It has been suggested that courts are more likely to commit attribution errors, since a trial tends to be focused heavily on the individual defendant and his culpability. Legislatures look more broadly at circumstances: the economics or sociological points that influence people's behavior and that the law might change.[108]

Self-serving bias interacts with attribution error in interesting ways that can be hard to untangle. People generally are less likely to commit the classic attribution mistake about themselves, because they notice and feel their own circumstances more keenly than those of others.[109] If you are frightened by a dog, you are likely to emphasize how big and scary the dog was; an onlooker is likely to notice that, too, but is much more likely to also conclude that you are scared of dogs—to interpret the story in a "dispositional" rather than just a "situational" way. If you are asked why you married your spouse, you are likely to talk mostly about various qualities your spouse has, not about your tastes. But if you are asked to explain why your friend George married his wife, Martha, your explanation will probably sound different: you will talk about Martha's qualities, but you are also more likely to talk about George's tastes, traits, and needs. Or simply think about losing your temper. In all these cases you are likely to interpret your own behavior mostly as a reaction to things outside yourself and to interpret the behavior of others as an outgrowth of their traits.

We would expect self-serving bias, however, to make people selective about all this—to make them more likely to attribute good outcomes to their own qualities and bad outcomes to their circumstances. There is evidence of such a pattern.[110] A student who does badly on an exam is likely to have a long and earnest story to tell about all the circumstances that contributed to the results; the student who does well goes around thinking it's just a reflection of his ability.[111] To see the point illustrated a few hundred more times, go to a sporting event and listen to the fans explain the successes and failures of their team and of their rivals. Or listen to lawyers explain their wins and losses. But the evidence on this issue isn't always consistent. These cognitive forces can run in different directions, with results that aren't always predictable. Political leaders who are praised for having all sorts of great virtues often will say that their decisions felt as though they were dictated by circumstance.[112]

An interesting question about self-serving bias is whether it necessarily is bad. Sometimes it can be hard to evaluate because it operates alongside more clearly benign cognitive tendencies from which it can be hard to separate: ordinary self-interest, and the fact that an actor knows himself, his tastes, and the feel of his experience better than anyone else does. Before a person spills coffee on himself, he thinks it preposterous that someone else who does this might collect a large award of damages from the maker of the drink. Once he himself has been burned, his view of the brewer's responsibility and the compensation it ought to pay may be very different. But there is no reason to infer from this change alone that in the latter instance the actor is subject to self-serving bias in any troublesome sense. It may be that he (and everyone else) is mistaken in cases where their own well-being is not at issue ("easy for *you* to say"), since they then lack an immediate stake in the decision; if the cost of coffee is salient to them but the experience of injury is not, they might be biased *against* the victim.

And sometimes a self-serving bias bestows advantages upon its holder.[113] The soldier charging over a hill, or the bride or groom stepping toward the altar, all may be helped by an exaggerated view of their prospects for success, in a way vaguely similar to how they might be helped by a stiff drink. (Would anyone do either of those things without a dash of self-serving bias?) This may be the case because the self-serving bias offsets distortions that run in the other direction, such as pessimism, or it may just be that too accurate a view of the stakes is likely to ruin the sense of confidence or conviction needed to make success most likely. (A shortage of self-serving bias appears to be linked to depression.)[114] Realism may cause a person to invest too little of himself in an enterprise because the costs and benefits don't seem favorable; yet they have the oddly self-fulfilling quality of becoming more favorable if he thinks they are. But notice the limits of the principle. The bias may be helpful at the moment of performance but not at the earlier node when one is deciding to undertake the activity in the first place. At that point—in deciding *whether* to enlist or marry—one wants a clear view of the consequences. Only once the decision to go forward has been taken is one better off with an unrealistically optimistic view. And even then there is an optimal amount of bias. Too much of it causes rashness or overinvestment, whether in a hopeless mission or a bad marriage.

All this is true from the perspective of the person with the bias. But acts motivated by bias can create benefits and costs for others, too. It may be bad for the soldiers themselves to exaggerate their expected fortunes when they decide to enlist, but good socially; we need the soldiers. This is why we invest in mythologies—stories, films, advertisements—that glorify and sanitize the soldier's experience: we feed the bias that exaggerates one's chances for glory and downplays the prospects for misery in order to bolster the self-serving bias and thus encourage acts that make everyone better off on net (though not necessarily the actor). State-sponsored advertisements for lotteries can be viewed the same way, as can celebrations of the success of entrepreneurs and other figures who have achieved success of whatever sort despite grim beginnings.

The application of these points to disputing is complex because it depends on a balance of private and social considerations that vary in different kinds of disputes. Sometimes disputants can expect better results if they are full of unwarranted righteousness or optimism. Those traits may make a client or lawyer a more convincing and formidable opponent or rival in negotiations.[115] They may help cow an opponent into wondering whether his case is weaker than he thought. They may generate a more generous settlement just because the other side must reconcile itself to its opponent's preferences; they may in particular cause an opponent to think more seriously about compromising because the enemy so evidently is committed to fighting to the bitter end.[116] These possibilities might reasonably cause a party to pause before taking a debiasing pill if one were available unless his adversary were to take one as well, for it may be a strategic disadvantage to see matters "objectively" in a heated conflict where everyone else is excessively convinced that they are right. Enlightenment can become a disadvantage if it produces a case where "The best lack all conviction, while the worst/Are full of passionate intensity."[117] A more prosaic disadvantage is that people free from bias are more likely to settle, and for less money, than people in the grip of it. In that case debiasing oneself becomes akin to cooperating in a prisoner's dilemma, which helps make the case for requiring it of both sides—if it could be done feasibly, which is far from clear.[118]

And now what of the external costs and benefits? One effect of self-serving bias is to prevent parties from caving in when an accurate view of their prospects would make it seem sensible to them to do so. Apart from whether this helps them in the long run, it might be a good thing in cases where the litigation creates benefits for those other than the parties. Public law litigation provides possible examples. The primary beneficiaries of such cases often are not parties to them; think of suits to enforce environmental laws or get rid of statutes that burden the rights of many—rights of religious expression, speech, freedom from search and seizure, and so on. An outcome either way may usefully clarify the law for others. Or consider areas of private law where litigation performs a particularly important regulatory function, as it does in the area of products liability. The plaintiff who presses on in the face of odds that are unfavorable when viewed coldly may be doing a public service in making more likely the creation of a valuable precedent. His fervor may also be a useful offset to attempts by the defense to spend heavily on the case to prevent an unhelpful precedent from being set.[119] At the same time, a *defendant's* exaggerated view of his chances to win might cause him to hold out in the face of socially undesirable litigation, refusing to settle and thus discouraging such cases from being brought in the future—a good thing. But the size of these good effects is a matter of pure conjecture.

SUGGESTIONS FOR FURTHER READING. Linda Babcock, George Loewenstein, and Samuel Issacharoff, *Creating Convergence: Debiasing Biased Litigants,* 22 Law & Soc. Inquiry 913 (1997); Linda Babcock and George Loewenstein, *Explaining Bargaining Impasse: The Role of Self-Serving Biases,* 11 J. Econ. Persp. 109 (1997); Ward Farnsworth, *The Legal Regulation of Self-Serving Bias,* 37 U.C. Davis L. Rev. 567 (2003); Ola Svenson, *Are We All Less Risky and More Skillful Than Our Fellow Drivers?* 47 Acta Psychologica 143 (1981); Jon Elster, Sour Grapes (1983); Lee Ross and Richard E. Nisbett, The Person and the Situation (1991); See Edward E. Jones and Richard E. Nisbett, *The Actor and the Observer: Divergent Perceptions of the Causes of Behavior, in* Attribution: Perceiving the Causes of Behavior 79 (Edward E. Jones et al. eds., 1971); Christine Jolls and Cass R. Sunstein, *Debiasing through Law,* 35 J. Legal Stud. 199 (2006).

PART V *Problems of Proof*

27 ⇥ Presumptions

Courts usually don't declare things true or false. That's too difficult. Usually they just try to estimate *likelihoods;* more precisely, they decide whether the evidence that a claim is true gets over a high enough bar to justify a decision—whether the decision is a criminal conviction, a verdict in a civil lawsuit, an opinion striking down a statute or regulation, or the reversal of a trial court's ruling on appeal.

This way of thinking helps explain the law's treatment of O. J. Simpson. He was prosecuted for murdering his ex-wife and a friend of hers, and he was acquitted. Then he was sued for damages by the families of the murder victims—and they won. How can that be? Is there not some contradiction between the first court's declaring him innocent and the second court's declaring him guilty? Not really, no; for that isn't quite what either of the courts really said. Simpson wasn't "found innocent" in the criminal court. His victory in that case was just a declaration that the evidence against him didn't satisfy the standard of proof used in criminal cases: proof beyond a reasonable doubt. Nor was he "found guilty" in the civil suit. The court only concluded that the evidence against him got over the lower bar used in civil lawsuits in the United States: proof by a preponderance of the evidence.[1] We will talk more about those different standards of proof in the next chapter, but you already can see the point. If the legal system concluded that Simpson was, say, 70 percent likely to have committed the murders, then the results in both cases were right. The evidence was enough to support a judgment that took away his wealth but not enough to support a judgment that took away his liberty. More generally the two cases illustrate our initial claim. The courts don't decide whether a defendant did a killing or didn't do it; they aren't in the business of declaring certainties. They decide whether the evidence in a case gets over the bar. Sometimes the evidence gets over one bar but not another.

These principles explain a lot about the way courts do their work generally. Courts make presumptions; they assign burdens of proof; they develop principles to say when some decision makers should defer to others; they create standards and then measure evidence and arguments against them. They set up default rules, then make comparative judgments about whether the reasons for doing otherwise are enough to set aside the background presumption. These approaches mean that in a lot of cases there is no need for a court to get to the bottom of the matter and find the right answer, whatever it may be. If the evidence is weak or the right answer to a question is too hard to figure out, as is often true, the default rule—the presumption—takes over and gives us a practical answer anyway.

We've seen how standards of proof can serve as an example of all this. So can *burdens* of proof. What's the difference? A standard of proof is a rule about the quality of the evidence that a party has to bring forward to win—how convincing it has to be. The burden of proof in a case sometimes is defined the same way, but it also can be viewed as an arrow indicating which side loses if there is no evidence on a question or if the answer is too hard to find. The arrow can change directions during a case. Thus the burden of proof in a civil lawsuit, such as a contract or tort claim, starts with the plaintiff. If he doesn't put in any evidence, or if it leads to no clear conclusion, then he loses; the defendant is presumed free from liability until proven otherwise. Now suppose the plaintiff's evidence is good, but the defendant says the case was brought too late—beyond, say, the three-year statute of limitations. That's called an affirmative defense, and this time the burden of proof is on the defendant. The suit is presumed timely until the defendant proves otherwise (which may or may not be easy to do). These rules are intuitive, but notice the work they do. They spare the courts the bother of needing to figure out what really happened with respect to each issue in every case. If it's too hard to say, the identity of the loser already has been declared in advance. The court doesn't have to decide whether the suit was on time; it can say that the defendant didn't come up with evidence on the point, make an assumption against him, and move on. (We could put the burden on the plaintiff to prove that the case *is* timely, but that would be wasteful; it would force the plaintiff to come up with evidence on a point that isn't really an issue in most cases.)[2]

Often the rules assigning burdens of proof are based on the cost to each side of figuring out there's a claim worth making in the first place and then coming up with evidence to support it. Whoever can do those things more easily is the automatic loser if they aren't done adequately.[3] Thus the plaintiff in a race discrimination case can start—and discharge his initial "burden of production"—by just showing he was a member of a racial minority, that he applied for a job for which he was qualified, and that the job went to someone who was white. That isn't much to ask a plaintiff to show, but the burden is light for a reason: the plaintiff isn't in a great position to show more, because much of the evidence about the hiring decision will be in the hands of the employer. So that small showing by the plaintiff causes the burden to shift. Now the employer has to offer a legitimate reason for the decision, or else lose. Coming up with such a reason usually isn't too hard, either (which is why the employer loses if it can't find one); and once that is done, the burden of showing that the reason is false shifts back to the plaintiff. That burden still may be hard to discharge, but at least this back-and-forth business has forced the employer to put forward an explanation that the two sides can argue about productively. This approach to burdens of proof, known as the *McDonnell Douglas* rule after the case that devised it, is unusual; it's a special feature of discrimination cases.[4] But it shows how initial burdens of producing proof and final burdens of persuasion can be jiggered to help force each party to make the contribution to the case that it is better positioned to offer. Sometimes burdens are assigned one way or another, or raised or lowered, in the service of other policies, as we will see in the next chapter.

A broadly similar logic gets rerun when one side loses its case in the trial court and decides to appeal. How should the appellate court decide whether the trial judge made a mistake? Of course the burden of proof is on the party taking the appeal; if he says nothing, the trial is presumed to have been fine and the resulting judgment stands. The more interesting question is the standard of proof the appellant has to satisfy—or, to use the language of appeals, what *standard of review* the court of appeals will use to measure a claim that the trial judge was mistaken. The judges hearing the appeal don't just look at everything the trial judge did and ask whether it was right. They use the same strategy as before: they set up a bar, and then ask whether the argument that the trial judge blundered is good enough to get over it. The height of the bar depends on the kind of mistake the trial judge is said to have made.

So suppose your case was tried to a judge rather than a jury (courts use a jury only when one of the parties asks for it). The judge concludes that one of your circus elephants stepped on the plaintiff and so requires you to pay damages.[5] You appeal on the ground that it wasn't your elephant. You probably will lose—even if it *wasn't* your elephant. The appellate judges aren't going to ask again whether the elephant was yours; they are going to strongly presume it was yours and ask whether your evidence is enough to overcome the presumption. The formal shape the presumption takes is a rule that decisions about facts made by a trial judge are reversed only if clearly erroneous. The reason for the rule is that the trial judge is in a better position to make the call than the appellate judges: he heard the witnesses and got a closer look at the evidence. This is a classic reason for the maker of one legal decision to defer to another. In practice it's a great time-saver. If the appellate judges aren't sure whose elephant it was, because the evidence is all too complicated or conflicting or obscure, they are left in position to announce a nice, clear decision. It was yours.

But now suppose you admit the elephant was yours and instead make a different claim on appeal: an elephant owner's liability for damage done by the animal shouldn't be automatic, as the trial judge thought; it should depend on whether the owner was careless in some way. This time the appellate court won't give any weight to what the trial judge thought. The decision will be made from scratch, or "de novo," so this time you will win if your arguments merely seem a little stronger than those of your opponent. The reason will be plain from a comparison to the previous case. Here the trial judge has no comparative advantage in deciding the issue. It's a question of *law* that will be answered not by listening to witnesses but by reading and thinking, which the appellate judges can do as well as the trial judge.

But then you still might wonder why the decision isn't left alone; since neither the trial judge nor the appellate judges have any better angle on it, is there any reason to think the appellate judges will answer it *better*? No, there really isn't. The issue, rather, is that any one appellate court supervises the work of lots of trial judges. A big reason for having appellate judges is to make sure all those trial judges are applying the same legal rules so that identical cases don't come out differently in different courtrooms. The only way to get that uniformity is to decide from scratch all issues of law, like the general rules governing animal owners; if the court of appeals gave deference to the trial judge on that point, the result would be that two judges could use different legal rules yet both be affirmed.[6] This isn't a problem when the question is purely factual—whether the elephant was *yours*—because we don't expect questions that specific to arise in lots of different courtrooms.

There are lots of decisions courts make that aren't purely matters of fact *or* law. They are somewhere in between, as when a judge decides that a case should go forward as a class action, or says that a lawyer should be hit with a monetary penalty for making a frivolous argument, or issues an injunction because the harm the defendant is inflicting on the plaintiff is held to be "irreparable." In all these cases the judge is applying a legal standard to a bunch of circumstances; the result is known as a mixed question of law and fact. There is no single standard of review for these sorts of decisions on appeal. It depends on the details. In the cases just sketched, review in the court of appeals usually will be deferential, whether it's called a search for "clear error" or an inquiry into whether there was an "abuse of discretion." As a practical matter these terms typically amount to the same thing. The decision is presumed correct, and anyone challenging it has the burden of making clear that it was wrong. If the court of appeals isn't sure, the decision stands. Very often the standard of review on appeal will make or break the complaining party's chance of success. That is why good appellate lawyers and judges are careful to settle it first thing.

Appellate judges don't just review the work of trial judges; and for everyone whose work they do review, there are rules about whether and to what extent to give deference—whether, that is, to presume the decision is right unless the complaining party can carry some more or less heavy burden of showing otherwise. But the reasons for giving or withholding deference may change. If the finding that you owned the elephant was made by a jury rather than a judge, the deference on appeal is even greater; indeed, it is nearly absolute. The Seventh Amendment to the Constitution forbids federal courts of appeal to second-guess facts found by juries.[7] (Sometimes there are ways around this: for example, you can argue that the evidence of your ownership was so weak that the issue never should have been given to the jury in the first place. But let's assume there was some evidence, the jurors were impressed by it, and you think they shouldn't have been.) This time the reason for the deference isn't just the comparative advantage of the decision maker on the front line. After all, that was already the reason for deferring to the trial judge, and now we're deferring even *more*. Here there's also a political point. The authors of the Constitution thought of juries as a political brake against the government; so if a jury found a fact, it should be hard for an officer of the government—a judge—to undo it.[8]

Sometimes federal courts review the decisions of state courts, as when a state prisoner seeks a writ of habeas corpus—a declaration by a federal judge that a state is holding him in violation of the Constitution. Perhaps it's your case; the state court concluded that you had an adequate trial lawyer, and you say otherwise. Your battle will be uphill all the way, because the federal statute allowing you to seek habeas corpus doesn't allow the federal judge to simply ask whether your lawyer was adequate. As usual, the question is reframed as a contest to see whether the evidence of your claim is strong enough to get over a series of hurdles. By now it will come as no surprise that any findings of fact made by the state courts are presumed correct by the federal. But the statute has also been read to require deference on questions of law: the prisoner has to show that the state court's reading of the Constitution not only was wrong—in other words, not only was it different from what the federal court would have said—but was unreasonable.[9] Here, as with the Seventh Amendment, the reason can be understood as political, though this time the politics are different. The authors of this part of the habeas corpus statute, which was enacted in 1996, didn't like the spectacle of federal courts meddling too much in the states' administration of criminal law, so they instructed federal judges to defer even on issues where there is no comparative advantage in the state judges and some need for uniformity. Congress did this in the interests of comity, or the mutual respect owed by one sovereign to another (in this case, by the federal government to the states). An alternative account is that the federal judges in habeas corpus cases were thought to be too quick to impose liberal readings of the Constitution on the states—readings that the authors of the statute didn't like. To curb that tendency and get better substantive results, they used a procedural method. They raised the bar for getting the writ issued. The point for us, in any event, is familiar. Federal judges reviewing what state courts have done don't make absolute judgments about it. They just say whether the likelihood of a mistake is great enough to satisfy a standard issued by Congress. Sometimes—often, perhaps—it's difficult to say for sure whether there was a mistake. Those look like hard cases, but actually they're easy. The prisoner loses.

Courts don't just review the work of other courts; they also review the work of agencies. Suppose the Environmental Protection Agency reads the Clean Air Act (a statute passed by Congress) to require you to build mile-high smokestacks on your factory. You go to court to complain. You might expect the court to decide for itself what the statute means for all the reasons we saw earlier: its meaning is a question of law, so nobody is in a better position than the judge to figure it out. But it might not work that way. If the statute is found to be ambiguous, the court usually will defer to whatever the agency thought it meant so long as it's reasonable; this is called *Chevron* deference, after the Supreme Court case that devised it.[10] Students of the case differ about why the deference is thought proper. It might be that an ambiguity in the statute is Congress's way of saying it wants the agency to decide what the statute should mean. Or it might be that the agency is in a better position to make sense out of the statute, a little like the way a trial court is in a better position to decide a question of fact—because it has a better understanding of the corner of the world that the question involves.[11] At any rate, notice how *Chevron* deference resembles the other burdens and standards we have considered. Where it applies, it means that the court doesn't have to be able to say for sure what a statute means, which might be very hard. It can simply say the question *is* hard and go with the default rule: the agency wins. The result is similar when an agency's own decision (not just its reading of a statute) is challenged in court. Usually the plaintiff has to show the agency's decision was "arbitrary and capricious," which is just another example of deferential review.

There are, of course, still other entities whose decisions get reviewed in the courts: legislatures, including Congress. People sue to get statutes declared invalid, or they claim the statutes are invalid when they are prosecuted under them. In either case the argument is that the statute violates the Constitution. You might think courts would resolve these claims by simply asking whether the statute is inconsistent with any rules found in the Constitution, but that rarely is how constitutional law works. The Constitution is full of things that do sound like rules, but the courts have turned many of them into standards that produce the same kinds of inquiries we have been discussing: presumptions, and then measurement against the standards they create. Laws that draw distinctions based on race, or forbid speech because of its content, or make it harder for someone to exercise rights the Supreme Court has said are "fundamental," aren't simply struck down. They get what the courts call "strict scrutiny," which usually is defined as asking whether the laws are "narrowly tailored to serve a compelling governmental interest." The court has to go through that inquiry. (*Then* it strikes the law down.) Other laws, like those restricting speech in ways neutral as to its content, or drawing distinctions based on sex, get "intermediate scrutiny"; the government has to show in either case that the law is "substantially related to an important governmental objective." These unsightly formulas seem distant from the Constitution, which speaks simply of the equal protection of the laws and the freedom of speech. But the courts don't want to ask directly whether a law violates those provisions. They are more comfortable restating constitutional commands as tests that create burdens and standards of proof.[12]

We have seen lots of different reasons for the creation of legal presumptions. Sometimes courts make presumptions for reasons that might be called political and that amount to orders from other sources—as with the habeas corpus statute or some provisions of the Constitution. Sometimes the presumptions are more squarely matters of epistemology or economics, as when one decision maker is thought to be in a better position than another to answer a question. Whatever the reasons, these general strategies for making decisions also help deal with threats of indeterminacy—the worry that information may be impossible to get or that the competition between complicated arguments may be impossible to resolve.[13] That threat can emerge easily; law generally and courtrooms in particular are full of uncertainties. We may never be sure whether the defendant committed the crime or who owned the elephant; we may never be certain whether the trial judge was right that the plaintiff suffered irreparable harm or that the prisoner's lawyer in the state court was competent; and we may never resolve what a statute means or whether it does more harm than good. That's often the normal state of things: we can't figure them out—which is why presumptions are so useful and so important to understand.

SUGGESTIONS FOR FURTHER READING. Gary Lawson, *Legal Indeterminacy: Its Cause and Cure,* 19 Harv. J.L. & Pub. Pol'y (1996); Bruce L. Hay and Kathryn E. Spier, *Burdens of Proof in Civil Litigation: An Economic Analysis,* 26 J. Legal Stud. 413 (1997); Randy E. Barnett, The Structure of Liberty ch. 10 (1998); Richard H. Gaskins, Burdens of Proof in Legal and Philosophical Discourse (1992).

28 ⤚ Standards of Proof

It's rare for people making decisions to be perfectly sure they are right, and this is as true in a courthouse as elsewhere. But how *much* confidence should we require in a decision? We find a lively set of studies in the problem in decisions courts make of the *what if* variety. A sailor falls over the side of a ship and is dragged to his death by a squid some moments later. He might have been saved if he had been thrown a rope, but the captain had mistakenly left all the rescue gear behind on shore. In a lawsuit resulting from this sort of case, it isn't enough for the sailor's kin to say it was blameworthy in the captain to have gone to sea ill-equipped (let's assume that it was). It also has to be shown that the rope would have made a difference—that it would have saved the sailor. Maybe it wouldn't have; maybe the squid was too quick. The normal thing would be to put together a jury and ask them to decide the question. But now suppose the jurors aren't entirely sure. They think a rope could well have saved him, but perhaps not. How sure must they be before they find against the captain?

It might seem a natural solution to have the jury assign a figure to its best guess and then have the captain pay over to the plaintiffs a share of money that corresponds to it. So suppose the sailor's death deprived his kin of $100,000 in earnings they otherwise had coming; if the jury thinks there is a 30 percent chance that a rope would have saved him, the captain would be obliged to pay the kin 30 percent of the earnings: $30,000. If the rope was 80 percent likely to have made a difference, then $80,000 would be due from the captain. The award would increase with our certainty of its justice.

Yet usually we do nothing of the kind. We tell the jury instead to answer a yes-or-no question: whether the plaintiff has shown by a preponderance of the evidence that a rope would have saved the sailor. Most courts regard this as equivalent to asking if the chance the rope mattered was better than 50 percent. If it wasn't—if the jury's best guess is that the rope was, say, 30 percent likely to have mattered—the plaintiff hasn't met the standard of proof and the captain pays nothing. But if there's a 60 percent chance that the sailor would have been rescued, the captain is held wholly responsible and pays the entire $100,000. The captain pays everything or nothing, though whether the rope would have helped may forever be a question to which our answer lies somewhere between those poles, and maybe near the middle.

Why this discrepancy; why does the law turn such modest confidence one way or the other into all-or-nothing results? The most likely reasons are practical. It might be hard for the parties to supply any decider—whether jury or judge—with the knowledge they would need to make more precise estimates. The trier of the facts would end up making guesses based on trivial foundations; the apparent precision of a finding that the rope was 70 percent likely to have saved the sailor from the squid would be an illusion. The judge or jury is more likely to be equal to the task if called on just to sort the case onto one side or another of the "more likely than not" threshold. Most of the time this allows the jury merely to consider the stories told by the two sides and compare their plausibility. The uncertainties about whether the rope was 20 percent or 30 percent or 45 percent likely to matter can be left unresolved, for they all mean the same thing in the end; likewise for distinctions between 60 percent and 80 percent. The general idea, which comes up a lot in law, is that sometimes a bad question that a court can answer relatively well is preferable to a better question that is more likely to be answered badly.

Another reason the 50 percent figure is so attractive involves the chance that the jury will decide the case wrong. One purpose of a standard of proof is to take the risk that the jury will err and distribute it between the parties. Getting back to the sailor who fell overboard, a low standard of proof for the plaintiff (in other words, a standard that is easy to meet) would mean we're ready to tolerate decisions that mistakenly blame the captain. A high standard means we're more ready to put up with mistakes that let the captain off the hook. In civil actions—cases where one citizen sues another over an accident or contract or other such claim—we set the standard right in the middle, which is a way of saying either mistake is equally unwelcome. At first this might sound wrong; if I sue you, wouldn't a false finding of liability be worse than a false decision leaving you alone? Perhaps not. An accident or breach of contract creates costs; the point of a lawsuit is to figure out who will pay them. There are two ways the suit can go wrong. It can leave you with the costs when I really should pay them, or it can stick me with the costs when they ought to be left with you or someone else. Either way the size and nature of the mistake are the same: the wrong person pays. From an economic standpoint neither mistake is preferable to the other, so the risk of error is assigned evenly to each side by putting the bar of confidence midway between us. (We set the bar higher when accusing someone of a crime, a point we will discuss later in the chapter.)

A still different part of the story behind the 50 percent rule involves how many lawsuits we want. Suppose we did give out damages in proportion to the jury's confidence; if the jurors think chances are 10 percent that the rope would have helped, the plaintiffs collect 10 percent of their damages from the captain. Plaintiffs who think their case looks exactly like this might well press forward with it. Indeed, any plaintiff might sue if he thinks he can show that someone else's blunder had *any* chance of mattering to him, even 5 percent or 1 percent, since he stands then to collect just that much from the defendant. Currently we don't see those suits much. Our more brutal rule—the 50 percent standard—usually extinguishes them early; if everyone at least can agree the rope *probably* wouldn't have mattered, the plaintiff has no case and doesn't bring one. Perhaps it seems unfair that the captain pays nothing in those cases even though the rope might have mattered, but we balance it out. Sometimes the sailor who falls overboard will bob around in the water long enough to make us think the rope was 60 percent or 70 percent likely to have saved him, and then the captain will pay everything—even though the rope might *not* have mattered.

Notice, then, that choosing a standard of proof has side effects, starting with consequences for the number of cases likely to be brought, and then spilling over into incentives for the possible defendants. Whether the requirement of proof by a preponderance of the evidence produces enough lawsuits for our liking depends on why we want them in the first place. Some say the only good thing lawsuits do is put pressure on people to behave themselves by putting the fear of litigation into them. (It's a strong form of the ex ante perspective laid out in the first chapter of this book.) On this view we probably will have enough suits if we make winners out of plaintiffs who can beat the 50 percent test. Those wins will give sea captains plenty to worry about. If the purpose of having lawsuits is different—if it includes, say, wanting to compensate the seaman's kin—then the 50 percent rule might seem harsh as well as crude; but then one also might wonder whether lawsuits are a very good way of supplying that compensation. It ends up being a quite expensive sort of insurance plan, with large shares of every dollar going to the lawyers.

These defenses of the preponderance of the evidence standard are uneasy, and in some cases they won't hold at all. This time suppose no one sees the sailor go overboard. Late that night he is found to be missing from the ship, and the captain determines that he probably has been gone five or six hours, having fallen into the sea perhaps a hundred miles east of the ship's current bearings in the Gulf of Mexico.[14] The captain decides against turning the ship around to search for him, preferring instead to press on to Corpus Christi. The first question is whether the captain acted badly; maybe failing to go back was like not having a rope on board in our earlier example, and in that case the captain is said to have committed a breach of his duty to the sailor. Assume so. But then our other question still persists: would it have made a difference if he *had* gone back? We might reasonably think the chances of finding the seaman after the passage of so much time and distance were less than even, in which event we have seen what result the rules require: no liability; the captain pays nothing.

Or do they? Think back to the earlier story about the sea captain—the one who was sued because he didn't have a rope to throw to a drowning sailor. We saw that the captain might win some cases where the sailor drowns because it won't be possible to show that the rope would have made a difference. But in advance, when the captain is deciding whether to bring rescue gear on the voyage, he can't know whether he'll get lucky in that way; he has to worry that anyone who falls overboard might stay afloat long enough to make it seem that the rope *would* have mattered. So there is legal pressure on the captain even though he may win some cases that he shouldn't. But this second case, where the captain doesn't go back for the sailor who fell off the boat six hours earlier, is different. Once a person has been overboard for that long, it may *never* be the case that a search probably would save him. It always will be a long shot. That means that if the captain never goes back to look, he'll never be held liable. A jury will never be able to say, by a preponderance of the evidence, that the captain's failure made any difference. And the captain will know this.

Here's another way to look at the same point. Perhaps one sailor in five will be found in cases like this where a search *is* made. But when the search isn't made we'll never know whether it was the one where the sailor would have been saved or one of the other four where it didn't matter. We'll be presented only with odds—a 20 percent chance every time—and under the more-likely-than-not rule we'll treat every case as though it were the second type, the kind where the search didn't matter. The standard of proof has produced a glitch: a situation where plaintiffs never are able to satisfy it no matter how many times the captain does wrong. Sometimes his mistakes matter, but all we can say after he makes them is that they probably didn't. The law is sensitive to these glitches, which sometimes have been called *recurring misses,* and often will reply by relaxing the standard of proof.[15] Thus in the case of the sailor gone overboard for six hours, the court held the captain (or rather his employer) liable despite protests that a search would probably have been futile.[16] The moral of the story is that asking whether the defendant's neglect more likely than not mattered is bearable so long as that question will catch enough captains to make them nervous. But if the rule will miss them all, the standard of proof has to be redrawn to set the pressure right.

This tale would be of only limited interest if its lesson were confined to misbehaving sea captains, but it turns out to have many applications elsewhere. Suppose a doctor misreads a patient's x-rays and so fails to see that he has cancer. Can it be said that an accurate reading of the x-ray would have made a difference? With respect to some cancers it surely cannot; finding the tumor a little earlier merely increases the patient's odds of survival, perhaps from 20 percent to 30 percent. Patients in these cases are like sailors long gone overboard. To most of them the right diagnosis makes no difference, but to some of them it will—and after the fact we may never know which were which. Again many courts excuse the plaintiff on such facts from the usual standard of proof, often by ordering what is called recovery for *loss of a chance*—recovery, in other words, in proportion to the chance for survival the doctor took away.[17] A doctor whose negligence cost the patient a third of his chances might pay a third of his damages. (But if the doctor's neglect cost the patient more than half his chances for survival, the doctor pays *all* his damages as usual—an asymmetry that has made some courts balk. If the doctor pays a little something when he takes away some of the plaintiff's chances, shouldn't he only pay *most* of the damages when he takes away *most* of his chances?)[18]

The examples so far have involved failures to take care which may or may not have caused an injury or death. But the preponderance of the evidence is the standard of proof in most sorts of civil cases, and as to all the questions within them, not just what would have happened if the defendant had been more careful; and elsewhere as well we find courts adapting the rule to cope with novel problems. So if you trespass on my land, leaving behind no trace, you will be made to pay me the market value of a license for the privilege. Normally I would have to prove what damage I suffered by the usual more-likely-than-not standard, but here that's probably impossible. The law thus gives me the benefit of a presumption about it, which helps ensure that you won't make a habit of trespassing.

Or, to take a case not on the civil side, imagine I am your lawyer in a murder trial. I sleep through most of it, and at the end you are found guilty. Now you say you want a new trial because I gave you ineffective assistance in the first one. This will require you to show—by a preponderance of the evidence—that my conduct fell below usual professional standards, which shouldn't be hard; but then you have to show also that the result of the trial would have been different if I had been awake. If the evidence against you was good, it might be hard to prove that my wakefulness more likely than not would have changed the outcome—so courts say that you needn't. You only are required to show a reasonable probability of a better outcome.[19] No one can say what number corresponds to that standard, but it evidently is less certainty than the usual rule needs. This time we find the standard relaxed not to discipline a wrongdoer but to make sure that the grasp of the state is properly checked and that your rights aren't canceled by the procedures used to vindicate them. In a broad sense the defendant with a bad case and a sleeping lawyer is like the sailor who was found to be missing six hours after he went overboard. The bad behavior by the lawyer or sea captain might not have mattered, but holding the complaining party to the usual tough standard—making him show that the bad behavior probably did matter—will make it too hard and cause him to lose too often.

We have been speaking of cases where the law relaxes its usual standards of confidence. Sometimes it stiffens them instead. If the *Daily Bugle* says the mayor takes bribes, he can sue for defamation only by showing the *Bugle* knew the claim was false or was reckless about its truth or falsity. More to our point, it's not enough for the mayor to prove that those things are more likely than not. He has to make his case by clear and convincing evidence.[20] No one can say what number corresponds to this standard, either, but it evidently is more certainty than the usual rule needs. Why raise the bar in this way? The Supreme Court has confessed that requiring clear and convincing evidence of the defendant's bad state of mind arguably "puts a premium on ignorance, encourages the irresponsible publisher not to inquire, and permits the issue to be determined by the defendant's testimony that he published the statement in good faith and unaware of its probable falsity."[21] Those are reasons why courts normally don't use such heightened standards, but in this case they are outweighed by other advantages. To see the point, it helps to distinguish between two types of errors: false positives and false negatives. A false positive means a finding of liability that is wrong. A false negative means a finding of no liability that is wrong. (These correspond to "Type 1" and "Type 2" errors discussed more commonly in the world of medicine.) We saw earlier that in a typical civil lawsuit we might consider those two kinds of mistakes equally bad; they both just mean that a bill will be paid by the wrong person. But in defamation lawsuits brought against the press, the public interest is greater than usual. We aren't indifferent between the two types of mistakes. False positives worry us more because the threat of them might cause the press to censor itself too much. So we set the standard of proof high, preferring to err on the side of the newspaper to preserve its incentive to err on the side of speaking.[22]

In criminal cases the standard of proof is highest of all: the familiar proof beyond a reasonable doubt. The reason, evidently enough, is that mistakenly convicting someone is thought worse than mistakenly letting him go. Thus Blackstone's claim that it's "better that ten guilty persons escape, than that one innocent suffer"—a fine example of comparing false positives and false negatives, though the right numbers that ought to be plugged into the maxim are open to debate.[23] But the high standard of proof also does something else. It helps offset other advantages that prosecutors enjoy against the defendant. The state has extensive powers to spy, search, and subpoena; it has the police and the warden; it has ambitious prosecutors with lots of resources. The defendant normally has little money, so he is supplied with other armor: the right to a free lawyer, a right to appeal, the right to have evidence suppressed if it was obtained wrongfully—and a presumption of innocence until it is overcome beyond a reasonable doubt. Try thinking of these points as packages that might be balanced against one another, with lots of edges where marginal adjustments can be made. When courts worry that the balance goes too far in favor of the state, they expand the rights of defendants; when legislatures think the balance tips too far toward the criminal, they make inroads along other margins, as we saw in chapter 3—cutting back on appeals, lengthening sentences, hiring police, and otherwise adding weights in the state's pan.[24] The standard of proof may thus be viewed as one part in an ongoing contest of inequalities. The substance of this point is more familiar than it may sound. We saw earlier in this chapter that civil standards of proof make up one piece of a system that regulates the flow of lawsuits and the incentives that result from them. The same goes for the standard on the criminal side, though this time the goals are different. The point for now is just to see again that standards of proof do more than set the bar for a jury's decision in a case. They have side effects.

The most interesting question about reasonable doubt is what it means to speak of it. Earlier we spoke interchangeably of a preponderance of the evidence, a more-likely-than-not standard, and confidence better than 50 percent, which most courts say all mean the same thing. Reasonable doubt has not lent itself so well to such restatement. Some say the phrase has a meaning too self-evident to bear elaboration,[25] but this is bluff; it does not survive the ample evidence that people—judges as well as laymen—have quite different ideas in mind when they speak and hear of reasonable doubt. The mighty Learned Hand didn't think much of the distinction between a preponderance of the evidence and reasonable doubt; he declined "to distinguish between the evidence which should satisfy reasonable men, and the evidence which should satisfy reasonable men beyond a reasonable doubt. While at times it may be practicable to deal with these as separate without unreal refinements, in the long run the line between them is too thin for day to day use."[26] This sounds startling to the modern ear. Is there not a massive difference between 51 percent confidence and, say, 90 percent confidence? Yet Judge Hand never should be dismissed lightly; perhaps the difference between the rules is indeed exaggerated. A juror's experience of believing something is more likely than not may be similar to thinking it true beyond reasonable doubt: as to any point offered in court, either you think it's true or you don't. Still, empirical studies do show that jurors (or at least mock jurors) are more likely to convict under lower standards of proof,[27] and later courts have all rejected Hand's view—but have left the difference between the standards imprecise. A survey was made of 171 federal judges, asking them to assign percentages to the certainty they associate with proof beyond reasonable doubt. Twenty-one said 100 percent, 25 said 80 percent or less, and the rest were scattered over various points in between, with the largest number—56—answering 90 percent.[28]

The range of numbers that judges attach to reasonable doubt may seem to cry out for a formal settlement of the matter: what *is* the right number? Nobody will say. A few years ago a judge in Nevada told a jury that reasonable doubt was "about seven and a half, if you had to put it on a scale" of zero to ten. The defendant's conviction was swiftly reversed, both because the number seemed wrong and because it was held wrong to speak in numbers at all.[29] No better, and reversed with as much dispatch, was the Connecticut judge who told the jury that "[y]ou don't have to go a hundred yards for a guilty finding. You got to go somewhere, I suppose, beyond the fifty yard line; where it is in there is up to you to decide."[30] There are appellate judges who have said in their written opinions that confidence beyond a reasonable doubt means "0.9 or so, with adjustments depending on the gravity of the offense,"[31] but there are no known cases of any court approving such a statement to a jury. What we want behind a conviction, it is said, is a felt sense of great confidence on the jury's part, not a belief that the probability of guilt has passed a high numerical threshold.

Might this give up a little too fast on the prospect of thinking in numbers? We already ask jurors to estimate various probabilities, especially in civil cases. They have to decide the chance that some wrong by the defendant caused an injury; or they have to figure the plaintiff's damages, which involves estimates of future wages and life expectancies—all matters of odds. People elsewhere lay down numerical gambles all the time when they make decisions about investments, formal or informal. The trouble is that inviting jurors to bet on the defendant's likelihood of guilt would be unappealing. To continue the analogy, perhaps the trouble is that they're playing with house money; they are deciding whether the terrible coercive power of the government should be unleashed on someone else. We can move away from all thoughts of betting on guilt or innocence, but it's surprisingly hard to come up with other ways of expressing the issue in numbers. For example, you wouldn't want to think in frequencies—to say an 80 percent likelihood of guilt means that if the facts were repeated 100 times, the defendant would be guilty in 80 of them. The real facts of criminal cases don't usually get repeated more than once, and asking jurors to imagine 100 of them invites errors of various sorts. One is a kind of hindsight bias, which we discussed in chapter 23: now that the jurors are presented with an outcome and a particular defendant, they might imagine him guilty more often than really would occur in a large number of rehearsals. It's all hard to say, precisely because the whole exercise is hypothetical. Indeed, in most cases—all those that don't hang on scientific evidence—a number is likely to be just a metaphor for a feeling. To say you are 90 percent sure of something usually reports a mental sensation of certainty rather than a real estimate of odds.

Apart from the true meaning of reasonable doubt is the question of the consequences for defendants of inviting a jury to think in figures. It might seem that putting a number on doubt would invite more convictions; if the approved figure were anything less than 100 percent, it would tell jurors to convict despite believing there is a clear, nameable risk that they have the wrong person—despite believing, perhaps, that if ten or so juries were to make a comparable judgment, one would be mistaken. So they will vote to convict more readily. But the result depends on just how the numbers are used. One study of the issue empaneled mock juries to decide a criminal case. All were told to decide whether the defendant was guilty beyond a reasonable doubt, but some were told as well that before doing so they should put a number on the defendant's probability of guilt. The group that did the latter exercise was less likely than the other to bring in a verdict of guilt. The process of staring the numerical point in the face evidently made the jurors shy about saying they had no reasonable doubts.[32] It goes to show what every good student of decisions knows. The act of quantifying things has psychological consequences, and they aren't always predictable. Since any utterance of a number seems fraught with risk and uncertainty, we don't give one to juries at all; and we don't ask juries to put numbers on their own views, either.

Since numbers are out, it falls to trial judges to offer words that will clarify the meaning of reasonable doubt. Courts turn out to be skittish about this, too. Some refuse to try; some obsess about detail. Upon reading the cases we learn that it's unlawful to tell jurors that reasonable doubt means they must have "an abiding or deep-seated belief of the defendant's guilt," but it's all right to say they must have an "abiding conviction" of it; the difference is that jurors are supposed to have convictions, not mere beliefs.[33] They can't be told that reasonable doubt means an "actual, substantial doubt," but they can be told they must be "firmly convinced" of the defendant's guilt.[34] They can be told not to convict if they have the sorts of doubts that would cause reasonable people to hesitate to act in their own important affairs, but the judge mustn't specify what those affairs might be.[35] Thus a judge will try telling the jurors that they should say the defendant murdered his wife only if they feel as sure of it as they did the last time they decided to buy a house or go in for heart surgery. Then the defendant loses and the court of appeals dutifully reverses, saying the trial judge trivialized the jury's assignment by comparing it to decisions familiar to them. These worries about specific analogies are understandable, for there really aren't any moments in ordinary life that much resemble deciding whether someone committed a crime for which the punishment is death or the loss of liberty. Perhaps we accept more risk in buying a house than we ought to impose on a defendant. The oddity, though, is that people have been put to death—they still are—on the strength of brief deliberation and evidence far too thin to be the basis of a plausible decision to buy or sell real estate. There are convictions with nothing more behind them than a single eyewitness of questionable pedigree. The convictions get affirmed by the same judges who complain that the reasonable doubt standard mustn't be diluted by analogies.

By this point you will detect a trend. Reasonable doubt can't be assigned a number because it's qualitative, not quantitative. It can't be compared to other life decisions, because that only trivializes the issue. If it can be paraphrased at all, it's only at great peril; the more words a court uses, the greater the chance of uttering a reversible gaffe. The law seems, in short, to have a nearly phobic aversion to clarity when it comes to its most important test. Why don't we do more to make sure its words mean the same thing to everyone? One reason may be that we don't want the test to always have the same meaning. Imprecision has its advantages. Lawyers learn this first with respect to contracts, statutes, or judicial opinions, where ambiguity creates spaces in which good things can happen as well as bad; an example of the good is that imprecision delegates the fine-tuning of a rule to someone who will come later and may be more sensitive to points that were out of the original author's view—facts, details, or changed circumstances (see chapter 17 for more on this idea). The reasonable doubt rule might be another case of strategic unclarity. There is reason to think that behind the screen of the standard, jurors demand better proof when a defendant is on trial for murder than they do in a case of petty larceny—the "adjustments depending on the gravity of the offense" we saw a court allude to earlier.[36] Since the cost of a mistake is a lot higher in the capital case, it may be convenient to have this subtle and informal way to raise the bar for conviction; perhaps jurors who have a feel for all the facts of a case can do it more precisely than a legislature could.

One can, of course, also imagine jurors making informal adjustments that are less appealing, or otherwise just differing randomly over the standard's meaning. Those are bad outcomes, but to an extent they may be inevitable under any statement of the standard; and in that case its imprecise phrasing has some offsetting benefits as well. It creates a valuable appearance of equal treatment. The reasonable doubt standard is the basis for thousands of criminal convictions every year. Some, as noted before, rest on most unimpressive evidence, while others are much better founded. But all those cases look as if they have been treated the same way when their results are laid before the public: in every one of them the system intones that there was guilt beyond a reasonable doubt. The vagueness of the standard also shores up confidence in the machinery of justice in another way, by glossing over differences in how people understand the words and the judgments they support. Everyone has some felt idea of what is meant by guilt beyond a reasonable doubt, and when they hear the standard applied by others they are free to fantasize that everyone shares their sense of it. A more explicit definition would cause controversy by forcibly exposing in every case the quality of the match between the evidence and the exact standard it is supposed to meet, which might be controversial.[37] We thus see further dividends of unclarity, as vague standards can serve as supports of a consensus at a high level of abstraction. Naturally this might be regarded in a less positive light, too—as chicanery on the part of the legal system—but on a more charitable view it's a bit of voluntary obscurity or unconsciousness that well serves its players, or at least most of them. In communities of any size—marriages, associations, countries—there are ideals everyone is content to agree upon only at a certain level of generality; they know they may differ on details but prefer not to know too much about them, and their mutual forbearance makes possible various practical achievements.

Now consider a different side of the problem. Earlier we saw that while judges won't instruct juries to think of reasonable doubt as a percentage, many of them are willing to try attaching the words to a number privately. The figures they give usually hover near 90 percent, which sounds pretty strong; on reflection, though, it seems to imply that a frightening share of convictions are mistakes—10 percent, to be exact. But that number probably is misleading. Remember that not all cases are prosecuted. Some are dropped. Others are settled by plea bargains. Prosecutors only can press a fraction to trial, and the high standard of proof may be enough to make them pick the ones where the likelihood of actual guilt is greatest, in turn keeping the real rate of error in the criminal courts very low.[38] In the end the rate of wrongful convictions is unknowable, but the general point, which goes back to the first chapter of this book, is to be careful in thinking about how well a rule works. It depends not only on what happens in the cases that go to court, but also on how the rule affects which cases are selected to appear there in the first place.

There is more reason to pause before moving from the extent of any juror's confidence to a conclusion about a jury's rate of mistake. The discussion so far has been written as though it fell to one person to decide a case; of course it really falls to a group, usually of twelve though sometimes as few as six, and in most states they must be unanimous to convict. Using a group to make the decision provides a second standard of proof along a different dimension. Each juror must be confident, but the group also must be confident. Just as any reasonable doubt within the mind of a juror spoils a conviction, so does the existence of any dissent within the group as a whole. We might think of the jury as if it were one mind—a many-brained creature that must find guilt beyond a reasonable doubt. Unlike a single person whose thinking and actual extent of doubt may be opaque, the many-brained creature reveals its confidence or want of it to the world in an open fashion, by votes from each of its members.

This makes a mild paradox of the Supreme Court's holdings that the reasonable doubt standard is required by the Constitution in criminal cases but that a unanimous jury is not.[39] Still, most states insist on unanimity anyway, so we can take it as the norm and ask how it might relieve worries that if the reasonable doubt standard amounts to 90 percent confidence it implies that one case in ten is wrongly decided. If twelve people each think that something is 90 percent likely to be true, perhaps its actual odds of being true are *better* than 90 percent. This is a rough application of the idea behind the Condorcet jury theorem. (We encountered the Marquis de Condorcet previously in chapter 15.) The theorem holds that under certain conditions, if each voter in a group is more likely than not to decide a question correctly, then the more voters there are in the group, the more likely their majority vote will be correct. The formal requirements of the theorem aren't satisfied by modern juries; it envisions voters who don't affect each other, for example, and are "enlightened" in various ways that may not hold for us.[40] But the idea that adding voters can increase their likelihood of being right is plausible and interesting, and some of the sense of the theorem may carry over to the criminal jury even if it doesn't fit here precisely. It's obvious enough that waiting until twelve jurors feel sure of the defendant's guilt makes an accurate conviction more likely than if only one juror is charged with the decision.[41] The question here is a little different, and more interesting: what does it mean when twelve people agree that the defendant is, say, 90 percent likely to be guilty? Does their agreement mean that he's *more* than 90 percent likely to be guilty, or merely that 90 percent is very likely to be an accurate statement of the odds of his guilt? The question lacks a settled answer.

Here is a final conundrum. Suppose a defendant has been arrested for trying to buy cocaine. He had found a dealer and offered to trade a gun for a couple of ounces of the drug; the dealer accepted, then announced that he was an undercover FBI agent and led the defendant off to jail; now he is being prosecuted under a statute that gives many years of prison to anyone who "uses a firearm" in relation to a drug trafficking offense. This raises a nice question: do you *use* a gun if you try to barter it for drugs, or do you only "use" a gun under the statute by putting it to work as a weapon? There are arguments to make either way; assume it's close but that the judge thinks the statute does cover the case. Well, but wait—how sure must the judge be? We know that in criminal cases the law throws almost the entire risk of error onto the government, so intolerable is the thought of convicting an innocent; that is what it means to require that the government prove guilt beyond a reasonable doubt or else lose the case. Presumably the same goes here. The defendant should get the long, hard sentence only if the judge is sure beyond a reasonable doubt that "use" in the statute covers the trade of a gun as well as the wielding of it. Except that isn't what judges do; they're not required to be convinced beyond a reasonable doubt before they say what the law is. Indeed, they don't confess to using any standard of proof at all when they interpret the law. They just say what they think the law means and that's the end of the case. If there are a few possible meanings of a statute, and the best of them seems just 40 percent likely to be right, that is the one the judges will adopt, however brutal the result may be for the defendant.[42]

At first it seems puzzling that the legal system would be so protective of defendants when juries find facts against them but so indifferent when judges find law against them. To grasp why the standard of proof for decisions of law is so weak, pause and imagine how the world would work if it were otherwise (this is frequently a sound strategy for making sense of strange rules). Let's go back to an example from early in this book. I spend all afternoon chasing a buffalo and at last am closing in on the animal as it starts to tire. At the last minute you emerge from behind a rock and deliver the lethal blow. I say it belongs to me. You say it belongs to you. I grab it and run; you follow and forcibly take the animal back from me. Alas, in our jurisdiction the rule governing this situation isn't written as clearly as we would like; its meaning certainly isn't clear beyond a reasonable doubt. So it follows (on our current assumption) that the law has nothing to say. I can't be prosecuted for theft because my guilt isn't clear beyond a reasonable doubt. (I confess to all the facts, but the *law* isn't clear enough.) But this is good news for you as well, for it also follows that you weren't committing a theft when you took the animal back. Any force you used might itself have been unlawful—unless, of course, it was just the force needed to stop me from stealing your animal, as you claim—a point on which the law (to repeat) is too unclear for a court to enforce. We're well on our way to a blood feud.

A lot of law consists of rules like ones saying who gets the buffalo: law settles disputes; it answers questions; it tells where our rights start and end. But those settlements and answers often aren't written well or with any great foresight; when invoked they may be found not to have meaning, or application to the facts, that can be called clear beyond a reasonable doubt or even by a preponderance of the evidence. To thus conclude that those laws don't count for anything would leave large tracts of conduct outside law altogether and regulated only by self-help. That undoubtedly is one way to run the world, but it fast can turn ugly—with results that explain the lack of popularity that anarchy historically has enjoyed.[43]

It would be too much to say that claims of law never are subject to standards of proof. Sometimes courts create so-called clear statement principles holding that unless statutes say so clearly, they will not be read to create some given result—retroactive application, for instance, or preemption of state authority, or the raising of hard constitutional questions.[44] These principles serve various purposes; they may force lawmakers to deliberate and be clear where those things are most wanted, or they can give courts a way not to deal with thorny problems unless they absolutely must. Anyhow, notice that any such rules require judges to say in a rough way not only what a law seems to mean but how likely that reading is to be right. It shows that courts do know how to apply standards of proof not only to questions of fact but to questions of law—when it suits them. At present the confidence of judges in their legal decisions almost always goes unremarked. They typically just pick whatever reading they think is the best available and then announce it with a strong but vague show of certitude. One could argue that judges should pay more attention to the point; for isn't there something bothersome about a defendant going to prison under a statute that has a questionable fit to the case?

As it happens there is a clear statement principle that bears on this last concern: the rule of lenity, a judge-made principle saying that ambiguities in penal statutes ought to be resolved in favor of the criminal defendant. The roots of the rule lie in the concerns similar to those that produce the high standard of proof for the factual side of a criminal charge. It's best for courts not to send people to prison, or worse, unless they are sure they should. This may appear to be the answer—at last—to your worry about being imprisoned for trying to trade a gun to a drug dealer. Whether you "used" the gun is open to two readings, so the rule of lenity requires that you should have the benefit of the doubt. Or so it might seem. But in the actual case of the traded gun the members of the Supreme Court argued at some length, disagreed, and then a majority of them said the statute did apply to the defendant.[45] They denied that the statute was ambiguous and so had no use for the rule of lenity. The defendant got a thirty-year sentence. The case ended as it did because the rule of lenity isn't a clear standard of proof after all. It's a rule of thumb that has been repeated in so many different words, some strong and some weak, that judges usually are free as a practical matter to invoke or ignore it at their pleasure.[46] We saw earlier that imprecision has its advantages; it has its drawbacks, too.

SUGGESTIONS FOR FURTHER READING. Joseph H. King Jr., *Causation, Valuation, and Chance in Personal Injury Torts Involving Preexisting Conditions and Future Consequences,* 90 Yale L.J. 1353 (1981); C. M. A. McCauliff, *Burdens of Proof: Degrees of Belief, Quanta of Evidence, or Constitutional Guarantees?* 35 Vand. L. Rev. 1293 (1982); Saul Levmore, *Probabilistic Recoveries, Restitution, and Recurring Wrongs,* 19 J. Legal Stud. 691 (1990); Daniel Farber, *Recurring Misses,* 19 J. Legal Stud. 727 (1990); Gary Lawson, *Proving the Law,* 86 Nw. U. L. Rev. 859 (1992).

29 ⟶ The Product Rule

How likely is it that two flips of a coin will both come up heads—and how do you *know* how likely it is? It is 25 percent likely. You know it because the chance that each flip will be heads is 50 percent, or .5; to get the chance that both flips will go that way, you multiply the chance of its happening each time: .5 times .5, which is .25, or 25 percent—the chance of two heads in a row. This is called the *product rule:* to figure out the chance of several probabilities all going a particular way, you multiply them by one another and find your answer in the product. That's all the math you need to understand for this chapter. It isn't much, but it's important; the legal system sometimes has a surprisingly hard time remembering it.

In the previous chapters we talked about various standards of proof: principally proof beyond a reasonable doubt and proof by a preponderance of the evidence, the latter rule amounting to a likelihood of better than 50 percent that the plaintiff's claims are right. But that sketch was too simple, for it assumed that there is just one issue in a case; in many of the examples we pondered, the one issue was causation—in plain terms, whether the defendant's wrong (not bringing a rope onto the ship, or not going back to search for the missing sailor) made a difference. But in most cases there isn't just one thing the plaintiff must prove. There is a list, known as the elements of the claim, and two or more of them may be in dispute. Think again of the forgetful sea captain we talked about last chapter. A member of his crew drowns. In an actual suit on these facts there might be two disputed things the plaintiff has to prove: that bringing a rope onto the ship would have made a difference, as we saw, and that it was *negligent* not to have a rope, which is a different point.

Well, now we have a problem. Let's imagine that the jury thinks the plaintiff is 60 percent likely to be right about each of those issues. It sounds like the plaintiff should win—but perhaps that's wrong. For how likely is it that the plaintiff is right on *both* points? If we apply the product rule we see that it is only 36 percent likely: .6 × .6 = .36. So there appears to be a 64 percent chance that the plaintiff's case is bad. Yet the plaintiff nevertheless will win, for juries typically are told to find for the plaintiff so long as they think *each* element of the case is proven by a preponderance of the evidence. No mention is made that the joint probability of the elements' being satisfied may be much less than that. So while we say a plaintiff has to win by a preponderance of the evidence, it appears that victory actually can be had with far less overall certainty than that.

No one has an entirely satisfying reply to this problem (sometimes known as the *conjunction paradox*), but various thoughts have been offered to help justify it. Maybe the reason juries are instructed to worry about each element by itself is to make sure they don't let the strength of one compensate for the weakness of another. If the jury is 95 percent sure that failing to bring a rope on board was wrongful, that doesn't mean that it should find for the plaintiff if it's only 10 percent likely that the rope would have made a difference; the 95 percent can't be used to make up for the 10 percent, and the typical instruction—that *each* element must be proven by a preponderance of the evidence—at least stops juries from making that mistake.[47] Or maybe the low total confidence we require in the verdict is balanced by the fact that juries have at least six people on them and usually they all have to agree before holding the defendant liable.[48] It's an appeal to the spirit if not the letter of the Condorcet jury theorem discussed last chapter, or (more modestly) just to the significance of conclusions drawn by supermajorities: if six people all agree that each element of a claim is more than 50 percent likely to be true, then the fact that they all agree might make the actual probability that the claims are true even greater than 50 percent—which might help offset a bit the fact that the product rule makes the decision *less* impressive than it looks. But again the conditions for the jury theorem aren't all satisfied here, so this argument has provoked its share of dissent.[49]

Another comfort is that sometimes the jury might just be comparing two stories: the plaintiff's and the defendant's. Richard Posner offers this example:

> Suppose, in a case in which the plaintiff's case has two elements—that a person hit him and that the person was the defendant's employee, elements which are independent of each other—the jury reckons the probability of the first element at .6 and of the second at .7, for a joint probability of .42. This still leaves the question: What did happen? Did the plaintiff fabricate his claim? Was he injured, but by someone else? If the injurer was not the defendant's employee, what was his status? Mulling over these questions, the jury may rationally conclude that the plaintiff's story, even though it

> has doubtful features, is more plausible than the alternative story told by the defendant, and therefore that the plaintiff should win.[50]

It might seem paradoxical that the plaintiff could win even if the jury thinks the elements of his case are only 42 percent likely to all be satisfied. But as Posner points out, if the jurors were confronted with the paradox they might go rethink their initial estimates of the probabilities to make them greater than 60 percent in the plaintiff's favor after all—and there would be nothing wrong with that sort of revision to reconcile the results.[51] Not all cases lend themselves to this sort of reasoning; sometimes there are lots of possible stories besides the ones the two parties are offering. But when a case does look like this—when it boils down to a choice between two stories—the law's failure to use the product rule isn't so troubling.

Notice, too, that a rigorous use of the product rule would make some types of cases hard to ever win. We have been thinking about cases with two issues in them. Now let's add a third and fourth. Imagine that a statute of limitations gives a sailor's kin two years after his death to bring suit. They file their claim a week late. They say they waited because they were trying to reach a compromise with the defendant—the sea captain—and he promised that he wouldn't complain if they waited past the deadline. Now he has reneged and is trying to have the suit dismissed. Let's assume that if all this is true the law will allow the late claim—but the captain denies saying any such thing, and denies as well that it would have been reasonable of the sailor's kin to rely on such a statement anyway. The court might submit all four issues to the jury: whether a rope ought to have been on the ship; whether it would have saved the sailor; whether the captain promised the plaintiffs more time to sue; and, if so, whether it was reasonable of the plaintiff to rely on him. The jury will be told to hold the captain liable if it finds for the plaintiffs on each of those four points by a preponderance of the evidence. If we take the product rule for all it's worth, it shouldn't be enough if the plaintiff proves he is 80 percent likely to be right about each of those things. That would still mean an overall likelihood of 41 percent that his whole case is right, which isn't good enough. But to ask for more than 80 percent certainty on each element gets us close to making the plaintiff meet the reasonable doubt standard from criminal law.

Speaking of which: what if the product rule applied in criminal cases? If reasonable doubt were to mean something like 95 percent certainty, as might be supposed, then it wouldn't be good enough for the jury to be 95 percent sure about each of the two or three elements in dispute—the defendant's identity, perhaps, and whether he was acting with the intent required by the criminal provision, and whether he was entrapped. The jury could be 98 percent sure about each of those things and still would come up short of 95 percent confidence in total once the product rule was applied. The example is artificial because juries don't think like that; we have seen that the legal system doesn't reduce reasonable doubt to a number. But the implication of the product rule is that proof beyond a reasonable doubt might become very hard to establish in some cases—even in some very strong cases—if there are multiple elements of proof in them. So the law's indifference to the product rule may reflect some sort of pragmatic judgment that the mathematically incoherent approach produces about as many verdicts of guilt and liability as we want. Or it may just reflect ignorance or neglect. Most judges and lawyers do not spend much time pondering it.

Another reason why ignoring the product rule might not be *so* bad is that the rule can get tricky to apply—and in ways that have implications which go beyond standards of proof. The classic example is *People v. Collins*,[52] a California case from the late 1960s. A woman was pushed down in an alley and her purse was snatched. A witness saw the thief running from the scene and described her as white with a blond ponytail; he said she got in a yellow car with a bearded black man, and they drove away. Later that day the police arrested a woman who matched that description—white with a blond ponytail, driving in a yellow car with a bearded black man. At her trial the prosecutor brought in a professor of mathematics to testify about the bearing of the product rule on the case. The prosecutor had supplied the professor with these assumptions about the probabilities of each feature of the witness's description:

The chance that any given car would be yellow was 1/10.
The chance that any given man would have a moustache was 1/4.
The chance that a girl would have a ponytail was 1/10.
The chance that a girl would have blond hair was 1/3.
The chance that a black man would have a beard was 1/10.
The chance that a car would contain an interracial couple was 1/100.

The prosecutor and the professor explained to the jury that the chance of all of those things happening could be estimated by multiplying them together: 1/10 × 1/4 × 1/10 . . . and so forth; with the result that there was only 1 chance in 12 million that any couple had all these characteristics, and thus 1 chance in 12 million that the defendant was innocent. The jury brought in a conviction.

The California Supreme Court reversed, holding all this an abuse of statistical argument. An initial problem was that the estimates the prosecutor was multiplying had no real foundation; he was just speculating. But the more interesting flaws in the argument ran deeper. The first, though not the most critical, was that the product rule applies only to probabilities that are independent of one another. If the chance that a man has a moustache is 1 in 4 and the chance that he has a beard is 1 in 10, that doesn't mean the chance that he has a moustache *and* beard is 1 in 40 (4 × 10)—because many people with beards also have moustaches; having one of them makes having the other more likely.

The point is important when, as here, we are trying to figure out the significance of various factors in the identification of a suspect. But it also might mitigate still further our earlier worry that the product rule is disregarded when juries decide civil lawsuits. It may be that the different elements of a plaintiff's case are, like a beard and a moustache, often interdependent. A finding that a rope should have been kept on the ship and a finding that it would have saved a man gone overboard, for example, are considered separate issues, but they might be far from independent; maybe one reason we're so sure the ship ought to have had a rope is that it would have been so likely to have mattered. Or maybe the jury's judgments on both scores will be influenced by the same thing—the sea captain's demeanor and credibility on the witness stand, let's say—and so again will overlap: if he's likely to lose on one issue, he's likely to lose on both of them. Thus if there are two elements in the plaintiff's case and they both are proven to a likelihood of 70 percent, their true joint likelihood may be greater than the 49 percent you get by multiplying them together; if they are interdependent in the ways just suggested, their joint likelihood probably is better than 50 percent after all. In some cases, at least, this may help take some of the edge off the fear that juries are holding people liable when the product rule suggests they shouldn't.

But now go back to case of the mugger with the blond ponytail. The deepest problem with the prosecutor's argument was different from either of the points just discussed. It's that the argument was illogical. Those identifying factors—the defendant's matching hair color, the color of the car, and so on—might have been very telling if they matched someone who was a suspect for other reasons (we will discuss an example like this in the next chapter). But if the match to those factors is the only evidence in the case, it's flimsy. The abuse of the product rule in *Collins* is known generally as the prosecutor's fallacy. The prosecutor points out that the chance of a random person matching some set of characteristics is small—say, 1 percent; and from this he invites the inference that since the defendant does have that set of characteristics, his chance of being guilty must be 99 percent.[53] It sounds plausible if you don't think about it too hard; if you do think about it, you discover it's wrong. But why?

The analysis is wrong because it is answering the wrong question. The issue in a criminal case is not how the defendant's chances of guilt compare to those of a random person. The issue is how the defendant's chances of guilt compare to the possibility that someone else—*anyone* else—did it. The defendant could be hundreds of times more likely than a random person to be guilty—but still be very likely to be innocent. If 1 person in 100,000 has that damning combination of traits, and there are 1 million people in the relevant population—the state or county—then there will be 10 people who fit the description. If you pick up any one of them just because they match, there are 9 chances in 10 that you've got the wrong person. In *Collins* the numbers were larger (1 in 12 million), but it still was reasonably likely that there was another couple fitting the same description in the area. (Yes, but what area? That was still another problem with the argument: one has to decide whether the relevant population is the neighborhood, city, state, or country.)[54] Using the product rule correctly isn't just a matter of getting the math right or making sure the inputs are independent. It's also a matter of being careful to ask the right question in the first place.

Linda is thirty-one years old, single, outspoken, and very bright. She majored in philosophy. As a student, she was deeply concerned with issues of discrimination and social justice, and she also participated in antinuclear demonstrations.

Which is more likely now?

1. Linda is a bank teller.
2. Linda is a bank teller and is active in the feminist movement.

This is a problem made famous by Amos Tversky and Daniel Kahneman, who offered it to many people and found that most of them—87 percent—picked (2).[55] That's wrong, of course; the product rule says that the chance of two things being true—that Linda is a bank teller *and* active in the feminist movement—is gotten by multiplying their chances together; the result always has to be smaller than the chance of either of them being true alone. To put it differently, (2) is a subset of (1), so it can't be more likely to be true. To suppose otherwise is sometimes known as the *conjunction fallacy*.

You probably didn't get caught by the Linda trap. After all, you have just been reading all about the product rule. But many people do fall for it. There are various ways to explain why. Maybe they can't help inferring that part of (1) is a statement that Linda *isn't* active in the feminist movement, and so regard themselves as just comparing two stories after the fashion we described earlier; but the result seems to hold in variations on the problem where that worry is not present. The authors' explanation of the study was that providing more detail about a story, as by describing Linda as a feminist, makes it easier to imagine—makes it more "representative" of a model they have in mind—and thus causes people to reckon it more likely, even though adding more details actually makes it less likely.

Another commentator suggests that the real difficulty in the problem is the way it invites us to think about probabilities; he recommends breaking problems like this down as if they involved large populations instead of abstract probabilities.[56] After all, when you say that Linda is more likely to be one thing rather than another, what do you really mean? One possibility is this: you mean that if there were a hundred Lindas, some share of them would have a given trait and the rest wouldn't. This way of thinking about problems sometimes make it easier to see them clearly. The Linda experiment was rerun, but this time the subjects were told there were a hundred people fitting the description in the opening paragraph; they were then instructed to guess how many of the hundred were bank tellers, and how many of the hundred were bank tellers active in the feminist movement. The number of subjects who committed "conjunction violations" dropped to 22 percent.

That trick—thinking in frequencies—is useful for understanding a lot of problems involving numbers. We will see other examples soon. But it doesn't solve all our problems. In another sequel to the Linda study, a bunch of experts on foreign policy were asked how likely it was that the United States would break off diplomatic relations with the Soviet Union within the next year. Another group was asked how likely it was that within the next year the Soviet Union would invade Poland and the United States would then break off diplomatic relations. The second group estimated the chances significantly higher than the first. Again this seems backwards: the second scenario had more elements than the first, and these needed to be multiplied, so the scenario must have been less likely to occur; yet it was predicted more often than the simpler and therefore more likely scenario.

Notice that this last study didn't lend itself so well to thinking in frequencies because the subjects here, unlike those in the Linda experiment, weren't being asked to compare the likelihood of two things. They simply were asked to estimate the chances of an outcome laid in front of them, with their results then compared to what others said. This is more often the situation in which lawyers and their audiences find themselves. Usually they aren't comparing two possibilities, one of which is the same as the other but with more details. Usually they're arguing about the likelihood that some given story is true: how a tort or crime occurred, or about what consequences might follow from a decision.

A valuable lesson of the "Poland variation" of the experiment is that stories often become more convincing when they are told in concrete detail, even if the details actually make the account less probable than it would otherwise be. That is why good lawyers don't speak in abstractions when they want to make an account or a prediction seem likely. They tell stories in detail. They might be suggesting to a jury how an accident occurred or trying to convince a judge that if such-and-such decision is made, it may lead to good or bad incentives or consequences down the line. Detailed examples make these kinds of arguments seem more convincing because they make the hazards involved easier to imagine and thus seem more likely to occur. That is why these principles are important for rhetoricians to grasp, not to mention their audiences.

SUGGESTIONS FOR FURTHER READING. Michael O. Finkelstein and William B. Fairley, *A Bayesian Approach to Identification Evidence,* 83 Harv. L. Rev. 489 (1970); Richard A. Posner, *An Economic Approach to the Law of Evidence,* 51 Stan. L. Rev. 1477 (1999); Saul Levmore, *Conjunction and Aggregation,* 99 Mich. L. Rev. 723 (2001); Ronald J. Allen and Sarah A. Jehl, *Burdens of Persuasion in Civil Cases: Algorithms v. Explanations,* 2003 Mich. St. L. Rev. 893; Amos Tversky and Daniel Kahneman, *Judgments of and by Representativeness, in* Judgment under Uncertainty: Heuristics and Biases 84 (Daniel Kahneman, Paul Slovic, and Amos Tversky eds., 1982); Gerd Gigerenzer, *Why the Distinction between Single-Event Probabilities and Frequencies Is Important for Psychology (and Vice Versa), in* Subjective Probability 129 (George Wright and Peter Ayton eds., 1994).

30 ↠ The Base Rate

We just talked about a principle of probability—the product rule—that is easy to grasp, though sometimes also easy to forget. There is one other such principle that we need to talk about. It's usually called the *base rate.*

After much study, the police determine—never mind how—that for every 100 people who ride on an airplane, one of them, on average, is carrying drugs. They bring a police dog named Merlin to the airport to help find the culprits. Merlin sniffs every passenger who exits a plane, and he barks when he smells drugs. Merlin is highly skilled. He *never* misses drugs when they're present. He occasionally is prone to giving false alarms, but not often; if no drugs are present, he is 90 percent likely to keep quiet. Smithers steps off the plane, and Merlin barks at him. How likely is it that Smithers is carrying drugs?

I pose this question because many people get it wrong; you should very much want to get it right, because it comes up in different ways all the time. It seems at first that Smithers probably has drugs. Merlin makes mistakes only 10 percent of the time; if he barks, Smithers is 90 percent likely to be carrying drugs, isn't he? No. The chance that Smithers has drugs is about 1 in 11 (or 9 percent, if you prefer). The trick is that you have to remember not just Merlin's chance of being right but also the background chance that Smithers has drugs in the first place, which is low. Think of it this way: for every 100 passengers that come off the plane, only one of them will be carrying drugs. Merlin will always bark in those cases. But then when the other 99 passengers come off the plane without drugs, Merlin also will bark some of the time—10 percent of the time, to be exact. So out of this batch of 100 passengers, maybe Smithers is the one with the drugs, but chances are better that he's one of the 10 Merlin will accuse wrongly. Here is another way to express the point: when you hear of a 10 percent rate of error, you need to carefully ask, 10 percent of what? It might seem to mean that 1 out of every 10 people Merlin barks at will be innocent, but in fact it means that 1 out of 10 people who are innocent get barked at anyway—which is not the same thing. So to make sense out of Merlin's barks, you need to know how likely each person in the pool is to be guilty in the first place. You need to know their background likelihood of guilt; you need to know the base rate.

To make the point even more intuitive, try it like this: imagine that *one person in the world*—call him Waldo—is carrying some rare drug. In search of him, Merlin starts to sniff every person on the planet—all 6,415,000,000 of them. Merlin will bark if he finds Waldo; he also will bark wrongly 10 percent of the time. Merlin barks at you. How likely is it that he just found Waldo? Not very. On his way to finding the real Waldo he is going to set off about 641,500,000 false alarms. You're probably in that group. Hey, wait: if he barks wrongly only 10 percent of the time, doesn't that mean you're 90 percent likely to be the right man? No, and now it's easy to see why: he has a 10 percent error rate in screening people, *almost all of whom are innocent.* That background likelihood of innocence is the dominant fact here, not Merlin's rate of error.

Our airport example is similar to the case of the one man in the world. It just involves less overwhelming background numbers: a less imposing base rate, as it is called, or less imposing prior odds. The first big lesson of this discussion is simply to remember base rates and not just the probabilities in the foreground of a problem. But our second task is to figure out how to get the actual right answer in the airport problem and others like it, and without doing messy mathematical calculations that will cause most readers to run screaming for the exits. I will do my best to explain it in words. It's important, and it isn't that hard.

Basically you want to build a fraction to show how likely Merlin is to be right—1 chance in 11, or something like that. *On top you put the number of times (in 100) that the dog will bark and be right. On the bottom you put the number of times (in 100) that the dog will bark at all—rightly or wrongly.* That's what you really want to know: how the number of correct barks compares with the number of total barks. Sometimes instead of using the number of times these things would happen in 100 tries, you might use the number of times in 1,000. It doesn't matter, so long as you use the same number (say, 100 or 1,000) in all of your thinking. We'll see an example in a minute. But to stick with the airport case, the number on top is the number of times in 100 that Merlin will bark at someone who does have drugs. That's easy here; we know that one person in 100 carries them, and that Merlin always finds him. So the number on top is 1. On the bottom we put the number of times Merlin will bark, rightly or wrongly, in the course of 100 sniffs. He will bark rightly 1 time in 100, as we just saw. He will bark wrongly in 10 percent of the remaining 99 cases—which we can round off to 10. That's a total of 11 alarms by Merlin. So the odds that his barking will lead to a find are about 1/11.

Let's do another. When he applies for a green card so that he can work in the United States, Smithers is required to take a test to see whether he has AIDS. The background chance that someone from his country has the disease is 1 in 250. The AIDS test he takes catches the disease in every person who has it. It also produces false positives 4 percent of the time. (Tests for AIDS nowadays are better than that, but bear with the example.) The test on Smithers comes up positive. What are the chances that he has AIDS? At first the chances look great: the test yields a false positive only 4 percent of the time, so that means he's 96 percent likely to have the disease, right? Wrong, of course, as you now understand. We have to account for the base rate—the background unlikelihood that he has the disease. And we know how to do this. We build a fraction. On top goes the number of times the dog will bark and be right, or, here, the number of times the test will be positive and will rightly find AIDS. Since 1 person in 250 has AIDS, and since the test catches all of them, that's 4 in 1,000 (we'll use thousands here so that we can work with whole numbers). So we can put a 4 on the top of the fraction. On the bottom goes the number of times the dog will bark, rightly or wrongly—or, here, the number of times the AIDS test will be positive, rightly or wrongly, in 1,000 tries. First there are the 4 *accurate* positives that we just mentioned. Then there are the *erroneous* positives, which happen 4 percent of the time. That's 4 times in 100, or about 40 times in 1,000. ("About" is the right word because we should have removed the 4 of those 1,000 cases that do have AIDS. But we're close enough.) The number on the bottom of the fraction thus is 44: 4 correct positives and 40 bad ones in every 1,000 tests. Now we can see the odds that Smithers has AIDS when his test says so: 4/44, or 1/11, or about 9 percent—roughly the same figure as in our airport case, as it happens.[57]

In the appendix to this chapter there are some more problems like these in case you are interested in playing with them; they will show a few other complications that can arise. In the meantime, you get the idea. You can go a long way with the technique of putting the correct barks on top and *all* the barks on the bottom. That won't be enough to solve complicated problems, but it will help with the simple ones, which otherwise leave most people flummoxed. Notice a key move in all the problems: turning the percentages into stories where you imagine a hundred or a thousand run-throughs, with some number of them coming out one way and the rest coming out the other. This technique—thinking in frequencies, as it sometimes is called—helps make problems involving percentages easier to understand.[58] You have to be careful with it, because a statement of a probability may not actually amount to a claim about how often the thing has happened or will happen. When we speak of a 60 percent chance that the plaintiff was run over by one of the defendant's taxicabs, we might imagine 100 such accidents, and suppose that the defendant's cabs were responsible in 60 of them—but there may really be no other accidents quite like the one in the plaintiff's case. When we speak of probabilities in a case like that, we just are expressing our subjective sense of confidence that the thing did happen—perhaps the odds we would use in placing a bet on the matter. But thinking in frequencies still is a useful tool to make numbers easier to picture in the mind's eye.

The general family of ideas we are considering here goes by the name of Bayesian methods, after Sir Thomas Bayes, a British mathematician who lived in the 1700s. He was the creator of Bayes' theorem, which is a way of getting from prior odds to so-called posterior odds; the methods of calculation offered above are essentially shortcut versions of what Bayes offered, and take you to the same place.

Now we have some useful tools for thinking about the likelihood that something is true. But when can you use them in court? Start by thinking of a civil trial where the jurors hear some piece of testimony. They are supposed to decide whether the plaintiff's claim more likely than not is true—whether, to say it numerically, the plaintiff's story is more than 50 percent likely to be right. Maybe the new testimony the jurors hear gets them over the 50 percent bar, or maybe it doesn't; but where do they *begin*? What should they assume are the background odds that the plaintiff is right? Jurors who hear new evidence are like the police who hear the dog bark, or the immigrant whose AIDS test comes back positive: none of them can know what to make of this new information unless they know the base rate, or the prior odds of whatever it is they are trying to decide. Another way to put the point is that when we get new information on a question—a barking dog, an AIDS test, or testimony at a trial—we don't hear it against a backdrop of no opinion at all. It always causes us to revise (or *update*, as Bayesians say) our earlier sense, however weak, of what the answer to the question probably was. So when a piece of evidence is shown at a trial, what is the base rate from which the jury should operate—the benchmark comparable to the one chance in a hundred that the passenger on the airplane had drugs?

It seems natural to reply that the jurors should start with even odds: a belief that the plaintiff is as likely to be right as wrong. This sounds consistent with the preponderance of the evidence standard and the usual view that it amounts to confidence better than 50 percent. But it would lead to embarrassing problems.[59] It would mean that any evidence at all in the plaintiff's favor would get him to 51 percent and to victory. Suppose the plaintiff was attacked by someone wearing a ski mask; all he could see was that the attacker had brown hair. Sixty percent of the people in the region have brown hair. The plaintiff picks one of them at random and sues him for damages. If the jurors start with a belief that the defendant is 50 percent likely to be the right person, then all the plaintiff might have to do is point out that the defendant has brown hair; for that makes it slightly *more* likely than 50 percent that the defendant was indeed the attacker. But that seems crazy. The plaintiff just picked any brown-haired person at random and sued him; he probably is innocent. The analysis of this problem is explained in the appendix to this chapter, but the basic reason for the bizarre result is that we *began* by assuming—in our usual fanciful fashion—that if the plaintiff were attacked 100 times, the defendant would be the attacker in 50 of them. There was just no reason to think that.

We could go through a similar example on the criminal side. A starting assumption that the defendant is 50 percent likely to be guilty might seem fine, since the prosecutor still has to get well to the north of that number to gain a conviction under the "reasonable doubt" standard. But that's still ungenerous to the defendant, since he is supposed to be presumed innocent. That doesn't mean the jurors should assume it's equally likely that he's guilty or innocent; it means they should start with the assumption that he *isn't* guilty. But just how strong should the assumption be? What we now see is that the presumption of innocence, or any other statement of where the burden of proof lies, can be viewed as the selection of a base rate—a background likelihood of guilt or innocence that will then be revised by the evidence in the case. Should the jury be told to start by assuming that the defendant is no more likely to be guilty of the crime than any random person on the street? So it has been suggested;[60] but then should the strength of the assumption depend on how many people there *are* on the street? Isn't a defendant in a small town more likely to be the right person than a defendant in New York City? Well, nobody says so.[61]

There aren't any settled answers to these questions. We have seen earlier that jurors aren't instructed to turn standards of proof into numerical tests. By the same token they certainly aren't told to think in the probabilistic ways we have been developing here, nor do judges talk this way. Jurors, like anyone, all start with priors about how likely the defendant is to be liable (in a civil case) or guilty (in a criminal one), but they are told only who has the burden of proof and what standards they have to meet. The details are left to the imagination.

So much for quantifying the burden of proof. Now what happens if a plaintiff wants to use a base rate—a statistical generalization—as his *only* evidence to meet it? The classic example involves a plaintiff run over by a bus. He remembers nothing. All we know this time is that 80 percent of the buses in town are owned by the defendant. Should this evidence alone make the plaintiff a winner? It does seem more likely than not that the defendant owned the bus, and that's the question in a civil case. Yet nobody thinks the plaintiff should win such a lawsuit without other evidence.[62] Various reasons have been put forward to explain the intuition. As explained earlier, in a case like this the real question is how confident the jurors are that the plaintiff is right; and if the statistics are the plaintiff's only evidence, the jurors might not have much confidence despite the strength of the numbers. They might reasonably wonder *why* that is the only evidence the plaintiff has put forward. Was the other possible evidence unhelpful to his case? Was he too cheap to do a more thorough investigation? The point can be turned into a claim about incentives: forbidding a case to go forward just on the strength of statistical statements forces plaintiffs to try to find better evidence than that, which we want them to do. Occasionally it might be impossible, but it's hard to tell when that's true and when the plaintiff merely is shirking—so we assume the latter. Apart from all this, allowing the plaintiff to win with that sort of evidence might cause the defendant to lose every such case despite being responsible in only, say, 80 percent of them. That's a hard result, and one that gives the wrong incentive both to the defendant and to the other bus company in town (which never gets held liable).

Another possibility is that the law won't stand for liability on these facts because it would violate the principle that guilt or liability ought to follow from individualized findings of wrongdoing, not mere statements of probabilities. But that principle has been known to bend. In the 1970s many women developed tumors because their mothers took a drug called DES during pregnancy. Unfortunately, by the time the disease appeared the women couldn't figure out which companies had filled the prescriptions their mothers took many years earlier. Many courts have allowed those plaintiffs to win anyway; otherwise these cases would involve recurring misses of the kind discussed in chapter 28. The interesting point was how the courts structured the right to recover. They decided to let each plaintiff collect an amount from each maker of DES that corresponded to the maker's share of the market for the drug.[63] This isn't quite like the bus case because here we know that each maker of DES really did injure some large number of plaintiffs. The base rate here, in other words, isn't just a statement of subjective confidence. It's a true statement of frequencies. If Squibb supplied 30 percent of the DES to the market, the point isn't that we're 30 percent sure Squibb caused the plaintiff's injuries; it's that we're 100 percent sure Squibb caused 30 percent of *all* plaintiffs' injuries. When companies are held liable this way (it isn't done often), there is less violence done to usual notions of fairness and efficiency than we might find in the bus case.

The DES cases are exceptional; base rates alone generally aren't enough to win a case. But then when should they be allowed into a case at all? Let's consider an example of a case where Bayesian reasoning might be helpful. A woman is stabbed to death, and a partial palm print is found on the knife. Only one person in 1,000 has a print that matches. Smithers is one of them, so evidently there's only 1 chance in 1,000 that he didn't do the crime, right? No, that's wrong, as we saw in chapter 29; it's called the prosecutor's fallacy. But in that discussion we were assuming there was no other evidence in the case. Suppose there *is* some other evidence against Smithers; now what are we to make of the handprint? Bayes' theorem provides a way to think about this question that is precise—but not necessarily desirable.[64] Try treating the matching palm print as a new piece of evidence that arrives, like the barking dog, against the backdrop of some given likelihood that the defendant is guilty. (We could have treated the palm print as establishing the base rate and the other evidence as the new information that calls for updated odds; the decision about which information to treat as "in the background" is arbitrary.) In the case of the palm print, the base rate is just the jurors' confidence that Smithers is guilty, based on whatever other evidence they have encountered *before* hearing about the palm print. Perhaps they have already learned that Smithers had a grudge against the victim, and as a result they think that he is 25 percent likely to have committed the crime. Or perhaps they think it's only 1 percent likely. What is the effect of the palm print, again assuming that it would match 1 person in 1,000 in the population at large?

Once more the math will be put in the appendix (problem two); here let's just consider the result. If the jurors thought the defendant's guilt was 25 percent likely before hearing of the handprint, their confidence after hearing about it—or rather the posterior odds of his guilt, strictly from a mathematical standpoint—should become 99 percent. Perhaps more interestingly, suppose the jurors started out thinking there was only a 1 percent chance that Smithers did it. Add the handprint and the odds then go from 1 percent to 90 percent. (We're leaving out some complications—that maybe the handprint does belong to Smithers but he was framed, for example; those could be accounted for with no great change in the outcomes.) This might seem to contradict some lessons from the chapter on the product rule. Wasn't the whole point that you shouldn't jump to conclusions just because the person who committed the crime has some rare trait that the defendant also has? Yes; but this example shows how quickly that reasoning changes if you have something else—even a little something else—to connect the defendant to the crime.

The points just explained aren't very intuitive, and they may not match the actual effect of such evidence on a typical juror's felt sense of confidence—for in practice jurors aren't told how Thomas Bayes would have them update their earlier sense of guilt in view of new evidence, and they aren't invited to think in the way just described. The interesting question is why. Maybe the reason is that jurors would make a botch of it, especially if we tried to add in those complications we left out—that Smithers might have been framed and so forth. Maybe asking jurors to think in terms of numbers does a disservice to the defendant, or to the ritual of the trial, or to our values concerning the meaning of guilt and liability. We want to avoid finding someone guilty because of their membership in a statistical class.

But then comes a last puzzle: sometimes math *does* play a significant role in a case; sometimes courts will allow statistical generalizations as evidence, and sometimes they won't, though it's hard to say quite when and why. In one case a woman was hurt by ice that slid off a passing truck. The truck had a Hertz logo on the side, so she sued Hertz; the court allowed evidence that Hertz owns 90 percent of the trucks with that logo, and as a result was willing to presume it owned this one.[65] In another case a child had been abused and the accused defendant was his father. A doctor told the jury that "eighty to eighty-five percent of child sexual abuse is committed by a relative close to the child"; this was held objectionable, the court saying it was difficult to understand "how statistical information would assist a trier of fact in reaching a determination as to guilt in an individual case."[66] The point can't be (or can't *just* be) that the second case was a criminal prosecution, for prosecutors sometimes are allowed to bring in statistical base rates, too. In a rape case where the victim couldn't identify anything about her attacker except his race, for example, a court allowed the jury to convict the defendant solely on the basis of testimony that the DNA found at the crime would match only 1 in 420 billion black people—and that it matched him.[67]

So sometimes courts do allow statistical generalizations into a case and sometimes they don't—but when? The best efforts to answer the question turn up no rules but a few noticeable tendencies.[68] Such evidence is most likely to be let in when the case has a clearly defined statistical structure (some employment discrimination cases are like this), or when one side wants to rebut the other's claim that some bad event happened by chance (as when two test-takers accused of cheating claim that their similar answers were just a coincidence), or when it will be hard for a plaintiff to come up with any evidence *other* than these sorts of generalities (think again of the DES cases; if the makers hadn't been held liable on a market-share theory, they might routinely have gotten off with no liability).

But the more general point to observe is the pattern of deep ambivalence the law displays about quantification. In a sense all knowledge is based on likelihoods, is it not? Yet courts avoid the explicit use of likelihoods habitually and allow it unpredictably, leaving many of their standards and conclusions unspoken, vague, and perhaps arbitrary because these are thought to be lesser evils than letting numbers play too significant a role in legal judgments. This state of affairs can be seen as part of a more general set of problems we have considered at other points, too: When do we want rigorous quantification in law, and when and why do we avoid it?

APPENDIX ➛ More Fun with Base Rates

1. *The brown-haired defendant.* In the main part of the chapter we considered a case where an attacker has brown hair, as does 60 percent of the population; the plaintiff sues one of the brown-haired people at random. The point of this silly-sounding case is to see what happens—and how the plaintiff wins—when we start with an assumption of even odds that the defendant is the culprit. Our goal is to build a fraction where the top

number is the number of times in 100 that the plaintiff would see brown hair and it would be the defendant's. *If* we assume prior odds of 50/50, then that means in half the cases—50 percent—the defendant *is* the attacker; in all of those the plaintiff would correctly observe brown hair. So the top number in the fraction is 50. The bottom number is 50 plus however many times the plaintiff would see brown hair and it *wouldn't* be the defendant's (like the dog barking when there are no drugs). Here we find that by taking the 50 times when the attacker isn't the defendant and multiplying it by 60 percent (the number of brunettes). That gets us 30. So our final fraction is 5/8, which means the defendant—a random brunette!—is 63 percent likely to be the attacker. But of course that's wrong; as you can see, the incorrect 50 percent base rate is what makes this train of thought end as it does.

2. *The palm print.* In the text we also saw a case where jurors start out thinking the defendant has a 1 percent chance of being guilty, then are shown that his palm print matches the one on the murder weapon—and there was 1 chance in 1,000 of such a match occurring at random. So what is the updated chance that the defendant did the crime? Build the fraction. On top goes the number of times that the dog would bark and be right—or, here, the number of times the palm print would match and be right; this time let's do it out of 10,000 imaginary run-throughs. We started with a 1 percent chance that Smithers was guilty. That means that in every 100 cases "like this," Smithers did it; and his handprint will match, we can suppose, in all of them. So that's 100 times (out of 10,000) that the handprint will match and correctly identify him as the killer. Now the bottom of the fraction consists of all the times the print will match, period—whether rightly or wrongly. It will happen 100 times, as we just saw—plus the times out of 10,000 when the handprint will match but Smithers *didn't* do it, which we need to figure out next. That will be a rare event. One person in 1,000 has the match, so we could expect a bad or mistaken match about 10 times in 10,000 trials. Okay; now we have the bottom of the fraction, too: 110 (the 10 mistakes plus the 100 correct hits). The result looks like this: 100/110. Do the division and you get about a 90 percent chance that Smithers did it.

3. *The O. J. Simpson case.* When O. J. Simpson was put on trial for the murder of his ex-wife, the prosecution attempted to bring in evidence that he had beaten her during their marriage. One of Simpson's lawyers, Alan Dershowitz, famously argued that only a tiny percentage of husbands who beat their wives—"certainly fewer than 1 of 2,500"—go on to murder them; for every 3 million incidents of abuse, there were only

about 1,500 murders (we have rounded off the numbers). How relevant are these statistics? Not very. You can see the problem clearly by structuring it like our other exercises in this chapter. Simpson's beating his wife is like the dog barking because he thinks he smells drugs. It *may* indicate that some underlying fact is present (that Simpson murdered his wife, or the passenger in fact is carrying drugs). To figure out the likelihood, we build a fraction. On top goes the number of times the foreground fact will be present (wife beating) and will correctly suggest guilt. This time let's do it out of 100,000 tries. The background population consists of battered women. If there are 100,000 of them, then some number will be murdered by their husbands—let's say 1 in 2,500, which is the same as 4 in 10,000, or 40 in 100,000. So 40 is the number that goes on top of our fraction. On the bottom of it goes the number of times that a battered wife is murdered by *anyone*, husband or not. Of course we begin with the 40 murders committed by husbands, then we add the number of times such women are murdered by other people. Ah, but this is a very small number: about .05 percent, or 5 out of 100,000. So we add the 5 to the 40, and now we have our fraction: 40/45—or about 89 percent. That is the rough likelihood that if a battered wife is found murdered, she was killed by her husband, at least using the raw numbers borrowed here. I don't vouch for their accuracy; but even if you change them around in plausible ways, it's still clear that the evidence that Simpson beat his wife was far more important than Dershowitz's argument caused it to seem.[69]

Can you summarize why the initial claim was misleading? It was answering the wrong question. The important issue isn't the rate at which battered women are murdered by their husbands. It's how that number *compares* to the rate at which battered women are murdered by anyone—just as we asked how the number of correct barks compared to the number of total barks by the drug-sniffing dog. Merlin's barking wasn't as impressive a piece of evidence as it seemed, because he had a large error rate and most people on a plane aren't carrying drugs. Simpson's abuse was a more impressive piece of evidence than his lawyer made it seem, though, because *once we know a battered woman has been murdered,* her husband's guilt is quite likely—much more likely than possession of drugs by some random passenger on a plane. To turn the point around, the background rates of innocence are different. The rate at which innocent passengers are barked at by the dog is large compared to the rate at which he finds drugs. But the rate at which battered wives are murdered by people other than their husbands is small compared to the rate at which their husbands are guilty.

4. *The taxicab problem.* Here is another classic puzzle. It's a little more complicated than the others.[70] Smithers is run over by a taxi. It was owned either by the Green Cab company or the Blue Cab company. Eighty-five percent of the cabs in the town are green; but Smithers is 80 percent sure the cab that hit him was blue. (Or instead of saying he is "80 percent sure," perhaps imagine that his judgments about these things have been shown 80 percent likely to be right.) Assuming there is no other evidence, what is the chance that he was hit by a blue cab? Remember the method. We build a fraction. On top goes the number of times the dog will bark and be right—or, here, the number of times (in a hundred imaginary accidents) that Smithers will say the cab was blue and be correct. This time it takes an extra minute to figure. The drug-sniffing dog caught the drugs every time they were there, and the AIDS test caught the AIDS every time it was there, but Smithers isn't like that. Even when the cab really was blue, he'll see it right just 80 percent of the time. But don't be distracted: we still want to know the same thing, which is just how many times out of a hundred incidents Smithers will see blue and be right. Think in frequencies. Here 15 cabs out of our 100 imaginary incidents will be blue (since 85 percent of them are green). Smithers will spot 80 percent of them. 80 percent of 15 is 12. That's the number on top of our fraction. On the bottom goes *all* the times Smithers will see blue. That will be the 12 we just counted, plus all the times when he says the cab was blue but is wrong. How many times will that happen? Well, the cab will be green in 85 of the 100 tries we are imagining, and he will get 20 percent of those *wrong* (that's his error rate). Twenty percent of 85 is 17. So now we have our fraction:

$$\frac{\text{12 (the number of times in 100 Smithers will say the cab was blue and be right)}}{\text{29 (the number of times he will say it was blue, whether it was or not—12 + 17)}}$$

This problem was harder than the others because we had to worry about false negatives as well as false positives. We had to take the times the car was blue and multiply it by the chance that he would see it rightly; and we had to take the times the car was green and multiply it by the chance he would see it wrongly. Those numbers together (12 and 17) give us the total number of times in a hundred he will say the car was blue. They are the only numbers we need here. The first one goes on top and both of them get added together on the bottom. (The 12/29 fraction we end with can itself be made a percentage, of course: there's a 41 percent chance the cab was blue.)

SUGGESTIONS FOR FURTHER READING. Michael O. Finkelstein and William B. Fairley, *A Bayesian Approach to Identification Evidence,* 83 Harv. L. Rev. 489 (1970); Laurence H. Tribe, *Trial by Mathematics: Precision and Ritual in the Legal Process,* 84 Harv. L. Rev. 1329 (1971); Richard A. Posner, *An Economic Approach to the Law of Evidence,* 51 Stan. L. Rev. 1477 (1999); Gerd Gigerenzer and Ulrich Hoffrage, *How to Improve Bayesian Reasoning without Instruction: Frequency Formats,* 102 Psychol. Rev. 684 (1995); Richard D. Friedman, *A Presumption of Innocence, Not Even Odds,* 52 Stan. L. Rev. 873 (2000); Jonathan J. Koehler, *When Do Courts Think Base Rate Statistics Are Relevant?* 42 Jurimetrics J. 373 (2002); Peter Tillers and Eric D. Green eds., Probability and Inference in the Law of Evidence: The Uses and Limits of Bayesianism (1988).

31 ⇝ Value and Markets

The chapters in this part began by discussing burdens and standards of proof. We then moved on to problems that arise in thinking about multiple pieces of evidence. Let's now conclude with some thoughts on the last stage of a case: the calculation of damages. It is a useful place to finish, since the interesting problems here raise many themes discussed in the other parts of the book.

A large share of law is devoted to saying what things are worth. When a civil wrong is committed—an act of negligence, say, or a broken contract, or a beating by a police officer—the law's usual reply is to make the wrongdoer pay whoever was injured by it. The payments are called damages. The question is how the size of the damages ought to be figured, which amounts to looking at the rights that the defendant destroyed and asking what they were worth. The same questions arise in a different setting when a government agency decides whether to adopt a regulation that will affect how some activity is carried out, whether it's flying an airplane, running a construction site, or operating a power plant. The regulations might make it safer to do those things; suppose they will prevent property damage, save lives, or avoid some injuries. But the regulations also will be expensive, so we have to decide whether they are worth the cost. Again it comes to a question of value: what is it worth to save property, life, or limb?

An interesting thread connects the law's answer to all these questions: the role of markets in which values can be measured. Sometimes the law searches hard for markets, and sometimes it avoids them. Begin with the simple case where I smash your car into an unrecognizable shape. Repairing it is out of the question. What do I owe you? A new car, you might suppose, but no; for I didn't destroy a new car. I destroyed a *used* car—used by you, at least. So what I owe you is another used car, or rather an amount that will permit you to buy one. We consult the market for used automobiles, figure out what the car I destroyed would have sold for, and then I pay you that amount. You can spend it on a fairly precise replacement for the car you once had or you can put it toward a new model. I owe you, in other words, the market value of that which

I demolished; since there is a good market for such things, this also will amount to its replacement cost.

So now you're happy—or are you? Perhaps not, if you were fond of your old car and so valued it at more than its market price. That extra value you put on your things—your subjective value of them—is lost without compensation when they are destroyed; the law generally won't even try to make it up to you. We saw the reason why in the discussion of administrative cost in chapter 6: trying to estimate how much you *really* value something, apart from how much the market values it, will be difficult, will result in lots of errors, and will make cases harder to settle. But sticking with market value as a measure of damages nevertheless does mean that in just about every case, a winning plaintiff gets less compensation than he should if our goal, so far as money will advance it, is to put him back into the position he had before he was wronged.

The point is that market measures may not be quite accurate. Indeed, sometimes they may be decidedly inaccurate. But when a market can be found, it's usually considered a cheaper and easier way to measure value than any other method. The perplexing difficulties arise when no market is handy, or when it is met with distrust by the courts. Thus a woman presents a camera store with a stack of her old home movies and pays to have them transferred into digital form. The films contain footage of weddings, holidays, little league baseball games, and the like; "they are my life," she tells the clerk, and she implores him not to lose them. He loses them. Now what? The store has a suggestion: it can pay her for the cost of replacement rolls of film. Of course the new rolls won't have any of the pictures that the old ones did, but what was the market value of those pictures anyway? Nothing; for nobody is interested in paying to watch someone else's home movies. And we have seen that the law generally declines to compensate for the extra subjective value someone puts on their goods. Generally—but not always. The court in the case on which this example is based couldn't quite stand to let the store get away with paying market value when it was such a small fraction of the value the plaintiff put on the film.[71] The jury was told to award an amount representing the value of the film to the owner. This, too, might seem a market-like solution: ask what she would have demanded to sell the film, not what anyone would have paid her for it. But that isn't quite what this court (or any other) was prepared to award; the court warned that the jury mustn't compensate for sentimental value, defining *sentimental* to mean "indulging in feeling to an unwarranted extent" or being "affectedly or mawkishly emotional." The plaintiff won $7,500.

Notice two ways of thinking about what the store might owe the customer here: what she would have demanded in payment to give up the film or destroy it outright, which might be an astronomical sum; or a payment worked out by asking what she would have demanded in advance to bear a small risk that the film would be destroyed. Imagine the clerk saying this to her: "I'll try to be careful, but one time in a thousand we do lose the film; if you're willing to pay an extra ten dollars, I can have it delivered by armored car and guarantee that it won't be lost." What would she have said? Perhaps she would have taken her chances; but perhaps she would have paid the $10—and let's suppose so. In that case we have another way to think of the value she put on the film. If we consider the $10 a premium for a kind of insurance, we can reason backwards to the value that the owner of the film put on it for these purposes. You wouldn't spend $10 to insure against a 1/1,000 chance of a misfortune that would cost you only $10 or $100—at least not if you were being economically rational. It wouldn't be worth it. In the long run you would end up paying more in insurance premiums than you ever would collect when the dreaded event occurs. Imagine paying $10 a day for 1,000 days, then collecting $100 on the day when the bad thing happens: it would be a bad deal. But if the loss were worth $1 million to you, the $10 payment to avoid the 1/1,000 chance of it would be a bargain. So to return to our case, if we assume $10 is the most you would pay to accept the 1/1,000 risk of lost film, the implication is that you value the film at $10,000.

We will see this style of reasoning used again in other settings below; let's pause here to ask why it is useful. After all, it might seem arbitrary to focus on the amount the owner of the film would have said it was worth for purposes of insurance. Why not ask instead how much she would have charged to destroy it on the spot? One reason is that when we decide how much compensation to award to the owner of the film, we also are putting a price on the misconduct of the camera store. (It's a simple application of points developed in the first chapters of this book.) The store will use this price when deciding how careful to be in the future, and how much to charge for its services—or whether to offer them at all. If the store has to pay a hundred thousand dollars when it loses a customer's movies because that is the amount the customer would have charged to sell them, the store will have to charge its customers a lot more in the first place to cover the cost of the occasional mishap. The question is whether everyone really wants to pay a lot more up front in order to have the right to collect a giant award of damages if the film is lost. Probably not, since if that's what many people wanted it would be in someone's interest to offer those terms to them.

The same logic can be applied to accidents. There are car accidents every day that cost people their lives. If the wrongdoer in such a case has to pay over the amount the victim would have charged to give up his life, the bill will be very large—not just for the victim, but for everyone else when they buy car insurance. We *could* all pay ten times as much for insurance and then give the victims of accidents ten times as much in compensation as we currently do. The result would be less driving, since owning a car would be far more expensive. The question is whether that is the world anyone wants. If it isn't, then giving mammoth awards of damages after an accident doesn't make sense. It gives victims more than they would have wanted to bargain for, given the costs of such a promise.

We have been comparing two ways of getting at the value of the film to its owner: asking what she would have sold it for, and asking how much insurance she might have thought worthwhile to buy against the chance of its loss. Another advantage of thinking about insurance is that it isn't as prone to exaggeration. The price you would have demanded to destroy the film is a matter of conjecture; there usually will be no way to falsify whatever you might say after the fact, and there is no reason not to claim an enormous sum. But when you are asked to state the value of things you want to insure, whatever you say will determine both how much you get if the thing is destroyed and how large your premiums will be in the meantime. The pressures running both ways help to discipline your estimates. Of course it's too late even for that exercise in the case of the lost film; thinking about the terms of an insurance contract may be a helpful thought experiment, but it, too, is conjectural once the damage is done.

Or is it? The kicker in the case of the lost film is that that the parties *did* have a contract of sorts. It was contained on the back of the customer's receipt. It said that the store's liability was limited to the replacement cost of the film. Yet the court refused to enforce these terms, saying they were unconscionable. The decision seems odd. Here there was no need to construct an artificial market or imagine hypothetical bargaining; there *was* a market, and the parties made a deal. The result of setting aside the deal was to put the court into the hard position of trying to say what the film was worth. Maybe the deal the court forced on the parties was an improvement over the deal they had made for themselves; maybe a higher price up front (which now is inevitable), and a $7,500 penalty if the film is lost, is closer to what they would have agreed upon if they had talked it over. Or maybe not. (Many other courts probably would have enforced the terms of the receipt and left it at that.) The general and interesting trend the decision illustrates is the ambivalence courts feel about markets. Sometimes they stretch to find one; sometimes they avoid resorting to one that is readily at hand.

As that brief reference to car accidents suggests, the sorts of problems we just saw—the struggle to find markets, and sometimes the aversion to them—are repeated when damage occurs to people rather than their property. When people are killed by acts of negligence, wrongful death statutes allow their kin to collect from whoever was to blame—but to collect what? The first item is lost support, which generally consists of whatever wages the victim had coming, with a deduction for whatever amounts he would have spent on himself rather than his family if he had lived. It's much costlier to kill an oil executive than a carpenter, as we saw in chapter 25; the spouse of the first may be awarded $9 million while the carpenter's wife collects an amount perhaps 5 percent of that size.[72] And then what happens if the victim was a housewife who received no paychecks? Here again the courts will try to find a market that can serve as a measure. They are likely to take evidence of the market value of the services the housewife provided: the hourly rate for a cook, a housekeeper, a day care provider, and so forth, multiplied in each case by the number of hours the wife spent on each of those tasks. Then the survivors can collect the sum of those totals.[73] If it seems demeaning to suppose that the contributions of a housewife can be measured in this way, notice that it is *plaintiffs'* lawyers who often try to introduce this evidence. They want to give the jury a solid basis for computing damages.

There is, in theory, another possibility. Suppose a woman graduates from law school and takes a job at a law firm in a big city at an annual salary of $100,000. After three years she quits so that she can raise her children. A couple of years later she is run over by a badly driven bus. Some economists have suggested that in a case like this, the starting point in measuring damages due to the decedent's family must be at least $100,000 per year. The logic is that regardless of the monetary cost of replacing the decedent's services around the house, her family must have considered those services to be worth more than $100,000—for that is the income that she gave up in order to stay at home. If her services had been worth less than $100,000 to the family, then presumably she would have kept her job. This measure of damages thus involves looking at the opportunity cost of the decedent's services. Of course that's a little too simple, because you would need to subtract from the $100,000 the amount the family then would have to spend on household help to make up for the fact that the wife was working. But that's a detail. Using the wife's opportunity cost as a benchmark would still result in much larger awards in some cases than we see now. It is a market measure, just a different one.

No court takes that approach to measuring tort damages. What would be the challenges in doing so? There would be administrative issues, of course—the difficulty of answering the questions accurately. And there would be the problem of disentangling the benefits the decedent got by staying home from the benefits her family got from it. Indeed, if you find the "opportunity cost" approach attractive, ponder a variation on it familiar from earlier in the book: suppose that an oil executive quits his job so that he can pursue his dream of becoming an oil painter, Zen master, or member of another such profession unlikely to be remunerative. He is then run over by a bus. Should his wife now collect, in lost support, the amount he would have made if he had kept the job at the oil company? What's the difference between this and the case of the housewife who left her law firm job? (For a suggestion about the answer, see the discussion similar to this one toward the end of chapter 4.)

A last interesting idea: we could try harder to find ways for people to assess their damages for themselves.[74] At first this sounds strange, but think back to the earlier discussion of the insurance that a film store's customer might have been willing to buy against the destruction of her movies. In effect, people who buy insurance are assessing their own damages—in advance. The key is to structure the job of assessment so that there is pressure not to exaggerate. Insurance policies do this, as we saw, by letting the amount you declare determine what you pay in premiums as well as what you get if the bad thing happens. We could import that logic here and tie the award of damages in a tort case to the amount of life insurance owned by the decedent's family on her life. If the family had no such insurance or very little, they might collect an amount set by statute; but if they did spend a lot on insurance, that could serve as solid proof of how they thought about the person's economic importance.

This, too, is never done. Still, once you start thinking about self-assessment, even more interesting and exotic possibilities (and even less likely, perhaps, to ever be used) come into view. Suppose the victim of an accident is injured but doesn't die, so life insurance is no help in figuring out what their damages might have been. This time you could look at any insurance they bought against disability or other injury, and figure that the benefits of that policy are what the guilty party should pay now. Or, to take the logic into a different field of law, consider the problem of deciding how much a house is worth so that a tax of the right size can be imposed on its owner. Usually an assessor hired by the town comes around to estimate the value of houses; might there be a way to use one of those self-assessment tricks here? The exciting idea isn't to look at how much fire insurance the homeowner bought (why might that be a bad measure of the house's value?). No, the exciting idea is to make the homeowner file a public statement of the value of the house—and then to have a rule that anyone in town can buy the house at that price if they wish. The owner will want to declare a low price to keep his taxes down, but if it gets too low someone who likes his house, or maybe just someone who wants to make him leave the neighborhood, can swoop in and force him to sell. What fun! (There are thoroughbred horse races like this, too, called claiming races. Your horse races against other horses of similar value—in, say, the $20,000 bracket. You can try to sneak your horse into a cheaper bracket where it is more likely to win the races, but you probably won't, because there is a catch: anyone can buy your horse for the price that defines the bracket.) But now we are drifting irresponsibly far from the chapter topic, so it's best to move on. The reader is invited to pursue these charming ideas through the reference to Saul Levmore's work in the margin.[75]

What about cases where someone wants compensation for pain and suffering? Those things, like companionship or the pictures on film, aren't bought and sold in markets, at least directly. (One can pay for painkilling drugs, but let's assume they won't help the victim now.) Even here lawyers often want to search for a market or near substitute that might help anchor the jury's intuitions—but this time it isn't allowed. A valiant effort was made in a case where the attorney for the plaintiff, one Faught, suggested to the jurors that they imagine a job offer:

> [I]f you take it you have to keep it for the rest of your life, you work seven days a week, no vacations, work daytime and night. The other thing is, you only get paid $3.00 a day. Here is your job—your job is to suffer Mr. Faught's disability.[76]

The argument was held improper, yet why? It might seem an ingenious and rational way to figure out what the plaintiff's pain is worth. But courts reject all such efforts—usually called "Golden Rule" arguments—on the ground that they invite the jurors to abandon their neutrality and identify with the plaintiff.[77] Another reason for objection goes back to the problem of the lost film. Awarding the plaintiff as much as he (or the jurors, or anyone) would demand to endure the injury puts a massive price on the infliction of it. That might sound good at first; nobody wants injuries. But again we have to remember that massive awards of damages make the activities to which they apply far more expensive—whether we are speaking of driving a car, performing surgery, or playing hockey. In effect the court in such a case is writing up a hypothetical insurance contract and awarding the benefits to the plaintiff. If the benefits are too small, the costs of the activity won't be brought home to those who participate in it. But if the benefits are too large—larger than the plaintiff would have thought worthwhile to insure in advance—then the activity will be made more expensive than anyone really wants it to be. You can, in all sorts of situations, produce useful and interesting results by asking what sorts of figures and other terms an imaginary insurance policy between the parties would have contained.[78] But courts avoid all semblance of explicit analytical method when they award damages for pain and suffering, so jurors are put back in the familiar position of flailing around arbitrarily. The resulting awards for similar injuries can vary enormously,[79] with the only discipline furnished by judges who, when deciding post-trial motions, make some effort to keep the awards in similar cases similar, whether they involve five figures, six, or seven.

How should lost *pleasures* of life be valued, as when a plaintiff loses the ability to play the violin? Again there are no obvious market measures available to use as benchmarks; many efforts have been made to find nonobvious measures, but they generally have met with resistance in the courts. The most prominent of these attempts are known as "willingness to pay" studies. They begin by trying to determine how much people value their lives by looking at how much they are willing to spend to reduce small risks of death.[80] Suppose, for example, that an airbag for an automobile costs $300, and suppose it is known that every 10,000 purchases of an airbag saves a life. In effect that means $3 million will be spent (by 10,000 consumers) to save that life. Put differently, each purchaser evidently is willing to spend $300 to obtain the benefit of the 1/10,000 chance that it will save his life—and this suggests that each values his own life at $3 million. (If airbags were $1,000 in this example, and people stopped buying them at that price, the economic inference would be that they value their lives at less than $10 million; they would rather accept a 1/10,000 chance of death than pay $1,000 to avoid it.)

Similar studies examine how much extra payment various types of workers demand to perform risky work. Assume window washers who work on top floors of tall buildings have a 1/10,000 greater chance of death than those who work near the ground; as a result, window washers are prepared to accept $300 less in wages to be assigned to low floors. Again, this would suggest that they value their lives at $3 million. Notice that this is similar to asking what the customer at the camera store would have paid for a guarantee that her film wouldn't be lost. There have been many efforts to combine the results of all these studies into an average sense of how much people seem to value their lives.[81] These inquiries are capable of generating widely disparate figures, but the averages they have generated lately are in the $7 million range.[82] That figure can quickly change across times and places and can vary according to the wealth of whoever is being studied. In the late 1990s the usual figure offered in the United States was in the range of $2–3 million.[83] At this writing the value of a life in Indonesia, measured the same way, appears to be about $1 million.[84]

It is true, of course, that people don't value every increment of risk the same way. They might be willing to pay nothing to eliminate a tiny risk and an enormous sum to eliminate a large one;[85] if they would be willing to spend no more than $60 to avoid a 1/100,000 risk of death, that doesn't mean they would be willing to spend no more than $6 million to avoid being killed on the spot. To say it more formally, people's willingness to pay to avoid risks can't be expected to be linear. But the kinds of risks on which the above studies are based tend to be similar in size to the kinds of risks created by defendants in accident cases. This shouldn't be surprising: remember that an important goal of this whole enterprise is to make damage awards that will give those defendants the right incentive to be careful in advance: neither too much nor too little.

Even if we do find a satisfactory way to put a value on a human life, however, that isn't the end of the inquiry; for the objective is to figure out how much someone valued lost *pleasures* in life. Some economists propose to do this by starting with a generic value of an "anonymous" life and then deducting the person's expected lifetime income. Whatever is left over must reflect the value the person assigned to the pleasures he expected to derive from living, as distinct from his expected economic gains. If the plaintiff is said (typically by an expert witness) to have lost

20 percent of the pleasure of living, then the plaintiff should be entitled to recover 20 percent of the sum designated as the value assigned to the enjoyment of life.[86]

These are the most ambitious attempts to tie the value of the lost pleasures of life to a market, but the courts have rejected them. They find these studies bizarre, or they reason more specifically that maybe some people *like* risky work, or take it (and arrive at their salary demands) for reasons other than the risks involved.[87] Courts may also worry that juries will make hash of these studies if they are invited to apply them. In any event, the lost pleasures of life, like pain and suffering and like emotional distress, generally end up measured by juries according to no yardstick in particular.

Those odd-sounding studies we just described may not appeal much to courts, but government agencies are another matter. The Federal Aviation Administration, the Nuclear Regulatory Commission, and other agencies have to make decisions about what precautions to require in the industries they supervise. As we noted at the outset of this chapter, requiring precautions is expensive; somehow agencies have to decide whether the precautions will save enough lives to be worth the cost. They sometimes use survey data of the kind just described to generate the figures they use for this purpose, and end up with numbers in the same range (the Environmental Protection Agency has been using a figure of about $6 million lately).[88] An alternative to that entire approach is "contingent valuation": one can perform surveys in which people are asked how much they would be willing to pay to avoid some result—leading to a finding, for example, that the average American household would be willing to spend $257 to avoid the extinction of the bald eagle.[89]

There are those who object vigorously to cost-benefit analysis as a way to decide whether to issue a regulation. They don't like the idea of deciding whether to ban the use of cellular phones in cars by valuing each life saved at, say, $6 million and then comparing that figure to the value of the work done by drivers on their phones, which may be large when you add up every example of it.[90] The challenge for the haters of such thinking is to come up with an alternative to it. They typically call for moral judgments about whether the lives saved are worth the cost of a regulation, though without reducing the lives to dollar figures. To many economists this sounds like an evasion of the trade-offs involved.[91] One consequence of using moral impressions rather than precise figures is that some regulations will end up saving many more lives than others for the same money; and then it becomes possible to show (it now *is* possible to show) that for the cost of regulation *x* that saves ten lives every year, we *could* have regulation *y* that would save thirty lives per year. Isn't it shocking? It's as if we're consigning an extra twenty people to die for no reason—or so goes the argument.

The comeback is that such an emphasis on what people are willing to pay, and what their lives cost, leads to repulsive results—that cigarette smoking might be a good thing because it causes people to die earlier and saves the money that would be spent keeping them alive in their old age; or that, as Lawrence Summers once suggested, it makes sense to dump toxic waste in countries with the lowest wages (because their willingness to pay to avoid it is lowest).[92] But the economist's dilemmas are not easily avoided. We do have to draw lines between lives worth saving and lives we will allow to be lost. The explicitly economic approach to these issues rings false for many people; they would prefer not to think and speak in that language, even if avoiding it means a measure of arbitrariness. Yet declining to think in terms of cost has a cost, and so it goes. Using markets and numbers to measure value and express judgments solves some problems and creates new ones. Sometimes we prefer one package of problems and sometimes we prefer the other. The debate between these camps is too elaborate to work out in detail here; but notice that it repeats in a new form a thread that runs throughout the law's attempts at valuation and proof, and through much of the discussion in this book—making it a good place to end.

SUGGESTIONS FOR FURTHER READING. W. Kip Viscusi, *Pain and Suffering: Damages in Search of a Sounder Rationale,* 1 Mich. L. & Pol'y Rev. 141 (1996); Margaret Jane Radin, *Compensation and Commensurability,* 43 Duke L.J. 56 (1993); Saul Levmore, *Self-Assessed Valuation Systems for Tort and Other Law,* 68 Va. L. Rev. 771 (1982); Eric A. Posner and Cass R. Sunstein, *Dollars and Death,* 72 U. Chi. L. Rev. 537 (2005); W. Kip Viscusi and Joseph E. Aldy, *The Value of a Statistical Life: A Critical Review of Market Estimates throughout the World,* 27 J. Risk & Uncertainty 5 (2003); Frank Ackerman and Lisa Heinzerling, *Pricing the Priceless: Cost-Benefit Analysis of Environmental Protection,* 150 U. Pa. L. Rev. 1553 (2002); Robert W. Hahn, *The Economic Analysis of Regulation: A Response to the Critics,* 71 U. Chi. L. Rev. 1021 (2004).

NOTES

PREFACE

1. I do not mean to disparage other texts written for newcomers. When I was heading to law school I remember reading Edward Levi's *Introduction to Legal Reasoning* and Karl Llewellyn's *The Bramble Bush.* Both books are interesting—classic, even—but neither was much help to me at that time, and neither overlaps with this project. Jay Feinman's *Law 101* provides the beginner with an overview of the American legal system, which some may find helpful, but it does not teach tools for thought. Larry Solum's online *Legal Theory Lexicon* (http://legaltheorylexicon.blogspot.com/) usefully discusses some of the ideas treated in this book (as well as various others that aren't), but not in the sort of detail or with the number or range of examples that I have in mind.
2. See Ward Farnsworth, *The Taste for Fairness,* 102 Colum. L. Rev. 1992 (2002).
3. See Richard H. Thaler, Quasi Rational Economics (1991).

ACKNOWLEDGMENTS

1. See Eric A. Posner, *Agency Models in Law and Economics,* in Chicago Lectures in Law and Economics (Eric A. Posner ed., 2000), which forms the basis of chapter 9.
2. See Saul Levmore, *Unconditional Relationships,* 76 B.U. L. Rev. 807 (1996), which forms the basis of chapter 16.
3. See Eugene Volokh, *Mechanisms of the Slippery Slope,* 116 Harv. L. Rev. 1026 (2003), which forms the basis of chapter 18.

PART ONE

1. Boyd v. Racine Currency Exch., 306 N.E.2d 39 (Ill. 1974).
2. See Frank H. Easterbrook, *The Court and the Economic System,* 98 Harv. L. Rev. 4, 21–29 (1984); Laurence H. Tribe, *Constitutional Calculus: Equal Justice or Economic Efficiency?* 98 Harv. L. Rev. 592 (1985).
3. For a more detailed discussion of these and other ex ante arguments in encroachment cases, see Richard A. Epstein, Principles for a Free Society: Reconciling Individual Liberty with the Common Good 225–29 (2002).
4. Jaffee v. Redmond, 518 U.S. 1 (1996).
5. See Easterbrook, *supra* note 2, at 21–29.
6. Ghen v. Rich, 8 F. 159 (D. Mass. 1881).

7. See generally Steven Shavell and Louis Kaplow, Fairness versus Welfare (2002).
8. See Fed. R. Civ. P. 51.
9. See, e.g., Brauner v. Peterson, 557 P.2d 359 (Wash. 1976).
10. For a famous expression of the point, see Guido Calabresi, Ideals, Beliefs, Attitudes, and the Law 1 (1985).
11. For the classic statement of this position and elaboration on it, see Richard A. Posner, *A Theory of Negligence,* 1 J. Legal Stud. 29 (1972).
12. Edwards v. Lee, 19 S.W.2d 992 (Ky. Ct. App. 1929). For discussion, see Richard A. Epstein, *Holdouts, Externalities, and the Single Owner: One More Salute to Ronald Coase,* 36 J.L. & Econ. 553 (1993).
13. See Richard A. Posner, The Economics of Justice ch. 4 (1981).
14. See Jules Coleman, Markets, Morals, and the Law (1988); Jeremy Waldron, *Criticizing the Economic Analysis of Law,* 99 Yale L.J. 1441 (1990); Richard S. Markovits, *A Constructive Critique of the Traditional Definition and Use of the Concept of "The Effect of a Choice on Allocative (Efficiency)": Why the Kaldor-Hicks Test, the Coase Theorem, and Virtually All Law-and-Economics Arguments Are Wrong,* 1993 U. Ill. L. Rev. 485.
15. See Anthony T. Kronman, *Wealth Maximization as a Normative Principle,* 9 J. Legal Stud. 229 (1980); Ronald M. Dworkin, *Is Wealth a Value?* 9 J. Legal Stud. 191 (1980); Guido Calabresi, *About Law and Economics: A Letter to Ronald Dworkin,* 8 Hofstra L. Rev. 553 (1980).
16. Cass R. Sunstein, *Legal Interference with Private Preferences,* 53 U. Chi. L. Rev. 1129 (1986).
17. Id.; Jon Elster, Sour Grapes: Studies in the Subversion of Rationality 109–40 (1983).
18. See Robert E. Goodin, Utilitarianism as a Public Philosophy (1995).
19. See Cass R. Sunstein and Richard H. Thaler, *Libertarian Paternalism Is Not an Oxymoron,* 70 U. Chi. L. Rev. 1159 (2003); Jeffrey J. Rachlinski, *Cognitive Errors, Individual Differences, and Paternalism,* 73 U. Chi. L. Rev. 207 (2006); Jon Hanson and David Yosifon, *The Situation: An Introduction to the Situational Character, Critical Realism, Power Economics, and Deep Capture,* 152 U. Pa. L. Rev. 129 (2003).
20. For discussion of this and other examples, see Frank H. Easterbrook, *The Court and the Economic System,* 98 Harv. L. Rev. 4, 12–14 (1984).
21. For discussion, see David Friedman and William Sjostrom, *Hanged for a Sheep—The Economics of Marginal Deterrence,* 22 J. Legal Stud. 345 (1993).
22. For an interesting empirical inquiry into the issue, see Thomas B. Marvell and Carlisle E. Moody, *The Lethal Effects of Three-Strikes Laws,* 30 J. Legal Stud. 89 (2001).
23. United States v. Fountain, 768 F.2d 790 (7th Cir. 1985) (Posner, J.).
24. See, e.g., City and County of Denver v. Kennedy, 476 P.2d 762 (Colo. App. 1970).

25. For further discussion of these examples and of the influence of strict liability on "activity levels," see Richard A. Posner, Economic Analysis of Law 180 (6th ed. 2002); Steven M. Shavell, *Strict Liability versus Negligence,* 9 J. Legal Stud. 1 (1980); Steven M. Shavell, Economic Analysis of Accident Law (1987).
26. Miranda v. Arizona, 384 U.S. 436 (1966).
27. For discussion of these arguments, see William Stuntz, *Miranda's Mistake,* 99 Mich. L. Rev. 975 (2001).
28. See Kathleen Sullivan, *Against Campaign Finance Reforms,* 1998 Utah L. Rev. 311.
29. Richard G. Lipsey and Kelvin Lancaster, *The General Theory of Second Best,* 24 Rev. Econ. Stud. 11 (1956).
30. The following discussion is condensed from Thomas S. Ulen, *Courts, Legislatures, and the General Theory of Second Best in Law and Economics,* 73 Chi.-Kent L. Rev. 189 (1998).
31. This example is adapted from the discussions in Richard S. Markovits, *Monopoly and the Allocative Inefficiency of First-Best-Allocatively-Efficient Tort Law in Our Worse-Than-Second-Best World: The Whys and Some Therefores,* 46 Case W. Res. L. Rev. 313, 320 n.7 (1996); John J. Donohue III, *Some Thoughts on Law and Economics and the General Theory of Second Best,* 73 Chi.-Kent L. Rev. 257 (1998).
32. See Richard S. Markovits, *Second-Best Theory and Law & Economics: An Introduction,* 73 Chi.-Kent L. Rev. 3 (1998); Donohue, *supra* note 31; Richard S. Markovits, *Second-Best Theory and the Obligations of Academics: A Reply to Professor Donohue,* 73 Chi.-Kent L. Rev. 267 (1998); Herbert Hovenkamp, *Antitrust Policy and the Social Cost of Monopoly,* 78 Iowa L. Rev. 371 (1993); Richard S. Markovits, *The Case for "Business as Usual" in Law-and-Economics Land: A Critical Comment,* 78 Iowa L. Rev. 387 (1993).
33. The argument of Ulen, *supra* note 30.
34. See Kenneth W. Simons, *The Hand Formula in the Draft Restatement (Third) of Torts: Encompassing Fairness as Well as Efficiency Values,* 54 Vand. L. Rev. 901, 904 n.12 (2001); Mark F. Grady, *Discontinuities and Information Burdens* (reviewing William M. Landes and Richard A. Posner, The Economic Structure of Tort Law (1987)), 56 Geo. Wash. L. Rev. 658 (1988).
35. See, e.g., Ward v. Rock against Racism, 491 U.S. 781 (1989).
36. 22 Eng. Rep. 27, 33 (Exch. Ch. 1862).
37. See United States v. Carroll Towing Co., 159 F.2d 169 (2d Cir. 1947).
38. Stephen G. Gilles, *The Invisible Hand Formula,* 80 Va. L. Rev. 1015 (1994).
39. See, e.g., Kershaw v. McKown, 196 Ala. 123 (1916).
40. 124 N.W. 221 (Minn. 1910).
41. On which see Eagle Terminal Tankers, Inc. v. Insurance Co. of the U.S.S.R., Ltd., 637 F.2d 890 (2d Cir. 1981); Thomas Schoenbaum, Admiralty and Maritime Law (2004).
42. Some of these rules have varied over time. For discussion of them, see Saul Levmore, *Rethinking Comparative Law: Variety and Uniformity in Ancient and*

Modern Tort Law, 61 Tul. L. Rev. 235 (1986). Levmore was a great help with these admiralty examples.

43. For extended discussion of these issues, see Richard A. Epstein, *Holdouts, Externalities, and the Single Owner: One More Salute to Ronald Coase,* 36 J.L. & Econ. 553 (1993).
44. See Henry C. Simons, Personal Income Taxation: The Definition of Income as Problem of Fiscal Policy 51–52 (1938).
45. The term was introduced in Guido Calabresi, The Costs of Accidents: A Legal and Economic Analysis (1970).
46. 1 Ex. 265 (1866); 3 H.L. 330 (1868).
47. See Stephen G. Gilles, *Negligence, Strict Liability, and the Cheapest Cost-Avoider,* 78 Va. L. Rev. 1291, 1331–32 (1992).
48. For discussion, see Steven Shavell, Economic Analysis of Accident Law (1987).
49. See id.; William M. Landes and Richard A. Posner, The Economic Structure of Tort Law 58–61 (1987).
50. See Guido Calabresi and Jon T. Hirschoff, *Toward a Test for Strict Liability in Torts,* 81 Yale L.J. 1055 (1972).
51. See Calabresi, *supra* note 45, at 150–64.
52. See Gilles, *supra* note 47, at 1332–34.
53. See Posner, *supra* note 25, at 181–82.
54. Gouled v. Holwitz, 113 A. 323 (N.J. 1921); for discussion, see Richard A. Posner and Andrew M. Rosenfield, *Impossibility and Related Doctrines in Contract Law: An Economic Analysis,* 6 J. Legal Stud. 83, 106 (1977).
55. See Posner and Rosenfield, *supra* note 54.
56. Transatlantic Fin. Corp. v. United States, 363 F.2d 312 (D.C. Cir. 1966).
57. O'Keeffe v. Snyder, 416 A.2d 862 (N.J. 1980).
58. See, e.g., Phelps v. McQuade, 115 N.E. 441 (N.Y. 1917).
59. See Saul Levmore, *Variety and Uniformity in the Treatment of the Good-Faith Purchaser,* 16 J. Legal Stud. 43 (1987).
60. Pierson v. Post, 3 Cai. 175 (N.Y. 1805).
61. For discussion of administrative cost and first-possession rules, see Richard A. Epstein, Simple Rules for a Complex World (1995).
62. See Landes and Posner, *supra* note 49, at 126–28; Kenneth S. Abraham, The Forms and Functions of Tort Law 58 (2002).
63. Golden Eagle Distrib. Corp. v. Burroughs Corp., 801 F.2d 1531 (9th Cir. 1986).
64. See Golden Eagle Distrib. Corp. v. Burroughs Corp., 809 F.2d 584 (9th Cir. 1987) (dissenting from denial of rehearing *en banc*).
65. 211 U.S. 149 (1908).
66. For vigorous criticisms of *Mottley* along these lines, see Donald L. Doernberg, *There's No Reason for It; It's Just Our Policy: Why the Well-Pleaded Complaint Rule Sabotages the Purposes of Federal Question Jurisdiction,* 38 Hastings L.J. 597 (1987).

67. See, e.g., Merrell Dow Pharmaceuticals v. Thompson, 478 U.S. 804 (1986).
68. For the best-known discussion of how this reasoning applies to the law of torts, see Calabresi, *supra* note 45.
69. The example is adapted from Posner, *supra* note 25, at 35–36.
70. For discussion and references, see Jonathan R. Macey, *Promoting Public-Regarding Legislation through Statutory Interpretation: An Interest Group Model,* 86 Colum. L. Rev. 223 (1986).
71. See Federalist 10 (1787).
72. See Jonathan R. Macey, *Transaction Costs and the Normative Elements of the Public Choice Model: An Application to Constitutional Theory,* 74 Va. L. Rev. 471 (1988).
73. See, e.g., W. Mark Crain and Robert D. Tollison, *The Executive Branch in the Interest-Group Theory of Government,* 8 J. Legal Stud. 555, 561 (1979); William Landes and Richard Posner, *The Independent Judiciary in an Interest-Group Perspective,* 18 J.L. & Econ. 875, 875–76 (1975).
74. For discussion, see John P. Fry, *The Treasure Below: Jurisdiction over Salving Operations in International Waters,* 88 Colum. L. Rev. 863 (1988).
75. See Mark F. Grady and Jay I. Alexander, *Patent Law and Rent Dissipation,* 78 Va. L. Rev. 305 (1992).
76. For discussion, see Stewart E. Sterk, *Information Production and Rent-Seeking in Law School Administration: Rules and Discretion,* 83 B.U. L. Rev. 1141 (2003).
77. See Todd J. Zywicki, *The Rise and Fall of Efficiency in the Common Law: A Supply-Side Analysis,* 97 Nw. U. L. Rev. 1551 (2003).
78. For citations to these criticisms and interesting discussion of them, see Frank B. Cross, *The First Thing We Do, Let's Kill All the Economists,* 70 Tex. L. Rev. 645 (1992).
79. Ronald H. Coase, *The Problem of Social Cost,* 3 J.L. & Econ. 1 (1960).
80. In the real case on which this story is loosely based, the baker lost. Sturges v. Bridgman, (1879) 11 Ch.D. 852. We don't know what actual values the parties put on their rights in *Sturges* or what, if anything, passed between them after judgment.
81. This scenario is discussed further in chapter 20.
82. See George J. Stigler, The Theory of Price 120 (4th ed. 1987).
83. See Posner, *supra* note 25, at 250.
84. See UCC § 2-305(1).
85. See UCC § 2-201.
86. See Ian Ayres and Robert Gertner, *Filling Gaps in Incomplete Contracts: An Economic Theory of Default Rules,* 99 Yale L.J. 87 (1989), from which the example in this paragraph is drawn. For other applications of a similar logic, see Ian Ayres and Eric Talley, *Solomonic Bargaining: Dividing a Legal Entitlement to Facilitate Coasean Trade,* 104 Yale L.J. 1027 (1995).
87. See Eric A. Posner, *There Are No Penalty Default Rules in Contract Law,* 33 Fla. St. U. L. Rev. 563 (2006); Ian Ayres, *Yah-huh: There Are and Should Be Penalty Defaults,* 33 Fla. St. U. L. Rev. 589 (2006).

88. See Pauline T. Kim, *Norms, Learning, and Law: Exploring the Influences on Workers' Legal Knowledge,* 1999 U. Ill. L. Rev. 447.
89. See Cass R. Sunstein, *Human Behavior and the Law of Work,* 87 Va. L. Rev. 205 (2001).
90. Ward Farnsworth, *Do Parties to Nuisance Cases Bargain after Judgment? A Glimpse Inside the Cathedral,* 66 U. Chi. L. Rev. 373 (1999).
91. For discussion, see Ward Farnsworth, *The Economics of Enmity,* 69 U. Chi. L. Rev. 211 (2002).
92. Robert C. Ellickson, *Order without Law: How Neighbors Settle Disputes* (1991).

PART TWO

1. See Paul G. Mahoney, *Mandatory Disclosure as a Solution to Agency Problems,* 62 U. Chi. L. Rev. 1047 (1995).
2. See Frank H. Easterbrook and Daniel R. Fischel, The Economic Structure of Corporate Law 171–73 (1991)
3. For good discussion of the agency problems raised by contingency fees, see Geoffrey P. Miller, *Some Agency Problems in Settlement,* 16 J. Legal Stud. 189 (1987).
4. See Larry E. Ribstein, *Ethical Rules, Agency Costs, and Law Firm Culture,* 84 Va. L. Rev. 1707 (1998).
5. The tale is well told in Thomas Sowell, Knowledge and Decisions (1980).
6. See Steven G. Calabresi, *Political Parties as Mediating Institutions,* 61 U. Chi. L. Rev. 1479 (1994).
7. The examples and analysis in this part are adapted from Saul Levmore, *Commissions and Conflicts in Agency Arrangements: Lawyers, Real Estate Brokers, Underwriters, and Other Agents' Rewards,* 36 J.L. & Econ. 503 (1993).
8. This style of analysis should be familiar from chapter 2.
9. See chapter 7, and compare this worry to the rationales for the doctrine of general-average contribution in admiralty, discussed in chapter 4.
10. Robert Axelrod, The Evolution of Cooperation (1984).
11. See Douglas R. Hofstadter, Metamagical Themas chs. 30–32 (1985).
12. See Anthony de Jasay, *Prisoners' Dilemma and the Theory of the State, in* The New Palgrave Dictionary of Economics and the Law 95 (1998).
13. See Frank H. Easterbrook, *Discovery as Abuse,* 69 B.U. L. Rev. 635 (1989); John K. Setear, *The Barrister and the Bomb: The Dynamics of Cooperation, Nuclear Deterrence, and Discovery Abuse,* 69 B.U. L. Rev. 569 (1989); Robert G. Bone, The Economics of Civil Procedure 222–24 (2003).
14. For discussion of related issues, see Robert C. Ellickson, Order without Law: How Neighbors Settle Disputes 167–83 (1991).
15. See Keith N. Hylton, *Efficiency and Labor Law,* 87 Nw. U. L. Rev. 471, 479–80 (1993).
16. This analysis is drawn from Eric A. Posner, *The Regulation of Groups: The Influence of Legal and Nonlegal Sanctions on Collective Action,* 63 U. Chi. L. Rev. 133 (1996), to which the reader is referred for more along the same lines.

17. The term originated with Garrett Hardin, *The Tragedy of the Commons,* 162 Science 1243 (1968).
18. See, e.g., Harold Demsetz, *Toward a Theory of Property Rights,* 57 Am. Econ. Rev. 347 (1967).
19. For discussion of this device as a solution to a prisoner's dilemma, see Thomas H. Jackson, *Bankruptcy, Non-bankruptcy Entitlements, and the Creditors' Bargain,* 91 Yale L.J. 857, 860–64 (1982); Robert E. Scott, *Through Bankruptcy with the Creditors' Bargain Heuristic,* 53 U. Chi. L. Rev. 690, 694–96 (1986).
20. See Randal C. Picker, *Law and Economics: Intellectual Arbitrage,* 27 Loy. L.A. L. Rev. 127 (1993).
21. For discussion, see David D. Friedman, Law's Order 91–92 (2000).
22. See, e.g., Milton Friedman, Capitalism and Freedom (1962); David D. Friedman, The Machinery of Freedom (1973); cf. David D. Friedman, *Problems in the Provision of Public Goods,* 10 Harv. J.L. & Pub. Pol'y 505 (1987).
23. See Gerrit de Geest, *The Provision of Public Goods in Apartment Buildings,* 12 Int'l Rev. L. & Econ. 299 (1992).
24. See Kenneth W. Dam, *Economic Underpinnings of Patent Law,* 23 J. Legal Stud. 247 (1994).
25. See Maureen A. O'Rourke, *Toward a Doctrine of Fair Use in Patent Law,* 100 Colum. L. Rev. 1177, 1184 (2000).
26. See Richard A. Posner, *Free Speech in an Economic Perspective,* 20 Suffolk U. L. Rev. 1, 19–20 (1986); Daniel A. Farber, *Free Speech without Romance: Public Choice and the First Amendment,* 105 Harv. L. Rev. 554 (1991).
27. See Richard A. Posner, Economic Analysis of Law 255 (6th ed. 2002).
28. The estimate, and interesting discussion, can be found in Rex E. Lee, *The American Courts as Public Goods: Who Should Pay the Costs of Litigation?* 34 Cath. U. L. Rev. 267 (1985); see also Posner, *supra* note 27, at 530–31.
29. Posner, *supra* note 27.
30. See Ellickson, *supra* note 14.
31. For discussion, see Robert D. Cooter, *The Theory of Market Modernization of Law,* 16 Int'l Rev. L. & Econ. 141, 149–61 (1996).
32. See Lee Anne Fennell, *Beyond Exit and Voice: User Participation in the Production of Local Public Goods,* 80 Tex. L. Rev. 1 (2001).
33. See Edward R. Becker et al., *The Federal Judicial Law Clerk Hiring Problem and the Modest March 1 Solution,* 104 Yale L.J. 207 (1994).
34. For interesting discussion of the solutions discussed in this paragraph and how segregation might more generally be viewed as an assurance game, see Abraham Bell and Gideon Parchomovsky, *The Integration Game,* 100 Colum. L. Rev. 1965 (2000).
35. 12 U.S.C. §§ 2901–8.
36. See Peter P. Swire, *The Persistent Problem of Lending Discrimination: A Law and Economics Analysis,* 73 Tex. L. Rev. 787 (1995); for criticisms of the Act, see Jonathan R. Macey and Geoffrey P. Miller, *The Community Reinvestment Act: An Economic Analysis,* 79 Va. L. Rev. 291 (1993).

37. See William N. Eskridge, *Channeling: Identity-Based Social Movements and Public Law,* 150 U. Pa. L. Rev. 419 (2001); Dennis Chong, Collective Action and the Civil Rights Movement (1991).
38. See William Poundstone, Prisoner's Dilemma 218–21 (1992).
39. See Dan M. Kahan, *The Logic of Reciprocity,* 102 Mich. L. Rev. 71 (2003).
40. Blankenship v. General Motors Corp., 406 S.E.2d 781, 783, 784 (W. Va. 1991).
41. See Michael I. Krauss, *Product Liability and Game Theory: One More Trip to the Choice-of-Law Well,* 2002 B.Y.U. L. Rev. 759.
42. See Robert E. Goodin, Utilitarianism as a Public Philosophy (1995).
43. See Robert Sugden, *Spontaneous Order,* 3 J. Econ. Persp. 85 (1989).
44. The Strategy of Conflict (1960).
45. N.L.R.B. v. General Electric Co., 418 F.2d 736 (2d Cir. 1969), quoted in Douglas G. Baird, Robert H. Gertner, and Randal C. Picker, Game Theory and the Law 43–45 & n.20 (1994), to which the reader is referred for more discussion.
46. 358 U.S. 1 (1958).
47. City of Boerne v. Flores, 521 U.S. 507 (1997).
48. United States v. Nixon, 418 U.S. 683 (1974).
49. See Laura Kalman, *Law, Politics, and the New Deal,* 108 Yale L.J. 2165 (1999).
50. See Larry D. Kramer, The People Themselves: Popular Constitutionalism and Judicial Review (2005); Mark V. Tushnet, Taking the Constitution Away from the Courts (1999).
51. Lisa R. Anderson and Charles A. Holt, *Information Cascades in the Laboratory,* 87 Am. Econ. Rev. 847 (1997).
52. See Sushil Bikhchandani, David Hirshleifer, and Ivo Welch, *Learning from the Behavior of Others: Conformity, Fads, and Informational Cascades,* 12 J. Econ. Persp. 151 (1998).
53. Id.
54. See David Hirshleifer, *The Blind Leading the Blind: Social Influence, Fads, and Information Cascades, in* The New Economics of Human Behavior (Mariano Tommasi and Kathryn Ierulli eds., 1995).
55. Elizabeth F. Loftus and Edith Greene, *Warning: Even Memory for Faces May Be Contagious,* 4 Law & Hum. Behav. 323 (1980); C. A. Elizabeth Luus and Gary L. Wells, *The Malleability of Eyewitness Confidence: Co-witness and Perseverance Effects,* 79 J. Applied Psychol. 714 (1994).
56. National Institute of Justice, U.S. Dept. of Justice, Eyewitness Evidence: A Guide for Law Enforcement (1999).
57. See Bikhchandani et al., *supra* note 52.
58. See Alex Cukierman, *Asymmetric Information and the Electoral Momentum of Public Opinion Polls,* 70 Pub. Choice 181 (1991).
59. See Eric Talley, *Precedential Cascades: An Appraisal,* 73 S. Cal. L. Rev. 87 (1999).
60. See Timur Kuran and Cass R. Sunstein, *Availability Cascades and Risk Regulation,* 51 Stan. L. Rev. 683 (1999).

61. For discussion, see Richard A. Posner, Catastrophe: Risk and Response (2005).
62. See Sushil Bikhchandani, David Hirshleifer, and Ivo Welch, *A Theory of Fads, Fashion, Custom, and Cultural Change as Informational Cascades,* 100 J. Pol. Econ. 992 (1992).
63 See Timur Kuran, Private Truths, Public Lies (1995).
64. For discussion, see Saul Levmore, *The Anonymity Tool,* 144 U. Pa. L. Rev. 2191 (1996).
65. See Lawrence Lessig, *The Regulation of Social Meaning,* 62 U. Chi. L. Rev. 943 (1995).
66. See Dan M. Kahan, *Social Influence, Social Meaning, and Deterrence,* 83 Va. L. Rev. 349 (1997).
67. A good general introduction to these possibilities is Daniel A. Farber and Philip P. Frickey, Law and Public Choice: A Critical Introduction (1991).
68. See Kenneth Arrow, Social Choice and Individual Values (1951).
69. For discussion, see Dennis C. Mueller, Public Choice II (1989).
70. See William H. Riker, Liberalism against Populism: A Confrontation between the Theory of Democracy and the Theory of Social Choice (1982).
71. See Gerry Mackie, Democracy Defended (2003), which takes issue with many of the empirical claims made by Riker.
72. On which see Daniel A. Farber and Philip P. Frickey, *The Jurisprudence of Public Choice,* 65 Tex. L. Rev. 873, 901–6 (1987); Kenneth A. Shepsle and Barry R. Weingast, *When Do Rules of Procedure Matter?* 46 J. Pol. 206 (1984).
73. See Saul Levmore, *Public Choice Defended,* 72 U. Chi. L. Rev. 777 (2005).
74. The classic discussion is Kenneth A. Shepsle, *Congress Is a "They," Not an "It": Legislative Intent as Oxymoron,* 12 Int'l Rev. L. & Econ. 239 (1992).
75. See Saul Levmore, *Voting Paradoxes and Interest Groups,* 28 J. Legal Stud. 259 (1999).
76. See Frank H. Easterbrook, *Ways of Criticizing the Court,* 95 Harv. L. Rev. 802 (1982); Lewis A. Kornhauser and Lawrence G. Sager, *Unpacking the Court,* 96 Yale L.J. 82 (1986).
77. National Mut. Ins. Co. of Dist. of Columbia v. Tidewater Transfer Co., 337 U.S. 582 (1949).
78. 28 U.S.C. § 1332.
79. For development of other examples, see Michael I. Meyerson, *The Irrational Supreme Court,* 84 Neb. L. Rev. 895 (2006).
80. For development of these points, see John M. Rogers, *"Issue Voting" by Multimember Appellate Courts: A Response to Some Radical Proposals,* 49 Vand. L. Rev. 997 (1996); David G. Post and Steven C. Salop, *Issues and Outcomes, Guidance, and Indeterminacy: A Reply to Professor John Rogers and Others,* 49 Vand. L. Rev. 1069 (1996).
81. See Lewis A. Kornhauser and Lawrence G. Sager, *The One and the Many: Adjudication in Collegial Courts,* 81 Cal. L. Rev. 1 (1993), from which the criminal example here is drawn.

82. See 8 U.S.C. § 1153(b)(5).
83. See 8 U.S.C. § 1186(b) (providing for termination of the resident status of entrepreneurs admitted under § 1153(b)(5)); 8 U.S.C. § 1184(d) (allowing the deportation of aliens admitted under § 1184 for failure to marry within three months).
84. See 8 U.S.C. § 1255(a)(2)(A).
85. See Marc Galanter and Thomas Palay, Tournament of Lawyers: The Transformation of the Big Law Firm (1991).

PART THREE

1. 384 U.S. 436 (1966).
2. See New York v. Quarles, 467 U.S. 649 (1984).
3. See William Stuntz, *Miranda's Mistake,* 99 Mich. L. Rev. 975 (2001).
4. Duncan Kennedy, *Form and Substance in Private Law Adjudication,* 89 Harv. L. Rev. 1685, 1773–74 (1976).
5. See Paul G. Cassell and Richard Fowles, *Handcuffing the Cops? A Thirty-Year Perspective on Miranda's Harmful Effects on Law Enforcement,* 50 Stan. L. Rev. 1055 (1998).
6. See Cass R. Sunstein, *Problems with Rules,* 83 Cal. L. Rev. 953, 975–76 (1995).
7. See Antonin Scalia, *The Rule of Law as a Law of Rules,* 56 U. Chi. L. Rev. 1175 (1989).
8. See Kathleen Sullivan, *The Justice of Rules and of Standards,* 106 Harv. L. Rev. 22, 67 (1992).
9. See Sunstein, *supra* note 6; David Schoenbrod, Power without Responsibility 76 (1993).
10. Woodson v. North Carolina, 428 U.S. 280 (1976); see Sunstein, *supra* note 6.
11. See Cass R. Sunstein, *Incompletely Theorized Agreements,* 108 Harv. L. Rev. 1733 (1995); Cass R. Sunstein, One Case at a Time: Judicial Minimalism on the Supreme Court (2001).
12. See Richard A. Posner, The Economics of Justice ch. 6 (1981).
13. See Louis Kaplow, *Rules versus Standards: An Economic Analysis,* 42 Duke L.J. 557 (1992).
14. See Richard A. Posner, Economic Analysis of Law 557 (6th ed. 2002).
15. See Isaac Ehrlich and Richard A. Posner, *An Economic Analysis of Legal Rulemaking,* 3 J. Legal Stud. 257 (1974).
16. See Kaplow, *supra* note 13.
17. See id.; Sunstein, *supra* note 6.
18. See Sunstein, *supra* note 6.
19. Oliver Wendell Holmes Jr., The Common Law (1888).
20. Baltimore & Ohio R.R. v. Goodman, 275 U.S. 66 (1927).
21. Pokora v. Wabash Ry. Co., 292 U.S. 98 (1934).
22. See Theisen v. Milwaukee Auto. Mut. Ins. Co., 118 N.W.2d 140 (Wis. 1963).

23. See Oona A. Hathaway, *Path Dependence in the Law: The Course and Pattern of Legal Change in a Common Law System,* 86 Iowa L. Rev. 601 (2001); Eric Talley, *Precedential Cascades: An Appraisal,* 73 S. Cal. L. Rev. 87 (1999).
24. For an interesting general discussion of the point, see Richard H. McAdams, *An Attitudinal Theory of Expressive Law,* 79 Or. L. Rev. 339 (2000).
25. For extended discussion of how legal rules about smoking can change attitudes toward it, see Lawrence Lessig, *The Legal Regulation of Social Meaning,* 62 U. Chi. L. Rev. 943 (1995).
26. Charles Krauthammer, *Disarm the Citizenry: But Not Yet,* Wash. Post, Apr. 5, 1996, at A19.
27. See David D. Friedman, Law's Order 182–83 (2000); T. H. White, The Once and Future King (1958).
28. Smith v. Maryland, 442 U.S. 735 (1979).
29. See, e.g., Eugene Volokh to Stewart Baker, *Civil Liberties in Wartime,* Slate, Sept. 20, 2001, http://slate.msn.com/?id=115633&entry=115888; Dave Kopel, *Don't Press the Panic Button,* Nat'l Rev. Online, Sept. 21, 2001, http://www.nationalreview.com/kopel/kopel092101.shtml.
30. See Eric A. Posner and Adrian Vermeule, *Should Coercive Interrogation Be Legal?* 104 Mich. L. Rev. 671 (2006).
31. See Eugene Volokh, *The Mechanisms of the Slippery Slope,* 116 Harv. L. Rev. 1026, 1058–59 (2003).
32. See Wisconsin v. Yoder, 374 U.S. 398 (1963); Sherbert v. Verner, 406 U.S. 205 (1972).
33. See Hernandez v. Commissioner, 490 U.S. 680 (1989); Lyng v. Northwest Indian Cemetery Protective Ass'n, 485 U.S. 439 (1988); Thomas v. Review Bd., 450 U.S. 707 (1981).
34. 381 U.S. 479 (1965).
35. 410 U.S. 113 (1973).
36. For fuller treatment of these cases as a study in slippery slopes, see Eugene Volokh, *Same-Sex Marriage and Slippery Slopes,* 33 Hofstra L. Rev. 1155 (2005).
37. 66 Tenn. 9 (1872).
38. See Stephen E. Weiss, *The Sorites Fallacy: What Difference Does a Peanut Make?* 33 Synthese 253 (1976).
39. For discussion, see Frederick Schauer, *Slippery Slopes,* 99 Harv. L. Rev. 361 (1985).
40. Jeremy Bentham, A Fragment on Government and an Introduction to the Principles of Morals and Legislation 430 (1776).
41. Meir Dan-Cohen, *Decision Rules and Conduct Rules: On Acoustic Separation in Criminal Law,* 97 Harv. L. Rev. 625 (1984).
42. Wayne R. LaFave, Substantive Criminal Law § 5.10 (2d ed. 2003).
43. Dan-Cohen, *supra* note 41.
44. See Dan M. Kahan, *Ignorance of Law Is an Excuse—But Only for the Virtuous,* 96 Mich. L. Rev. 127 (1997); Dan-Cohen, *supra* note 41.

45. This discussion draws on Emily L. Sherwin, *Law and Equity in Contract Enforcement,* 50 Md. L. Rev. 253 (1991).
46. See Melvin A. Eisenberg, *The Divergence of Standards of Conduct and Standards of Review in Corporate Law,* 62 Fordham L. Rev. 437 (1993).
47. Id.
48. See Patricia A. McCoy, *A Political Economy of the Business Judgment Rule in Banking: Implications for Corporate Law,* 47 Case W. Res. L. Rev. 1 (1996).
49. See Cass R. Sunstein, *Problems with Rules,* 83 Cal. L. Rev. 953 (1995).
50. See Dan-Cohen, *supra* note 41.
51. See Carol S. Steiker, *Counter-revolution in Constitutional Criminal Procedure? Two Audiences, Two Answers,* 94 Mich. L. Rev. 2466 (1996).
52. 85 Harv. L. Rev. 1089 (1972).
53. See chapter 3.
54. The classic statement of this view is in Oliver Wendell Holmes Jr., *The Path of the Law,* 10 Harv. L. Rev. 457 (1897).
55. See Guido Calabresi, *Remarks: The Simple Virtues of the Cathedral,* 106 Yale L.J. 2201 (1997).
56. See Guido Calabresi and A. Douglas Melamed, *Property Rules, Liability Rules, and Inalienability: One View of the Cathedral,* 85 Harv. L. Rev. 1089, 1124 (1972).
57. See Posner, *supra* note 14, at 205–6.
58. See Calabresi and Melamed, *supra* note 56, at 1127.
59. Ploof v. Putnam, 81 A. 188 (Vt. 1908).
60. London Borough of Southwark v. Williams, [1971] Ch. 734 (A.C. 1970).
61. See Calabresi and Melamed, *supra* note 56, at 1105.
62. See chapter 13; Posner, *supra* note 14, at 60–61.
63. See, e.g., Ian Ayres and Eric Talley, *Solomonic Bargaining: Dividing a Legal Entitlement to Facilitate Coasean Trade,* 104 Yale L.J. 1027 (1995); Louis Kaplow and Steven Shavell, *Do Liability Rules Facilitate Bargaining? A Reply to Ayres and Talley,* 105 Yale L.J. 221 (1995).
64. See, e.g., Ward Farnsworth, *Do Parties to Nuisance Cases Bargain after Judgment? A Glimpse Inside the Cathedral,* 66 U. Chi. L. Rev. 373 (1999).
65. See Calabresi and Melamed, *supra* note 56, at 1116 ff.
66. Spur Indus. v. Del E. Webb Dev. Co., 494 P.2d 700 (Ariz. 1972).
67. See Guido Calabresi, *Neologisms Revisited,* 64 Md. L. Rev. 736 (2005).
68. Joel Dobris, *Boomer Twenty Years Later: An Introduction, with Some Footnotes about "Theory,"* 54 Alb. L. Rev. 171 (1990).
69. A. Douglas Melamed, *Remarks: A Public Law Perspective,* 106 Yale L.J. 2209 (1997).
70. James E. Krier and Stewart J. Schwab, *Property Rules and Liability Rules: The Cathedral in Another Light,* 70 N.Y.U. L. Rev. 440 (1995).
71. See Eugene Kontorovich, *Liability Rules for Constitutional Rights: The Case of Mass Detentions,* 56 Stan. L. Rev. 755 (2004).
72. 334 U.S. 1 (1948).

73. See Herbert Wechsler, *Toward Neutral Principles of Constitutional Law,* 73 Harv. L. Rev. 1, 29–30 (1959).
74. 198 U.S. 45 (1905).
75. See, e.g., Robert Hale, *Rate Making and the Revision of the Property Concept,* 22 Colum. L. Rev. 209 (1922).
76. See, e.g., West Coast Hotel Co. v. Parrish, 300 U.S. 379, 399 (1937). The leading discussion of these events as a series of baseline problems is Cass R. Sunstein, *Lochner's Legacy,* 87 Colum. L. Rev. 873 (1987). For a dissenting interpretation, see David Bernstein, *Lochner's Legacy's Legacy,* 82 Tex. L. Rev. 1 (2003).
77. See Lucas v. South Carolina Coastal Council, 505 U.S. 1003 (1992).
78. 482 U.S. 691 (1987).
79. See the discussion in Louis Michael Seidman, *The Problems with Privacy's Problem,* 93 Mich. L. Rev. 1079 (1995).
80. See, e.g., Randy E. Barnett, Restoring the Lost Constitution: The Presumption of Liberty (2004); Richard A. Epstein, *Takings, Exclusivity, and Speech: The Legacy of* PruneYard v. Robins, 64 U. Chi. L. Rev. 21 (1997).
81. See Cass R. Sunstein, *Legal Interference with Private Preferences,* 53 U. Chi. L. Rev. 1129 (1986).

PART FOUR

1. Daniel Kahneman, Jack L. Knetsch, and Richard H. Thaler, *Experimental Tests of the Endowment Effect and the Coase Theorem,* 98 J. Pol. Econ. 1325 (1990).
2. See discussion in D. A. Redelmeier, P. Rozin, and D. Kahneman, *Understanding Patients' Decisions: Cognitive and Emotional Perspectives,* 270 J. Am. Med. Ass'n 72 (1993).
3. See J. H. Dales, *Pollution, Property and Prices* (1968); William J. Baumol, *On the Taxation and the Control of Externalities,* 62 Am. Econ. Rev. 307 (1972); Bruce A. Ackerman and Richard B. Stewart, *Reforming Environmental Law,* 37 Stan. L. Rev. 1333 (1985); Nathaniel E. Keohane, Richard L. Revesz, and Robert N. Stavins, *The Choice of Regulatory Instruments in Environmental Law,* 22 Harv. Envtl. L. Rev. 313 (1998).
4. See David S. Brookshire and Don L. Coursey, *Measuring the Value of a Public Good: An Empirical Comparison of Elicitation Procedures,* 77 Am. Econ. Rev. 554 (1987); Don L. Coursey, John L. Hovis, and William D. Schulze, *The Disparity between Willingness to Accept and Willingness to Pay Measures of Value,* 102 Q.J. Econ. 679 (1987).
5. See John A. List, *Does Market Experience Eliminate Market Anomalies?* 118 Q.J. Econ. 41 (2003).
6. See Herbert Hovenkamp, *Legal Policy and the Endowment Effect,* 20 J. Legal Stud. 225 (1991).
7. See Daniel A. Farber, Eco-pragmatism (1999); Christopher H. Schroeder, *Clear Consensus, Ambiguous Commitment,* 98 Mich. L. Rev. 1876 (2000).

8. See Jack Beermann and Joseph W. Singer, *Baseline Questions in Legal Reasoning: The Example of Property in Jobs,* 23 Ga. L. Rev. 911 (1989); Russell Korobkin, *The Endowment Effect and Legal Analysis,* 97 Nw. U. L. Rev. 1227 (2003).
9. See, e.g., David Charny, *Economics of Death,* 107 Harv. L. Rev. 2056, 2067 (1994).
10. See Daniel Kahneman and Amos Tversky, *The Simulation Heuristic, in* Judgment under Uncertainty: Heuristics and Biases (Daniel Kahneman ed., 1982).
11. Thomas Gilovich and Victoria H. Medvec, *The Temporal Pattern to the Experience of Regret,* 67 J. Personality & Soc. Psychol. 357 (1994); Chris Guthrie, *Panacea or Pandora's Box? The Costs of Options in Negotiations,* 88 Iowa L. Rev. 601, 647–48 (2003).
12. See Janet Landman, *Regret and Elation following Action and Inaction: Affective Responses to Positive versus Negative Outcomes,* 13 Personality & Soc. Psychol. Bull. 524 (1987).
13. See Amos Tversky and Daniel Kahneman, *Loss Aversion in Riskless Choice: A Reference-Dependent Model,* 107 Q.J. Econ. 1039 (1991); Daniel Kahneman, Jack L. Knetsch, and Richard H. Thaler, *The Endowment Effect, Loss Aversion, and Status Quo Bias,* 5 J. Econ. Persp. 193 (1991); Jeffrey J. Rachlinski, *The Psychology of Global Climate Change,* 2000 U. Ill. L. Rev. 299.
14. See Russell Korobkin, *Inertia and Preference in Contract Negotiation: The Psychological Power of Default Rules and Form Terms,* 51 Vand. L. Rev. 1583 (1998), for discussion of this possibility and a good general treatment of regret, its origins, and its implications.
15. See Korobkin, *supra* note 8.
16. See, e.g., Massimo Paradiso and Antonella Trisorio, *The Effect of Knowledge on the Disparity between Hypothetical and Real Willingness to Pay,* 33 Applied Econ. 1359 (2001).
17. See Owen D. Jones and Timothy H. Goldsmith, *Law and Behavioral Biology,* 105 Colum. L. Rev. 405 (2005).
18. See Cass R. Sunstein, *Social Norms and Social Roles,* 96 Colum. L. Rev. 903 (1996).
19. See Ward Farnsworth, *Do Parties to Nuisance Cases Bargain after Judgment? A Glimpse Inside the Cathedral,* 66 U. Chi. L. Rev. 373 (1999).
20. See Mark Kelman, *Consumption Theory, Production Theory, and Ideology in the Coase Theorem,* 52 S. Cal. L. Rev. 669 (1979).
21. See Richard H. Thaler, Quasi Rational Economics 7–8 (1991).
22. See Cass R. Sunstein, *Incommensurability and Valuation in Law,* 92 Mich. L. Rev. 779 (1994).
23. Baruch Fischhoff, *Hindsight [not=] Foresight: The Effect of Outcome Knowledge on Judgment under Uncertainty,* 1 J. Experimental Psychol. 288 (1975).
24. Id.

25. Neal V. Dawson et al., *Hindsight Bias: An Impediment to Accurate Probability Estimation in Clinicopathologic Conferences,* 8 Med. Decision Making 259 (1988).
26. See Jeffrey J. Rachlinski, *A Positive Psychological Theory of Judging in Hindsight,* 65 U. Chi. L. Rev. 571 (1998).
27. See Kim A. Kamin and Jeffrey J. Rachlinski, *Ex Post [not=] Ex Ante: Determining Liability in Hindsight,* 19 Law & Hum. Behav. 89 (1995); Reid Hastie and W. Kip Viscusi, *What Juries Can't Do Well: The Jury's Performance as a Risk Manager,* 40 Ariz. L. Rev. 901 (1998). For criticism and cautionary suggestions, see Richard Lempert, *Juries, Hindsight, and Punitive Damage Awards: Failures of a Social Science Case for Change,* 48 DePaul L. Rev. 867 (1999).
28. Tarasoff v. Regents of the Univ. of Cal., 551 P.2d 334 (Cal. 1976).
29. Susan J. LaBine and Gary LaBine, *Determinations of Negligence and the Hindsight Bias,* 20 Law & Hum. Behav. 501 (1996).
30. Id.
31. See Chris Guthrie, Jeffrey J. Rachlinski, and Andrew J. Wistrich, *Inside the Judicial Mind,* 86 Cornell L. Rev. 777, 799–805 (2001); Hastie and Viscusi, *supra* note 27; Lempert, *supra* note 27.
32. See Baruch Fischhoff, *Perceived Informativeness of Facts,* 3 J. Experimental Psychol.: Hum. Perception & Performance 349, 354–56 (1977); D. Sharpe and J. G. Adair, *Reversibility of the Hindsight Bias: Manipulation of Experimental Demands,* 56 Organizational Behav. & Hum. Decision Processes 233 (1993); Kamin and Rachlinski, *supra* note 27.
33. Merrie Jo Stallard and Debra L. Worthington, *Reducing the Hindsight Bias Utilizing Attorney Closing Arguments,* 22 Law & Hum. Behav. 671 (1998).
34. D. Jordan Lowe and Philip M. J. Reckers, *The Effects of Hindsight Bias on Jurors' Evaluations of Auditor Decisions,* 25 Decision Sci. 401 (1994).
35. See, e.g., The T.J. Hooper, 60 F.2d 737 (2d Cir. 1932) (Hand, J.).
36. See Rodi Yachts, Inc. v. National Marine, Inc., 984 F.2d 880 (7th Cir. 1993) (Posner, J.).
37. See Rachlinski, *supra* note 26; Hall v. Hilbun, 466 So. 2d 856 (Miss. 1985); for objections, see Philip G. Peters Jr., *Hindsight Bias and Tort Liability: Avoiding Premature Conclusions,* 31 Ariz. St. L.J. 1277 (1999).
38. See David B. Wexler and Robert F. Schopp, *How and When to Correct for Juror Hindsight Bias in Mental Health Malpractice Litigation: Some Preliminary Observations,* 7 Behav. Sci. & L. 485 (1989); Hal R. Arkes and Cindy A. Schipani, *Medical Malpractice v. The Business Judgment Rule: Differences in Hindsight Bias,* 73 Or. L. Rev. 587 (1994).
39. Christine Jolls, Cass R. Sunstein, and Richard Thaler, *A Behavioral Approach to Law and Economics,* 50 Stan. L. Rev. 1471 (1998).
40. Russell B. Korobkin and Thomas S. Ulen, *Law and Behavioral Science: Removing the Rationality Assumption from Law and Economics,* 88 Cal. L. Rev. 1051 (2000).

41. Fed. R. Evid. 407; see Kimberly Eberwine, *Hindsight Bias and the Subsequent Remedial Measures Rule: Fixing the Feasibility Exception,* 55 Case W. Res. L. Rev. 633 (2005).
42. Dan L. Burk and Mark A. Lemley, *Biotechnology's Uncertainty Principle,* 54 Case W. Res. L. Rev. 691 (2004).
43. See Rachlinski, *supra* note 26.
44. For development of this view, see Charles Yablon, *Hindsight, Regret, and Safe Harbors in Rule 11 Litigation,* 37 Loy. L.A. L. Rev. 599 (2004).
45. Itamar Simonson and Amos Tversky, *Choice in Context: Tradeoff Contrast and Extremeness Aversion,* 29 J. Marketing Res. 281 (1992).
46. Id.
47. Mark Kelman, Yuval Rottenstreich, and Amos Tversky, *Context-Dependence in Legal Decision-Making,* 25 J. Legal Stud. 287 (1996).
48. Id.
49. Id.
50. See Daniel Kahneman and Amos Tversky, *Prospect Theory: An Analysis of Decision under Risk,* 47 Econometrica 263 (1979).
51. See Daniel Kahneman and Amos Tversky, *Conflict Resolution: A Cognitive Perspective, in* Barriers to Conflict Resolution 44 (Kenneth Arrow et al. eds., 1995); Chris Guthrie, *Insights from Cognitive Psychology,* 54 J. Legal Ed. 42 (2004).
52. Amos Tversky and Daniel Kahneman, *Rational Choice and the Framing of Decisions,* 59 J. Bus. S251 (1986).
53. Amos Tversky and Daniel Kahneman, *Advances in Prospect Theory: Cumulative Representation of Uncertainty,* 5 J. Risk & Uncertainty 297 (1992); Chris Guthrie, *Framing Frivolous Litigation: A Psychological Theory,* 67 U. Chi. L. Rev. 163 (2000).
54. See Jeffrey J. Rachlinski, *Gains, Losses and the Psychology of Litigation,* 70 S. Cal. L. Rev. 113 (1996).
55. Id.
56. Id.
57. Id.; see also Russell Korobkin and Chris Guthrie, *Psychology, Economics, and Settlement: A New Look at the Role of the Lawyer,* 76 Tex. L. Rev. 77 (1997).
58. Guthrie, Rachlinski, and Wistrich, *supra* note 31, at 796–97.
59. See Thomas C. Schelling, *Economic Reasoning and the Ethics of Policy,* 63 Pub. Int. 37 (1981).
60. See B. J. McNeil et al., *On the Elicitation of Preferences for Alternative Therapies,* 306 N. Eng. J. Med. 1259 (1982).
61. See Aaron D. Twerski and Neil B. Cohen, *Informed Decision Making and the Law of Torts: The Myth of Justiciable Causation,* 1988 U. Ill. L. Rev. 607.
62. Paul Slovic, Baruch Fischhoff, and Sarah Lichtenstein, *Facts versus Fears: Understanding Perceived Risk, in* Judgment under Uncertainty: Heuristics and Biases (Daniel Kahneman, Paul Slovic, and Amos Tversky eds., 1982).

63. S. Plous, *Thinking the Unthinkable: The Effects of Anchoring on Likelihood Estimates of Nuclear War,* 19 J. Applied Soc. Psychol. (1989).
64. Gretchen B. Chapman and Brian H. Bornstein, *The More You Ask for, the More You Get: Anchoring in Personal Injury Verdicts,* 10 Applied Cognitive Psychol. 519 (1996); John Malouff and Nicola S. Schutte, *Shaping Juror Attitudes: Effects of Requesting Different Damage Amounts in Personal Injury Trials,* 129 J. Soc. Psychol. 491 (1989).
65. Verlin B. Hinsz and Kristin E. Indahl, *Assimilation to Anchors for Damage Awards in a Mock Civil Trial,* 25 J. Applied. Soc. Psychol. 991 (1995).
66. Mollie W. Marti and Roselle L. Wissler, *Be Careful What You Ask For: The Effect of Anchors on Personal Injury Damages Awards,* 6 J. Experimental Psychol. 91 (2000).
67. See Chapman and Bornstein, *supra* note 64.
68. See Edie Greene and Brian H. Bornstein, Determining Damages: The Psychology of Jury Awards 154 (2003).
69. Id.; Marti and Wissler, *supra* note 66.
70. Russell Korobkin and Chris Guthrie, *Opening Offers and Out-of-Court Settlement: A Little Moderation May Not Go a Long Way,* 10 Ohio St. J. Disp. Resol. 1 (1994).
71. See Robert B. Cialdini et al., *Reciprocal Concessions Procedure for Inducing Compliance: The Door-in-the-Face Technique,* 31 J. Personality & Soc. Psychol. 206 (1975).
72. See Guthrie, Rachlinski, and Wistrich, *supra* note 31.
73. Pescatore v. Pan Am. World Airways, 887 F. Supp. 71 (E.D.N.Y. 1995).
74. Landers v. Ghosh, 491 N.E.2d 950 (Ill. App. Ct. 1986) (affirming $400,000 award).
75. See Cass R. Sunstein et al., Punitive Damages: How Jurors Decide (2002). For criticism and suggestions that compensatory and punitive damages have rational links, see Neil Vidmar, *Experimental Simulations and Tort Reform: Avoidance, Error, and Overreaching in Sunstein et al.'s* Punitive Damages, 53 Emory L.J. 1359 (2004).
76. See Chapman and Bornstein, *supra* note 64.
77. See Andrew J. Wistrich, Chris Guthrie, and Jeffrey J. Rachlinski, *Can Judges Ignore Inadmissible Information? The Difficulty of Deliberately Disregarding,* 153 U. Pa. L. Rev. 1251 (2005).
78. See Fed. R. Evid. 408.
79. See Cass R. Sunstein, Daniel Kahneman, and David A. Schkade, *Assessing Punitive Damages (with Notes on Cognition and Valuation in Law),* 107 Yale L.J. 2017 (1998).
80. See Jennifer K. Robbennolt and Christina A. Studebaker, *Anchoring in the Courtroom: The Effects of Caps on Punitive Damages,* 23 Law & Hum. Behav. 353 (1999).

81. See Greg Pogarsky and Linda Babcock, *Damage Caps, Motivated Anchoring, and Bargaining Impasse,* 30 J. Legal Stud. 143 (2001).
82. See Jeffrey J. Rachlinski, *The Uncertain Psychological Case for Paternalism,* 97 Nw. U. L. Rev. 1165 (2003).
83. See Marcel Kahan and Michael Klausner, *Path Dependence in Corporate Contracting: Increasing Returns, Herd Behavior and Cognitive Biases,* 74 Wash. U. L.Q. 347 (1996).
84. Frederick Schauer, *Do Cases Make Bad Law?* 73 U. Chi. L. Rev. 883 (2006).
85. Oliver Wendell Holmes Jr., *Codes, and the Arrangement of the Law,* 5 Am. L. Rev. 1 (1870).
86. See Jeffrey J. Rachlinski, *Bottom-Up versus Top-Down Lawmaking,* 73 U. Chi. L. Rev. 933, 951–60 (2006).
87. Shelley E. Taylor, Positive Illusions: Creative Self-Deception and the Healthy Mind 10–11 (1989); Ola Svenson, *Are We All Less Risky and More Skillful Than Our Fellow Drivers?* 47 Acta Psychologica 143 (1981); David G. Myers, Social Psychology 85 (1983).
88. For discussion and references, see Christine Jolls, *Behavioral Economic Analysis of Redistributive Legal Rules,* 51 Vand. L. Rev. 1653 (1998).
89. Christine Jolls and Cass R. Sunstein, *Debiasing through Law,* 35 J. Legal Stud. 199 (2006).
90. See chapter 14; and see Paul Slovic, The Perception of Risk (2000); Cass R. Sunstein, *The Laws of Fear,* 115 Harv. L. Rev. 1119 (2002).
91. Neil D. Weinstein and William M. Klein, *Resistance of Personal Risk Perceptions to Debiasing Interventions, in* Heuristics and Biases: The Psychology of Intuitive Judgment (Thomas Gilovich, Dale Griffin, and Daniel Kahneman eds., 2002).
92. See Jolls and Sunstein, *supra* note 89.
93. Linda Babcock, George Loewenstein, and Samuel Issacharoff, *Creating Convergence: Debiasing Biased Litigants,* 22 Law & Soc. Inquiry 913 (1997).
94. Fed. R. Civ. P. 68.
95. See Michael D. Young, *Bottom Line Negotiating,* 49 Fed. Law. 20, 20 (2002). For discussion and other suggestions with a different focus, see generally David A. Anderson, *Improving Settlement Devices: Rule 68 and Beyond,* 23 J. Legal Stud. 225 (1994); Geoffrey P. Miller, *An Economic Analysis of Rule 68,* 15 J. Legal Stud. 93 (1986).
96. See generally James Friedrich, *On Seeing Oneself as Less Self-Serving Than Others: The Ultimate Self-Serving Bias?* 23 Teaching Psychol. 107, 107–9 (1996).
97. See Frank B. Cross, *In Praise of Irrational Plaintiffs,* 86 Cornell L. Rev. 1 (2000).
98. For discussion of the rule, exceptions to it, and consequences, see Samuel R. Gross and Kent D. Syverud, *Getting to No: A Study of Settlement Negotiations and the Selection of Cases for Trial,* 90 Mich. L. Rev. 319, 361, 371–72 (1991).

99. See Samuel R. Gross, *We Could Pass a Law . . . What Might Happen if Contingent Legal Fees Were Banned,* 47 DePaul L. Rev. 321, 328 (1998).
100. See id. at 328–30.
101. See Richard J. Reifenberg, *The Self-Serving Bias and the Use of Objective and Subjective Methods for Measuring Success and Failure,* 126 J. Soc. Psychol. 627 (1986).
102. See Lee Ross and Richard E. Nisbett, *The Person and the Situation: Perspectives of Social Psychology* 77–89 (1991).
103. E. E. Jones and V. A. Harris, *The Attribution of Attitudes,* 3 J. Experimental Soc. Psychol. 1 (1967).
104. See Neal R. Feigenson, *The Rhetoric of Torts: How Advocates Help Jurors Think about Causation, Reasonableness, and Responsibility,* 47 Hastings L.J. 61 (1995).
105. See Richard H. McAdams, *The Political Economy of Entrapment,* 96 J. Crim. L. & Criminology (1995); Kevin A. Smith, *Psychology, Factfinding, and Entrapment,* 103 Mich. L. Rev. 759 (2005).
106. See Eva S. Nilsen, *The Criminal Defense Lawyer's Reliance on Bias and Prejudice,* 8 Geo. J. Legal Ethics 1 (1994).
107. See Craig Haney, *Violence and the Capital Jury: Mechanisms of Moral Disengagement and the Impulse to Condemn to Death,* 49 Stan. L. Rev. 1447 (1997).
108. See Rachlinski, *supra* note 86, at 948–49.
109. See Edward E. Jones and Richard E. Nisbett, *The Actor and the Observer: Divergent Perceptions of the Causes of Behavior, in* Attribution: Perceiving the Causes of Behavior 79 (Edward E. Jones et al. eds., 1971), from which the examples in this paragraph are drawn. See also Shelley E. Taylor and Susan T. Fiske, *Salience, Attention, and Attribution: Top of the Head Phenomena, in* 11 Advances in Experimental Social Psychology 249 (Leonard Berkowitz ed., 1978).
110. See D. T. Miller and M. Ross, *Self-Serving Biases in the Attribution of Causality: Fact or Fiction?* 82 Psychol. Bull. 213 (1975).
111. See Jones and Nisbett, *supra* note 109.
112. Id.
113. See Jon Elster, Sour Grapes 157 ff. (1983); Jolls, *supra* note 88.
114. See L. B. Alloy and L. Abramson, *Judgment of Contingency in Depressed and Nondepressed Students: Sadder but Wiser?* 108 J. Experimental Psychol. 441 (1979).
115. See James Boyd White, *The Ethics of Argument: Plato's Gorgias and the Modern Lawyer,* 50 U. Chi. L. Rev. 849 (1983).
116. See Thomas Schelling, The Strategy of Conflict (1960).
117. W. B. Yeats, *The Second Coming, in* The Collected Poems of W. B. Yeats (R. Finneran ed., 1964).
118. See Jolls and Sunstein, *supra* note 89.
119. See Owen Fiss, *Against Settlement,* 93 Yale L.J. 1073 (1984); Cross, *supra* note 97.

PART FIVE

1. For interesting comparisons to the standard of proof used in civil law countries, see Kevin M. Clermont and Emily Sherwin, *A Comparative View of Standards of Proof,* 50 Am. J. Comp. L. 243 (2002); Kevin M. Clermont, *Standards of Proof in Japan and the United States,* 37 Cornell Int'l L.J. 263 (2004).
2. See Richard A. Posner, Economic Analysis of Law 618 (6th ed. 2002).
3. See Bruce L. Hay and Kathryn E. Spier, *Burdens of Proof in Civil Litigation: An Economic Analysis,* 26 J. Legal Stud. 413 (1997).
4. See McDonnell Douglas v. Green, 411 U.S. 792 (1973).
5. A fact pattern adapted from Behrens v. Bertram Mills Circus, (1957) 2 Q.B. 1.
6. See Posner, *supra* note 2, at 600–601.
7. For discussion of some complications, see the majority and dissenting opinions in *Gasperini v. Center for the Humanities,* 518 U.S. 415 (1996).
8. See generally Charles W. Wolfram, *The Constitutional History of the Seventh Amendment,* 80 Harv. L. Rev. 289 (1966).
9. See Williams v. Taylor, 529 U.S. 420 (2000).
10. Chevron U.S.A. v. Natural Resources Defense Council, 467 U.S. 837 (1984).
11. For discussion and references, see Antonin Scalia, *Judicial Deference to Administrative Interpretations of Law,* 1989 Duke L.J. 511.
12. For related discussion, see chapters 3 and 17.
13. See Gary Lawson, *Legal Indeterminacy: Its Cause and Cure,* 19 Harv. J.L. & Pub. Pol'y (1996).
14. Gardner v. National Bulk Carriers, 310 F.2d 284 (4th Cir. 1962).
15. See Daniel Farber, *Recurring Misses,* 19 J. Legal Stud. 727 (1990); Saul Levmore, *Probabilistic Recoveries, Restitution, and Recurring Wrongs,* 19 J. Legal Stud. 691 (1990).
16. Gardner v. National Bulk Carriers, *supra* note 14.
17. See, e.g., Herskovits v. Group Health Coop. of Puget Sound, 664 P.2d 474 (Wash. 1983); Joseph H. King Jr., *Causation, Valuation, and Chance in Personal Injury Torts Involving Preexisting Conditions and Future Consequences,* 90 Yale L.J. 1353 (1981).
18. See Fennell v. Southern Md. Hosp. Ctr., 580 A.2d 206 (Md. 1990).
19. Strickland v. Washington, 466 U.S. 668, 694 (1984).
20. New York Times v. Sullivan, 376 U.S. 254 (1964).
21. St. Amant v. Thompson, 390 U.S. 727, 731–32 (1968).
22. For discussion of the difference between false positives and false negatives, see Robert G. Bone, The Economics of Civil Procedure 128–32 (2003); Posner, *supra* note 2, at 618–20.
23. 4 William Blackstone, Commentaries on the Laws of England 359 (Univ. of Chicago Press 2002) (1769); Alexander Volokh, *N Guilty Men,* 146 U. Pa. L. Rev. 173 (1997).
24. See Richard A. Posner, *The Cost of Rights: Implications for Central and Eastern Europe—and for the United States,* 32 Tulsa L.J. 1 (1996).

25. See, e.g., Murphy v. Holland, 776 F.2d 470 (4th Cir. 1985).
26. United States v. Feinberg, 140 F.2d 592, 594 (2d Cir. 1944).
27. Norbert L. Kerr et al., *Guilt beyond a Reasonable Doubt: Effects of Concept Definition and Assigned Decision Rule on the Judgments of Mock Jurors,* 34 J. Personality & Soc. Psychol. 282–94 (1976).
28. See C. M. A. McCauliff, *Burdens of Proof: Degrees of Belief, Quanta of Evidence, or Constitutional Guarantees?* 35 Vand. L. Rev. 1293, 1325 (1982); United States v. Fatico, 458 F. Supp. 388, 409 (E.D.N.Y. 1978) (Weinstein, J.).
29. McCullough v. State, 657 P.2d 1157, 1157 (Nev. 1983).
30. State v. DelVecchio, 464 A.2d 813, 818 (Conn. 1983).
31. Branion v. Gramly, 855 F.2d 1256, 1263 n.5 (7th Cir. 1988) (Easterbrook, J.).
32. Rita James Simon and Linda Mahan, *Quantifying Burdens of Proof: A View from the Bench, the Jury, and the Classroom,* 5 Law & Soc'y Rev. 319 (1971).
33. Proctor v. United States, 685 A.2d 735, 738–39 (D.C. 1996).
34. Cage v. Louisiana, 498 U.S. 39, 41 (1990) (per curiam).
35. See Victor v. Nebraska, 511 U.S. 1 (1994).
36. See Elisabeth Stoffelmayr and Shari S. Diamond, *The Conflict between Precision and Flexibility in Explaining "Beyond a Reasonable Doubt,"* 6 Psychol. Pub. Pol'y & L. 769 (2000); Norbert L. Kerr, *Severity of Prescribed Penalty and Mock Jurors' Verdicts,* –36 J. Personality & Soc. Psychol. 1431 (1978).
37. See Charles Nesson, *Reasonable Doubt and Permissive Inferences: The Value of Complexity,* 92 Harv. L. Rev. 1187 (1979).
38. See Richard A. Posner, *An Economic Approach to the Law of Evidence,* 51 Stan. L. Rev. 1477, 1506 (1999).
39. Apodaca v. Oregon, 406 U.S. 404 (1972); Burch v. Louisiana, 441 U.S. 130 (1979).
40. See Ronald J. Allen and Sarah A. Jehl, *Burdens of Persuasion in Civil Cases: Algorithms v. Explanations,* 2003 Mich. St. L. Rev. 893, 906–15.
41. See Saul Levmore, *Conjunction and Aggregation,* 99 Mich. L. Rev. 723 (2001).
42. See Gary Lawson, *Proving the Law,* 86 Nw. U. L. Rev. 859 (1992).
43. See Larry Alexander, *Proving the Law: Not Proven,* 86 Nw. U. L. Rev. 905 (1992).
44. For discussion, see William N. Eskridge Jr., Dynamic Statutory Interpretation (1994); William N. Eskridge Jr. and Philip N. Frickey, *Quasi-Constitutional Law: Clear Statement Rules as Constitutional Lawmaking,* 45 Vand. L. Rev. 593 (1992); Cass R. Sunstein, *Nondelegation Canons,* 67 U. Chi. L. Rev. 315 (2000).
45. Smith v. United States, 508 U.S. 223 (1993).
46. See Ward Farnsworth, *Signatures of Ideology: The Case of the Supreme Court's Criminal Docket,* 104 Mich. L. Rev. 67, 97–99 (2005).
47. See Posner, *supra* note 38.
48. See Levmore, *supra* note 41.
49. See Allen and Jehl, *supra* note 40.
50. See Posner, *supra* note 38, at 1513.

51. Id.
52. 68 Cal. 2d 319 (1968).
53. See William C. Thompson and Edward L. Schumann, *Interpretation of Statistical Evidence in Criminal Trials: The Prosecutor's Fallacy and the Defense Attorney's Fallacy,* 11 Law & Hum. Behav. 167 (1987).
54. For good discussions of *Collins,* see Michael O. Finkelstein and William B. Fairley, *A Bayesian Approach to Identification Evidence,* 83 Harv. L. Rev. 489 (1970); Jonathan J. Koehler, *One in Millions, Billions, and Trillions: Lessons from* People v. Collins *(1968) for* People v. Simpson *(1995),* 47 J. Legal Ed. 214 (1997).
55. See Amos Tversky and Daniel Kahneman, *Judgments of and by Representativeness, in* Judgment under Uncertainty: Heuristics and Biases 84 (Daniel Kahneman, Paul Slovic, and Amos Tversky eds., 1982).
56. See Gerd Gigerenzer, *Why the Distinction between Single-Event Probabilities and Frequencies Is Important for Psychology (and Vice Versa), in* Subjective Probability 129 (George Wright and Peter Ayton eds., 1994).
57. For discussion of this problem and some variations, see Charles A. Holt and Lisa Anderson, *Classroom Games: Understanding Bayes' Rule,* 10 J. Econ. Persp. 179 (1996); Gerd Gigerenzer, *Why Do Frequency Formats Improve Bayesian Reasoning? Cognitive Algorithms Work on Information, Which Needs Representation,* 19 Behav. & Brain Sci. 23 (1996).
58. For extended discussion, see Gerd Gigerenzer and Ulrich Hoffrage, *How to Improve Bayesian Reasoning without Instruction: Frequency Formats,* 102 Psychol. Rev. 684 (1995).
59. See Richard D. Friedman, *A Presumption of Innocence, Not Even Odds,* 52 Stan. L. Rev. 873 (2000), from which the example given here is adapted.
60. Id.
61. See Stephen E. Fienberg and Michael O. Finkelstein, *Bayesian Statistics and the Law,* in Bayesian Statistics 5 (1996) (remarks of H. W. Lewis).
62. See Smith v. Rapid Transit, Inc., 58 N.E.2d 754 (Mass. 1945), which gave rise to the large literature on the "bus problem"; for important contributions to the discussion and sources for the discussion in the text, see Laurence H. Tribe, *Trial by Mathematics: Precision and Ritual in the Legal Process,* 84 Harv. L. Rev. 1329 (1971); Posner, *supra* note 38.
63. See, e.g., Sindell v. Abbott Labs., 607 P.2d 924 (Cal. 1980).
64. See Finkelstein and Fairley, *supra* note 54; Tribe, *supra* note 62.
65. Kaminsky v. Hertz Corp., 288 N.W.2d 426 (Mich. App. 1979).
66. Stephens v. State, 774 P.2d 60 (Wyo. 1989).
67. Roberson v. State, 16 S.W.3d 156 (Tex. App. 2000).
68. See Jonathan J. Koehler, *When Do Courts Think Base Rate Statistics Are Relevant?* 42 Jurimetrics J. 373, 373–402 (2002), from which these examples are derived.
69. This example and the numbers it uses are adapted from Gerd Gigerenzer, Calculated Risks: How to Know When Numbers Deceive You (2002).

70. See Steven C. Salop, *Evaluating Uncertain Evidence with Sir Thomas Bayes: A Note for Teachers,* 1 J. Econ. Persp. 155 (1987); Amos Tversky and Daniel Kahneman, *Causal Schemas in Judgments under Uncertainty, in* Progress in Social Psychology 49 (M. Fishbein ed., 1980).
71. Mieske v. Bartell Drug Co., 593 P.2d 1308 (Wash. 1979).
72. Pescatore v. Pan Am. World Airways, 887 F. Supp. 71 (E.D.N.Y. 1995) (affirming $9 million award); Landers v. Ghosh, 491 N.E.2d 950 (Ill. App. Ct. 1986) (affirming $400,000 award).
73. See, e.g., Haddigan v. Harkins, 441 F.2d 844 (3d Cir. 1970).
74. See Saul Levmore, *Self-Assessed Valuation Systems for Tort and Other Law,* 68 Va. L. Rev. 771 (1982), from which this paragraph and the next one are derived.
75. Id.
76. Faught v. Washam, 329 S.W.2d 588 (Mo. 1959).
77. Id.; Red Top Cab Co. v. Capps, 270 S.W.2d 273 (Tex. Civ. App. 1954); Edward J. McCaffery, Daniel J. Kahneman, and Matthew L. Spitzer, *Framing the Jury: Cognitive Perspectives on Pain and Suffering Awards,* 81 Va. L. Rev. 1341 (1995).
78. W. Kip Viscusi, *Pain and Suffering: Damages in Search of a Sounder Rationale,* 1 Mich. L. & Pol'y Rev. 141 (1996).
79. See, e.g., Olin Corp. v. Smith, 990 S.W.2d 789 (Tex. App. 1999) (affirming $5,580,000 award for suffering from loss of leg); Williams v. United States, 747 F. Supp. 967 (S.D.N.Y. 1990) ($500,000 award for suffering from loss of leg).
80. For general discussion, see Thomas C. Schelling, Choice and Consequence 113 (1984).
81. See W. Kip Viscusi and Joseph E. Aldy, *The Value of a Statistical Life: A Critical Review of Market Estimates throughout the World,* 27 J. Risk & Uncertainty 5 (2003); W. Kip Viscusi, *The Value of Life: Estimates with Risks by Occupation and Industry,* 42 Econ. Inquiry 29 (2004).
82. Viscusi and Aldy, *supra* note 81.
83. See Victor E. Schwartz and Cary Silverman, *Hedonic Damages: The Rapidly Bubbling Cauldron,* 69 Brook. L. Rev. 1037 (2004).
84. See Richard A. Posner, *Efficient Responses to Catastrophic Risk,* 6 Chi. J. Int'l L. 511, 513 n.8 (2006).
85. See Joanne Linnerooth, *The Value of Human Life: A Review of the Models,* 17 Econ. Inquiry 52 (1979).
86. See Ted R. Miller, *Willingness to Pay Comes of Age: Will the System Survive?* 83 Nw. U. L. Rev. 876 (1989).
87. See, e.g., Mercado v. Ahmed, 974 F.2d 863 (7th Cir. 1992); for further criticisms, see Andrew J. McClurg, *It's a Wonderful Life: The Case for Hedonic Damages in Wrongful Death Cases,* 66 Notre Dame L. Rev. 57 (1990).
88. For discussion and references, see Eric A. Posner and Cass R. Sunstein, *Dollars and Death,* 72 U. Chi. L. Rev. 537 (2005); John F. Morrall III, *A Review of*

the Record, Regulation, Nov./ Dec. 1986, at 25; Lisa A. Heinzerling, *Regulatory Costs of Mythic Proportions,* 107 Yale L.J. 1981 (1998).

89. John B. Loomis and Douglas S. White, *Economic Benefits of Rare and Endangered Species: Summary and Meta-analysis,* 18 Ecological Econ. 197, 199 (1996).

90. See Frank Ackerman and Lisa Heinzerling, Priceless: On Knowing the Price of Everything and the Value of Nothing (2004).

91. See, e.g., Robert W. Hahn, *The Economic Analysis of Regulation: A Response to the Critics,* 71 U. Chi. L. Rev. 1021 (2004).

92. For references, see Ackerman and Heinzerling, *supra* note 90.

AUTHOR INDEX

SUBJECT INDEX

- Highway 59 (South)
- Loop 610
    - ↳ 610 East
    - ↳ Down to sign "Pasadena H/W 225"
- H/W 225 E
    - ↳ get off Pasadena Blvd
    - ↳ turn right on PB
    - ↳ Stay till ~~B~~ Burke Ave
- ~~[illegible]~~ (Right onto Burke)
- Left onto Cherrybrooke
- Right on Dabney
- Left onto S. Fisher Ct